Class Action Strategy & Practice Guide

Gregory C. Cook and
Jocelyn D. Larkin, Editors

Cover design by Amanda Fry/ABA Design

The materials contained herein represent the opinions of the authors and/or the editors, and should not be construed to be the views or opinions of the law firms or companies with whom such persons are in partnership with, associated with, or employed by, nor of the American Bar Association or the Section of Litigation unless adopted pursuant to the bylaws of the Association.

Nothing contained in this book is to be considered as the rendering of legal advice for specific cases, and readers are responsible for obtaining such advice from their own legal counsel. This book is intended for educational and informational purposes only.

Printed in the United States of America.

22 21 20 19 18   5 4 3 2 1

Library of Congress Cataloging-in-Publication Data

Names: Cook, Gregory C., editor. | Larkin, Jocelyn D., editor.
Title: Class action strategy & practice guide / edited by Gregory Cook and Jocelyn Larkin.
Description: First edition. | Chicago : American Bar Association, 2018. | Includes bibliographical references and index.
Identifiers: LCCN 2018037998 (print) | LCCN 2018038210 (ebook) | ISBN 9781641052740 (ebook) | ISBN 9781641052733 (print : alk. paper)
Subjects: LCSH: Class actions (Civil procedure)—United States.
Classification: LCC KF8896 (ebook) | LCC KF8896 .C5295 2018 (print) | DDC 347.73/53—dc23
LC record available at https://lccn.loc.gov/2018037998

Discounts are available for books ordered in bulk. Special consideration is given to state bars, CLE programs, and other bar-related organizations. Inquire at Book Publishing, ABA Publishing, American Bar Association, 321 N. Clark Street, Chicago, Illinois 60654-7598.

www.ShopABA.org

Contents

Chapter 4: Responding to the Class Action Complaint. 91
Robert J. Herrington

Chapter 7: Class Certification Strategy 215
Catha Worthman and Andrew J. McGuinness

Chapter 8: Managing Multiple Class and Enforcement Actions 255
Gregory C. Cook and Daniel R. Karon

About the Contributors

FRED BURNSIDE is co-chair of Davis Wright Tremaine LLP's Class Action Defense Group and focuses on consumer class actions and consumer financial services litigation. Mr. Burnside was part of the Members Consultative Group that helped draft the American Law Institute's treatise on class actions, "The Principles of Aggregate Litigation." He has been in practice for 18 years; has successfully litigated a class action to the U.S. Supreme Court, *Microsoft v. Baker*, 137 S. Ct. 1702 (2017); has more than 30 appellate victories; and has litigated more than 70 class actions, including a victory in a two-week class action jury trial alleging damages of $175 million. Mr. Burnside has been a member of the Planning Committee and a presenter at the ABA's National Institute on Class Actions for the past ten years. Mr. Burnside is also a coordinating editor for the ABA's Annual Survey of State Class Action Law and author of the Oregon chapter and co-author of the Washington chapter. Mr. Burnside was named one of America's Leading Lawyers for Business in Litigation by Chambers USA. Mr. Burnside is licensed and active in Washington, Oregon, and California.

GREGORY C. COOK is a partner in the Birmingham, Alabama, law firm Balch & Bingham LLP where he has practiced since 1991 and now chairs the firm's Financial Services Litigation Practice Group. He is a graduate of Duke University, magna cum laude, and Phi Beta Kappa. He received his law degree from Harvard Law School, magna cum laude, and served as the executive editor of the *Harvard Journal of Law and Public Policy*. His practice centers on complex commercial litigation with a concentration on defending class actions (over 60). Mr. Cook has spoken and written widely on civil procedure and class actions. He served for three years as co-chair of the ABA Class Action and Derivative Suits Committee, as a past chair of the Business Torts and Antitrust Section of the Alabama State Bar and as past chair of the Birmingham

Bar Association Civil Courts Procedure Committee. He is a member of the Alabama Supreme Court's Standing Committee on the Rules of Civil Procedure. Mr. Cook is a fellow of the Birmingham Bar and of the American Bar Association. He has served on numerous bar committees including the Alabama Bar Disciplinary Rules and Enforcement Committee, the Alabama Lawyer Board of Editors, the Alabama State Board of Bar Examiners (Subject Matter Expert), Alabama Bar Unauthorized Practice of Law Committee, Birmingham Bar Bulletin Committee, Birmingham Bar Professional Ethics Committee, and Birmingham Bar Continuing Legal Education Committee. He is admitted to practice in Alabama and Texas; the U.S. Courts of Appeal for the Second, Ninth, and Eleventh Circuits; and the Supreme Court of the United States. He has been recognized by many rating services including as a BTI Client Service All-Star twice, Benchmark, Best Lawyers, Martindale Hubbell, and Super Lawyers. Mr. Cook served in the U.S. Air Force, rising to the rank of captain.

STEVEN CORHERN is an associate in the Birmingham office of Balch & Bingham LLP. His practice focuses on complex, appellate, and insurance coverage litigation. He has litigated class actions in both state and federal court, involving defective products, civil rights violations, consumer protection statutes, and contractual agreements. Prior to joining Balch & Bingham, Mr. Corhern clerked for the Honorable Emmett R. Cox, Senior Circuit Judge on the Eleventh Circuit, and the Honorable Virginia Emerson Hopkins of the Northern District of Alabama. Mr. Corhern is a graduate of the University of Alabama School of Law and Mississippi State University.

JAMES M. FINBERG is a partner at Altshuler Berzon LLP in San Francisco, where he specializes in employment discrimination and wage/hour class actions. Mr. Finberg received a BA in 1980 from Brown University and a JD in 1983 from the University of Chicago Law School, where he was executive editor of the *University of Chicago Law Review*. In 2005, he served as president of the Bar Association of San Francisco. From 2008 to 2010 and from 1997 to 1998, he served as co-chair of the Lawyers' Committee for Civil Rights of the San Francisco Bay Area. He is a fellow of the American College of Labor and Employment Lawyers. Since 2005 he has been listed in "The Best Lawyers in America" for labor and employment law. Mr. Finberg was listed as one of the Top

100 "Super Lawyers" in Northern California from 2005 to 2013. In 2009, he was named a "California Lawyer of the Year" by *California Lawyer* in the field of civil rights.

REBECCA FRANCIS is a litigation partner at Davis Wright Tremaine LLP. She focuses on consumer class action defense, complex commercial and regulatory litigation, health care litigation, and appellate law. Ms. Francis's trial experience includes successfully co-trying a class action before a jury trial in federal court, and she regularly appears before the American Arbitration Association. Ms. Francis also enforces consumer arbitration agreements and terms of use, and counsels clients on online terms of use and arbitration agreements.

CHRISTOPHER K. FRIEDMAN is an associate in the Financial Services Litigation Practice Group at Bradley Arant Boult Cummings LLP. He regularly represents financial institutions, mortgage companies, investors, and similar entities in claims brought in state and federal court, and has experience litigating a wide range of complex litigation, class actions, mass tort litigation, and civil rights claims brought under 42 U.S.C. § 1983. Mr. Friedman also has experience defending brokerage firms against claims asserted by customers in proceedings before the Financial Industry Regulatory Authority. Mr. Friedman received his BA in religion from Birmingham-Southern College, a masters in theological studies from Vanderbilt University, and his JD from Cumberland School of Law, summa cum laude.

ROB HERRINGTON is co-chair of the National Class Action Defense Practice at Greenberg Traurig LLP. His practice focuses on defending consumer products companies in complex litigation including false advertising, unfair competition, and multi-plaintiff product liability litigation. Mr. Herrington is the author of the best-selling book *Verdict for the Defense* (Sutton Hart Press 2011) and a co-author of *The Class Action Fairness Act: Law and Strategy* (ABA Publishing 2013). Mr. Herrington was recognized as the "Class Action Litigation Lawyer of the Year" in 2017 by the Century City Bar Association. In 2013, 2014, and 2015, Mr. Herrington was named in *Law360*'s list of "Top Attorneys Under 40" for class actions.

KATHRYN HONECKER is chair of the Class Action Department at Rose Law Group, PC, the largest women-owned law firm in Arizona's history. Her practice focuses on class actions in federal and state courts throughout the United States, representing plaintiff classes in major consumer fraud, civil rights, employment, securities, and insurance sales practices and other complex litigation. She is a 1998 graduate of Creighton University School of Law. Ms. Honecker has previously served as co-chair of the ABA Section of Litigation's Class Actions and Derivative Suits Committee and currently serves as co-chair of its Consumer Litigation Committee.

DANIEL R. KARON manages Karon LLC. He represents plaintiffs and defendants in consumer fraud and antitrust class action lawsuits. He is a lecturer in law at Columbia Law School and was a lecturer in law at Cleveland State University's Cleveland-Marshall College of Law. He lectures on class actions at the Ohio State University College of Law and has lectured at other law schools, including Columbia, Michigan, Vanderbilt, Notre Dame, Georgia, and Tulane. He chairs the ABA's National Institute on Class Actions, writes a bimonthly column on class actions for *Law360*, and serves on Loyola University Chicago School of Law's Institute for Consumer Antitrust Studies' U.S. Advisory Board. He has published multiple law review and bar journal articles on class action topics, and he lectures nationally for the ABA and other bar associations.

JOCELYN D. LARKIN is the executive director of the Impact Fund, a legal foundation in Berkeley, California, that provides funding and representation in support of complex public interest litigation. Her practice focuses on complex employment discrimination and class action practice on behalf of plaintiffs. Ms. Larkin has served as class counsel in many major class actions, including *Dukes v. Wal-Mart Stores*, *Ellis v. Costco Wholesale Corp.*, *Parra v. Bashas' Inc.*, *Williams v. City of Antioch*, and *Stender v. Lucky Stores*. For many years, Ms. Larkin spearheaded the Impact Fund's complex litigation training program, including the development of its Class Action Training Institute and its annual Class Action Conference. Ms. Larkin is a frequent speaker and author on issues concerning class actions, employment law, ethics, and civil rights. She is a graduate of the University of California, San Diego, and the University of California, Los Angeles School of Law. Ms. Larkin is the past co-chair of the ABA Section of Litigation's Class Actions and Derivative Suits Committee and a member of the ABA Federal Practice Task Force.

ANDREW J. MCGUINNESS practices complex litigation, with a focus on class actions, antitrust, consumer, and securities trials and appeals. He serves on the planning committee for the ABA National Institute on Class Actions and co-chairs the ABA Section of Litigation Class Action and Derivative Suit's Antitrust Subcommittee. He teaches "Class Actions 101," a course he designed, at the National Institute. He is past co-editor of *Securities Litigation News* and regularly publishes articles on class actions and related legal topics. Mr. McGuinness served for eight years as lead MDL counsel for an OEM motor vehicle manufacturer in the largest auto recall by number of vehicles. He is listed in "Best Lawyers" and has been designated a "Super Lawyer." After graduating magna cum laude from the University of Michigan Law School, Mr. McGuinness clerked for the Honorable Frank M. Coffin of the U.S. Court of Appeals for the First Circuit; practiced commercial litigation at Skadden, Arps, Slate, Meagher & Flom in Chicago; and headed the class action defense practice for Dykema Gossett PLLC before establishing his own complex litigation boutique in Ann Arbor, Michigan. He can be reached through www.topclasslaw.com.

DENA SHARP is a partner with Girard Sharp who devotes her practice to representing plaintiffs in complex litigation throughout the United States. She currently serves as co-lead counsel in the *In re Lidoderm Antitrust Litigation* and *In re Restasis Antitrust Litigation* pharmaceutical MDLs, and as a member of the End-Payer Plaintiffs' Steering Committee in the *In re Generic Pharmaceuticals Pricing Antitrust Litigation.* Outside the courtroom, Ms. Sharp serves on the board of directors of the Impact Fund—a nonprofit organization that supports litigation on behalf of marginalized communities—and is a co-author of the widely cited *Sedona Principles: Best Practices and Principles for Electronic Document Production (Third Edition)*. She is also a vice chair of the Advisory Council for the Duke Law School Center for Judicial Studies. Ms. Sharp received her law degree from University of California, Hastings College of the Law and her undergraduate degree from Brown University.

JASON B. TOMPKINS is a partner at Balch & Bingham LLP, where his practice focuses on consumer finance litigation and appeals across the country. He has handled hundreds of individual and class actions involving the Fair Debt Collection Practices Act, Fair Credit Reporting Act, and Telephone Consumer Protection Act. Mr. Tompkins coordinates nationwide defense strategy for several financial services company clients and was counsel for one of the nation's largest debt buyers in *Midland Funding, LLC v. Johnson*, 137 S. Ct. 1407 (2017). Mr. Tompkins currently serves as co-chair of the ABA Consumer Litigation Committee and vice-chair of the Appellate Section of the Alabama State Bar. He is a member of the New York, District of Columbia, and Alabama bars.

CATHA WORTHMAN is a founding partner of Feinberg, Jackson, Worthman & Wasow, where she represents individuals and public interest organizations in wage and hour, civil rights, and benefits litigation, as well as in policy advocacy and election law matters. She graduated from the University of California, Berkeley, School of Law, Order of the Coif, in 2003.

The contributors to this book would like to thank and acknowledge the following individuals for their assistance on this book:

Kim K. Ellis, Legal Assistant at Balch & Bingham LLP

John B. Isbister, Partner at Tydings & Rosenberg LLP

Lindsay Nako, Director of Litigation & Training at Impact Fund

Candice Sherman, Paralegal at Balch & Bingham LLP

Matthew M.K. Stein, Associate at Skadden, Arps, Slate, Meagher & Flom LLP

Jonathan Udell, Associate at Rose Law Group PC

Fabrice N. Vincent, Partner at Lieff Cabraser Heimann & Bernstein, LLP

Clark Wu, Associate at Rose Law Group PC

Paloma Nikolic, Administrative Assistant, Altshuler Berzon

Foreword

As class actions have evolved, they have become larger and more complex, requiring mastery of and compliance with ever-evolving case law. Authors and editors Gregory Cook and Jocelyn Larkin, master class action strategists and litigators, worked with other seasoned class action lawyers to produce this essential practice guide for lawyers, judges, and advocates and decision makers at every level.

As lead counsel in the VW Diesel Emissions settlement, which strove to set new standards for size, speed, and class member participation in a high-profile consumer class action, I have learned that the more I learn, the more I learn there is to learn about effective class action litigation strategies.

The thorough, comprehensive, and sophisticated treatment and discussion of all aspects of class action litigation makes this text a vital and necessary addition to the libraries of class action veterans and newbies alike.

Jocelyn Larkin's extraordinary contributions to class action jurisprudence, as longtime executive director of the Impact Fund, give her unique and extraordinary insights into successful prosecution of class action, insights thoroughly and eloquently shared in this one of a kind publication. Co-editor Gregory Cook's decades of work defending numerous complex class actions well balances this text with perceptive and discerning practice tips and wisdom for practitioners and courts alike.

This exciting and detailed new book promises to give an edge to practitioners in an area where thoughtful strategizing can make the difference on pleading issues, trial plans, class definitions, experts, class certification, and successful settlements.

—Elizabeth J. Cabraser

Introduction

Gregory C. Cook and Jocelyn D. Larkin

Why a book on class action strategy? Like any area of the law, there is a need for practical answers to a myriad of "how to" issues and this book certainly covers those. But, class actions present a unique problem for lawyers. These complex and high-risk cases turn many, if not most, of a lawyer's normal instincts on their head. In a class action, advocates on both sides are forced to play a kind of three-dimensional chess. They must repeatedly rethink strategies as the case evolves, monitor or disrupt parallel litigation in other courts, and even, at times, join hands with their opponents. In what other kind of case would a defense lawyer call it a victory if she loses the claims pled by the individual plaintiff so long as she defeats class certification? Other than in a class action, when would a plaintiff's lawyer intentionally simplify his case and drop some lucrative damage claims?

Lawyers who have not been down this path before risk missing key strategic decisions because they have not thought their arguments all the way through to the end of the case. For a novice, the difficulty of understanding these complex decisions is exacerbated by the long duration of a typical class action. An associate may spend several years working on just one phase of a class action (e.g., class certification and an interlocutory appeal of that order) without the ability to connect that work with the decisions at the outset of the case or the intricate compromises made in the settlement of the dispute. The full arc of the case, as well as the detours along the path, are both essential to understanding class action strategy.

Further, a class action practitioner must always consider the reaction of the lawyer on the other side of the "v" or risk missing critical strategy calls. Indeed, a class action is never actually bilateral because the court and potentially dissatisfied class members can each in their own way profoundly influence the outcome of the litigation. All of this complexity is amplified by the fact that the class certification decision (the decision that truly drives the value of the case) is a discretionary decision for the trial judge and thus often impossible to predict with any certainty for clients.

For those and many other reasons, most chapters in this book are co-authored by a team composed of both a plaintiff and defense lawyer. Where appropriate, we have allocated entire chapters to the unique concerns of one side or the other. We provide here a brief roadmap.

Chapter 2 focuses on what plaintiff counsel needs to do to prepare for filing a class action. How does one choose the right plaintiffs—a critical decision? Are they adequate? What claims do they personally have? What law will govern their claims? In what venue can they bring their claims? Will they tell a compelling story to the press? To the court? To a mediator? To the defendant? Are their claims typical? Did they have individualized contacts with the defendant? Are they serial plaintiffs? Will they agree to take a "pickoff" settlement offer? Will they be willing to persevere over years of long and contentious litigation? Do they fully understand their responsibilities as class representatives?

What is the ideal number of plaintiffs? Can too many class representatives hurt the case or invite dissension? Is one plaintiff just too risky if the fate of the entire case turns on his or her answers in deposition? Should counsel sign up other plaintiffs in case the named plaintiff is found inadequate? Perhaps plaintiff counsel should have a mass sign-up for everyone who might be a plaintiff so that counsel can negotiate from strength if the class certification motion is denied.

Those named plaintiff questions cannot be considered in a vacuum, though, because they interconnect with a series of other decisions. Where should class counsel bring the case? What is the most favorable forum for the claims and do the prospective named plaintiffs have venue there? What happens if the case is transferred to a distant forum as part of a multi-district litigation (MDL) proceeding?

Class counsel must also determine how to define the class. How broadly should they define the class? In contrast to normal cases, the wrongdoing must be carefully and precisely defined—especially in the class definition. Class counsel must determine what is certifiable—what can they prove with common evidence? What claims should be included? What is a fail-safe class definition and how can it be avoided? Must the class members be identifiable at the time of certification (depending upon the legal standard in the relevant circuit)? What time period should be covered (for instance, statute of limitation issues can sometimes be used as an argument to defeat predominance)?

In Chapter 3, we explore the defendant's forum choices and again the correct strategy decision will be a multi-layered analysis, leading at times to a counterintuitive result. Moreover, the defendant often has very little time to react to the forum choice, even though it is perhaps the most important question in the case. Should the defendant opt to remove the case from state to federal court? Is it better to have a federal judge who has time to fully review the briefs and arguments and will likely apply a more rigorous evidentiary standard to expert testimony? But, will removing the case cause other plaintiff's counsel to notice the litigation and more sophisticated counsel to become involved? Will removing the case make settlement more difficult and affect the structure of the settlement as well as its costs? How will standing issues play out in each forum? Is the potential of a motion to transfer the case to an MDL after removal good news or bad? Perhaps the state court offers better class certification law, broader discovery, or an easier appeal mechanism than federal court.

That's not all. Practitioners must consider if there is a forum selection clause in the mix. Also, is a venue motion likely to deliver the defendant to safer waters? What are the advantages or disadvantages of various alternative venues?

And, of course, can the defendant compel private arbitration, particularly where the proceeding will be taken outside of public view? Is the inevitable fight over arbitration worth the money and time? What about the dangers of arbitrators applying equity and splitting the baby rather than sticking to legal doctrine? Is it worth the risk of giving up a full appeal from a final decision? If the case is truly dangerous and will involve hundreds or thousands of individual cases and damaging public relations, should the defendant take the opportunity to settle and resolve a problem with a global class action settlement rather than risking piecemeal arbitration?

Chapter 4 addresses the defendant's options in responding to the complaint. What are the steps for a full and complete early case assessment? Are there ways to resolve the individual complaint, either before filing or after? Could early concessions or a voluntary change to a challenged practice lead to an argument by plaintiff's counsel that they are entitled to catalyst attorneys' fees? Maybe the case is significant enough (or so insignificant) that an early class settlement is the best move for the client?

Is it worth it to file a motion to dismiss? What are the best arguments for dismissal? Perhaps the goal of educating the court is worth filing an early motion. Perhaps it will cause plaintiff's counsel to file a narrowed complaint. On the other hand, filing a motion to dismiss may merely educate the plaintiff's lawyers about the problems with their complaint and their class representatives, allowing them to solve the problems early. Should the defendant take the offense and file a motion to strike the class allegations? If no motion is filed, what are the affirmative defenses or counterclaims to include in an answer and/or cross-complaint?

In Chapter 5, our authors tackle class action discovery from both sides' perspective. Should the court grant a stay of discovery while considering a motion to dismiss? Should the defendant agree to broader discovery in the hope of demonstrating the presence of individualized issues? How broadly should discovery be drafted? What type of agreement on Electronically Stored Information (ESI) is appropriate? Can the defendant make predominance arguments regarding varying facts without allowing broad discovery on those facts? Is bifurcation of discovery between merits and class issues still a viable option after the Supreme Court has made clear that merits issues can overlap with the elements of class certification? Are communications allowed with class members before and/or after certification and on what terms? Is the list of class members discoverable? Is discovery allowed from absent class members and, if so, in what forms?

Chapter 6 discusses summary judgment options, a strategy that has evolved over the years. Can and should a defendant move for summary judgment before class certification? Are there advantages even if the motion will not win the case (for instance, narrowing the case, causing the plaintiff to respond in an individualized way). Should the plaintiff agree that the court should hear the defendant's summary judgment motion before class certification? What standard should the court apply?

Chapter 7 is a rich resource on the class certification arguments for both sides, covering each of the elements of the Federal Rule 23 and the typical arguments for and against class certification. The lesson of Chapter 7 is that class certification is discretionary and difficult to predict. As a result, both sides need to focus on providing the court with a complete evidentiary record—not merely hypothetical or boilerplate legal arguments.

Among the many issues covered: What are the main issues that courts focus on during class certification? How does counsel establish (or challenge) each element of Rule 23? Are courts more skeptical of certifying classes when the merits appear weak? Why is it vital that plaintiff counsel keep their case simple and their class definitions precise? Why is it important to rely upon the defendant's documents, policies, and Rule 30(b)(6) depositions during the class certification motion? What is ascertainability and why is this such a controversial topic? What are the differences among (b)(1), (b)(2), and (b)(3) classes and how to determine which fits and does not fit your case?

Chapter 8 takes on how to manage multiple class actions (and government enforcement actions, especially criminal actions). For instance, when and why should counsel file for MDL consolidation? What does the MDL Panel find most important in deciding whether to consolidate and where? How many cases must exist before consolidation? Can consolidation backfire on defendants? To what districts or judges are cases most likely to be transferred? Are there trends in consolidation decisions? Once consolidated, how do plaintiff lawyers organize their steering committees? How do counsel on both sides try to coordinate MDL proceedings?

What are the risks to both sides from consolidation? What law applies if the actions are consolidated? Are there any rights of review for consolidation decisions?

If no MDL is created, how can both sides consolidate multiple actions, especially if parallel cases are pending in state and federal courts? What about managing competing civil and criminal cases?

Class actions, like other civil cases, ordinarily settle, but the process is vastly more complicated, requires court approval, and offers a bevy of traps for the unwary. Settlement and all that it entails is covered in Chapter 9. Practitioners must consider settlement from the very beginning of the case and the desire for a final global resolution can drive decisions that would otherwise seem upside down. Defendants may decide not to remove or compel arbitration; plaintiffs may avoid issuing press releases to avoid copycat cases. Settlement creates some of the most interesting strategic issues. When the defense has decided to settle, they will normally want the most expansive class definition and the broadest release, even though they have vociferously opposed any certification earlier in the case. Plaintiffs in turn will find themselves downplaying the value of a claim that they once touted as a blockbuster. When the terms of a settlement are finally hammered out, plaintiff and defense counsel share a common goal of obtaining approval and will then join forces to this end and against any objectors who oppose the accord.

The value of this chapter to practitioners cannot be overstated. Settlement is driving proposed changes to Rule 23 and new case law. It is clearly the hottest topic in class actions—notice, settlement approval factors, emphasis on the preliminary approval stage, distribution methods, claims processing, unclaimed proceeds and cy pres, coupon settlements, class representative payments, objector payments, conflicts of interest, among many other topics. What should be part of a term sheet as opposed to part of a side agreement? How will attorney fees be calculated? When should they be negotiated?

Occasionally class actions go to trial and, even when they do not, courts often demand trial plans at the class certification stage. Chapter 10 explains trial plans. In the past, the question of actually conducting a class action trial was often not actively considered (and even more rarely conducted). While trial plans were rare 20 years ago, many federal courts treat them as essential today. Defendants frequently argue that a class trial will devolve into endless individual-by-individual testimony. Plaintiffs must be prepared to respond by explaining how they propose to try the case with a focus on methods of macro-proof, such as statistics or admissions. This chapter both discusses the elements of a good trial plan and provides examples of trial plans. There is simply no other similar resource available and this chapter is reason enough to buy this book.

Finally, we cover expert witnesses in class actions. Today, it is rare that a motion to certify a class is filed without an accompanying expert witness report. Likewise, virtually every opposition brief uses an expert. The competing expert testimony typically centers on whether the claims can be proven with common evidence although they can be used for many other purposes (e.g., numerosity, feasibility of notice, merits issues). *Daubert* motions, which test the admissibility of expert testimony, are an essential part of almost every class certification fight today, and the Supreme Court has focused on expert testimony in several of its recent class certification decisions. Does the court apply the same *Daubert* standard at class certification as it does before trial? Does the expert rely upon admissible evidence? Does the testimony "fit" the legal theory and claims? Would the testimony be admissible in an ordinary single plaintiff case? Should the plaintiff or defendant hire a consulting expert to assist in litigating the case? How can an expert use sampling to support claims of class-wide liability or impact?

All of this is to say that class actions involve decisions on strategy at every turn. The positions of the parties are constantly changing, and counsel must always be looking ahead and, at the same time, carefully watching their flank. We hope this book helps all practitioners identify and answer those key strategy questions and also recognize the choices that their opponent is similarly struggling to make.

2

Investigating and Filing a Class Action

Jocelyn D. Larkin and Dena C. Sharp

INTRODUCTION

Class actions are complex. Before filing a class action, counsel must conduct a thorough investigation and make a series of key strategic decisions. The nature of the investigation and evaluation will, of course, vary based on the clients, the facts, and the substantive area of the law. This chapter provides an overview of the process of investigating and filing a complaint.

The core questions to be resolved before filing a class action are:

- proposed named plaintiffs;
- proper defendants;
- legal theories to be pled;
- remedies to be sought;
- venue;
- class definition;
- appropriate time period;
- appropriate geographic area;
- litigation team and roles; and
- resources required.

While this checklist may look fairly straightforward, the challenge is that the questions are inextricably *interrelated*. Consider these issues. One of your clients (and potential named plaintiffs) may be able to allege some legal theories, but not others, or only for a limited time period. Some potential plaintiffs may have strong claims but be located in less favorable venues. Adding a particular defendant in a class case based on state law may create diversity jurisdiction, triggering removal to federal court under CAFA (Class Action Fairness Act). A case with nationwide scope might have the greatest impact, but might require resources that counsel does not have or cannot prudently risk.

Often it can take several months or a year to complete a class action investigation and make these crucial decisions. But, in some cases, counsel will not have that luxury. Counsel may be facing an expiring statute of limitations or the risk that competing class actions will be filed first. In such circumstances, decisions will need to be made under pressure and based only on the information available.

Finally, in deciding whether to file a class action, counsel must balance the interests and goals of his or her individual client (or clients) with the demands and duties of a class action. Once a putative class action is filed, counsel and the named plaintiffs may owe some types of fiduciary duties to the unnamed class members. Thus, the client must fully understand the unique nature of a class action versus an individual lawsuit, as well as his or her responsibilities to the class.

EVALUATING A POTENTIAL CLASS ACTION: THE BASICS

Could This Case Be a Class Action?

Few civil cases are suitable for a class action. While this and later chapters discuss class requirements in depth, it is useful to start with a basic definition of what kind of case *might* be a class action. For a class action, counsel must identify *a legal wrong common to a group that is susceptible to a common remedy*.

Here are a few examples to illustrate what could be a class action and what could not.

- A telecommunications company adds a service charge to the bills of all of its cellphone customers in a particular geographic area. The service charge appears to violate a statute or regulation.

- Yes. Common legal question, common harm, common remedy.
- A publicly traded company holds a press conference and announces a new product that it plans to launch, which in fact is far from ready and suffering from major problems. Those who purchased stock after the announcement want to sue for securities fraud.
  - Yes. Common legal question, common harm, common remedy.
- Ten African American and Asian employees of a large company allege discrimination, including unequal pay, excessive discipline including termination, and sexual harassment. They want to sue for back pay and damages.
  - Probably not, or at least not all in one case. Injuries are too diverse and might not uniformly affect a sufficiently large group.
- Following a chemical spill at a factory, nearby residents and business owners want to bring claims for illness and personal injuries caused by the emissions, loss of property value, and business interruption.
  - Probably not in one case. Injuries are too diverse and damages are individualized.
- Applicants for food stamps claim that the welfare office does not process their applications within the 21-day time period required by statute. They seek injunctive relief to enforce the statutory time limit.
  - Yes. There is a common wrong that affects a group, which can be remedied with a court order requiring compliance with the statutory time period.
- A slumlord fails to make timely and necessary repairs to houses that he owns throughout a large metropolitan area. A group of tenants wants repairs made, rent abatement, and emotional distress damages.
  - Probably not. Lease terms might vary and there might be questions about when and how the tenant put the landlord on notice of the need for repairs. There is also not likely to be a common method of proving the need for and cost of repairs at each individual house. Personal injury claims are not typically suitable for class actions.

- A local government official spends tax revenues to remodel his personal and vacation residences.
  - Generalized public injury rather than an injury to specific class members; no common remedy.

In making this threshold "could this be a class" determination, counsel should review case law to see whether similar claims have been successfully brought as class actions.

Advantages and Disadvantages of a Class Action

Even if a case could be a class action, it does not mean that it should be. Counsel should weigh the advantages and disadvantages of a class action.

The most obvious advantage of a class action is that, if successful, the outcome will have a much *greater impact*. A defendant will likely pay much larger damages for its conduct in a class action, and be deterred from risky business practices in the future. Far more victims will be aware of—and compensated for—their losses. A class action can also result in systemic injunctive relief to reform practices or prevent further illegal conduct, often subject to future court monitoring. Such relief is not typically available in an individual lawsuit.

Advantages

- Greater impact
- More attention from media
- Broader discovery
- Pressure on defendants

The impact of a class action will often go well beyond the parties to the litigation. Class actions get far more *attention from the media* than ordinary lawsuits. Companies in the same industry will monitor the litigation and might be deterred from similar actions by the prospect of class-wide liability. The public also gets greater access to information about illegal conduct that might present a risk to public safety.

Class actions can also present advantages in discovery. Courts generally allow *broader discovery* in a class action than in a single plaintiff case to permit the plaintiffs a fair opportunity to meet certification requirements. Moreover, the focus of discovery (and litigation) tends to be on the challenged conduct of the defendant, rather than on the named plaintiff's conduct.

Given the high stakes of class actions, defendants might be more interested in talking settlement in a class action than in an individual case, where even a loss would simply be dismissed as a cost of doing business.

There is an equally compelling list of disadvantages to class litigation. The cases are *procedurally complex* and require tremendous time, attention, and expertise. Class certification presents a daunting hurdle, which makes class actions particularly *risky*. Because of the high stakes, counsel can expect defendants to hire highly qualified counsel and to mount an *aggressive defense*. Class cases are also very *expensive*, requiring extensive deposition and document and e-discovery, expert testimony, and class notice, all paid for by class counsel. These cases typically take much *longer to litigate* than ordinary litigation, and resolution can be delayed for years by interlocutory and post-judgment appeals. Clients may well *receive less* for their claims in a class action than in an individual case and must be so advised. Class actions are subject to *judicial oversight* and approval, which can limit how and when cases are settled or dismissed. Even when the parties reach a judicially sanctioned settlement, a third-party *objector* can challenge the settlement and take an appeal. Finally, your *client's goals* might simply not align with the goals and demands of a class action.

Disadvantages
• Procedurally complex
• Expensive, risky, and time-consuming
• Duration
• Aggressive defense
• Judicial oversight
• Alignment of client and class goals

Alternatives to Class Actions

In evaluating whether or not to file a class action, counsel should consider whether alternatives exist that can provide some or all of the same benefits without the time and expense of a class action. Again, the alternatives available will depend on the relevant substantive law and jurisdiction.

One alternative to a class action is civil enforcement by a government agency, such as the Equal Employment Opportunity Commission (EEOC), the Department of Justice (DOJ), or the Securities and Exchange Commission (SEC). Some government agencies have broad investigative and subpoena authority and will use it to pursue alleged wrongdoing. In some cases, your client can file a report or complaint of alleged systemic malfeasance with the appropriate agency. However, counsel should recognize that neither you nor your client will control if and when the agency actually investigates or institutes an enforcement action. (See also discussion of class actions litigated parallel to governmental enforcement actions at Chapter 8.) Counsel will generally not receive compensation for the work done investigating the allegations or preparing the complaint unless paid by the client for the work.

Your client may also be able to obtain the desired relief through an individual declaratory or injunctive relief claim, provided that he or she has been directly injured by the challenged conduct. For example, a claim that a statute or regulation is unconstitutional may not require a certified class action, since a finding of unconstitutionality will necessarily apply to all those affected by the law. Similarly, some states allow taxpayer standing to challenge allegedly illegal use of governmental funds.

Finally, your client can send a demand letter and attempt to reach a negotiated resolution without the necessity of filing a class action. For defendants eager to avoid publicity, a confidential pre-litigation settlement might be a viable alternative. However, a settlement will not bind other putative class members unless a case is actually filed, certified, and settled through the Rule 23 or equivalent state law class action mechanism.

PRE-FILING INVESTIGATION AND DISCOVERY

Every case investigation will differ, based on the facts and legal issues, but there are some steps common to many cases. The goals of the investigation are to determine if the conduct has affected a broad group—or just your clients—and whether a sufficient level of injury or amount of monetary loss is at stake.

Clients

Practitioners should use communications with their clients to drive the initial stages of the investigation, including identifying potential fact resources, securing relevant documents, and obtaining witness statements. It is critical to determine whether the clients have signed arbitration agreements that the defendant will argue apply to the challenged conduct, further discussed later in the chapter.

Potential Defendants

An enormous amount of information about potential defendants is available through public sources and those sources should be plumbed.

It is necessary to identify the proper defendants, including assessment of the circle of potential liability in any defendant family. Investigate the specific role of each defendant in connection with the conduct at issue. If possible, the investigation should determine where the alleged misconduct occurred, as design, manufacturing, or relevant communications might have occurred somewhere other than the defendants' domicile. Practitioners should also research and monitor public statements made by the defendants or others concerning the conduct or product at issue. You will want to investigate the financial health of the potential defendant, to avoid a successful outcome resulting in a defendant filing for bankruptcy.

Related Litigation or Investigations

Investigate what other cases are or have been filed against this defendant or concerning this type of conduct. Also counsel should ascertain whether there are pending investigations of the conduct by state or federal government enforcement agencies.

Evidence Preservation

You should take steps to preserve evidence, as it might disappear. Your client, of course, needs to understand his or her duty to retain evidence. You should advise your client in writing to retain bank, telephone, and tax records as well as electronic mail. If it is a consumer case, the client should request transaction records from the potential defendant and, if there is a customer portal, also download the client's records there. Relevant information on a website should be printed or recorded in a way that will be admissible later. If information is in the hands of third parties, formal steps must be taken to ensure that it is not destroyed. You may want to send an evidence retention demand to the defendant, although it will obviously alert them to your investigation. Important information can be lost (for instance, payment records which could identify the class for particular years) if you delay in sending such a hold notice to the defendant.

Experts

You may want to contact industry experts or insiders who might have knowledge of the conduct. Consider retaining an expert as a consultant. He or she may be able to assist with the investigation, assess liability, or verify that the product or conduct implicated the potential plaintiffs. After the Supreme Court's decision in *Tyson Foods, Inc. v. Bouaphakeo*,[1] defendants are likely to aggressively challenge statistical experts and methodology at the class certification stage, using *Daubert* motions. The sooner that experts are retained, the more prepared they and counsel will be to address these challenges.

IDENTIFYING CLASS REPRESENTATIVES

When victims become aware of a legal wrong, they often turn to the Internet and perhaps others in the same situation to determine what recourse may be available. Dozens or even hundreds of individuals or entities willing to serve as class representatives may come forward. Determining which of many class members should serve as a class representative involves several interrelated considerations.

Typicality

The first question is whether the person (or entity) is sufficiently typical under Rule 23(a)(3). His claims must arise from the same event, practice, or course of conduct that affected other class members, and his claims must be based on the same legal or remedial theory.

Another question is whether the proposed class representative has standing to assert claims on behalf of the class, or some portion of the class. Among the relevant inquiries are whether the prospective class representative has documentation or other proof of the relevant purchase or transaction, and whether he has signed any releases or arbitration agreements that may negate his ability to pursue claims in the class context.

Watch out for the "uninjured" plaintiff. A class member who has received a refund from the defendant or has otherwise obtained restitution might be unfit to represent the class. What constitutes injury? The Supreme Court recently took that question on in *Spokeo, Inc. v. Robins*,[2] holding that whether an asserted invasion of statutory rights meets the Article III standing requirements turns on whether the plaintiff's injury is "'real,' and not 'abstract.'" The Court advised that "intangible injuries can nevertheless be concrete," and that "both history and the judg-

---

1. Tyson Foods, Inc. v. Bouaphakeo, 577 U.S. ___, 136 S. Ct. 1036 (2016).
2. Spokeo, Inc. v. Robins, ___ U.S. ___, 136 S. Ct. 1540, 1548 (2016).

ment of Congress play important roles" when it comes to evaluating whether an intangible harm is sufficiently concrete (or "real") to give rise to standing.[3] *Spokeo*'s standing discussion is limited to general principles and, in its only reference to class actions (which was relegated to a footnote), the Court confirmed that a named plaintiff even in a class action must demonstrate his Article III standing.[4]

It is up to plaintiffs' counsel to make sure that the injuries in the case are sufficiently "real" to merit the time and resources of the parties and the court. Class actions about seemingly minor injuries or violations— too little rosehips in a blended tea bag, or nominal statutory infractions—may constitute technical injuries or violations, but does bringing that case advance any genuine interests? And how difficult will it be to show that the defendant profited from the conduct? (In cases brought under statutes that establish minimum damages, the "profit" question might fall away, but it might still be necessary to plead some actual injury to your client and the putative class.)

Beyond pleading and proof requirements, an important consideration for the attorneys in the case and for the bar in general is whether the case is likely to "turn off" the judge, potentially resulting in bad precedent for the next, more meritorious case that comes along. Make sure that any named plaintiff candidates are not subject to unique arguments or defenses, such as notice triggering a statute of limitations defense, that would control the outcome of their individual claims. Counsel should thoroughly vet class representatives, including a discussion regarding their knowledge of the alleged wrongdoing and how they came to be affected by it.

One of the most significant defenses to investigate is whether the potential class representative signed an *arbitration agreement* and, if so, whether it contains a class action waiver. Ascertaining the circumstances in which the client signed the arbitration agreement may also be relevant. The U.S. Supreme Court has repeatedly (some might say aggressively) upheld a defendant's use of an arbitration agreement with

---

3. *Id.* at 1549; *see, e.g., In re* Horizon Healthcare Servs. Inc. Data Breach Litig., 846 F.3d 625 (3d Cir. 2017) (lead opinion concluded that the plaintiffs subjected to data breach had standing based on congressional action, while concurring judge looked to common law privacy concepts); Van Patten v. Vertical Fitness Grp., LLC, 847 F.3d 1037, 1042–43 (9th Cir. 2017) (affirming summary judgment but holding that the plaintiff had Article III standing under Telephone Consumer Protection Act: "Congress identified unsolicited contact as a concrete harm, and gave consumers a means to redress this harm.").

4. 136 S. Ct. at 1547 n.6 (citation omitted).

class action waiver to foreclose the use of the class mechanism to challenge alleged wrongdoing.[5] As a result of these defense-friendly rulings, many more corporations have adopted arbitration agreements to limit the class remedy for consumers and employees. As a result, plaintiffs' counsel have discovered many good class action cases stymied at the outset by these agreements. See discussion at Chapter 3.

Potential class representatives should also be vetted for characteristics or circumstances that might subject them to distracting or debilitating attacks, including criminal history, bankruptcy, service as a "serial" plaintiff in multiple class actions, or an expressed willingness to place his interests ahead of those of class members. Before proceeding with any given plaintiff, counsel should run comprehensive searches of social media, court and bankruptcy records, and other available sources to "dig up any dirt" about that person—you can rest assured your adversaries will. And maybe it should go without saying, but make absolutely sure that the person is actually a member of the class as defined.

Adequacy

Another question is whether the potential class representative is likely to pass muster under Rule 23(a)(4)'s adequacy test. The ideal class representative is responsive and credible. He wants to effect the change or redress the wrong that the lawsuit seeks to address, and is willing and able to focus on the best results for the class as a whole. He understands that complex litigation often takes years to resolve and is willing to stay involved for the long haul if necessary.

Even the most typical class representative cannot effectively serve the interests of the class if he is not willing to fulfill his duties and "fairly" protect the interests of the class, as required by Rule 23(a)(4). His attorneys must explain to him the duties associated with representing a class, and should usually do so in the attorney representation agreement to avoid any doubt. A class representative's duties generally fit into two categories: (1) loyalty to the class and (2) participation in the lawsuit.

With regard to loyalty, the representative has a duty to stand in the shoes of class members, and must not place his personal interests ahead

---

5. *See* Am. Express Co. v. Italian Colors Rest., 570 U.S. 228, 133 S. Ct. 2304 (2013); AT&T Mobility v. Concepcion, 563 U.S. 333, 131 S. Ct. 1740 (2011).

of the interests of other members of the class. As a practical matter, this means he must not accept a "pick-off" settlement offer from the defendant that would benefit him but not his fellow class members.

As to the duty to participate in the lawsuit, the class representative must generally stay informed about the lawsuit and work with his attorneys. Fulfilling his duties typically requires acquiring a basic understanding of the claims and the class he seeks to represent; staying in close contact with his attorneys and overseeing his counsel's prosecution of the case; providing information and documents to his attorneys as necessary; reviewing and providing input on pleadings; making himself available to provide testimony at a deposition or in the courtroom; and staying apprised of and providing input on settlement offers.

The most often cited adequacy attack is whether there is a conflict of interest between the interests of the class representative and the class (or a portion of the class). For instance, former landowners may have significantly different objectives (maximizing monetary recovery) from current landowners (future land use rules). If these conflicts rise to the level of being "fundamental," subclasses may be necessary, including separate class representatives for each, and perhaps even separate counsel. Such conflicts are not always evident at the outset of the litigation and can require careful planning to avoid.

How Many Class Representatives?

Often it makes sense for several individuals or entities to serve as class representatives, particularly when they collectively represent the interests of class members affected by the full spectrum of products or conduct at issue. Class representatives from around the country may also provide important coverage for claims brought under the laws of various states, as many courts have construed the viability of state law claims at the motion to dismiss phase as an Article III standing issue, rather than a Rule 23 adequacy issue.

It can also be helpful to have "back up" class representatives when others become unavailable or decline to participate. Some attorneys may take the "back up" plan farther, signing up as many potential plaintiffs as possible. Doing so might lend credibility to the case in the eyes of the court, showing that class members really care about the outcome and will likely provide the attorneys with valuable insight into the facts of the case. In the event the court denies class certification, moreover, the plaintiffs' attorneys may turn to willing plaintiffs to proceed by way of a "mass action" to avoid Rule 23's procedural hurdles—provided their attorneys thought ahead and included in engagement agreements the possibility of proceeding as either a class or mass action.

The interest in comprehensive coverage must be weighed against the burden, expense, and risk associated with including numerous class representatives, each of whom requires a significant investment of attorney time and vetting. With several plaintiffs being deposed on the same or similar topics, for example, defense counsel has a real opportunity to elicit testimony that tends to show that individualized issues will predominate over common ones or to otherwise pit one plaintiff's testimony against another.

American Pipe Tolling

The Supreme Court has clearly held that the filing of a class action tolls the statute of limitations for putative class members.[6] However, many issues still remain in the application of this tolling, including whether it applies cross-jurisdictionally and how broad the tolling applies.

The Supreme Court recently held that *American Pipe* tolling does not apply to a subsequent class action filed after an earlier class action is not certified.[7]

In determining whether to file individual actions on behalf of clients or whether to add additional class representatives, counsel should consider the benefits (and the limits) of such tolling in their jurisdiction.

ASSEMBLING A TEAM OF CO-COUNSEL

Considerations of risk, expense, and available resources will drive the decision about which lawyers should be on your team. Prosecuting a complex case on a contingency fee basis against well-heeled corporate defendants represented by top law firms almost invariably equates to substantial risk and expense. Assembling a team of co-counsel to jointly prosecute the case allows the attorneys or firms to split both the financial risk and the work.

---

6. Am. Pipe & Constr. Co. v. Utah, 414 U.S. 538, 554 (1974).
7. China Agritech, Inc. v. Resh, __ U.S. __, 138 S. Ct. 1800 (2018).

Practical considerations that may inform the composition of the team include:

- the court's preferences or directives;
- which firms or organizations filed cases, and when;
- whose clients are best suited to serve as class representatives, including considerations of typicality, adequacy, and covering the spectrum of claims or issues in the case;
- which firms have relevant subject matter expertise;
- the respective firms' demonstrated work ethic, record of success, reputation, and credibility;
- available attorney and supporting resources;
- the firms' financial wherewithal and ability to contribute to ongoing litigation expenses; and
- familiarity with the court, including use of local counsel.

Closely related to these practical considerations are the criteria the court will typically consider when appointing counsel or interim counsel for the class (under Federal Rule of Civil Procedure 23(g) or state law analogues): (1) the work counsel has done in identifying or investigating potential claims in the action; (2) counsel's experience in handling class actions, other complex litigation, and the types of claims asserted in the action; (3) counsel's knowledge of the applicable law; and (4) the resources that counsel will commit to representing the class.

Counsel filing a motion for appointment should consider accompanying the motion with a proposed case management order describing lead counsel's duties and ability to delegate work and the responsibilities of any executive or steering committee of counsel. (See the section titled "Determining Leadership and Working Protocols" in Chapter 8).

SELECTING WHICH CLAIMS TO ASSERT

The business of selecting claims to assert on behalf of the class will profoundly affect the outcome of any case. From a substantive standpoint, counsel must decide whether to assert federal or state law claims (or both) and must determine which causes of action are available given the products or conduct at issue. And, from a procedural standpoint, the amenability to certification of the menu of available claims must be carefully considered not at class certification (when it will be too late) but instead when the complaint is filed. Each set of considerations is discussed briefly in the following sections.

Assessing the Available Claims

There is no one-size-fits-all class action complaint. While a plaintiff's lawyer may be accustomed to pleading very broadly, with many causes of action, in a non-class case, this is generally not an effective pleading strategy in a class action. For a complaint to stand a chance, the claims asserted must be tailored to the subject matter and conduct at issue. While a complaint in a non-class action may include many allegations and legal theories, a complaint in a class action should be focused on legal theories that can be proven with common evidence. This requires both a review of the legal claims available and the particular theory of the case. A products liability case against a California company may be filed under that state's consumer protection statute, for example, while a securities fraud case will likely involve claims under federal and possibly state securities statutes. The selected claims must provide the relief your client and the prospective class seek, and relevant questions in that regard include whether the available causes of action provide for injunctive or declaratory relief, or monetary damages (or both).

The parameters of the proposed class (in terms of geography, time frame, and other objective criteria) must also be taken into account. If proposed class members live in multiple states or across the country, asserting federal claims (if they are available) might avoid complex choice of law and manageability issues often associated with claims brought under the laws of many states. (See "Addressing Choice of Law Issues" below for more on choice of law issues.) When some critical mass of the class is comprised of residents of one or only a few states, by contrast, counsel should analyze available remedies under state law. In addition, counsel should make sure they file their case in a forum with a meaningful connection to their claims. The days of rote allegations that personal jurisdiction is appropriate because a defendant "does business" in a forum appear to be over, given the Supreme Court's decision in *Bristol-Myers Squibb Co. v. Superior Court*.[8]

---

8. Bristol-Myers Squibb Co. v. Superior Court, __ U.S. __, 137 S. Ct. 1773, 1781 (2017) ("What is needed—and what is missing here—is a connection between the forum and the specific claims at issue.").

Asserting state law claims and filing the case in state court may inure to the benefit of the plaintiff, but making an early assessment about whether the case will end up in federal court (because of CAFA or diversity jurisdiction issues, for example) could ultimately save valuable time that will otherwise be lost while the case lingers in procedural purgatory. Careful analysis of and compliance with any given state's pre-filing and pleading requirements, including pre-suit demand letters and the like, will also help avoid unnecessary delay and distraction.

Counsel considering asserting state law claims on behalf of a proposed class should also make sure the relevant state statutes allow for class actions. California and New York may, for example, while Tennessee and Illinois may not. The Supreme Court, in its 2010 decision in *Shady Grove Orthopedic Associates v. Allstate Insurance Co.*, weighed in on the related question of whether a federal court may exercise CAFA jurisdiction over a proposed class action that could not be pursued on a class-wide basis had it been filed in the state court across the street.[9] The Court concluded that the answer is yes, and that Rule 23 preempted a New York state statute prohibiting class actions for recovery of penalties. The result was that the plaintiff was allowed to pursue a state law class action in federal court, even though it would have been barred from doing so in state court. The Court analyzed the Rules Enabling Act and issued fractured opinions on the question of whether Rule 23 abridges, enlarges, or modifies a New York substantive right. Justice Stevens' concurring opinion—which is the controlling opinion because it was decided on the narrowest grounds—explained that when the Federal Rules conflict with a state procedural rule, the Federal Rules control in federal court. What is left to lower courts faced with similar inquiries is the determination of whether the relevant state law provision is procedural or substantive, and whether application of Rule 23 to preempt it would abridge, enlarge, or modify a substantive right.

Amenability to Certification

Even the best substantive claims may be ill-suited for certification under Rule 23. Waiting until class certification to find out if the claims are likely to be certified is a mistake. Instead, that assessment should be among the primary factors taken into account when counsel is selecting claims to include in a class action complaint.

---

9. Shady Grove Orthopedic Associates v. Allstate Ins. Co., 559 U.S. 393 (2010).

The following table includes examples of the types of claims and causes of action that might or might not be amenable to certification:

Likely Class Claims	Unlikely Class Claims
Claims based on written representations provided to all or virtually all class members	Claims based on oral or written representations that varied materially during the class period
Claims that focus on the defendants' conduct	Claims that focus on class members' reliance, knowledge, or perceptions
Statutes that include presumptions based on objective criteria	Statutes that include presumptions based on subjective criteria
An issue class for victims of a single event	Personal injury claims arising from multiple events

The analysis is not rote, and the unique facts of the case and characteristics of class members must of course be taken into account. Even claims that focus on the defendants' conduct might be subject to criticisms under Rule 23(b)(3)'s "predominance" requirement or the implicit, court-constructed "ascertainability" requirement, if the class definition includes persons or entities that were "uninjured" by the conduct at issue or who are otherwise difficult to identify using objective criteria. (See "Components of a Good Class Definition" later in the chapter for more on defining the class.)

SELECTING A VENUE

Practitioners will want to carefully consider the best available venue for filing their class action. Possible venues will depend on, among other things, which causes of action are alleged, where the parties reside, where the conduct occurred, whether the case is brought in state or federal court, whether the case is subject to removal from state to federal court under CAFA, and whether a multi-district litigation (MDL) proceeding has been established. Depending on how important counsel perceive the venue selection to be, that determination can drive which parties to name, which claims to allege and what class to represent.

In evaluating competing venues, counsel must carefully review the relevant local rules for specific rules about class actions, as well as more generally on motion practice, trial deadlines and pre-trial publicity. Local rules vary markedly even among counties within a single state, and among federal districts within a single circuit. For example, some archaic local rules, which are arguably inconsistent with Federal Rule of Civil Procedure 23, mandate the filing of a motion for class certification within 90 days of the filing of the case.[10]

Federal Court Actions

Venue in the federal courts is determined by statute; there are no venue rules specific to class actions. There is a general venue provision for many federal cases.[11] There are also special venue provisions, applicable to particular statutes or kinds of actions.[12] Practitioners need to research which venue provision applies to each cause of action alleged.

The general venue provision looks to where the defendant "resides" or where "a substantial part of the events or omissions giving rise to the claim occurred."[13] For a corporate entity, its residence is any judicial district in which it "is subject to the court's personal jurisdiction."[14] Some specific venue statutes focus on the plaintiff's residence.[15] In the context of a class action, the venue determination is based on where the named plaintiffs live, not where absent class members reside.

Venue and MDL

Selecting the perfect venue may be only temporary if the case is subject to transfer to an existing MDL. Counsel should research whether similar federal cases have been, or are likely to be, consolidated for pretrial purposes in one court (MDL). While theoretically a case will be returned to the home forum for trial, as a practical matter, that rarely happens. See Chapter 8, Managing Multiple Class and Enforcement Actions.

State Court Actions and CAFA

States have their own venue rules that dictate where a case may properly be filed. However, under the Class Action Fairness Act (CAFA), many state law class actions are subject to removal to federal court. So,

---

10. *See, e.g.,* C. D. Cal. Local Civil Rule 23-3.
11. 28 U.S.C. § 1391.
12. *Id.*
13. *Id.*
14. *Id.* § 1391(b)(1).
15. *See, e.g.,* 42 U.S.C. § 2000e-5(f)(3) (Title VII).

in selecting a forum, counsel should determine the proper state venue and also evaluate whether the case is subject to CAFA removal. CAFA contains certain exceptions to removal and, if keeping the case in state court is a high priority, then counsel should evaluate whether the case satisfies any of these exceptions.[16]

Other Factors to Weigh in Selecting Venue

Assuming that venue is available in more than one court, counsel should consider some other strategic and practical factors in selecting the best option:

- **Research substantive case law.** What are the key rulings in the circuit on your particular cause of action? How have similar cases been treated?
- **Research procedural law, local rules, and custom.** Has the forum been receptive to class actions generally? Does the forum have local rules about when class certification must be filed or how discovery is handled? How are out-of-town counsel treated when litigating in that forum?
- **Research judges and jury pools.** Are the class action cases assigned to a single department or judge? What is the track record for that judge? While your case is not likely to go to trial, evaluate whether the jury pool is likely to favor your case.
- **Consider your resources.** Do you have the capacity and resources to litigate in a distant forum? Is the cost of traveling and staying in a hotel in that jurisdiction particularly high?
- **Identify local counsel.** Can you identify a competent and trusted local counsel? What can local counsel tell you about the culture of the forum in which they practice?
- **Explore local media.** Are the local media likely to be interested in and sympathetic to your case? Class actions tend to get a lot of attention from the media and, if possible, you want it to favorably portray your case.

---

16. *See generally* THE CLASS ACTION FAIRNESS ACT: LAW AND STRATEGY (Gregory C. Cook ed., 2013).

ADDRESSING CHOICE OF LAW ISSUES

Mention "choice of law" and even the most dedicated practitioner's eyes are likely to glaze over. But getting the choice of law analysis right at the outset of a case can determine whether the claims will survive motions to dismiss and class certification challenges. Further, if there is an argument that a single state's law should apply (or federal law should apply), class certification should be much easier.

Choice of law issues in class actions are typically implicated in federal diversity jurisdiction cases, that is, cases prosecuted in federal court that do not involve federal questions. The first question is whether the parties to the litigation are bound by an enforceable choice of law agreement. Ironically, this can be a benefit to plaintiff counsel. If such agreement applies, and if it clearly sets forth the substantive law that will govern any relevant dispute, it is usually determinative. If not, the analysis can become more convoluted, raising the specter of the *Erie* doctrine and other flashbacks to law school.

What follows is a brief overview of some choice of law issues to consider in the early stages of investigating and pleading a class case. The substantive and procedural analyses can be intricate, however, and significant choice of law issues requires a more in-depth analysis that is beyond the scope of this chapter.

Which Choice of Law Rules Apply?

Absent an enforceable choice of law agreement, the parties and the court are first faced with the question of which jurisdiction's *choice of law* rules apply. The short answer is that the forum state's rules typically govern. Under long-standing Supreme Court precedent, a federal court sitting in diversity that is faced with more than one potentially applicable law typically uses the choice of law rules of the state court.[17] And state courts apply their own choice of law rules (described later).

What Substantive Law Applies?

The next question is what *substantive law* applies. The federal choice of law statute (28 U.S.C. § 1652) directs a federal court sitting in diversity to apply state law on the merits. In *Erie Railroad Co. v. Tompkins*,[18]

---

17. Klaxon Co. v. Stentor Electric Mfg. Co., 313 U.S. 487, 496 (1941).
18. Erie R.R. Co. v. Tompkins, 304 U.S. 64 (1938).

the Supreme Court interpreted section 1652 to mean that federal courts should apply both state statutory and state common law to resolve the merits of a case.

While states have adopted an array of choice of law rules to answer this question, they generally fit into four categories (with some states having adopted hybrids of the categories):

- **Most significant relationship test.** A majority of courts apply the "most significant relationship test" adopted by the Restatement (Second) of Conflict of Laws. Under this test, the court first analyzes the substantive legal issue in the case (*e.g.*, tort, contract, etc.), and then analyzes which state has the most significant relationship to the relevant occurrence(s) and parties.

- **Government interest analysis.** This policy-driven approach requires the court to first identify relevant policies underlying the potentially applicable state's laws. The court then analyzes those policies in conjunction with the state's contacts to the occurrence(s) and parties to the litigation, and will generally apply the law of the state that the court determines has the greatest interest in having its laws applied to the dispute.

- **Lex loci.** Under this traditional approach to choice of law issues, the court determines the substantive rights of an injured party based on the law of the state in which the injury occurred.

- **Lex fori.** Infrequently applied nowadays, this approach favors the law of the state in which the action is brought without further analysis. Very few states (like Louisiana and Michigan) continue to apply the lex fori test, and only in tort cases.

Choice of Law Issues in MDLs and Transfers

Multi-district litigation cases (MDLs) raise particularly thorny choice of law issues. An MDL often includes some cases that were transferred and some that were not; some class cases and some individual cases; some federal question cases and some diversity cases; some cases that assert state law claims, others that assert federal claims. The resulting bramble of procedural and substantive issues and the overlay of often conflicting claims render the choice of law rules as they apply to MDLs difficult, if not impossible, to summarize.

With that said, the general proposition that the presiding court will apply the choice of law rules of the forum state generally appears to hold true in MDLs. How the MDL court decides federal procedural issues, however, is subject to an analysis too intricate to be explored fully here. Suffice to say that the likelihood that the MDL court will apply its own circuit's precedent when it comes to substantive federal issues makes the determination of where an MDL ultimately lands an important—and sometimes dispositive—issue for the litigants. See further discussion on this topic in Chapter 8.

The choice of law issues raised by transfer under 28 U.S.C. § 1404 (for the convenience of the parties and witnesses) or under 28 U.S.C. § 1406 (for jurisdictional reasons) are beyond the scope of this chapter, but likewise often require complex choice of law analyses.

Strategic Calls Relating to Choice of Law

While choice of law issues might be confusing to say the least, they also may present the savvy practitioner with the opportunity for strategic decision making.

Streamlining, for example, should be a top priority for anyone considering asserting the laws of several states in a single case. Look at the applicable state laws and determine whether you can argue that the laws of the various states do not conflict and present no manageability concerns for the court. Cases in which these types of arguments may be effective include consumer claims brought under the similar consumer protection statutes of several states, or antitrust claims brought under the *Illinois Brick* repealer statutes of several states.

Making the tough calls early in the case is also often difficult, but should yield rewards in the long run. Even if the laws of several states may be available, will it ultimately benefit your clients and the class to assert them all? Consider stipulating early in the litigation to apply the substantive law of only a few key states, and toll claims under the laws of other states. Reducing the state laws in play will make the court's job easier, which usually translates to greater chances of success. On the other hand, pleading only one or a few states' laws carries risks as well. For example, if the court determines that the relevant choice of law precludes the class representative from asserting the selected state's claim, the entire case could be dismissed. Either way, in other words, choice of law decisions can be dispositive at the pleading stage.

Class certification is often where the choice of law issues have the biggest impact. Don't wait until you see a blistering opposition to certification to decide how these issues should play out. When the laws of many states are in play, you should decide well before you move for class certification—and perhaps before you even file your complaint—whether to seek certification of a class in each of those states (leaving most of the work to the court—usually not advisable); seek certification of one nationwide class under the laws of one or more states (often very difficult but not impossible); or seek certification of subclasses grouped by similar state laws (a middle road that might give the court some much needed options). Relevant inquiries include whether injured class members are found in only certain states and whether a nationwide class or multiple-state class will ultimately benefit class members, as weighed against the attendant certification challenges.

DEFINING THE CLASS

In preparing to file a class action, defining the class (or classes) is a critical task, one which is often not given sufficient attention. Most fundamentally, the class definition determines the scope of the action, and distinguishes the case from similar or overlapping cases (if any). It will also determine *which* claims are tolled and for *whom*, up until the class certification determination is finally resolved.[19] In recent years, defendants have been increasingly successful in defeating class certification based on arguments challenging the class definition. While a district court can re-write a proposed definition to address a defendant's concerns, practitioners should not assume a court will step in to correct problems. Where possible, get it right the first time.

Components of a Good Class Definition

Class member characteristics. At the most basic level, the class definition should describe the kind of person who is in the class (e.g., "purchaser," "employee," "customer," "plan participant," "resident," "loan officer").

---

19. Am. Pipe & Constr. Co. v. Utah, 414 U.S. 538, 553 (1974) ("the commencement of the original class suit tolls the running of the statute for all purported members of the class . . .").

Defendant and conduct. The definition should describe the defendant, and the conduct, policy, or product at issue (e.g., "all purchasers of Acme auto company's 2016 Model L," "all uniformed officers subject to the Cincinnati Police Department's overtime policy").

Temporal scope. The class definition should include a time period during which the challenged conduct by the defendant is alleged to have occurred. Depending on the case, the "opening" date for the class may be a function of the facts (e.g., when the conduct started or when the first named plaintiff was affected) or the law (e.g., statute of limitations or other statutory provision). If the allegedly illegal conduct was only for a limited period and no injunctive relief is sought, the definition may also have an end date.

Geographical scope. The class definition also should specify the geographic scope of the class. That might be driven, for example, by the location of the defendant's facilities (e.g., "all sales reps employed in Acme's Northwest region") or by the state in which the class members reside ("all Colorado customers of Cable Company who were assessed a 'rewiring' fee").

No fail-safe classes. While it seems counterintuitive, case law prohibits a class definition that defines the class with reference to a finding of liability. In other words, the class cannot be "all persons *injured by* the conduct of X company" or "all African American workers *discriminated against* based on their race." A liability-based definition is known as a "fail-safe" class. The rationale for the rule prohibiting fail-safe classes is twofold. At class certification, no merits determination of who has been injured has yet been made, so there is no way to know who is in the class or who should receive a class notice prior to trial. The more frequently cited explanation is that, if the defendant wins on liability at trial, the universe of class members bound by the judgment will be zero since, by definition, no one was injured.

Not based on subjective state of mind. Related to the fail-safe class problem, the class cannot be defined based upon the subjective state of mind of class members. So, a class defined as "all persons who believed and relied on the statements of X company" would also not be sufficient because there is no way to know who is in the class without the individual testimony of each member. Again, to whom could class notice be sent prior to trial?

Not overly complex or vague. In a laudable effort to be precise, class definitions can become hyper-technical or prolix. Work hard to avoid this. There is no reason that the definition should be one long, complicated sentence with multiple clauses and qualifiers. It can be a series of short simple sentences. Potential class members should be able to read the class definition and know whether or not they are members of the class. Similarly, one might be tempted to make the class definition somewhat vague either because no discovery has yet occurred or in an effort to ensure broad discovery. Again, this can be risky if not corrected by the time of any motion practice.

Exclude class members with obvious conflicts. Defendants often argue that there are conflicts of interest among class members. To the extent you can anticipate those arguments, explicitly exclude those class members from the class definition from the outset. ("This class does not include any consumers of X product who are currently employed by X company or whose immediate family members are employed by X company.")

Multiple Classes and Subclasses

Sometimes, a need might arise for more than one class or for a subclass, because of differences among the affected group. Some class members may be entitled to certain remedies (like injunctive relief or restitution), while other class members are not. In a multi-state case, class members from one state may have additional legal claims based on their particular state's laws.

Keep in mind that every class or subclass must independently satisfy the specific class certification requirements in Rule 23, and have their own class representatives. The additional class might be absolutely necessary and appropriate, but because each class or subclass complicates the case and creates additional hurdles for certification, counsel should carefully evaluate them.

Class Definition and Ascertainability

Recent decisions from the Third Circuit have held that plaintiffs must satisfy an implied requirement that class members are "ascertainable," meaning that there is a "reliable and administratively feasible" way to identify class members.[20] Specifically, the Third Circuit has suggested

---

20. *See* Carrera v. Bayer Corp, 727 F.3d 300 (3d Cir. 2013); Marcus v. BMW of North America, LLC, 687 F.3d 583 (3d Cir. 2012).

that class member self-identification by affidavit might not satisfy its ascertainability rule, particularly if the defendant would not have the opportunity to cross-examine the class member. Thus, defendant's business records may be necessary in some cases. This heightened requirement is particularly troublesome in consumer class actions where there often exist *no* records of purchases of inexpensive consumer goods.

The Third Circuit's ascertainability requirement is controversial and has been rejected by at least two circuits.[21] The Seventh Circuit's decision in *Mullins* provides the most thorough repudiation of the reasoning and policy arguments underlying the Third Circuit's *Carrera* decision. It held that questions of how to identify class members should properly be evaluated as part of the manageability analysis of Rule 23(b)(3) and should be balanced against the consequences of having no class action.[22]

The Supreme Court has, to date, declined to accept review of a case squarely presenting these differing views of "ascertainability." Until the Supreme Court has addressed and resolved the question, practitioners should be familiar with the case law in their circuit and anticipate how they can satisfy it or plan discovery to determine that question. This issue is most consequential in consumer cases involving relatively inexpensive products, typically purchased with cash or without records to identify the discrete purchase. It would also be significant in other consumer cases such as the Telephone Consumer Protection Act (TCPA).

DRAFTING THE COMPLAINT AND CLASS ALLEGATIONS

The product of your investigation and your decisions about parties, venue, claims, remedies, class definition, and co-counsel will then be used to prepare the class action complaint. The elements that must be pled will vary based on the substantive area of the law and the claims selected. However, some general practice points apply regardless of the kind of class action you are filing. As in all circumstances, check the local rules for any specific pleading requirements.

---

21. Mullins v. Direct Digital LLC, 795 F.3d 654 (7th Cir. 2015); Rikos v. Proctor & Gamble Co., 799 F.3d 497 (6th Cir. 2015).

22. *Mullins*, 795 F.3d at 672. Indeed, in another post-*Carrera* decision, the Third Circuit itself seemed to walk back some of the more far-reaching interpretations of *Carrera*. Byrd v. Aaron's Inc., 784 F.3d 154 (3d Cir. 2015).

Plausible Set of Facts, Not Bare Allegations or Legal Conclusions

The Supreme Court's decision in *Bell Atlantic Corp. v. Twombly*[23] altered the landscape for federal pleading and particularly for class actions. By its terms, Federal Rule of Civil Procedure 8(a)(2) requires only "a short and plain statement of the claim showing that the pleader is entitled to relief." In *Twombly*, the Court held that the facts must suggest a "plausible claim."[24] The Court affirmed the dismissal of alleged antitrust violations among defendant telephone companies, concluding that the class complaint pled insufficient facts to show a conspiracy.[25] Two years later, in *Ashcroft v. Iqbal*,[26] the Supreme Court went further and encouraged courts to "draw on [their] judicial experience and common sense" in determining whether a claim was plausible.[27]

Thus, to defeat a motion to dismiss, counsel must plead specific facts to satisfy the heightened *Twombly/Iqbal* requirements. This task is easier said than done because counsel will not have had access to discovery. Errant corporations and government agencies rarely advertise their wrongdoing. *Twombly* underscores the importance of a thorough investigation.

Media-Friendly Introductory Paragraph

Counsel will want to begin with a pithy introductory paragraph that explains why the case is righteous. If media is planned in connection with the filing, this introduction will provide reporters with an easy-to-comprehend synopsis. Your paragraph(s) should be legalese-free (really!) and should answer four questions: who are the parties, what happened, what does the class want, and what's the broader significance of the case. It should be "quotable," but keep in mind that the court will also read it—perhaps as its first introduction to the case—so it should also have a serious and professional tone.

---

23. Bell Atlantic Corp. v. Twombly, 550 U.S. 544 (2007).
24. *Id.* at 555–56.
25. *Id.*
26. Ashcroft v. Iqbal, 556 U.S. 662 (2009).
27. *Id.* at 679.

Class Definition and Class Allegations

The complaint should include the class definition (discussed earlier) as well as specific allegations mirroring the requirements of Rule 23(a) and 23(b). Those allegations should not simply be a recitation of the language of the rule. For each requirement, the allegations should include facts specific to the case (e.g., a list of common questions, an estimate of the number of class members).

Compelling Individual Stories with a Caution

The allegations about your named plaintiffs should tell a compelling and detailed narrative that highlights the real-world consequences of the alleged wrongdoing. The media will use those stories to explain the case to a lay audience. Keep in mind, however, that your named plaintiff must be typical of the class. Do not include extraneous facts or circumstances that will create typicality arguments for the defendant or suggest potentially damaging avenues of discovery.

Non-Class Claims for Named Plaintiffs?

Named plaintiffs often have claims in connection with the wrongdoing that are purely individual, and not suited to be class claims. For example, a worker who has blown the whistle on fraud by the employer may have suffered retaliation as a result. Because these individual claims usually arise from the same set of facts, it may be necessary to plead them in the class complaint or risk losing them. Be thoughtful about whether those individual claims will invite an argument by the defense that your plaintiff is an inadequate class representative because he or she will be more concerned about their individual claim than zealously pursing the class claims. A motion to sever or stay the individual claim while the class claims are litigated can defuse that threat.

Selection of Remedies

Counsel should carefully consider which remedies to seek for the class. In a large class, remedies requiring individual class member testimony (e.g., emotional distress damages) may create manageability concerns. If injunctive relief is sought, there must be a class representative with standing, meaning someone who could benefit if injunctive relief is granted. Other types of equitable relief might be easier to certify (for instance, a claim for rescission of an illegal contract, void transactions, unconscionable sale, or a claim for an accounting).

MEETING DEMAND OR EXHAUSTION REQUIREMENTS

For some kinds of cases, the law imposes a requirement that a plaintiff exhaust administrative remedies or otherwise make a demand. Municipalities often require the submission of a government tort claim prior to filing suit. A plaintiff must file a charge of discrimination with the Equal Employment Opportunity Commission or equivalent state fair employment agency before filing a discrimination lawsuit. Some state deceptive trade claims also include the requirement of sending a written demand. Counsel should research and comply with any applicable exhaustion requirements as part of the pre-filing preparation.

The demand should allege the class nature of the allegation to foreclose any argument that exhaustion was only effective for the individual, and not the class. Including language such as "on behalf of themselves and all similarly situated persons" may be sufficient. Where possible, the demand should specify what relief is requested.

Even where demand or exhaustion is not legally required, a demand letter may be a smart move. Where liability is reasonably clear, it may allow the case to be resolved swiftly, and short of contested litigation. Where the defendant places a high value on avoiding, or at least managing, publicity about the underlying conduct, a plaintiff has the best opportunity to leverage that advantage for the benefit of the class *before* the case is filed. While a class action cannot be settled confidentiality, the media story is very different when the press release is about a settlement and the language has been negotiated. Sometimes, a courtesy heads-up to the other side before filing will garner good will with defense decision makers; sometimes not.

A demand letter can be very useful later in supporting a motion for attorneys' fees to demonstrate that the defendant had an opportunity to avoid the expense of plaintiffs' fees but chose to litigate instead. Under California law, plaintiffs must send a demand letter if their counsel will later seek attorneys' fees based on the catalyst theory (i.e., that the litigation prompted the defendant to "voluntarily" change the challenged practice).[28]

---

28. Graham v. DaimlerChrysler Corp., 34 Cal. 4th 553, 560 (2004).

The downside of sending a demand letter is that it alerts a defendant that a lawsuit is coming and allows it to begin preparing a defense and a media response. Surprise is a huge natural advantage for plaintiffs and should be sacrificed only with care.

DEVELOPING A CASE NARRATIVE AND COMMUNICATION STRATEGY

Media is ordinarily an important part of a plaintiff's class action strategy. Press coverage can be extremely useful in identifying witnesses and potential class members. In many cases, defendants will have sophisticated public relations support so counsel will want to ensure that plaintiffs get their "spin" on a case out first. As the representative of the plaintiff, counsel will have the advantage of developing an affirmative media strategy before the case is filed.

Themes and Case Narrative

Counsel should identify some simple case themes that fit the case. Like jury arguments, those themes tend to paint the case in terms of good and bad. ("Company tricked most vulnerable elderly consumers," "Female applicants just want employer to provide a level playing field," "Big bank used incomprehensible fine print to cheat homeowners.")

Use those themes to build a case narrative. A good case narrative tells a story, with a beginning, a middle, and a proposed ending (the outcome of the lawsuit). It should be a one or two paragraph explanation of the case, which identifies the parties, the challenged conduct, the relief, and the significance of the case. The narrative should be written in simple language and be free of legalese. Be careful about being too specific because the facts may change as the case evolves (e.g., claims dismissed, unforeseen discovery). The case narrative should be used in preparing press releases, sound bites, and clients for media appearances.

Communication Tools

Counsel should develop a case website that class members and the media can access. It should be clear and easy to navigate, and provide links to important information or pleadings. They should include an FAQ section and a toll-free method for contacting counsel. In appropriate cases, counsel should also develop social media tools for providing information about the case.

Media Strategy

Before developing a media strategy, counsel should research any local court rules regulating media in connection with litigation. While such rules are disfavored, one does not want to appear to be attempting to taint the jury pool. There may be other reasons to avoid media that should be evaluated (e.g., identity of minor client is confidential). If your team is not familiar with the jurisdiction, you might want to consider hiring a local media consultant.

Counsel should determine the audience and target media based upon the specific case. The business press might be your focus if you are trying to reach your potential witnesses in a securities class action. If you have a predominantly Spanish-speaking class of low-income workers, Spanish language radio may be your best option. If you are trying to influence a government enforcement agency, you need to determine the relevant outlets followed by its key decision makers. You may also want to cultivate influential bloggers in the appropriate substantive area. If there is a particular media outlet from which you especially want coverage, counsel should consider providing an exclusive to that organization.

Counsel should identify which named plaintiffs and lawyers can best speak for the case. Named plaintiffs should be well-prepared and sympathetic. Lawyers need to be persuasive and speak in simple sound bites. Consider whether allies (e.g., a union or consumer group) can convey specific helpful messages.

In connection with the filing of a complaint, counsel may want to hold a press conference or issue a press release.

CONCLUSION

Given the high stakes, risk, and expense of a class action, there is no substitute for thorough investigation, analysis, and preparation. That investment will create early momentum in the litigation and credibility with defense counsel and the court.

3

Defendant's Options for Forum Selection

Gregory C. Cook and Steven C. Corhern

FORUM OPTIONS FOR DEFENDANTS

It is often said that the plaintiff is the "master of the complaint." Perhaps for that reason, courts will almost always honor the plaintiff's choice of forum. Defendants, on the other hand, have no reason to respect that choice. Plaintiffs choose courts that favor them, and there are many reasons a defendant might desire to disrupt the plaintiff's choice—ranging from mere inconvenience to overt judicial hostility.

This chapter discusses what options a defendant has to change the plaintiff's chosen forum. The bulk of this discussion focuses on arbitration. The proliferation of arbitration agreements in recent years combined with the numerous Supreme Court decisions on the topic have created an enormous body of case law in this area. This chapter identifies some of the more important strategic considerations defendants should evaluate before moving to compel arbitration. In addition to arbitration, this chapter addresses other methods of disrupting the plaintiff's chosen forum, including forum selection clauses, motions to transfer venue, removal to federal court, and personal jurisdiction motions as to the class. This chapter concludes with a discussion of the options defendants have for avoiding litigation in multiple forums.

MOVING TO COMPEL ARBITRATION

Courts have also shown an increasing willingness to honor arbitration agreements and to resolve doubts about arbitrability in favor of arbitration. Indeed, the Federal Arbitration Act (FAA) preempts most state law rules that can be used to defeat arbitration.[1] Thus, arbitration is one of the best ways to defeat the plaintiff's chosen forum and defeat the class action before it even begins.

Advantages and Disadvantages of Arbitration

There are many advantages to arbitration. First, arbitration agreements can include a class action waiver, which is a provision that simply states that the plaintiff cannot bring a claim on behalf of a class.[2] In 2011, the Supreme Court affirmed the validity of such waivers in *AT&T Mobility LLC v. Concepcion*.[3] Since then, these waivers have become common place. A defendant whose contract contains such a waiver might have to arbitrate the individual claim, but the specter of class litigation or arbitration can be avoided.

Second, a motion to compel arbitration is essentially a separate proceeding often divorced from the merits of the underlying lawsuit. Thus, the court should focus on the arbitration agreement and whether it is valid and enforceable, not whatever terrible things the plaintiff may have alleged in the complaint.

Third, there is an extensive body of case law on compelling arbitration. Most questions related to the enforceability of an arbitration agreement have been litigated in some form or another. This body of case law should make it easier for a defendant to assess whether a motion to compel will be successful. It should also make it easier for the court to make a decision, which can speed up the time to resolution.

---

1. "Section 2 [of the Federal Arbitration Act] is a congressional declaration of a liberal federal policy favoring arbitration agreements, notwithstanding any state substantive or procedural policies to the contrary. The effect of the section is to create a body of federal substantive law of arbitrability, applicable to any arbitration agreement within the coverage of the Act." Moses H. Cone Mem'l Hosp. v. Mercury Constr. Corp., 460 U.S. 1, 24 (1983).

2. For example, the class action waiver in the Supreme Court's decision in *AT&T Mobility LLC v. Concepcion* required that claims be brought in the parties' "individual capacity, and not as a plaintiff or class member in any purported class or representative proceeding." *See* 563 U.S. 333, 336 (2011).

3. *Concepcion*, 563 U.S. at 336.

Perhaps most importantly, the Federal Arbitration Act makes a ruling on arbitration immediately appealable. The defendant will not need to slog through discovery, dispositive motions, class certification, or a trial—spending large sums on costs and attorney fees; they can instead immediately seek relief from an incorrect result. In other words, trial judges are especially careful to reach the correct result, perhaps, in part, because they can be almost immediately reversed for failing to follow this well-developed body of law.

> The Federal Arbitration Act makes a ruling on arbitration immediately appealable.

Arbitration also has numerous advantages that are not specifically related to class certification but might be relevant to the defendant's forum decision. The process is usually faster and cheaper than litigation, it uses simplified procedural rules, and often markedly limits the discovery available. Most arbitration agreements allow the parties to choose the arbitrator, who will usually have some training in the law or subject matter of the dispute and, thus, will be more predictable than a lay jury. Finally, arbitration is often a private affair that does not result in a published opinion or media attention though there is no positive legal requirement that arbitrations be kept confidential.[4] Parties that desire confidentiality can achieve this result by incorporating a confidentiality requirement into their arbitration agreements. Such provisions are generally enforceable, though a few courts have found such confidentiality provisions unconscionable.

Of course, arbitration has some disadvantages. First, arbitration awards are usually final. This means that a defendant will not have an opportunity to appeal and correct errors in the arbitrator's ruling, even errors of law (which can be a significant consideration if the major defenses center on legalities rather than equities). In fact, a court can generally overturn an arbitration award in only very narrow circumstances, such as fraud, corruption, evident bias, misconduct, or acting outside the scope of his powers.[5] As Justice Kagan explained in *Oxford Health Plans LLC v. Sutter*:

---

4. Amy J. Schmitz, *Untangling the Privacy Paradox in Arbitration*, 54 U. KAN. L. REV. 1211 (2006); Laurie Kratky Doré, *Public Courts Versus Private Justice: It's Time to Let Some Sun Shine in on Alternative Dispute Resolution*, 81 CHI.-KENT L. REV. 463, 466 (2006); Jean R. Sternlight, *Creeping Mandatory Arbitration: Is It Just?*, 57 STAN. L. REV. 1631, 1647 (2005).
5. *See* 9 U.S.C. § 10.

A party seeking relief [from an arbitration award] bears a heavy burden. It is not enough to show that the arbitrator committed an error—or even a serious error. Because the parties bargained for the arbitrator's construction of their agreement, an arbitral decision even arguably construing or applying the contract must stand, regardless of a court's view of its (de)merits.[6]

Importantly, most courts hold that parties cannot alter the grounds for vacating an arbitrator's award by agreement (meaning that the arbitration clause cannot create an appeal right in court no matter what contractual language is used).[7]

The lack of appellate rights leads directly to the second and most significant disadvantage—the possibility of class arbitration. As the name suggests, class arbitration is arbitration on a class-wide basis. This is likely only a possibility if the arbitration clause is silent as to class action procedure. While recent Supreme Court precedent and more carefully crafted arbitration provisions have made the possibility of class arbitration less likely, it is a dangerous proposition and one that defendants should always consider before moving to compel arbitration. As Justice Scalia explained in *Concepcion*:

[C]lass arbitration greatly increases risks to defendants. Informal procedures do of course have a cost: The absence of multilayered review makes it more likely that errors will go uncorrected. Defendants are willing to accept the costs of these errors in arbitration, since their impact is limited to the size of individual disputes, and presumably outweighed by savings from avoiding the courts. But when damages allegedly owed to tens of thousands of potential claimants are aggregated and decided at once, the risk of an error will often become unacceptable. Faced with even a small chance of a devastating loss, defendants will be pressured into settling questionable claims.[8]

A third disadvantage is that the motion to compel arbitration might turn into a mini-lawsuit with discovery on issues of contract formation as well as defenses such as unconscionability. For example, the dispute in *Concepcion* went all the way to the Supreme Court before the lower court ever passed on the merits. The lawsuit was first filed in 2006 and the dispute over arbitration was finally decided by the Supreme Court in 2011, five years later. While most arbitration disputes will not last as long as the one in *Concepcion*, defendants should be aware that moving

6. Oxford Health Plans LLC v. Sutter, 569 U.S. 564, 569 (2013).
7. Hall St. Assocs., L.L.C. v. Mattel, Inc., 552 U.S. 576, 586 (2008) (holding that § 10 and § 11 of the FAA provide the exclusive grounds for vacating an arbitration award).
8. 563 U.S. at 350.

to compel arbitration could drastically extend the duration of litigation. Of course, this can sometimes work to the defendant's advantage if the plaintiff has neither the will nor the resources for a protracted fight.

Fourth, and along the same lines, some judges are openly hostile to arbitration agreements. California courts, for example, have long disfavored arbitration and will often stretch to find ways around them. In fact, many of the Supreme Court's decisions on arbitration—including *Concepcion*—started in California. Similarly, the former Chief Judge of the Alabama Supreme Court recently stated (in dissent) that all pre-dispute arbitration agreements violate the Seventh Amendment.[9] If the judge particularly disfavors arbitration, a defendant might anger the judge by moving to arbitrate. If the defendant's argument for compelling arbitration is not a strong one, the judge might deny the motion, leaving the defendant in court with an angry judge. Of course, this is a strategic decision that necessarily depends on the facts of each case.

Fifth, moving to compel arbitration might foreclose a class-wide settlement. As discussed in Chapter 9, class settlements can be advantageous because a defendant can effectively purchase finality in one stroke (except for those few individuals who opt out). For defendants facing a slew of individual cases or even multiple, competing class actions, this option might be preferable to engaging in years of protracted litigation on multiple fronts.[10] The Volkswagen emissions scandal is a recent example. Faced with thousands of individual cases and

---

9. Am. Bankers Ins. Co. of Fla. v. Tellis, 192 So. 3d 386, 401 (Ala. 2015) (Moore, C.J., dissenting) ("I do not agree that the Supreme Court's interpretation of the FAA is a law I am required to apply, because that interpretation does not conform to the United States Constitution I am sworn to uphold and support. What if a state court is presented with a constitutional question the United States Supreme Court has not yet considered? As far as my research shows, the United States Supreme Court has not yet considered whether its interpretation of the FAA violates the Seventh Amendment.").

10. Sullivan v. DB Investments, Inc., 667 F.3d 273, 339 (3d Cir. 2011) (Scirica, J., concurring) ("A responsible and fair settlement serves the interests of both plaintiffs and defendants and furthers the aims of the class action device. Plaintiffs receive redress of their claimed injuries without the burden of litigating individually. Defendants receive finality. Having released their claims for consideration, class members are precluded from continuing to press their claims . . . . A defendant, therefore, may be motivated to pay class members a premium and achieve a global settlement in order to avoid additional lawsuits, even ones where it might be able to file a straightforward motion to dismiss for failure to state a claim.").

a public relations nightmare, Volkswagen opted for a global settlement rather than protracted litigation.[11]

Additionally, defendants should consider whether compelling arbitration is likely to put an end to the matter. If the damages are high and the plaintiff's counsel already has secured multiple potential plaintiffs, the defendant might have to compel arbitration and actually arbitrate against each one of the plaintiffs. With modern social media and the potential for efficiently managing large numbers of individual arbitrations (for instance, reusing depositions and paper discovery), this possibility should be carefully reviewed.[12] A global settlement might be preferable in this situation. If a defendant believes that a class-wide settlement would be advantageous, then it should explore that option before moving to compel arbitration.

Should I move to compel arbitration to avoid the plaintiff's chosen forum?

Benefits of Arbitration	Downsides of Arbitration
• Agreement might contain a class action waiver	• Arbitrator's decision on merits is final; appeal is essentially not available
• Decision is divorced from the merits	• Possibility of class-wide arbitration
• Extensive body of case law	• Fight over arbitration might turn into mini-trial; judge might be openly hostile to arbitration
• Adverse decision immediately appealable	
• Faster, cheaper, confidential, and in front of experienced practitioner rather than a jury	• Forecloses possibility of class-wide settlement
	• Plaintiff's counsel might recruit large number of individual plaintiffs

Having discussed the strategic advantages and disadvantages of arbitration, we now turn to the specific questions defendants should ask before moving to compel arbitration.

---

11. Order Granting Final Approval, *In re* Volkswagen "Clean Diesel" Marketing, Sales Practices, & Products Liability Litigation (MDL 2672), Case No. 3:15-md-2672-CRB, (N.D. Cal. Oct. 25, 2016), ECF No. 2102.

12. Gregory C. Cook, Comment, *Why American Express v. Italian Colors Does Not Matter and Coordinated Pursuit of Aggregate Claims May Be a Viable Option After Concepcion*, 46 U. Mich. J.L. Reform Caveat 104 (2012).

Is There a Written Agreement to Arbitrate?

The FAA provides that

> [a] written provision in any maritime transaction or a contract evidencing a transaction involving commerce to settle by arbitration a controversy thereafter arising out of such contract or transaction . . . shall be valid, irrevocable, and enforceable, save upon such grounds as exist at law or in equity for the revocation of any contract.[13]

The first question, then, is whether there is a valid and enforceable agreement to arbitrate.

First, the agreement to arbitrate must be in writing. Thus, defense counsel should always ask: What written contracts are potentially applicable to this dispute? In our modern society, most commercial transactions will involve some kind of written agreement. For example, consumer products are usually sold with an express warranty. Cell phone companies require a written service contract. Financial institutions require customers to sign a deposit agreement. Online merchants require customers to agree to terms and conditions before completing a purchase. Each of these written contracts could contain a written arbitration provision. [14]

Assuming an agreement to arbitrate exists, the second question is whether the agreement is broad enough to cover the dispute. Again, courts will look to state contract law to answer this question. Language such as "arising out of" or "relating to" have been construed broadly to encompass nearly any dispute.[15] Yet, even broad language such as "arising out of" or "relating to" is not enough if the dispute does not relate to the contract containing the arbitration agreement.[16] Because this is a matter of state law contract interpretation, a defendant should consult the law of the relevant jurisdiction,

> Non-signatories can sometimes enforce an arbitration agreement.

---

13. *See* 9 U.S.C. § 2.

14. Brian T. Fitzpatrick, *The End of Class Actions?* 57 Ariz. L. Rev. 162 (2015).

15. *See* Title Max of Birmingham, Inc. v. Edwards, 973 So. 2d 1050, 1054 (Ala. 2007); Serra Chevrolet, Inc. v. Hock, 891 So. 2d 844, 847 (Ala. 2004). "[T]he words 'relating to' in the arbitration context are given a broad construction.").

16. *See* Carroll v. W.L. Petrey Wholesale Co., 941 So. 2d 234, 241 (Ala. 2006) (denying motion to compel arbitration; even though contract contained an arbitration provision covering all disputes arising from or related to the contract, the dispute did not relate, even indirectly, to the contract).

including any choice of law provisions, to determine the scope of the arbitration clause.

Defendants should be aware that non-signatories can sometimes enforce an arbitration agreement. For example, the defendant's contract might incorporate by reference a contract containing an arbitration provision. A defendant can also sometimes enforce an arbitration provision when it is the third-party beneficiary of the contract containing the arbitration provision. And, if the non-signatory asserts claims that are "intertwined with" or "related to" the contract, then a defendant can sometimes compel arbitration.[17] Again, whether a defendant can enforce an arbitration provision in these situations is governed by state contract law. Thus, a defendant should carefully consult the law of the state at issue, including the relevant choice of law rules, when assessing whether the arbitration agreement will be enforceable.

Is the Written Agreement Enforceable?

If there is a written agreement to arbitrate, the next question is whether that agreement will be enforceable. While section 2 of the FAA directs courts to enforce them, the last clause in section 2 (commonly referred to as the "savings clause") allows a court to invalidate an arbitration agreement "upon such grounds as exist at law or in equity for the revocation of any contract."[18] Thus, courts look to state contract law to determine enforceability.

Before *Concepcion*, plaintiffs had some success in arguing that arbitration agreements containing class action waivers were unconscionable, especially in the consumer context. They pointed out that these agreements effectively insulated defendants from liability for small value claims because those claims are more expensive to prove than the plaintiff could ever hope to recover in an individual action. In fact, *Concepcion* involved a California state court rule that invalidated class action waivers when the waiver "becomes in practice the exemption of the party from responsibility for its own fraud, or willful injury to the person or property of another."[19]

---

17. *See* Hanover Ins. Co. v. Atlantis Drywall & Framing LLC, 579 F. App'x 742, 745 (11th Cir. 2014), *on reh'g*, 611 F. App'x 585 (11th Cir. 2015) (describing situations when a non-signatory could enforce an arbitration provision under state law).

18. *See* 9 U.S.C. § 2.

19. *Concepcion*, 563 U.S. at 340.

Concepcion expressly rejected this argument and held that the FAA preempts any state law rule that is inconsistent with the FAA's command to "enforce arbitration agreements according to their terms." Writing for the majority, Justice Scalia acknowledged that this holding might lead to undesirable results but concluded that state law rules should yield to congressional directives:

> The dissent claims that class proceedings are necessary to prosecute small-dollar claims that might otherwise slip through the legal system. But States cannot require a procedure that is inconsistent with the FAA, even if it is desirable for unrelated reasons.[20]

In the aftermath of *Concepcion*, plaintiffs tried to limit its reach to state law rules. Pointing to a footnote in a 1985 Supreme Court decision, plaintiffs argued that public policy prohibits the prospective waiver of federal statutory rights. Plaintiffs then argued that an arbitration agreement containing a class action waiver amounts to a prospective waiver of these rights in practice because the costs of proving a claim on an individual basis far exceeded the value of the claim itself.[21] This argument was referred to as the "effective vindication" argument.

In *American Express v. Italian Colors Restaurant*, the Supreme Court rejected this argument and held that there is no public policy exception requiring the effective vindication of federal statutory rights. In *Italian Colors*, the plaintiff, a merchant, claimed that American Express had violated the antitrust laws in relation to certain credit card fees. The plaintiff pointed out that proving the antitrust violation would require an economic regression analysis. This analysis, in turn, required the plaintiff to hire an economist at a cost of at least half a million dollars. The plaintiffs argued that this enormous expense meant the class action waiver in their arbitration agreement amounted, in effect, to a waiver of their statutory rights under the Sherman Act. Justice Scalia, writing for the majority, rejected this argument saying:

> [T]he fact that it is not worth the expense involved in proving a statutory remedy does not constitute the elimination of the right to pursue that remedy. The class-action waiver merely limits arbitration to the two contracting parties.

---

20. The Supreme Court's decision in DIRECTV, Inc. v. Imburgia, 136 S. Ct. 463, 469 (2015) removes any doubt that courts must treat arbitration agreements consistent with other contracts. In that case, the Supreme Court reversed the decision of a California appellate court which was purportedly based on an interpretation of the parties' contract. The Court's opinion makes clear that it is unlikely to tolerate efforts to undermine *Concepcion*.

21. *See* Am. Exp. Co. v. Italian Colors Rest., 570 U.S. 228, 235 (2013) .

The Supreme Court continued this trend in *Epic Sys. Corp. v. Lewis*.[22] In that case, an accountant brought a class action under the Fair Labor Standards Act. His employment agreement included an arbitration provision with a class action waiver. The district court enforced the waiver and compelled arbitration, but the Ninth Circuit reversed. It concluded that "an agreement requiring individualized arbitration proceedings violates the [National Labor Relations Act] by barring employees from engaging in the 'concerted activity.'"[23] The Supreme Court granted certiorari to resolve a circuit split and, in a 5–4 decision, held that the National Labor Relations Act (NLRA) did not mandate the availability of classwide proceedings. Thus, employers can enter (and enforce) arbitration agreements with employees that include a class action waiver. In reaching this conclusion, the majority acknowledged that class actions enhance the enforcement of the NLRA by spreading the costs of litigation, but concluded that this was a policy decision that was more appropriately left to Congress. Following *Concepcion*, *Italian Colors*, and *Epic Systems*, the argument that class action waivers in arbitration agreements are unenforceable because the costs of pursuing a claim on an individual basis outweigh the value of the potential recovery seems all but dead.

That does not mean, however, that plaintiffs cannot challenge arbitration provisions. Following are some of the arguments that plaintiffs are currently using to defeat a motion to compel arbitration.[24]

Contract Formation Defenses

As the Supreme Court has consistently made clear, arbitration is premised on *an agreement* to submit a dispute to arbitration. If the parties never agreed to arbitrate (with a few exceptions), then they cannot be compelled to arbitration.[25] Thus, plaintiffs might attempt to defeat

---

22. 138 S. Ct. 1612, 1619 (2018).

23. *See id.* at 1620.

24. There are substantive areas of the law where arbitration may not be available: (1) perhaps some employment relationships (D.R. Horton, Inc. v. NLRB, 737 F.3d 344 (5th Cir. 2013)); (2) most lending to military members (10 U.S.C. § 987; 32 C.F.R. § 232.8); (3) home mortgages (Reg. Z, 12 C.F.R. § 1026.36(h)(1)). The CFPB recently made a significant effort to prohibit arbitration clauses with class action waivers in the financial industry but was ultimately overruled by Congress. It is fair to expect future regulatory or legislative action in the area of arbitration and perhaps more modest prohibitions including barring the use of arbitration in particular contexts.

25. *See* Rent-A-Ctr., W., Inc. v. Jackson, 561 U.S. 63, 70 n.2 (2010) (noting that "[t]he issue of [an] agreement's 'validity' is different from the issue whether any agreement between the parties 'was ever concluded'").

arbitration by arguing that a valid contract was never formed for a wide variety of reasons. Such defenses have become the main field of dispute over arbitration agreements. For example, a plaintiff might argue that a signature is a forgery, that it was procured by fraud ("I did not know what I was signing"), or that he was under duress when he signed the contract. If faced with one of these defenses, a defendant should take full advantage of the opportunity to emphasize the individualized inquiries that would be needed to adjudicate these defenses. Even if the court ultimately declines to order arbitration as to the named plaintiff, the need to examine each contract's signature individually would decrease the likelihood of finding predominance.[26]

> A challenge to the underlying contract as a whole should be one for the arbitrator to decide.

After identifying each potentially applicable arbitration agreement, a defendant should ensure that the agreements are not internally inconsistent or contradictory. In analyzing any arbitration agreement, a court should begin by determining "whether the parties agreed to arbitrate the dispute."[27] Generally, courts will ask whether (1) there was an agreement to arbitrate and (2) whether the dispute in question is covered by that agreement.

If the contract (or contracts) creates an ambiguity, it can open the door to judicial interpretation. Checking for inconsistencies or contradictions is especially important when there are multiple, potentially applicable arbitration agreements. To illustrate, automobile purchases often involve both a purchase and sales agreement and a financing document that might or might not cross-reference one another. Thus, certain types of claims arising from the transaction might be covered by an arbitration agreement while others might not. The resolution of such questions will turn on state contract law. It is important to remember that the presumption in favor of arbitrability does not apply to the contract formation analysis.[28] So, to the extent an ambiguity exists as to

---

26. *In re* Titanium Dioxide Antitrust Litig., 962 F. Supp. 2d 840, 862 (D. Md. 2013) (individualized review of contracts would defeat class certification); Lozano v. AT & T Wireless Servs., Inc., 504 F.3d 718, 728 (9th Cir. 2007) (predominance defeated when state-by-state review of arbitration contracts was necessary).

27. Will-Drill Res., Inc. v. Samson Res. Co., 352 F.3d 211, 214 (5th Cir. 2003).

28. Dasher v. RBC Bank (USA), 745 F.3d 1111, 1115–16 (11th Cir. 2014) ("[W]hile doubts concerning the scope of an arbitration clause should be resolved in favor of arbitration, the presumption does not apply to disputes concerning whether an agreement to

whether an agreement was actually formed, a court is not required to resolve that dispute in favor of arbitration.

Contract formation will often be a simple matter. If the contract bears the plaintiff's signature, the plaintiff will have to show that the signature is a fraud to avoid it. If the plaintiff has sued for breach of contract, he will be estopped from denying the validity of the contract.[29] A plaintiff can also agree to arbitrate through conduct, such as using a service or product after being made aware of the arbitration agreement.[30] Even if the plaintiff does not have actual notice of the arbitration provision, he often will be unable to avoid arbitration when he knew he could have discovered the arbitration provision through a reasonable investigation.[31] Even if a plaintiff is successful on any of these arguments, he will have highlighted an individualized issue that will likely torpedo his case at class certification.

In other situations, the formation issue will not be as simple. One common dispute occurs when the arbitration provision was added through an amendment to the original contract and the defendant must prove it followed the proper procedures for amending the contract (for instance, that the amendment was mailed to the plaintiff at their correct address or that there was an opportunity to refuse the amendment and cease doing business with the defendant).[32] A defendant should be careful to document its procedures and to keep detailed records. It should submit this evidence with its motion to compel arbitration.

---

arbitrate has been made.") (quoting Applied Energetics, Inc. v. NewOak Capital Mkts., LLC, 645 F.3d 522, 526 (2d Cir. 2011)).

29. *See* Bahamas Sales Assoc., LLC v. Byers, 701 F.3d 1335, 1342 (11th Cir. 2012) ("In essence, equitable estoppel precludes a party from claiming the benefits of some of the provisions of a contract while simultaneously attempting to avoid the burdens that some other provisions of the contract impose.") (citing Blinco v. Green Tree Servicing LLC, 400 F.3d 1308, 1312 (11th Cir. 2005)); Custom Performance, Inc. v. Dawson, 57 So. 3d 90, 97 (Ala. 2010) ("A plaintiff cannot simultaneously claim the benefits of a contract and repudiate its burdens and conditions.").

30. Galloway v. Santander Consumer USA, Inc., 819 F.3d 79, 87 (4th Cir. 2016) (finding that plaintiff's actions of "making payment in the revised amount CitiFinancial requested and then continuing to make those payments for several years without complaint can only be interpreted as an assent to the terms of the Amended Agreement as slightly modified by the company"); *Ex parte* Rush, 730 So. 2d 1175, 1178 (Ala. 1999) (plaintiffs accepted contract containing arbitration provision by paying service fees under contract).

31. *See Tellis*, 192 So. 3d at 390.

32. *See* Moore-Dennis v. Franklin, 201 So. 3d. 1131, 1145 (Ala. 2016) (Shaw, J., concurring in result) (concluding that defendant's effort to modify a deposit agreement to include an arbitration provision was ineffective because the defendant did not follow the modification procedures set forth in the deposit agreement).

This dispute frequently arises in Internet contracts, when the question is whether to enforce "clickwrap" or "browsewrap" agreements when the defendant failed to prove the plaintiff received actual notice of the arbitration provision.[33] Again, a corporation should ensure that actual notice is provided and should retain this evidence and should consider submitting sworn proof of such matters (for instance, that the consumer clicked "accept" on the screen with the arbitration clause and submit exemplars of the screens that would have appeared). A recent example of the shrink-wrap issue is *Norcia v. Samsung Telecommunications America*,[34] in which the Ninth Circuit held that no agreement to arbitrate had been formed when Samsung placed a warranty brochure containing an arbitration clause within a product box, but neither the box nor the cover of the brochure prominently disclosed the clause.

Likewise, a recent example of the clickwrap issue is *Bazemore v. Jefferson Capital Systems, LLC* in which the Eleventh Circuit refused to enforce the arbitration clause because the defendant introduced no evidence "that the Internet web page or pages that [plaintiff] viewed, or upon which she applied for her [credit card], displayed or referred to any terms or conditions of the credit card she sought, much less that she was required to consent to any such terms in order to obtain her credit card."[35]

In rare circumstances, courts have refused to compel arbitration when the arbitration provision was obscured such that the consumer did not understand that he was agreeing to arbitrate, usually in extreme circumstances.[36] However, as noted earlier, courts must treat arbitration clauses exactly as they would any other contract clause under state law.

Another contract formation defense that has been met with mixed success is that the contract fails because the consideration is illegal or insufficient. A good example is a case involving an agreement with

---

33. Nguyen v. Barnes & Noble Inc., 763 F.3d 1171, 1176 (9th Cir. 2014) (declining to compel arbitration because provision did not appear on defendants' website, was available only through a hyperlink at the bottom of the webpage, and consumer had no other notice that she was agreeing to arbitration provision).

34. Norcia v. Samsung Telecomm. Am., LLC, 845 F.3d 1279 (9th Cir. 2017).

35. Bazemore v. Jefferson Capital Sys., LLC, 827 F.3d 1325, 1327 (11th Cir. 2016).

36. *See* Noble v. Samsung Elecs. Am., Inc., No. 16-1903, 682 F. App'x 113, 116 (3d Cir. Mar. 3, 2017) (explaining that an arbitration clause buried on the 97th page of a document titled "Health and Safety and Warranty Guide" and included in the packaging for a smart watch did not evidence an agreement to arbitrate because "when [a] writing does not appear to be a contract and the terms are not called to the attention of the recipient, there is no reasonable notice and the terms cannot be binding") (internal citations and quotation mark omitted).

a casino to arbitrate certain claims. Because gambling is illegal in many states, plaintiffs have argued that the agreement to arbitrate is illegal and, therefore, unenforceable. Some courts have rejected this argument,[37] but others have not.[38] Similarly, courts have refused to enforce arbitration agreements when some provision in the underlying contract violated state law. The reasoning of these decisions are suspect given the Supreme Court's clear statement in *Prima Paint* and its progeny that a challenge to the underlying contract as a whole should be one for the arbitrator to decide.[39] The lesson for defendants is that many courts (especially state courts) remain hostile to arbitration.

Contract Formation Considerations

Was contract signed? Is the signature authentic?
Was electronic consent given by clickwrap or browsewrap?
Was the contract correctly amended by the defendant corporation? Did it follow the correct procedures? Can it prove compliance? Did the amendment process make the contract illusory?
Are there multiple overlapping arguments that create ambiguity?
Is a non-signatory able to enforce?

Unconscionability

Concepcion did not hold that unconscionability does not apply to arbitration agreements. Instead, it held that states cannot adopt rules about unconscionability that treat arbitration agreements differently than other contracts. Therefore, a court can still hold an arbitration agreement

---

37. Johnson v. Jefferson Cnty. Racing Ass'n, Inc., 1 So. 3d 960 (Ala. 2008); Sokaogon Gaming Enter. Corp. v. Tushie-Montgomery Assocs., Inc., 86 F.3d 656, 659 (7th Cir. 1996) ("Although the arbitration clause is contained in a contract that the tribe contends is illegal, the tribe rightly does not argue that the illegality of the contract infects the arbitration clause.").

38. *See* Macon Cnty. Greyhound Park v. Hoffman et al., No. 1131273, 226 So. 3d 152, 167 (Ala. Dec. 23, 2016) (holding that arbitration agreement was founded on gambling consideration and, therefore, unenforceable under state law); Greenburg v. SNA Consultants, Inc., 866 N.Y.S. 2d 115, 116–17 (N.Y. App. Div. 2008) (refusing to enforce arbitration provision because defendant had failed to obtain architect's license and, therefore, the service contract containing the arbitration agreement was illegal and unenforceable); Rapid Settlement, Ltd. v. Symetra Life Ins. Co., 234 S.W.3d 788, 800 (Tex. Ct. App. 2007) (refusing to enforce arbitration agreement located in contract that required certain payments in violation of state law).

39. *See* Prima Paint Corp. v. Flood & Conklin Mfg. Co., 388 U.S. 395, 403–04 (1967); *Rent-A-Ctr.*, 561 U.S. at 70.

to be unconscionable as long as it does so for reasons apart from the agreement being one to arbitrate. Generally, this defense requires a showing of both procedural and substantive unconscionability,[40] but again the precise test will vary according to the law of the relevant jurisdiction.

An example of a successful, post-*Concepcion* attack on an arbitration provision is the Eleventh Circuit's decision in *In re Checking Account Overdraft Litigation*.[41] In that case, the arbitration agreement contained a cost-shifting provision that allowed the defendant to recover its costs from the plaintiff even if the plaintiff prevailed on the merits. Further, the cost-shifting provision was buried in the contract such that an ordinary consumer would not realize it applied to the arbitration provision on the first page. The Eleventh Circuit concluded that, under South Carolina's law of unconscionability, the cost-shifting provision made the contract both procedurally and substantively unconscionable. The Eleventh Circuit still compelled arbitration, however. Under South Carolina law, unconscionable provisions can be severed from the remainder of the contract. The Eleventh Circuit found that the unconscionable provision operated independent of the arbitration clause and that the operation of either provision was not impaired by the invalidation of the other, and therefore, the cost-shifting provision could be severed.[42] Today, most arbitration agreements contain sophisticated severance clauses.

> Today, most arbitration agreements contain sophisticated severance clauses to avoid allegations of unconscionability as to particular provisions.

Arbitration Forum Truly Inaccessible

While *Italian Colors* foreclosed the effective-vindication argument, it left the door open to the argument that the arbitral forum is truly inaccessible for the vindication of federal statutory rights.[43] In *Italian Colors*, Justice Scalia provided some examples of what might make the forum

---

40. Blue Cross Blue Shield of Alabama v. Rigas, 923 So. 2d 1077, 1087 (Ala. 2005) ("To avoid an arbitration provision on the ground of unconscionability, the party objecting to arbitration must show both procedural and substantive unconscionability.").

41. MDL No. 2036, 685 F.3d 1269, 1277 (11th Cir. 2012).

42. In drafting an arbitration contract, defendants should carefully consider the placement of the arbitration provision so that it will survive should a different provision of the same contract be held unconscionable.

43. *See Italian Colors*, 570 U.S. at 236 (explaining that the public policy exception for prospective waivers of federal statutory rights might invalidate an arbitration agreement when the arbitral forum is truly inaccessible).

inaccessible. He noted that an outright prohibition on certain federal statutory rights would certainly fall in this category, and he suggested that administrative fees that are so high that they make arbitration impractical might also fall into this category. While not mentioned by Justice Scalia, it is possible that other requirements—such as a provision that requires a consumer arbitration to occur in a foreign country or a foreign language—might make the arbitral forum inaccessible. The touchstone appears to be whether the arbitral forum presents a fair (albeit less advantageous) alternative to litigation.

While not based on the effective-vindication rationale, the Eleventh Circuit recently concluded that an arbitral forum was inaccessible. In *Inetianbor v. CashCall, Inc.*, the agreement required arbitration to occur before an authorized representative of the Cheyenne River Sioux Tribe and pursuant to the Tribe's rules for consumer dispute resolution.[44] After the district court initially compelled arbitration, the plaintiff tried to commence arbitration proceedings with the Tribe. He was told that the Tribe had nothing to do with "this business." Effectively, the Tribe said it was not going to conduct an arbitration as required by the arbitration contract. The plaintiff returned to the district court, which agreed the arbitral forum in that case was truly inaccessible. The court then vacated its order compelling arbitration.

On appeal, the Eleventh Circuit affirmed. It concluded that the arbitration agreement was premised on the participation of the Cheyenne River Sioux Tribe and did not allow for the selection of a substitute arbitral forum. *Inetianbor* perhaps represents an extreme example; the arbitration agreement literally required the arbitration to occur in a forum that affirmatively refused to conduct arbitration. It is also possible to draft around *Inetianbor* by including a provision in the arbitration agreement that allows for the appointment of a substitute arbitral forum if the primary choice is unavailable. Still, defendants and their counsel should be aware of this result because arbitration agreements are not always updated to reflect the most recent changes in the law.

Waiver: "Substantially Invoking the Litigation Process"

Arbitration agreements, like other contractual provisions, can be waived. The test for waiver varies with each jurisdiction, and different jurisdictions often reach different results on the same facts. The federal

---

44. *See* Inetianbor v. CashCall, Inc., 768 F.3d 1346, 1351 (11th Cir. 2014), *cert. denied*, 135 S. Ct. 1735, (2015).

circuit courts illustrate this phenomenon. To find waiver, all circuit courts require at least some conduct that is inconsistent with the right to arbitrate—that is, substantially invoking the litigation process. Some courts have found that filing an answer or participating in discovery might waive the right to compel arbitration. However, the circuits have different requirements on whether the party opposing arbitration must show prejudice before the right to arbitrate is waived.

The Fourth, Fifth, and Ninth Circuits require a high showing of prejudice while the First Circuit requires only a modicum of prejudice.[45] The Second, Third, Eighth, and Eleventh Circuits fall somewhere between the heavy burden and modicum of prejudice. The Tenth Circuit includes prejudice as a consideration in a multifactor test for waiver.[46] The Seventh and D.C. Circuits do not require a showing of prejudice at all.[47]

In the jurisdictions that require a showing of some prejudice, a defendant might be tempted to engage in some litigation with the knowledge that a motion to compel arbitration can always be brought later. This is not advisable. It is almost impossible to know in advance what facts will trigger a finding of prejudice. Thus, a defendant should assert his right to compel arbitration at the earliest possible juncture.

Even if a defendant waives his right to compel arbitration, that right can be revived if the complaint is later amended in a way that significantly alters the scope of the lawsuit.[48] *Krinsk v. SunTrust Banks, Inc.* is an example.[49] In that case, the putative class was small—it encompassed a three-month time frame and only included Florida residents over the age of 65 who had had their home equity lines of credit suspended for failing to provide updated financial information. Later, the plaintiff expanded her class definition to encompass a three-year time frame and any Florida resident who had their home equity lines of

---

45. *See* Thomas J. Lilly, Jr., *Participation in Litigation as a Waiver of the Contractual Right to Arbitrate: Toward a Unified Theory*, 92 NEB. L. REV. 86, 102 (2013).

46. *See* Lamkin v. Morinda Properties Weight Parcel, LLC, 440 F. App'x 604, 610 (10th Cir. 2011).

47. *See* Lilly, *supra* note 45; Ivax Corp. v. B. Braun of Am., Inc., 286 F.3d 1309, 1316 (11th Cir. 2002).

48. Manasher v. NECC Telecom, 310 F. App'x 804, 807 (6th Cir. 2009) (amendment that did not alter the scope of the litigation was insufficient to revive right to compel arbitration); Brown v. Green Tree Servs., LLC, 585 F. Supp. 2d 770, 782 (D.S.C. 2008) (amendment that altered scope of lawsuit revived right to arbitration); Envirex, Inc. v. K.H. Schussler Fur Umwelttechnik GMBH, 832 F. Supp. 1293, 1296 (E.D. Wis. 1993) (same).

49. 654 F.3d 1194, 1203 (11th Cir. 2011).

credit suspended for any reason. The Eleventh Circuit concluded that this amendment had dramatically altered the scope of the lawsuit such that the defendant's previously waived right to compel arbitration was revived.

Who Decides Whether the Arbitration Agreement Is Enforceable?

Because some courts are hostile to arbitration provisions, the question of "who decides" a particular defense to arbitration might determine whether that agreement is enforceable. Generally, a challenge to the validity of the contract containing the arbitration provision, as a whole, will be a question for the arbitrator.[50] As Justice Scalia explained in *Rent-a-Center, West, Inc. v. Jackson*, a challenge to the entire contract "either on a ground that directly affects the entire agreement (*e.g.*, the agreement was fraudulently induced), or on the ground that the illegality of one of the contract's provisions renders the whole contract invalid" is not "relevant to a court's determination whether the arbitration agreement at issue is enforceable."[51]

A challenge to the arbitration provision itself, on the other hand, is normally a question for the court. The Supreme Court has made it difficult to bring these challenges, however. To raise a question of "arbitrability," the party opposing arbitration must specifically assert that the arbitration provision itself was obtained by fraud, is unconscionable, or is otherwise invalid. Failure to specifically challenge the arbitration provision will usually result in an order compelling arbitration.

The threshold issues of arbitrability can be delegated to an arbitrator. In *First Options of Chicago, Inc. v. Kaplan*, the Supreme Court held that

> [j]ust as the arbitrability of the merits of a dispute depends upon whether the parties agreed to arbitrate that dispute, so the question "who has the

---

50. Prima Paint Corp. v. Flood & Conklin Mfg. Co., 388 U.S. 395, 403–04 (1967) ("[I]f the claim is fraud in the inducement of the arbitration clause itself—an issue which goes to the 'making' of the agreement to arbitrate—the federal court may proceed to adjudicate it. But the statutory language does not permit the federal court to consider claims of fraud in the inducement of the contract generally.") (footnotes and some internal quotation marks omitted).

51. *Rent-A-Ctr.*, 561 U.S. at 70. Justice Scalia reached this conclusion based on the *Prima Paint* line of cases, which hold that § 2 of the FAA dictates that agreements to arbitrate are valid and enforceable regardless of the enforceability of the contract in which they are found. Interestingly, Justice Scalia stated in passing that "neither party has asked us to overrule" this line of cases. *Id.*

primary power to decide arbitrability" turns upon what the parties agreed about *that* matter.[52]

This holding makes sense because the general rule is that arbitration provisions are severable from the contract in which they are found.[53] Therefore, if the parties agree that issues of arbitrability can be arbitrated, then *that* agreement can be severed from the main contract and enforced even though no one has yet determined whether the merits of the dispute are subject to arbitration (even though the main agreement might later be found to be unenforceable). The only requirement is that the parties clearly and unmistakably evidence their intent to submit issues of arbitrability to arbitration.

Contractual provisions that delegate issues of arbitrability to the arbitrator are commonly referred to as a delegation provision or delegation clause. Such provisions can take several forms, but one that arises frequently is a statement that the rules of the American Arbitration Association will govern the arbitration proceedings. These rules state that an arbitrator shall have the authority to decide issues of his own jurisdiction, and many courts have interpreted this authority (which is incorporated into the party's agreement by reference) as delegating to the arbitrator the authority to decide all issues of arbitrability.[54]

---

52. 514 U.S. 938, 943 (1995).

53. Buckeye Check Cashing, Inc. v. Cardegna, 546 U.S. 440, 445 (2006) ("[A]s a matter of substantive federal arbitration law, an arbitration provision is severable from the remainder of the contract.").

54. *See, e.g.*, Petrofac, Inc. v. DynMcDermott Petroleum Operations Co., 687 F.3d 671, 675 (5th Cir. 2012) (noting that most federal circuit courts have adopted this position), Terminix Int'l Co. v. Palmer Ranch Ltd. P'ship, 432 F.3d 1327, 1332 (11th Cir. 2005) ("By incorporating the AAA Rules, including Rule 8, into their agreement, the parties clearly and unmistakably agreed that the arbitrator should decide whether the arbitration clause is valid" and collecting cases), and Joe Hudson Collision Ctr. v. Dymond, 40 So. 3d 704, 711 (Ala. 2009). Until recently, some argued that the Tenth Circuit had adopted a different approach. The Tenth Circuit put an end to this argument in January 2017, stating "Some courts have suggested that the Tenth Circuit is the only federal appellate court that has deviated from this consensus . . . . We disagree . . . ." Belnap v. Iasis Healthcare, 844 F.3d 1272, 1284 (10th Cir. 2017). It went on to adopt the general rule followed in other circuits.

It is important to note, however, that merely mentioning the rules of the American Arbitration Association may not be enough to send issues of arbitrability to arbitration. In Chambers v. Groome Transp. of Ala., 41 F. Supp. 3d 1327, 1337–38 (M.D. Ala. 2014), the supposed delegation provision stated that "[a]rbitration shall be administered and conducted *under the Mediation Rules* by mediators of the American Arbitration Association ("AAA")." *Id.* The court concluded that this statement was unclear because the defendant

What Does the Agreement Say about Class-Wide Proceedings and Who Decides?

As mentioned earlier, the possibility of class-wide arbitration poses a significant danger for defendants because it combines the potential for crushing liability with the informality of the arbitration process. Without any procedural safeguards in place, all but the most stalwart defendants would be pressured to settle rather than risk an adverse decision. While the Supreme Court's jurisprudence on this issue has evolved, the Court held in *Stolt-Nielsen S.A. v. AnimalFeeds International Corp.* that "a party may not be compelled . . . to submit to class arbitration unless there is a contractual basis for concluding that the party agreed to do so."[55] The Court reaffirmed this conclusion in *Concepcion* when it discussed at length how class-wide arbitration differs from one-on-one proceedings.

Given that most modern arbitration agreements incorporate a class action waiver—an express provision prohibiting the plaintiff from proceeding in arbitration on behalf of a class—it seems unlikely that many defendants will face the specter of class-wide arbitration. However, as noted earlier, it is possible that an arbitrator might hold a class action waiver unenforceable and the arbitration clause might not include a "blow-up" clause to send the matter back to court.

Still, the answer to this question will turn on the language of the particular arbitration agreement. For that reason, defendants should carefully examine their arbitration agreements for any language that could be interpreted as authorizing or permitting class-wide arbitration. If such language is found, then the defendant might want to avoid arbitration all together rather than risk the possibility of class-wide arbitration.

Additionally, the Supreme Court has not yet provided a clear answer to the question: Who decides whether an agreement authorizes class-wide arbitration? While *Concepcion* decried the dangers of class-wide arbitration, the Court was also clear that the purpose of the FAA is to ensure that arbitration agreements are enforced according to their terms. It follows then that a clause delegating certain threshold matters to the arbitrator might permit the arbitrator to determine whether class-wide arbitration is permissible. Indeed, a plurality of the Supreme

---

had not pointed the court to the supposedly applicable "Mediation Rules" and the court's own research had not uncovered any such rules. Thus, the court held that it was unclear what the parties had agreed to on arbitrability and declined to compel arbitration.

55. Stolt-Nielsen S.A. v. AnimalFeeds Int'l Corp., 559 U.S. 662, 684 (2010).

Court endorsed this approach in *GreenTree Financial v. Bazzle*.[56] However, later decisions have disavowed the rationale of *Bazzle*[57] and the Third, Fourth, and Sixth Circuits have rejected it entirely.[58] The Fourth Circuit's discussion in *Dell Webb Communities, Inc. v. Carlson* is illustrative. In that case, the Court noted that *Bazzle* was a plurality opinion and that, in *Oxford*, the Court dropped a footnote that essentially undermined the continued validity of the *Bazzle* decision. Turning next to other post-*Bazzle* Supreme Court cases and its own precedents, the Fourth Circuit determined that the primary benefit of bilateral arbitration—procedural informality—must be abandoned in class arbitration proceedings. Because this primary benefit is "dramatically upended in class arbitration," the Court held that the decision on class arbitration is for the court unless the arbitration agreement "unmistakeably provide[s] that the arbitrator [will] decide whether [the] agreement authorizes class arbitration."

Not all courts agree that *Bazzle* has been abrogated. In *Robinson v. J & K Administrative Management Services, Inc.*,[59] the Fifth Circuit adhered to its decision in *Pedcor Management Co. Welfare Benefit Plan v. Nations Personnel of Texas, Inc.*[60] and held that an arbitrator should decide the issue of class-wide arbitration. In *Robinson*, a plaintiff requested class-wide arbitration of her FLSA claims and, after the defendant failed to answer, moved to compel arbitration. The district court compelled arbitration and also held that the class-wide arbitration issue should be decided by the arbitrator. The defendant appealed, arguing that *Stolt-Nielson* had invalidated *Bazzle* as well as prior circuit precedent holding that a broad arbitration clause, "such as [one] submitting 'all disputes, claims, or controversies arising from or relating to' the agreement to arbitration," was enough to submit the "availability of class or collective arbitration" to the arbitrator. The Fifth Circuit rejected this argument, saying that

56. GreenTree Financial Corp. v. Bazzle, 539 U.S. 444, 452 (2003) (plurality opinion).

57. *Oxford Health Plans*, 569 U.S. at 569 & n.2; Opalinski v. Robert Half Int'l Inc., 761 F.3d 326, 331–34, 335–36 (3d Cir. 2014).

58. Dell Webb Communities, Inc. v. Carlson, 817 F.3d 867 (4th Cir. 2016); Opalinski v. Robert Half Int'l Inc., 761 F.3d 326, 332 (3d Cir. 2014); LexisNexis Div. v. Crockett, 734 F.3d 594, 597–99 (6th Cir. 2013). The Ninth Circuit has also endorsed this view in an unpublished opinion. *See* Eshagh v. Terminix Int'l Co., L.P., 588 Fed. Appx. 703, 704 (9th Cir. 2014).

59. Robinson v. J & K Admin. Mgmt. Servs., Inc., 817 F.3d 193 (5th Cir.), *cert. denied*, 137 S. Ct. 373, (2016).

60. Pedcor Mgmt. Co. Welfare Benefit Plan v. Nations Pers. of Texas, Inc., 343 F.3d 355, 357 (5th Cir. 2003).

Stolt-Nielson had not spoken to the issue of who decides whether class arbitration is available when the arbitration agreement is silent. Further, the Fifth Circuit explained that *Stolt-Nielson*'s holding that a party cannot be required to arbitrate matters to which it has not agreed to arbitrate did not apply in *Robinson* because the question of who decides the issue of class-wide arbitration is different from the question of whether class arbitration is contractually permissible. Accordingly, in the Fifth Circuit's view, *Stolt-Nielson* was insufficient to overrule *Bazzle* and *Pedcor*.[61]

In *Epic Systems*, Justice Gorsuch noted "courts may not allow a contract defense to reshape traditional individualized arbitration by mandating classwide arbitration procedures without the parties' consent."[62] Justice Gorsuch did not elaborate, however, on what constitutes "consent." The Supreme Court may soon answer this question. In April 2018, the Court granted certiorari in *Varela v. Lamp Plus, Inc.* In that case, an arbitration agreement was silent on class arbitration but expressly waived the right to all "civil actions or proceedings."[63] The Ninth Circuit concluded this phrase was ambiguous and that the most reasonable interpretation was that it included class as well as individual actions. Construing this agreement against the defendant drafter, the Ninth Circuit ordered class-wide arbitration.[64] The defendant petitioned for certiorari on the question: "Whether the Federal Arbitration Act forecloses a state-law interpretation of an arbitration agreement that would authorize class arbitration based solely on general language commonly used in arbitration agreements."[65] Accordingly, it seems likely that the Court will soon address what language constitutes consent to class-wide arbitration.

A word of warning to defendants: agreeing to submit the matter of class arbitration to the arbitrator will very likely prevent that defendant from later challenging an adverse determination. In *Oxford Health Plans LLC v. Sutter*, the parties both interpreted *Bazzle* as requiring that

---

61. A district court in the Southern District of New York recently adopted the Fifth Circuit's reasoning in *Robinson*. *See* Wells Fargo Advisors, L.L.C. v. Tucker, 195 F. Supp. 3d 543, 549 (S.D.N.Y. 2016). The Second Circuit affirmed without deciding whether class arbitration was an issue of arbitrability. Wells Fargo Advisors, LLC v. Sappington, 884 F.3d 392, 2018 WL 1177230 (2d Cir. 2018).

62. 138 S. Ct. at 1623.

63. Varela v. Lamps Plus, Inc., 701 F. App'x 670, 672 (9th Cir. 2017), *cert. granted*, 138 S. Ct. 1697 (2018).

64. *Id.*

65. Pet. Cert., Lamps Plus, Inc. v. Varela, No. 17-988 (U.S. 2018), 2018 WL 389119, at *i.

the issue of class arbitration be submitted to the arbitrator. After an adverse ruling on that issue, the Supreme Court decided *Stolt-Nielsen*. The defendant moved the arbitrator to reconsider its decision, but the arbitrator adhered to his previous determination. The defendant then moved the federal court to invalidate the decision under section 10(a)(4) of the FAA as beyond the scope of the arbitrator's power. The Supreme Court rejected this effort, stating that:

> A party seeking relief under [Section 10(a)(4)] bears a heavy burden. It is not enough to show that the arbitrator committed an error—or even a serious error. Because the parties bargained for the arbitrator's construction of their agreement, an arbitral decision even arguably construing or applying the contract must stand, regardless of a court's view of its (de)merits. Only if the arbitrator acts outside the scope of his contractually delegated authority—issuing an award that simply reflects his own notions of economic justice rather than drawing its essence from the contract—may a court overturn his determination.[66]

Thus, a defendant should contest the class arbitration issue at the outset. Agreeing to submit the issue to the arbitrator will likely preclude a later challenge to an adverse decision on that issue.

What If Some Members of the Class Are Subject to Arbitration but the Named Plaintiff Is Not?

Often, a defendant will be faced with a class action in which some class members are subject to arbitration but others are not. The law appears settled that an individual who is bound by an arbitration clause cannot represent a class in federal court.[67] The converse of this situation—the named plaintiff is not subject to arbitration but putative class members are—is more complicated. At the very least, courts appear to agree that plaintiffs who are bound by an arbitration provision (or a forum-selection or other unique contractual provision) are not similarly situated to members of the putative class.[68] The courts are split, however, on whether this precludes class certification.[69]

---

66. *Oxford Health Plans*, 569 U.S. at 569 (internal alterations and citations omitted).
67. 1 JOSEPH M. MCLAUGHLIN, MCLAUGHLIN ON CLASS ACTIONS § 4:18 (13th ed. 2016).
68. *See In re* Titanium Dioxide Antitrust Litig., 962 F. Supp. 2d 840, 861–62 (D. Md. 2013).
69. *Compare* Tan v. Grubhub, Inc., No. 15-CV-05128-JSC, 2016 WL 4721439, at *4 (N.D. Cal. July 19, 2016) (refusing to certify class because some class members were subject to individual arbitration provisions), *with* Mora v. Harley-Davidson Credit Corp.,

Even if an arbitration provision with absent class members cannot be used to defeat class certification, a defendant should still insist that this limitation be incorporated into the class definition. A failure to do so can result in the arbitration defense being waived.[70] However, a defendant cannot move to compel arbitration against absent class members until a class is certified, as these individuals are not actually parties to the action. As such, no court order compelling these individuals to arbitration would be binding.[71]

MOVING TO ENFORCE A FORUM SELECTION CLAUSE

A forum selection clause is a contractual agreement to bring specified types of lawsuits in a particular forum. Like agreements to arbitrate, they are matters of contract and the defendant's analysis of these provisions should begin with a review of all contracts that are potentially relevant to the transaction. If a forum selection clause is found, the defendant should then assess whether the specified forum is actually preferable to the plaintiff's chosen forum. There is no point in jumping out of the proverbial frying pan only to end up in the fires of tort-hell.

There can be many reasons for preferring one judicial forum over another. One might have more favorable law, a more favorable jury pool, judges with more favorable temperament, and so on. For example, most judicial forums in the Eleventh Circuit will be more conservative

---

No. 1:08-CV-01453-AWI, 2012 WL 1189769, at *13 (E.D. Cal. Apr. 9, 2012) ("Courts have likewise held the presence of agreements to arbitrate with some of the unnamed Class members does not defeat class certification."); *see* McLaughlin, *supra* note 67 (noting that most courts will not deny class certification merely because some putative class members may be subject to arbitration).

70. *In re Citigroup, Inc.*, 376 F.3d 23, 27 (1st Cir. 2004) (defendant waived right to compel arbitration of some class members claims by waiting until 18 months after class certification to move to compel arbitration).

71. *In re* Checking Account Overdraft Litig., 780 F.3d 1031, 1037 (11th Cir. 2015) (explaining that, until a class is certified, "the unnamed putative class members are not yet before the court," and that in "the absence of both live claims and cognizable plaintiffs, the District Court's pronouncement purporting to definitively foreclose the arbitration of the hypothetical claims that might be raised in the future by hypothetical plaintiffs cannot be regarded as anything but an impermissible advisory opinion on an abstract proposition of law.") (internal quotation marks, alterations, and citations omitted); *Mora*, 2012 WL 1189769, at *15 (explaining that a defendant had not waived its right to compel arbitration because "until a class is certified and the opt-out period has expired, unnamed Class members are not parties to this action, and their claims are not at issue.").

on class certification issues than any judicial forum in California. Sometimes there are variations in the law between the forums that can be dispositive on important issues. In the Fifth Circuit, it is near impossible to certify a class action when reliance is an element of the claim.[72] In other circuits, class-wide evidence of reliance might be possible for certain claims.[73] In the Second Circuit, a class must be defined such that each person within the class would have standing.[74] The Seventh Circuit, on the other hand, has taken a more liberal view of the relationship between the class definition and standing.[75]

As discussed later, following a transfer based on a valid forum selection clause, a defendant can take advantage of these variations in the law. Additionally, the defendant might gain a procedural advantage in a different judicial forum. For example, Rule 23 does not set a deadline for filing a motion for class certification, but some jurisdictions have created a 90-day deadline in their local rules.[76] Such 90-day deadline is enforceable and courts have struck class allegations for failure to comply with it.[77]

If the defendant identifies a favorable forum selection clause, the defendant should next determine whether the clause is enforceable. This analysis somewhat differs between federal and state courts. In federal court, the analysis must proceed under 28 U.S.C. § 1404. This statute does not apply to state courts, so defendants must determine the applicable state law governing forum selection clauses. This answer might be embodied in a statute or the defendant might have to look to state contract law.

The Supreme Court has made clear that forum selection clauses will normally be enforced. In *Atlantic Marine Construction Co. v. U.S.*

---

72. Sandwich Chef of Texas, Inc. v. Reliance Nat'l Indem. Ins. Co., 319 F.3d 205, 219 (5th Cir. 2003) ("The pervasive issues of individual reliance that generally exist in RICO fraud actions create a working presumption against class certification.").

73. CGC Holding Co., LLC v. Broad & Cassel, 773 F.3d 1076, 1089 (10th Cir. 2014) ("Sometimes issues of reliance can be disposed of on a classwide basis without individualized attention at trial.")

74. Denney v. Deutsche Bank AG, 443 F.3d 253, 264 (2d Cir. 2006) (taking the position that a class must be defined in such a way that anyone within it would have standing).

75. Kohen v. Pac. Inv. Mgmt. Co. LLC, 571 F.3d 672, 677 (7th Cir. 2009) (explaining that a class will often include people who were not injured by the defendant's conduct but that this fact will not preclude class certification).

76. *See, e.g.,* C.D. Cal. R. 23-3; N.D. Ga. R. 23.1(B); N.D. Tex. 23.2.

77. *See* Watson v. Schwarzenegger, 347 F. App'x 282, 284–85 (9th Cir. 2009).

District Court for Western District of Texas,[78] the Supreme Court made clear that the analysis of a motion to enforce a forum selection clause brought in federal court must proceed under a modified version of the test for transferring venue under § 1404 (but not § 1406). In that case, a Texas subcontractor sued a Virginia-based contractor in the Western District of Texas. The parties' contract, however, required all suits to be brought in the Eastern District of Virginia. The contractor argued that venue was wrong under § 1406 or, alternatively, that the court should transfer venue under § 1404. The district court denied both motions because most of the subcontractor's witnesses would not be subject to compulsory process in Virginia. The Supreme Court concluded the district court was wrong to refuse transfer under § 1404. Relying on its earlier decision in *Stewart Organization, Inc. v. Ricoh Corp.*,[79] the Court explained that a valid forum selection clause should be given "controlling weight in all but the most exceptional cases."[80] The Court also articulated three significant differences in the § 1404 analysis when a forum selection clause is at issue. First, the Court explained that the burden of proof actually shifts to the plaintiff to show why "transfer to the forum for which the parties bargained is unwarranted."[81] Second, the district court must not consider any private interest factors. "When parties agree to a forum-selection clause, they waive the right to challenge the preselected forum as inconvenient or less convenient for themselves or their witnesses, or for their pursuit of the litigation."[82] Third, the Court held that the original venue's choice of law rules will not follow the case to the new venue. As the Court explained,

> [W]hen a party bound by a forum-selection clause flouts its contractual obligation and files suit in a different forum, a § 1404(a) transfer of venue will not carry with it the original venue's choice-of-law rules—a factor that in some circumstances may affect public-interest considerations.[83]

---

78. 571 U.S. 49, 52 (2013).

79. 487 U.S. 22, 30 (1988).

80. *Atl. Marine Constr. Co.*, 571 U.S. at 63 ("For that reason, and because the overarching consideration under § 1404(a) is whether a transfer would promote 'the interest of justice,' 'a valid forum-selection clause [should be] given controlling weight in all but the most exceptional cases.'") (quoting Stewart Org., Inc. v. Ricoh Corp., 487 U.S. 22, 33 (1988)).

81. *Id.* at 63.

82. *Id.* at 64.

83. *Id.*

Thus, after *Atlantic Marine*, "a [federal] district court should transfer the case [to the parties' chosen forum] unless extraordinary circumstances unrelated to the convenience of the parties clearly disfavor a transfer."[84]

> The Supreme Court has made clear that forum selection clauses will normally be enforced.

The Supreme Court did not explain what might constitute extraordinary circumstances sufficient to disregard the parties' chosen forum, but the tenor of the Court's opinion suggests transfer will almost always be appropriate.

Atlantic Marine also answered how a federal district court should proceed when the chosen forum is a state or foreign court. In that situation, the court should dismiss under the doctrine of forum non conveniens.[85]

The enforceability of a forum selection clause may differ, however, if the case is pending in state court. Most state courts, as a matter of state contract law, will enforce a valid forum selection clause. For example, Alabama state courts will enforce a forum selection clause unless the party challenging the clause can show that it was obtained by fraud, undue influence, overwhelming bargaining power, or that the selected forum would be seriously inconvenient.[86]

REMOVING TO FEDERAL COURT

For class actions filed in state court, a defendant's knee jerk reaction might be to immediately remove the case to federal court. This is usually a good strategy, but not always. Depending on the facts of any particular case, state courts might offer strategic advantages that make it

---

84. *Id.* at 62.

85. *Atl. Marine Constr. Co.*, 571 U.S. at 60("[T]he appropriate way to enforce a forum-selection clause pointing to a state or foreign forum is through the doctrine of *forum non conveniens*. Section 1404(a) is merely a codification of the doctrine of *forum non conveniens* for the subset of cases in which the transferee forum is within the federal court system; in such cases, Congress has replaced the traditional remedy of outright dismissal with transfer.").

86. *Ex parte* D.M. White Const. Co., Inc., 806 So. 2d 370, 372 (Ala. 2001) ("An outbound forum-selection clause is enforceable unless the challenging party can establish that enforcement of the clause would be unfair on the basis that the contract was affected by fraud, undue influence, or overweening bargaining power or enforcement would be unreasonable on the basis that the selected forum would be seriously inconvenient. The burden on the challenging party is difficult to meet.") (internal citations and alterations omitted).

superior to federal courts. Therefore, a defendant should carefully consider its overall strategy before filing a notice of removal.

The Advantages and Disadvantages of State Court

Federal courts offer several advantages to state courts in complex litigation. First, federal courts often have more resources and will likely have more experience with complex litigation. In many state courts, the judge might not even have a law clerk, which means he or she will be reading all the briefs and conducting all the legal research on his or her own. Additionally, state court judges often have larger caseloads than federal court judges.

Second, the procedural rules and requirements of federal court might be outcome determinative. For example, since the Supreme Court's decisions in *Bell Atlantic Corp. v. Twombly* and *Ashcroft v. Iqbal*, federal courts have taken motions to dismiss more seriously and will more frequently dismiss claims at the pleading stage. This pleading standard is not available in most state courts. Similarly, some federal courts are willing to strike class allegations early in the litigation.[87] This can significantly decrease the scope of discovery and might deter plaintiffs' counsel from pursuing the case. For class actions based on fraud, the federal requirement that allegations of fraud be stated with particularity might be dispositive.[88] Federal courts have also shown a greater willingness to deny class certification in "no injury" class actions. These courts reason that establishing the existence of an actual injury will be an individualized issue that will overwhelm the class action.[89] Many state courts, on the other hand, do not require plaintiffs to prove that every member of the putative class was actually injured to grant class certification.[90]

---

87. FED. R. CIV. P. 23(d)(1)(D); *see* MCLAUGHLIN, *supra* note 67, § 3:4.

88. *See* FED. R. CIV. P. 9(b); Kearns v. Ford Motor Co., 567 F.3d 1120, 1125 (9th Cir. 2009); Morgan v. AT & T Wireless Servs., Inc., 177 Cal. App. 4th 1235, 1256, 99 Cal. Rptr. 3d 768, 785 (2009) ("But [defendant's] argument fails to recognize the distinction between common law fraud, which requires allegations of actual falsity and reasonable reliance pleaded with specificity, and the fraudulent prong of the UCL, which does not.").

89. *See, e.g.*, Kohen v. Pac. Inv. Mgmt. Co. LLC, 571 F.3d 672, 677 (7th Cir. 2009) (stating that "a class should not be certified if it is apparent that it contains a great many persons who have suffered no injury at the hands of the defendant"); Denney v. Deutsche Bank AG, 443 F.3d 253, 264 (2d Cir. 2006) ("[N]o class may be certified that contains members lacking Article III standing. The class must therefore be defined in such a way that anyone within it would have standing.") (internal citations omitted).

90. *See* Evans v. Lasco Bathware, Inc., 178 Cal. App. 4th 1417, 1422 (2009).

Worth noting is that the Supreme Court's recent decision in *Spokeo, Inc. v. Robins* raises serious questions about whether no-injury class actions are ever possible in federal court.[91] Many post-*Spokeo* courts have dismissed class actions for lack of standing because the plaintiff failed to allege a particularized injury. Other courts have been less strict in their application of the particularized injury requirement.[92] The law will continue to develop in this area, and it seems likely that this issue will return to the Supreme Court in the near future.

A third advantage of federal courts is the likelihood of containing (or at least avoiding) significant discovery-related litigation costs. Federal courts are more likely to bifurcate discovery or phase discovery prior to class certification, which will, in theory, limit the scope of discoverable issues to the requirements of Rule 23. Similarly, federal courts are often more likely to limit the scope of discovery on the merits. Indeed, recent amendments to the Federal Rules of Civil Procedure have highlighted the proportionality requirements of those rules. This change is in sharp contrast to many state courts, where wide-open discovery is the norm.[93] If discovery of electronically stored information will be an issue (which it almost certainly will be), then a federal court judge will likely have more experience than their state court counterparts. Further, the rules impose special requirements on discovery of electronically stored information that might offer greater protection from burdensome document requests than in some state courts.

---

91. Spokeo, Inc. v. Robins, 136 S. Ct. 1540, 1548, (2016), *as revised* (May 24, 2016) (holding that, to establish an injury in fact, a plaintiff must allege a particularized injury—one that has affected him in a concrete and individual way).

92. *Compare* Meyers v. Nicolet Rest. of De Pere, LLC, 843 F.3d 724, 728 (7th Cir. 2016) (no standing to bring class action under FACTA when the plaintiff failed to allege any particularized harm from the statutory violation); Hancock v. Urban Outfitters, Inc., 830 F.3d 511, 514 (D.C. Cir. 2016) (no standing where plaintiffs alleged that department store clerk violated District of Columbia consumer protection statutes by asking for their zip codes, but alleged no injury caused by the violation such as "any invasion of privacy, increased risk of fraud or identity theft, or pecuniary or emotional injury"), *with In re* Nickelodeon Consumer Privacy Litig., 827 F.3d 262, 274 (3d Cir. 2016) (finding standing when plaintiff's confidential information was disclosed even though the disclosure had not resulted in any additional injury to the plaintiff).

93. *See* Ala. R. Civ. P. 26(b)(1) ("Parties may obtain discovery regarding any matter, not privileged, which is relevant to the subject matter involved in the pending action, whether it relates to the claim or defense of the party seeking discovery or to the claim or defense of any other party, including the existence, description, nature, custody, condition and location of any books, documents, or other tangible things and the identity and location of persons having knowledge of any discoverable matter. It is not ground for objection that the information sought will be inadmissible at the trial if the information sought appears reasonably calculated to lead to the discovery of admissible evidence.").

A fourth advantage is that federal courts offer several means for consolidating or otherwise preventing the simultaneous prosecution of multiple class actions. One option discussed later in the chapter under the heading "Moving to Transfer Venue" is moving to transfer venue under 28 U.S.C. § 1404. Another option discussed in Chapter 8 is moving the judicial panel on multi-district litigation to consolidate under 28 U.S.C. § 1407 (or, shorthand, MDL). Other options, such as the first-filed rule, are discussed later in the chapter.

Fifth, federal judges are more likely to be independent. State court judges—especially in states were judges are elected—might be perceived by some defendants to lean toward the local plaintiff rather than the out-of-town corporate defendant. Similarly, plaintiffs' attorneys are more likely to have a relationship with the local state court judge. And even the best state court judges are disinclined to grant dispositive motions. By contrast, federal courts will take dispositive motions seriously, and have the time and staff to research and study such motions.

Despite these considerable benefits, federal court will not always be the best strategic option. Prior to filing a notice of removal, defendants should always consider if there are any benefits to staying in state court. One possible advantage is it will likely be far easier to obtain court approval for any settlement, dismissal (perhaps an individual settlement), and any attorney fees. State courts have far less stringent rules governing class action settlements. For example, the Tennessee rule governing class action settlements simply states:

> A certified class action shall not be voluntarily dismissed or compromised without approval of the court, and notice of the proposed dismissal or compromise shall be given to all members of the class in such manner as the court directs.[94]

The rules of many other states are similar.[95] Additionally, many states do not have express rules governing an award of attorney fees. To illustrate, the Tennessee Rule requires attorneys to file a motion and direct notice to class members in a reasonable manner but, unlike Federal Rule 23(g), there is no express requirement that the court hold a hearing and state its findings of fact and conclusions of law. Georgia's version of Rule 23 does not even mention attorney fees.[96]

The current version of Federal Rule 23(e) (and federal case law), on the other hand, imposes relatively stringent requirements on any class

---

94. TENN. R. CIV. P. 23.05.
95. *See* ALA. R. CIV. P. 23(e); *see* GA. CODE ANN. § 9-11-23(e).
96. GA. CODE ANN. § 9-11-23.

action settlement. For instance, Rule 23(e)(5) allows any class member to object to even dismissals and provides that an objection to a settlement (or dismissal) may only be withdrawn with the court's approval. A federal court is also likely to scrutinize the attorney fee award more carefully than a state court.[97] Further, a provision of the Class Action Fairness Act (CAFA) makes coupon settlements unlikely in federal court.[98] The strong trend in federal courts to carefully scrutinize class action settlements is covered in detail in Chapter 9.

A second benefit of state courts is that the state's class action law might be more favorable to the defendant on certain important issues. For example, Georgia allows for an appeal of right from an order certifying a class action.[99] In the federal system, the Courts of Appeals have discretion about whether to accept an appeal from a certification order and rarely exercise that discretion unless the issue presents a truly novel and unsettled point of law.

The standard for the admission of expert testimony can be another major difference between state court and federal court. The federal *Daubert* test is well established. State courts, on the other hand, have been slow to adopt *Daubert*. If the plaintiff's expert is likely to have difficulty passing muster under *Daubert*, then removal might be the best choice. The converse is also true. If the defendant's expert is unlikely to pass muster under *Daubert*, then it might be best to remain in state court.

Some states are actually more hostile to class action treatment than their federal counterparts. Alabama, which used to be a class-friendly state, has taken a much more stringent view of the class certification requirements in recent years. As a result, it might actually be more difficult to certify a class action in Alabama state court than in federal court. Removing to federal court might also cause a defendant to lose protections provided

---

97. Park v. Thomson Corp., 633 F. Supp. 2d 8, 11–12 (S.D.N.Y. 2009) ("At the fairness hearing, this Court expressed its concerns with the Initial Settlement, particularly the $40 cap on damages and the creation of a *cy pres* fund. While this Court essentially invited the parties to amend their proposed settlement in light of the Court's misgivings, the Objectors helped transform the fairness hearing into a 'truly adversarial proceeding.' Accordingly, Objectors' counsel are entitled to an award of fees.") (internal citation omitted).

98. *See* 28 U.S.C. § 1712.

99. *See* ALA. CODE § 6-5-642 ("A court's order certifying a class or refusing to certify a class action shall be appealable in the same manner as a final order to the appellate court which would otherwise have jurisdiction over the appeal from a final order in the action."); GA. CODE ANN. § 9-11-23 ("A court's order certifying a class or refusing to certify a class shall be appealable in the same manner as a final order to the appellate court which would otherwise have jurisdiction over the appeal from a final order in the action. The appellate courts shall expedite resolution of any appeals taken under this Code section.").

by state law. For example, the Alabama Deceptive Trade Practices Act (ADTPA) includes a provision that prohibits a plaintiff from pursuing a private cause of action under that statute on behalf of a class.[100] In *Lisk v. Lumber One Wood Preserving, LLC,* the Eleventh Circuit held that this provision does not apply in federal court.[101] Thus, removing an ADTPA class action to federal court would actually be counterproductive.

Another example is Federal Rule 23(c)(4), which provides that: "[w]hen appropriate, an action might be brought or maintained as a class action with respect to particular issues."[102] Although many states incorporate this language into their state version of Rule 23, some do not.[103] If issue certification is a realistic possibility, a defendant might consider staying in state court that does not allow it.

If a defendant desires to delay resolution of the class action for some reason, then staying in state court might be a good idea. As mentioned earlier, most state courts have fewer resources and carry heavier caseloads. Further, state court judges are less likely to have as much experience in complex litigation and, therefore, might need additional time to understand the issues presented. In some state courts, it is not unusual for a case to lay dormant for years awaiting a ruling on a dispositive motion or a certification order.

On the other hand, some states and municipalities have special dockets or a special panel of judges for complex litigation. The Orange County Superior Court in California is an example.[104] These special panels are often made up of excellent judges and might have specialized rules that are beneficial to litigants. Before removing, a defendant should check to see if one of these specialized complex litigation panels or dockets is available.

Finally, class actions filed in state court generally receive less publicity than class actions filed in federal court. Removing the case to federal court might alert the media to its existence and also runs the risk of encouraging copycat suits by other potential plaintiffs. Depending on

---

100. *See* ALA. CODE § 8-19-10(f).

101. Lisk v. Lumber One Wood Preserving, LLC, 792 F.3d 1331, 1335 (11th Cir. 2015). Following the Eleventh Circuit's decision in *Lisk*, the Alabama legislature amended the ADTPA in an effort to overturn the *Lisk* decision and make the ADTPA's class action bar applicable in federal court. No court has yet addressed the effect of this amendment.

102. FED. R. CIV. P. 23(c)(4).

103. *See* MASS. R. CIV. P. 23; Fletcher v. Cape Cod Gas Co., 394 Mass. 595, 602, 477 N.E.2d 116, 121 (1985) ("We are unwilling to read into either the rule or the statute the authority for issue certification expressly provided by the drafters of the Federal rule.").

104. *See* http://www.occourts.org/directory/civil/complex-civil/fact-sheet.pdf.

the size of the class as pleaded, there might be advantages to staying in state court to avoid publicity until the statute of limitations has run.[105] Along the same lines, removing the case to federal court will require the defendant to make certain assertions on the record regarding the size of the class and the potential damages involved. To remove under CAFA, a defendant must make these types of determinations in a very short time frame. If the answer to these questions is unclear, staying in state court might be preferable.

Should I remove to federal court to avoid the plaintiff's chosen forum?

Benefits of Removal	Downsides of Removal
• Federal courts have more resources than state courts; judges are less likely to be perceived as favoring local parties over out-of-state parties	• State court analysis of class action settlements is often less rigorous than in federal court
• Federal procedural rules might help determine the ultimate outcome	• State court rules or judges might be more favorable than federal court
• Federal court is more likely to restrain discovery	• If a defendant desires to delay a resolution, state courts often have less resources and carry heavier caseloads, which will likely delay a resolution
• Federal courts offer opportunities to consolidate or forestall competing actions	
• Generally more attention to class certification issues including need to review merits related to elements of Rule 23	• State court class actions often receive less publicity than federal court actions
• *Daubert*	• Some state statutes provide for automatic right of appeal for class certification decisions
• Generally more attention to dispositive motions	• Federal courts might disregard state procedural limits or class actions (*Shady Grove*)
• Availability of discretionary appeals of class certification unavailable in some states	

---

105. Generally, the statute of limitations is tolled for all members of a putative class during the pendency of a class action. Therefore, this logic would not apply if the plaintiff is seeking a nationwide class. On the other hand, a class that is limited in scope, time, or geography might not provide the same tolling for members of the putative class. For example, a class that is limited to a single state should not toll the statute of limitations for individuals in other states. In keeping the litigation low-key until the statute of limitations has run, the defendant might be able to avoid similar litigation in those other states.

Procedures for Removal

Prior to 2005, class actions had to be removed (with a few exceptions) under the ordinary removal statute, 28 U.S.C. § 1441. But removal under this statute was problematic because the defendant had to establish an independent basis for subject matter jurisdiction. Plaintiffs were able to easily avoid this problem by pleading only state law claims or by joining a non-diverse defendant.[106] Further, a state law complaint would almost never reach the required $75,000 amount in controversy because aggregation of the claims of the class members was not considered.[107] The CAFA was enacted to combat this problem.

A full discussion of the precise requirements for removal under CAFA is beyond the scope of this chapter. However, a brief overview of CAFA's jurisdictional hurdles is appropriate here. First, CAFA does not apply if the proposed class involves fewer than 100 people. Second, CAFA does not apply if the amount in controversy, exclusive of interest and costs, does not exceed $5 million. Third, CAFA does not apply if there is not at least minimal diversity. Even if all these requirements are met, the court will not have jurisdiction if the "local controversy" or "home state" exceptions apply. Even then, the court might have discretion to decline jurisdiction in certain situations.[108]

The party asserting federal court jurisdiction will have the burden to show that removal is appropriate. Thus, the defendant's notice of removal will need to establish that the controversy involves more than 100 individuals, that it involves more than $5 million, and that minimal diversity exists. For strategic reasons, this might be more difficult than it sounds. A defendant only has 30 days from the time it receives the complaint to file a notice of removal. A defendant might be unable to determine the size of the putative class or the total amount in controversy in that short a period. Even if the defendant can make this determination, the defendant might still be unable to gather the evidence to prove these requirements. And even then, the defendant might not want to put its method for determining the size of the class or the

106. Scott P. Nelson, *CAFA in the Congress: The Eight-Year Struggle, in* THE CLASS ACTION FAIRNESS ACT: LAW & STRATEGY 23, 23–25 (Gregory C. Cook ed. 2013).

107. Exxon Mobil Corp. v. Allapattah Servs., Inc., 545 U.S. 546, 571 (2005).

108. For concise overview of these requirements, *see* Gregory C. Cook & Jocelyn D. Larkin, *Introduction and Overview, in* THE CLASS ACTION FAIRNESS ACT: LAW & STRATEGY 3, 4–11 (Gregory C. Cook ed. 2013). For a more thorough discussion, see the accompanying chapters.

amount in controversy in a publicly available court document for fear that it undermine its case on the merits or damage its reputation.

Generally, the procedures for removal are the same as the ordinary removal statute, 28 U.S.C. § 1446, with two important exceptions. First, the absolute bar on removal more than one year after the case was filed does not apply.[109] Thus, a case can be removed at any time, as long as it is done within 30 days of the defendant receiving an "amended pleading, motion, order or other paper from which it might first be ascertained that the case is one which is or has become removable."[110] Second, any defendant can remove the action without the consent of any other defendant.[111]

Numerous other questions can arise regarding the timing of the notice of removal. For example, does amending the complaint to add a defendant commence a new action for purposes of removal? Again, the answers to these questions are beyond the scope of this chapter. The strategic significance of these changes is that a defendant might be unable to remove when initially served but might be able to remove the case later. If removal is desired, then the defendant should determine what facts would trigger their right to remove. When those triggers appear, the notice of removal should be filed right away.

MOVING TO TRANSFER VENUE

If arbitration and a forum selection clause are unavailable, the defendant should assess the advantages and disadvantages of the plaintiff's chosen forum and determine whether a different judicial forum would be preferable. If the answer is yes, the defendant should consider moving to transfer venue.

This venue analysis should begin with the relevant venue statute. The federal venue statute, 28 U.S.C. § 1391, provides that venue is proper in (1) the judicial district where the defendant resides, (2) the district where a "substantial portion of the events or omissions giving rise to the claim occurred," or (3) if there is no such district, then any district where the defendant is subject to personal jurisdiction.[112]

---

109. 28 U.S.C. § 1453.
110. *Id.* § 1446(b)(3).
111. *Id.* § 1453.
112. *Id.* § 1391(b).

Most states have similar venue provisions, though they might be broader than the federal version. The Texas venue statute, for example, allows the plaintiff, in certain situations, to sue in the county where he or she resided at the time the cause of action accrued.[113]

Defendants should also be aware that some federal statutes have unique venue provisions that might supersede the general federal venue statute. For example, the Securities Act of 1934 contains a special venue provision that allows a defendant to be sued in essentially any judicial district where an important act or omission giving rise to the violation occurred.[114] Courts have interpreted this special provision to be broader than the general federal venue statute.[115]

If venue is improper, then the defendant can move to dismiss under Federal Rule of Civil Procedure 12(b)(3) or the appropriate state law analog. Given that federal and state venue statutes make it proper to sue a corporation in most judicial districts along with the fact that savvy plaintiffs' counsel seldom selects an improper venue, a motion to dismiss for improper venue will rarely be available. Moreover, federal courts have authority to transfer a case filed in an improper venue to a proper one.[116] Nonetheless, moving to dismiss might still be advisable because it will bring the issue to the judge's attention and allow the judge to "split the baby" by transferring venue rather than dismissing it outright. The goal of avoiding the unfavorable forum will be accomplished and there is at least the possibility that the judge might simply dismiss the case rather than transferring it. If so, the plaintiff might be sufficiently discouraged or inconvenienced that he or she might not refile in the appropriate venue.

Even if the plaintiff's chosen venue is proper, a defendant can always move to transfer venue under 28 U.S.C. § 1404. This motion is almost entirely discretionary and requires the judge to weigh a number of factors and decide whether fairness and the interests of justice make a

---

113. Tex. Civ. Prac. & Rem. Code Ann. § 15.002; *see also* Ala. Code § 6-3-7(3).

114. *See* 15 U.S.C. § 78aa; First Fed. Sav. & Loan Ass'n of Pittsburgh v. Oppenheim, Appel, Dixon & Co., 634 F. Supp. 1341, 1350 (S.D.N.Y. 1986) ("Under this standard any non-trivial act in the forum district which helps to accomplish a securities law violation is sufficient to establish venue.").

115. Wichita Fed. Sav. & Loan Ass'n v. Landmark Grp., Inc., 674 F. Supp. 321, 329 (D. Kan. 1987).

116. *See* 28 U.S.C. § 1406 ("The district court of a district in which is filed a case laying venue in the wrong division or district shall dismiss, or if it be in the interest of justice, transfer such case to any district or division in which it could have been brought.").

different venue more appropriate.[117] Despite their discretionary nature, a motion to transfer venue can be an effective tool for avoiding a forum that is inconvenient because it is distant, has an unfavorable jury pool, or has a hostile bench. But it will rarely allow a defendant to avoid unfavorable substantive law. Under the Supreme Court's decision in *Van Dusen v. Barrack*, the transferee court must apply the choice-of-law rules of the transferor court in most circumstances.[118] This means that the defendant will be stuck with the law that would have been applied by the transferor court.

To be entitled to a transfer, the defendant must make a substantial showing that transfer is warranted. This showing must also be supported by record evidence. Courts have broken the transfer analysis into three steps. First, a court should consider whether the case could have been brought in the defendant's chosen forum. This analysis requires the court to consider whether the action could have been commenced in the proposed transferee district.[119] While courts have articulated different tests, they generally consider whether the proposed transferee court would have had personal and subject matter jurisdiction, whether venue would be proper in that court, and whether the defendant would be subject to service of process in that forum.[120]

The second step involves the consideration of a number of private interest factors. A common articulation of these six factors is:

> (1) the plaintiffs' choice of forum . . .; (2) the defendants' choice of forum; (3) whether the claim arose elsewhere; (4) the convenience of the parties; (5) the convenience of the witnesses of the plaintiff and defendant, but only to the extent that the witnesses may actually be unavailable for trial in one of the fora; and (6) the ease of access to sources of proof.[121]

---

117. *See* Stewart Org., Inc. v. Ricoh Corp., 487 U.S. 22, 29 (1988).

118. 376 U.S. 612, 639 (1964) ("We conclude, therefore, that in cases such as the present, where the defendants seek transfer, the transferee district court must be obligated to apply the state law that would have been applied if there had been no change of venue. A change of venue under § 1404(a) generally should be, with respect to state law, but a change of courtrooms.").

119. Hatch v. Reliance Ins. Co., 758 F.2d 409, 414 (9th Cir. 1985) ("Whether an action 'might have been brought' in a district, the court looks to whether the action initially could have been commenced in that district.") (citing Hoffman v. Blaski, 363 U.S. 335, 344 (1960)).

120. Kay v. Nat'l City Mortgage Co., 494 F. Supp. 2d 845, 849 (S.D. Ohio 2007) (court must have jurisdiction, be proper venue, and defendant must be subject to service of process); Delorenzo v. HP Enter. Servs., LLC, 79 F. Supp. 3d 1277, 1280 (M.D. Fla. 2015) (court must have personal and subject matter jurisdiction and be proper venue).

121. Greater Yellowstone Coal. v. Bosworth, 180 F. Supp. 2d 124, 127 (D.D.C. 2001).

Courts usually consider each of the six factors separately. They will state whether the factor weighs for or against transfer and whether it should be given great or little weight. A number of rules have developed to help aid the court in its analysis. For example, courts often will defer to the plaintiff's chosen forum unless the plaintiff has little or no connection to it.

The most important factor in this analysis is normally the convenience of the witnesses, especially non-party witnesses.[122] The court will assess the importance of the witness to the case and should not simply count how many potential witnesses live in the opposing forums. Courts will also consider the power of the transferee court to bring non-party witnesses into court. The new geographical limits of Federal Rule of Civil Procedure 45 prohibit a court from requiring a defendant to appear and testify at a location more than 100 miles from where he resides, is employed, or regularly transacts business.[123] Therefore, the fact that a key non-party witness lives in the transferee district should weigh strongly in favor of transfer to that district unless the witness has voluntarily agreed to testify in the plaintiff's chosen forum.

There are strategic reasons for filing such a motion to transfer even if the court ultimately rules for the plaintiff. For example, if the defendant argues that key witnesses are located in the proposed transferee district, the plaintiff might counter by arguing that some or all of the witnesses are not important to their case. Even if the court ultimately denies transfer, this on-the-record statement might allow the defendant to narrow the scope of discovery.

Only slightly less important than the convenience of witnesses is the named plaintiff's connection (or lack thereof) to the chosen forum. While courts typically defer to the plaintiff's choice of forum, they have not hesitated to transfer cases when the plaintiff resides in a different district or appears to be forum shopping.[124] Similarly, courts have held that the plaintiff's chosen forum is entitled to less weight in the class

---

122. *See* 15 CHARLES WRIGHT & ARTHUR MILLER, FEDERAL PRACTICE & PROCEDURE § 3851 (4th ed.) ("The convenience of witnesses, particularly nonparty witnesses important to the resolution of the case, is often cited as the most significant factor in ruling on a motion to transfer under 28 U.S.C.A. § 1404(a).").

123. *See* FED. R. CIV. P. 45(c).

124. Brown v. SunTrust Banks, Inc., 66 F. Supp. 3d 81, 84 (D.D.C. 2014) (explaining that a plaintiff's chosen forum is entitled to less deference when the chosen forum has no particular ties to the controversy and no particular interest in the outcome).

action context.[125] Therefore, when a plaintiff's residence in the chosen forum is merely "fortuitous," courts will transfer the case, especially if other factors weigh strongly in favor of it.[126]

Another factor to consider is the pendency of other related matters. Transfer to another jurisdiction where other cases are pending can help to coordinate the litigation, reduce discovery costs, improve the possibility of settlement, and reduce the possibility of inconsistent judgments. The case of *Hawkins v. Gerber Products Co.*,[127] is an example of a defendant using a motion to transfer to avoid inconsistent judgments and a plaintiff-friendly venue. In *Hawkins*, the plaintiff filed a class action against Gerber and its parent company Nestle alleging claims for violations of California, Michigan, and New Jersey law. Ten other class actions were filed, but the MDL panel refused to consolidate the cases. Instead, a number of them were transferred to New Jersey and consolidated in that district. The California district court found that "the transfer of this action to the District of New Jersey would serve the interest of justice due to the possible consolidation of discovery and the conservation of time, energy and money, and the avoidance of the possibility of inconsistent judgments."[128]

The third step involves considering the "interests of justice."[129] While the articulation of these considerations differs by judicial districts, courts have considered factors such as (1) the interests of judicial economy, (2) the difficulty of applying the law of a distant forum, (3) the relative congestion of the two court's dockets, and (4) the interest in

---

125. Hawkins v. Gerber Products Co., 924 F. Supp. 2d 1208, 1214 (S.D. Cal. 2013) ("Though generally, a plaintiff's choice of forum receives deference in a motion to transfer venue, in class actions, a plaintiff's choice of forum is often accorded less weight.") (citing Lou v. Belzberg, 834 F.2d 730, 739 (9th Cir. 1987)) (internal citations omitted); Jaramillo v. DineEquity, Inc., 664 F. Supp. 2d 908, 914 (N.D. Ill. 2009) ("[T]he plaintiff's choice of forum is given less deference "when another forum has a stronger relationship to the dispute.").

126. Job Haines Home for the Aged v. Young, 936 F. Supp. 223, 227 (D.N.J. 1996) (transferring case filed in New Jersey to California because defendants and documents were all in California as was their attorney, alleged wrongdoing occurred in California, defense witnesses were all in that state and representatives' only named nonparty witness did not object to going to California to testify, California courts were intimately familiar with matter, and only New Jersey contact was fortuitous circumstance that representative happened to reside in state.).

127. *Hawkins*, 924 F. Supp. 2d at 1215.

128. *Id.* at 1214.

129. *See* WRIGHT & MILLER, *supra* note 122, at § 3854.

having local controversies decided at home.[130] Some courts have found the interests of justice factor determinative even when other factors weighed strongly for or against transfer.[131] Courts often find that the interest of justice favors transfer when there are multiple suits pending in multiple districts. While the interest in avoiding inconsistent judgments is certainly a large part of this, the public's interest in judicial economy and avoiding duplicative litigation is also important.

OPTIONS FOR DEFENDANTS FACING MULTIPLE CLASS ACTIONS IN MULTIPLE FORUMS

Class litigation often results in multiple lawsuits in varying jurisdictions. As discussed in Chapter 8, the filing of multiple suits might warrant consolidation in an MDL. However, if there are only a handful of lawsuits or the suits are not pending in federal court, MDL consolidation is likely not an option. Nonetheless, defendants do have procedural tools available to them that should allow them to avoid litigation in multiple forums.

The First-Filed Rule: Multiple Suits Pending in Federal Court

The first-filed rule protects the interests of judicial economy and the defendant's right not to be sued for the same dispute in two different courts.[132] Simply stated, when two duplicative actions are pending in courts of concurrent jurisdiction, the court with the earlier filed case should hear the dispute.[133]

---

130. *Id.*; Greater Yellowstone Coal. v. Bosworth, 180 F. Supp. 2d 124, 127 (D.D.C. 2001).

131. Research Automation, Inc. v. Schrader-Bridgeport Int'l, Inc., 626 F.3d 973, 978 (7th Cir. 2010) ("The interest of justice may be determinative, warranting transfer or its denial even where the convenience of the parties and witnesses points toward the opposite result.").

132. Worthington v. Bayer Healthcare, LLC, No. CIV.A. 11-2793 ES, 2012 WL 1079716, at *7 (D.N.J. Mar. 30, 2012) ("If nationwide classes were certified in both actions, each of the named plaintiffs would be included in the other's class. This Court cannot allow a parallel action to proceed which involves putative absent class members from an earlier-filed class action. Such a situation would cause substantial duplication of effort, and worse, potentially inconsistent rulings. This would frustrate one of the primary purposes of the rule, which is to avoid the embarrassment of conflicting judgments.").

133. Collegiate Licensing Co. v. Am. Cas. Co. of Reading, Pa., 713 F.3d 71, 78 (11th Cir. 2013) ("The first-filed rule provides that when parties have instituted competing or parallel litigation in separate courts, the court initially seized of the controversy should hear the case."); 1 Cyc. of Federal Proc. § 2:171 (3d ed. 2016).

The first-filed court will also decide whether the disputes are duplicative and whether the second suit "must be dismissed, stayed, or transferred and consolidated."[134] The second-filed court also has discretion to dismiss or stay the second-filed action.[135] It is not usual for the second-filed court to stay the proceedings pending a decision from the first-filed court. The first-filed rule is usually available only when the two actions are pending in federal court,[136] though there is some authority that suggests it should apply when the prior pending action is in state court.[137]

In applying the first-filed rule, courts consider three factors: (1) chronology of the two actions, (2) similarity of the parties, and (3) similarity of the issues.[138] The first factor—chronology of the two actions—usually looks only at the date the initial complaint was filed, even if that complaint was later amended.[139] If one of the two actions was originally filed in state court and later removed to federal court, the date the complaint was filed in state court is the relevant date.[140]

For the second factor, most courts only require a substantial similarity of the parties,[141] though some courts have required exact identity.[142] The test applied on this factor is especially important in class litigation because the named representatives in two simultaneously pending class actions will rarely if ever be the same person. If exact identity is

---

134. *Collegiate Licensing Co.*, 713 F.3d at 78.

135. McReynolds v. Merrill Lynch & Co., 694 F.3d 873, 888 (7th Cir. 2012) ("The district court has broad discretion to dismiss a complaint for reasons of wise judicial administration whenever it is duplicative of a parallel action already pending in another federal court.") (internal quotation marks and citation omitted).

136. Sini v. Citibank, N.A., 990 F. Supp. 2d 1370, 1375 (S.D. Fla. 2014).

137. Merrill Lynch, Pierce, Fenner & Smith, Inc. v. Haydu, 675 F.2d 1169, 1174 (11th Cir. 1982) ("The matter was first presented to the state court which first decided the question. In absence of compelling circumstances, the court initially seized of a controversy should be the one to decide the case.").

138. Wallerstein v. Dole Fresh Vegetables, Inc., 967 F. Supp. 2d 1289, 1293 (N.D. Cal. 2013).

139. NCR Corp. v. First Fin. Computer Servs., Inc., 492 F. Supp. 2d 864, 866 (S.D. Ohio 2007).

140. Aluminum Banking Co. v. Callery/Conway/Mars HV, Inc., No. CIV. 06-12038, 2006 WL 2193007, at *2 (E.D. Mich. Aug. 2, 2006) ("[E]very court to consider that question has held that the date the case was filed in state court is the relevant date.").

141. *Wallerstein*, 967 F. Supp. 2d at 1295; Whitten Ranch, Inc. v. Premier Alfalfa, Inc., 2009 WL 1844482 (D. Neb. 2009).

142. Lac Anh Le v. Pricewaterhousecoopers LLP, No. C-07-5476 MMC, 2008 WL 618938, at *1 (N.D. Cal. Mar. 4, 2008) (holding that two class actions were not the same because neither class had been certified and therefore the two suits involved only the individual plaintiffs).

required, this element will almost never be met. For class actions, courts have found substantial similarity when both classes seek to represent at least some of the same individuals.

Though the test for the third factor varies by jurisdiction, most courts require only substantial similarity.[143] Substantial similarity usually means that the two lawsuits overlap so that the adjudication of the first lawsuit will effectively answer the issues raised in the second lawsuit. Courts have found substantial similarity even when the claims are not entirely the same[144] or the relief sought is different.[145]

The hallmark of the first-filed rule is discretion and ample authority exists that a judge can decide to depart from the first-filed rule even when all factors counsel in favor of its application.[146] Courts have recognized three reasons not to apply the first-filed rule: (1) the first action was brought in bad faith, (2) it is an anticipatory suit, or (3) it is a blatant attempt at forum shopping. Few cases have considered the bad faith exception, but defendants should always be aware that this argument exists. The second exception, anticipatory suits, is unlikely to apply in the class action context.[147] Finally, the forum shopping exception usually requires clear proof. Courts have suggested that artificially dividing the class into separate actions might be sufficient to find forum shopping.[148]

---

143. 1 Cyclopedia of Federal Procedure § 2:177 (3d ed.).

144. *Worthington*, 2012 WL 1079716, at *5 (finding substantial similarity even though the two actions asserted claims under different state laws).

145. Catanese v. Unilever, 774 F. Supp. 2d 684, 689 (D.N.J. 2011) ("Where two actions filed in different districts involve the same parties and the same issues, and differ only as to the remedy sought, the first-filed rule applies.") (internal quotation marks and citations omitted).

146. DigiTrax Entmt, LLC v. Universal Music Corp., 21 F. Supp. 3d 917, 925 (E.D. Tenn. 2014).

147. A suit is anticipatory for purposes of the second exception "when the plaintiff files suit upon receipt of specific, concrete indications that a suit by the defendant is imminent." Youngevity Int'l, Inc. v. Renew Life Formulas, Inc., 42 F. Supp. 3d 1377, 1383 (S.D. Cal. 2014). While this exception might apply in ordinary litigation where parties might file an anticipatory lawsuit rather than waiting to be sued—this would never happen in a class action because a defendant would never file an action against a class of persons who might sue it later.

148. Wiley v. Trendwest Resorts, Inc., No. C 04-4321 SBA, 2005 WL 1910934, at *5 (N.D. Cal. Aug. 10, 2005) (refusing to apply the first-filed rule when the plaintiff filed a second lawsuit rather than amending his original complaint and articulated no reason for splitting the two suits between Nevada and California).

A defendant faced with multiple class actions in different federal courts should consider whether the first-filed rule would bar the second-filed action. If the two lawsuits involve the same common nucleus of facts and/or similar claims (even if asserted under the laws of different states), the defendant has a good argument that the first-filed rule applies and the second-filed action should not proceed. Other factors—for example, plaintiffs' counsel is the same in both actions—should bolster the chances of success. If one of the actions is pending in state court, the defendant should consider whether it is possible and advantageous to remove the state court action to federal court to take advantage of the first-filed rule.

There are several reasons for wanting to stop the second-filed action. First, the costs of litigating in two separate forums will be higher than litigating in a single forum. Second, a defendant who is litigating in two places runs the risk of providing inconsistent discovery responses or taking inconsistent positions that can be exploited by plaintiffs' counsel. Third, defendants run the risk of inconsistent court orders. For instance, one court might conclude that certain documents are privileged when another court might conclude that they are not. Fourth, the judge in the second-filed action might be less favorable than the judge in the first-filed action. Fifth, a judge who is unaware of the other pending action might be angry if he discovers it independently. Thus, bringing the action to the judge's attention might be of benefit to the defendant, even if the judge ultimately concludes the actions are not parallel.

On the other hand, situations exist in which the defendant might want to let the second-filed action proceed. If the judge in the second-filed action is more favorable to the defendant, the defendant should consider fast-tracking the second action so that it reaches judgment before the first-filed action. The defendant might reach the same conclusion if the court with the second-filed action has more favorable law, a better jury pool, or is more convenient to the defendant.

Before departing the first-filed rule, it is worth mentioning that a defendant facing multiple class actions in the same federal district court should consider whether a motion to consolidate is available under Rule 42. This option is not available when the matters are pending in different federal districts, but this fact might encourage one court to transfer the matter to that district for purposes of consolidation. A defendant should consult the local rules of the jurisdiction regarding the procedures for filing a motion to consolidate. Consistent with the first-filed rule, the first-filed court will normally decide a consolidation motion but it is possible that this might vary based on the particular situation or the particular jurisdiction.

State Law Abatement Statutes: Multiple Suits Pending in the Courts of the Same State

The first-filed rule will not help defendants facing multiple state court actions in the same state. In that situation, the defendant has the option of removing both actions to federal court in hopes of applying the first-filed rule. Alternatively, the defendant should consider whether a state law analog to the first-filed rule is available.

Many states have statutes that prohibit plaintiffs from prosecuting two simultaneous actions against the same defendant.[149] For example, Alabama has a statute prohibiting a plaintiff from prosecuting two actions against the same defendant at the same time.[150] In this spirit of this statute, Alabama appellate courts have required lower courts to stay later-filed class actions until the court in the first-filed action has ruled on class certification.[151] If the court certifies the class, then the action must be abated. Though Georgia has an almost identical statute, it does not appear Georgia's courts have applied the abatement rule in the class action context.

Colorado River Abstention: Federal Abstention in Favor of a Pending State Court Action

The *Colorado River* doctrine has its origins in *Colorado River Water Conservation District v. United States*.[152] In that case, the state of Colorado had a complex and comprehensive scheme for determining water allocations from the Colorado River. The United States sought to adjudicate certain rights to that water in federal court rather than the state system for water allocation. The district court abstained from exercising its jurisdiction and the U.S. Supreme Court affirmed this decision, holding that "a number of factors clearly counsel against concurrent federal proceedings."[153] First and foremost was a federal statute indicating a policy against piecemeal adjudication of water rights. The Court also noted that the lack of

---

149. *See* ALA. CODE § 6-5-440; GA. CODE ANN. § 9-2-5.

150. *See* ALA. CODE § 6-5-440; GA. CODE ANN. § 9-2-5.

151. *Ex parte* J.E. Estes Wood Co., Inc., 42 So. 3d 104, 110 (Ala. 2010).

152. Colorado River Water Conservation Dist. v. United States, 424 U.S. 800 (1976).

153. *Id.* at 819.

proceedings in the federal action, the convenience of the parties, and the state court's assumption of jurisdiction over the property at issue.

Abstention under the *Colorado River* doctrine is rare. As the Supreme Court explained in *Colorado River*, the doctrine is premised on concerns about "wise judicial administration, giving regard to conservation of judicial resources and comprehensive disposition of litigation."[154] Because a federal court has a "virtually unflagging obligation of the federal courts to exercise the jurisdiction given them," and given

> the absence of weightier considerations of constitutional adjudication and state-federal relations, the circumstances permitting the dismissal of a federal suit due to the presence of a concurrent state proceeding for reasons of wise judicial administration are considerably more limited than the circumstances appropriate for abstention.[155]

Still, these situations do exist and numerous federal courts have applied the doctrine to justify abstention when concurrent state-court proceedings are ongoing.

The *Colorado River* analysis proceeds in two parts. First, a court must ask whether the state and federal proceedings are truly parallel. Actions are generally considered parallel when they "involve substantially the same parties and substantially the same issues."[156] A primary consideration in this analysis is whether the two proceedings will require the presentation of the same evidence.[157] Exact parallelism is not required and two actions involving completely different causes of action can still be parallel if they involve the same issues.[158] Relevant to the class action context, different named plaintiffs in the state and federal action will not prevent the court from finding that the two actions are parallel.[159] As can be expected, the parties or the court's characterization of the issues might play a role in the outcome of this analysis.

---

154. *Id.* at 817.

155. *Id.* at 817–18.

156. Ambrosia Coal & Const. Co. v. Pages Morales, 368 F.3d 1320, 1330 (11th Cir. 2004).

157. Tyrer v. City of S. Beloit, Ill., 456 F.3d 744, 752–53 (7th Cir. 2006); New Orleans Pub. Serv., Inc. v. Council of City of New Orleans, 911 F.2d 993, 1005 (5th Cir. 1990).

158. *See Tyrer*, 456 F.3d at 752–53; Bosdorf v. Beach, 79 F. Supp. 2d 1337, 1344 n.13 (S.D. Fla. 1999).

159. *See* Romine v. Compuserve Corp., 160 F.3d 337, 340 (6th Cir. 1998) (explaining that "where the interests of both the named plaintiffs and the identical putative classes they seek to represent are congruent," the cases are parallel "notwithstanding the non-identity of the named parties"); Gintz v. Jack In The Box, Inc., No. C 06-02857 CW, 2006 WL 3422222, at *4 (N.D. Cal. Nov. 28, 2006) (staying class action under Colorado River doctrine).

If the actions are not parallel, then the analysis is over. If the court finds that the actions are parallel, then it proceeds to the second part of the analysis and considers whether several factors favor abstention. A standard articulation of the *Colorado River* factors is as follows: (1) whether one of the courts has assumed jurisdiction over property, (2) the inconvenience of the federal forum, (3) the potential for piecemeal litigation, (4) the order in which the forums obtained jurisdiction, (5) whether state or federal law will be applied, and (6) the adequacy of the state court to protect the parties' rights.[160]

No one factor is determinative and the court must apply the factors "in a pragmatic, flexible manner with a view to the realities of the case at hand."[161] For example, a federal court can still abstain under the Colorado River doctrine even if the state court action was filed later in time. As the Supreme Court explained in *Moses H. Cone Memorial Hospital*, this factor is not as concerned with "which complaint was filed first, but rather . . . how much progress has been made in the two actions."[162] If the state court action is further along than the federal court action, then this factor might weigh in favor of abstention.

The first factor, whether the court has assumed jurisdiction over property, is generally restricted to in rem proceedings and, thus, is unlikely to arise in the class action context.[163] However, this factor will weigh heavily in favor of abstention, so it should always be considered.[164] Similarly, the desire to avoid piecemeal litigation appears to be a primary objective when courts abstain under the *Colorado River* doctrine.[165] In particular, courts want to avoid the possibility of conflicting and inconsistent judgments.[166] The mere potential for inconsistent judgments is usually not enough to warrant abstention.

---

160. *See* Am. Bankers Ins. Co. of Fla. v. First State Ins. Co., 891 F.2d 882, 884 (11th Cir. 1990).

161. Moses H. Cone Mem'l Hosp. v. Mercury Constr. Corp., 460 U.S. 1, 21 (1983).

162. *Moses H. Cone Mem'l Hosp.*, 460 U.S. at 21.

163. *See* Jackson-Platts v. Gen. Elec. Capital Corp., 727 F.3d 1127, 1141 (11th Cir. 2013).

164. *See* R & R Capital, LLC v. Merritt, No. CIV. A. 07-2869, 2007 WL 3102961, at *13 (E.D. Pa. Oct. 23, 2007).

165. *See* Spectra Commc'ns Grp., LLC v. City of Cameron, Mo., 806 F.3d 1113, 1121 (8th Cir. 2015) ("The third factor, the risk of piecemeal litigation, is the "predominant factor") (citation omitted); Federated Rural Elec. Ins. Corp. v. Arkansas Elec. Cooperatives, Inc., 48 F.3d 294, 297 (8th Cir. 1995) ("The Supreme Court cases make it clear that this is the predominant factor.").

166. *See* Sini v. Citibank, N.A., 990 F. Supp. 2d 1370, 1379 (S.D. Fla. 2014); *Bosdorf*, 79 F. Supp. 2d 1337; Shields v. Murdoch, 891 F. Supp. 2d 567, 582–83 (S.D.N.Y. 2012) ("Abstention is more appropriate where the parties to both suits are not identical because there is a

A final consideration that might arise in the *Colorado River* analysis is "the vexatious or reactive nature of either the federal or the state litigation."[167] Numerous federal courts have abstained under the *Colorado River* doctrine after concluding that the federal lawsuit was vexatious or reactive.[168]

CHALLENGING PERSONAL JURISDICTION FOR CLASS MEMBERS IN THE WAKE OF *BRISTOL-MEYERS SQUIBB*

In June 2017, the Supreme Court held that state courts lack personal jurisdiction to adjudicate controversies brought by nonresident plaintiffs against a nonresident defendant(s). This is true even though the nonresident plaintiffs desire to join their claims with claims brought by resident plaintiffs. In *Bristol-Myers Squibb Co. v. Superior Court of California, San Francisco City*, more than 600 plaintiffs from multiple states joined together in a single lawsuit in California. The defendant was the maker of Plavix, a blood thinner, that is sold nationwide. All plaintiffs claimed that the drug had injured them in some way. Importantly, the case was not brought as a class action but as a "mass action."[169]

Ordinarily, a defendant must "purposely avail" itself of the forum state before that state can exercise jurisdiction over the defendant—that is, the state can make the defendant litigate in its courts. Bristol-Myers argued that the California state court did not have personal jurisdiction over it, at least as to the plaintiffs who were not residents of California. The California Supreme Court disagreed. It noted that the claims of the nonresidents were nearly identical to the claims of the 86 California residents. Further, Bristol-Myers had a research lab in California where it conducted non-Plavix research and approximately 1 percent of Bristol Myer's revenue was based off of sales in California. Thus, the California Supreme Court concluded that Bristol-Myers had sufficient minimum contacts to subject it to claims by plaintiffs from outside California.

---

possibility that the parties who are not bound by the prior judgment may cause inconsistent judgments in subsequent lawsuits.") (internal alterations and citation omitted).

167. *Moses H. Cone Mem'l Hosp.*, 460 U.S. at 17 n.20.

168. *See* Allen v. La. State Bd. of Dentistry, 835 F.2d 100, 105 (5th Cir. 1988) (affirming district court's stay where sequence of events indicates federal suit was vexatious or reactive); Nakash v. Marciano, 882 F.2d 1411, 1417 (9th Cir. 1989) (affirming district court's abstention because federal suit was attempt to avoid adverse ruling in state court); *Bosdorf*, 79 F. Supp. 2d at 1346; *see also* Fuller Co. v. Ramon I. Gil, Inc., 782 F.2d 306, 309–10 (1st Cir. 1986).

169. 137 S. Ct. 1773, 1775 (2017).

The Supreme Court reversed in an 8–1 decision authored by Justice Alito. The Court explained that there are two types of personal jurisdiction—general and specific. General jurisdiction means that a party is so at home in that forum that it is fair to subject that party to any type of claim there. For a corporation, general jurisdiction only exists in the state where it is incorporated or in the state where it has the base of its operations. California did not have general jurisdiction over Bristol-Myers because the company was incorporated in Delaware and had its base of operations in New Jersey.

Specific jurisdiction, on the other hand, exists when a corporation has purposefully directed its activity toward that state *in relation to* the events giving rise to the lawsuit. As for the 86 California residents, the California courts had specific jurisdiction because Bristol-Myers had sold Plavix to them in California. But for the out-of-state residents, the California courts lacked jurisdiction. This was true even though the in-state and out-of-state plaintiffs were asserting the same type of claim against the same defendant for the same product. Thus, even if the plaintiffs could properly join their claims together under California's joinder rules, that did not mean that the California courts had jurisdiction to adjudicate those claims. Accordingly, the due process clause of the 14th Amendment prohibited the nonresident defendants from forcing Bristol-Myers to litigate their claims in a California state court. While Bristol-Myers' personal jurisdiction defense did not take the entire lawsuit out of California state court, it significantly reduced the number of plaintiffs from more than 600 to less than 90. Further, it is likely that many of the dismissed plaintiffs will not refile a new lawsuit in their home states.

Scholars, courts, and practitioners are still wrestling with the meaning of *Bristol-Myers*. Plaintiffs have argued that *Bristol-Myers* is limited to mass actions and, therefore, does not apply to cases brought under Rule 23. Some courts have already accepted this argument.[170] For example, the

---

170. *In re* Chinese-Manufactured Drywall Prods. Liab. Litig., MDL No. 09-2047, 2017 WL 5971622, at *14 (E.D. La. Nov. 30, 2017) ("Class actions, nonetheless, are different from mass torts. In particular, for a case to qualify for class action treatment, it needs to meet the additional due process standards for class certification under Rule 23—numerosity, commonality, typicality, adequacy of representation, predominance and superiority. Often, mass torts cannot qualify for class action treatment because they are unable to satisfy these standards, and at other times, actions can begin as a mass tort but ultimately be resolved as a class action in the settlement context because in that context, manageability concerns are alleviated.") (internal citations omitted); Fitzhenry-Russell v. Dr. Pepper Snapple Grp., Inc., No. 17-CV-00564 NC, 2017 WL 4224723, at *5 (N.D. Cal. Sept. 22, 2017) ("*Bristol-Myers* is meaningfully distinguishable based on that case concerning a mass tort action, in which

court in *In re: Chinese-Manufactured Drywall Products Liability Litigation* concluded that class actions contain additional procedural safe guards (the requirements of numerosity, commonality, typicality, adequacy, predominance, and superiority) that often cannot be met in the mass action context. Given these procedural safeguards, defendants cannot complain that it is inappropriate to adjudicate the claims of out-of-state plaintiffs in a forum that bears little connection to their claims.[171] In reaching this conclusion, the court noted that the U.S. Supreme Court had approved the use of nationwide class actions in *Phillips Petroleum Co. v. Shutts* as long as the appropriate state substantive law was applied to each plaintiff's claim.[172] The *Chinese Drywall* court reasoned that it could address the concern about applying the appropriate substantive law through choice-of-law principles. The court then further distinguished *Bristol-Myers*, saying:

> [s]imply put, in [*Bristol-Myers*], the individual non-resident plaintiffs desired to disregard their own states' laws and instead apply California's consumer protection laws before a California jury. The Supreme Court rightly halted this form of forum shopping.[173]

Defendants, on the other hand, argue that *Bristol-Myers* applies equally to both mass actions and class actions. Thus, out-of-state plaintiffs whose claims bear no connection to the forum cannot force them to litigate in that forum.[174] For example, in *Spratley v. FCA US LLC*,[175]

---

each plaintiff was a named plaintiff. The Court acknowledges [the defendant's] criticism that the plaintiffs manipulated the complaint so as to not run afoul *Bristol-Myers*. That fact does not change that the plaintiffs are the masters of their complaint.").

171. *Chinese Drywall*, 2017 WL 5971622, at *15.

172. *See* Phillips Petroleum Co. v. Shutts, 472 U.S. 797, 821–23 (1985).

173. *Chinese Drywall*, 2017 WL 5971622, at *16.

174. *See* McDonnell v. Nature's Way Prod., LLC, No. 16 C 5011, 2017 WL 4864910, at *4 (N.D. Ill. Oct. 26, 2017) ("Purchasers of [defendant's product] and the other sixty-nine products described in paragraphs 22 and 24 who live in Florida, Michigan, Minnesota, Missouri, New Jersey, New York, or Washington have no injury arising from [the defendant's] forum-related activities in Illinois. Instead, any injury they suffered occurred in the state where they purchased the products. Because the only connection to Illinois is that provided by [the plaintiff's] purchase of [the product], which cannot provide a basis for the Court to exercise personal jurisdiction over the claims of nonresidents where [the defendant] has no other connection to this forum, the Court dismisses all claims . . . brought on behalf of non-Illinois residents or for violations of Florida, Michigan, Minnesota, Missouri, New Jersey, New York, and Washington law without prejudice."); *In re* Dental Supplies Antitrust Litig., No. 16CIV696BMCGRB, 2017 WL 4217115, at *9 (E.D.N.Y. Sept. 20, 2017) ("The constitutional requirements of due process does not wax and wane when the complaint is individual or on behalf of a class. Personal jurisdiction in class actions must comport with due process just the same as any other case."); Plumbers' Local Union No. 690 Health Plan v. Apotex Corp., No. CV 16-665, 2017 WL 3129147, at *8 (E.D. Pa. July 24, 2017).

175. No. 317CV0062MADDEP, 2017 WL 4023348, at *7 (N.D.N.Y. Sept. 12, 2017).

seven plaintiffs from seven different states joined together in an action brought in the Southern District of New York to sue Chrysler for an alleged defect in its vehicles. Chrysler moved to dismiss the non-New York plaintiffs for lack of jurisdiction. The district court first concluded that it lacked general jurisdiction over Chrysler. It then concluded that it also lacked specific jurisdiction over Chrysler for the plaintiff who had not purchased his or her vehicle in New York. The court explained,

Essentially, Plaintiffs argue that the out-of-state Plaintiffs' claims need not arise from Chrysler's New York activities because the out-of-state Plaintiffs' claims are the same as the New York Plaintiffs' claims and arise out of Chrysler's nationwide activity. However, the Supreme Court recently rejected this very theory of personal jurisdiction.[176]

Because "the out-of-state Plaintiffs [had] shown no connection between their claims and Chrysler's contacts with New York," the court "lack[ed] specific jurisdiction over [their] claims."[177]

After *Bristol-Myers*, counsel for defendants should consider challenging personal jurisdiction in any mass or class action that (1) spans more than one state and (2) is brought in a state where the defendant is not subject to general jurisdiction. However, because the law is unsettled, counsel should always check the most recent case law for its jurisdiction. New cases will be further defining and refining the contours of *Bristol-Myers* during the next several years, and any meaningful analysis must take this new case law into account.

Assuming that a *Bristol-Myers* motion is possible, there are several benefits. First, the successful motion will effectively limit the plaintiff's claims to the forum state. This might be especially useful in multi-plaintiff cases where forum plaintiff's claims lack merit or are questionable, but the claims of other, non-forum plaintiffs are meritorious. Under *Bristol-Myers*, the court would still lack personal jurisdiction over these meritorious claims. This is true even if they are properly pled. Another potential benefit is that moving under *Bristol-Myers* might make it impossible to meet the numerosity requirement for class certification. Even if the out-of-state plaintiffs are likely to refile in their home states, defendants might still want to break the case up to escape an unfavorable venue.

As always, there are other strategic considerations that must factor into a defendant's decision to move under *Bristol-Myers* even when

176. *Id.* at *6.
177. *Id.* at *7.

such a motion is possible. First, Rule 12(h) provides that the defense is waived as a matter of law unless it is raised in a Rule 12(b) motion or a responsive pleading.[178] Thus, defendants must raise this defense early in the case. If the defendant has already responded or begun litigating, it might be too late to challenge personal jurisdiction under *Bristol-Myers*. Assuming it is not too late, some defendants might want to waive personal jurisdiction for the same reasons they might want to forgo compelling arbitration or removing a case to federal court. For example, if a defendant desires a quick and comprehensive settlement, it would be easier to accomplish that in a single jurisdiction in front of a single judge. Additionally, a defendant might like the judge assigned to the case or like the substantive law of the plaintiff's chosen forum. If it is likely that out-of-state plaintiffs will refile in their home state, it might be better to consent to jurisdiction in a single forum. Counsel should carefully consider such strategic benefits before moving to break a single large case into several smaller ones.

There might be other reasons that a *Bristol-Myers* motion is undesirable. For example, if the plaintiffs assert that the defendant or defendants harmed them through a conspiracy, a portion of which was carried out in the forum state, such an allegation might satisfy the minimum contacts requirement for claims by out-of-state plaintiffs. Even if the conspiracy allegations are factually untrue, a challenge to personal jurisdiction could lead to limited discovery on that issue. Defendants might find such discovery undesirable for any number of reasons.

CONCLUSION

Defendants should explore all of their forum options, and must do so immediately upon receiving the complaint, because time is very short. Forum can be case dispositive and defendants might have a number of options depending upon the claims, the applicable contracts, and the location.

---

178. *See* FED. R. CIV. P. 12(h).

4

Responding to the Class Action Complaint

Robert J. Herrington

This chapter addresses strategic considerations for responding to a class action complaint. We begin by discussing early case assessments and how they can be used to defend class actions more efficiently and effectively. Next, we discuss early resolution strategies, including individual settlements, pre-litigation refunds, Rule 68 offers of judgment, and voluntary market actions. We then discuss jurisdiction and venue, including strategies for moving the case to a forum that may be more advantageous for the defense. We also address motion-to-dismiss strategies and options for challenging class allegations early in the case. We also cover filing an answer to the class action complaint, including affirmative defenses that can help defeat class certification. Finally, we address the importance of developing an overall defense narrative that can be woven into each case filing.

EARLY CASE ASSESSMENTS

Many defense lawyers use a standard playbook for defending a class action. The complaint is filed and the first step is to file a motion to dismiss. The motion is briefed and decided somewhere between two and six months (or more) later. In many cases, little happens in the meantime. If the motion is granted with prejudice, great; you're a hero. If leave to amend is granted, another round of briefing and waiting follows. If the motion is denied, the case proceeds to discovery and briefing on class certification, with plaintiffs feeling like they have momentum and can now exert pressure.

This is not to say that motions to dismiss are bad. To the contrary, they can be a critical part of effectively responding to a class-action complaint. But they are just one part of an effective defense strategy. Where appropriate, many sophisticated defense lawyers use another tool as well: the early case assessment. And many in-house counsel— justifiably concerned about the costs of class litigation—are insisting on early case assessments as a way to better understand and guide the case to a successful resolution.

So, what is an early case assessment? It is a proactive, case-management process that involves investigating a claim within the first two to six months, evaluating the strengths and weakness, analyzing and quantifying the risk, and developing a comprehensive defense strategy.

Investigating the Claim

The core premise of an early case assessment is to be proactive rather than reactive. That means understanding the facts of a case as early as possible so better decisions can be made. Here is an example: imagine that a consumer class action alleges that your client's new, "hot" product has a defect that causes a certain percentage to fail after just three months. Also imagine that the allegations have merit (i.e., the product does have a material defect), but you will not know this information until someone interviews the lead engineer for the project and reviews the engineering team's documents. Would the strategy for defending the case be different if you knew that the defect allegations had merit? Would it be better to have that information near the beginning of the case, rather than only after the lead engineer's deposition is noticed? The answers seem obvious, yet in many cases, critical information remains unknown until the class action reaches deep into the discovery phase, after hundreds of hours have been spent on work that may never have been undertaken had this information been known earlier.

The initial phase of an early case assessment involves conducting a reasonably fulsome fact investigation. Who are the key witnesses? Interview them. What are the key documents and electronic information?

Use predictive coding or another tool to identify and analyze them. Create a chronology. Create a "hot" documents list. What are the five to ten best facts and documents? The five to ten worst? Investigate the facts that likely will drive class certification. If the case involves labeling or advertising, did the ads and labels vary and in what ways? What about the product formulation or design? Did it vary? In a product defect case, investigate whether the circumstances of the defect vary. Is the alleged defect present in every unit or does it vary? Under what circumstances will the defect manifest in a way that affects consumers? Do those circumstances vary?

Analyze the individual plaintiff's allegations and any documents the client might have on that individual. Do a background investigation on the plaintiff. Is this a serial plaintiff, or maybe one with a family or other relationship with plaintiff's counsel or perhaps a criminal record or bankruptcy that may be disqualifying? Does the time line suggest that the plaintiff was recruited to buy the product and sue?

Evaluating the Case

As the facts are assembled, objectively analyze the legal elements of the claims, how the facts may fit the elements, and prepare an overview of the case to be used in developing an overall case strategy. Many experienced class action defense lawyers might believe that they have a "good handle" on the relevant case law and think they can skip this step, but the facts of every case are different. It is worth the effort to dig deeply into the relevant legal issues to identify the cases most like the one you are defending so you can more accurately predict how a motion to dismiss, motion for summary judgment, and class certification will be decided. What cases have addressed allegations and facts most similar to yours and how were they decided? How has the judge assigned to your case addressed the key issues that might be raised in a motion to dismiss or for class certification? Keep in mind that the law governing critical procedural or substantive issues may be better in another venue. It is important to understand those differences so you can evaluate whether to try to move the case.

Recently, more district courts have been analyzing class certification on an element-by-element basis. One helpful strategy is to develop, very early in the case, your own element-by-element analysis of the claims and defenses, including the likely jury instructions and how the facts fit those instructions. Using the results of the fact investigation, you can then assess which legal elements likely are common to putative class members and which truly vary in material ways. This assessment will help in developing a more accurate prediction on class certification and allow you to focus discovery and briefing efforts as the case progresses.

The critical point is to prepare an *objective* case evaluation, early in the case, that summarizes the key legal issues and how the facts appear to fit. The point here is not to evaluate "how to win." That step will come. The case overview should objectively evaluate the complaint's allegations, as well as the likelihood of a series of possible outcomes. The overview can then serve as a baseline for assessing the value of the case and developing the overall defense strategy.

Analyzing and Quantifying the Risk

An early case assessment should include a risk analysis—that is, what risks does the class action present to the company? The most obvious risk is an adverse monetary judgment. To assess and quantify this risk, you need to understand the size of the putative class and how much money is potentially at issue. In a consumer class action, the complaint usually will attempt to put "at issue" a significant portion of the revenue associated with a product, service, or business practice, as well as the revenue of "similar" products and services the named plaintiff may not have purchased.

To quantify the risk, start by analyzing the largest universe of products that may potentially be at issue and the revenue associated with those products. What is the plaintiff's "best day in court," assuming everything goes his way? Then analyze the likelihood of success on the key procedural or substantive steps in the case. What is the likelihood the court will agree with each of the arguments in a motion to dismiss and how would that affect risk? Ask the same question for the other key procedural and substantive issues in the case. Take those percentages and use a decision tree analysis or other tool to model different outcomes and assess the overall risk of an adverse monetary judgment. A risk analysis is only as good as the inputs, so consider having different members of the litigation team independently provide estimates on each key issue. Model each team member's estimates, as well as the average.

Although money is one aspect of class action risk analysis, it is far from the only risk. If the case seeks injunctive relief, you need to analyze the impact of any injunction, both in terms of costs of compliance and impact on revenue. Also consider reputational risk. The litigation may generate adverse press, and a "loss" at various stages of the case could generate additional media coverage. Your opponent also may attempt to generate coverage, either by providing press releases and interviews or by working with investigative reporters. The class certification process tends to generate media coverage, plus an adverse certification ruling often means notice to the company's customers or client base. These risks often are more difficult to quantify, but they should be included in the risk analysis as real possibilities.

Developing a Defense Strategy

At this point in the process, the team can develop an overall case strategy. Depending on the company's goals and risk tolerance, the strategy may range from seeking an immediate resolution to litigating each and every reasonably debatable issue. The idea is to use the early case assessment to inform proactive strategy decisions that help position the case to achieve the optimal case outcome in the most cost-effective way.

For example, again imagine a product defect class action where the early case assessment shows that the product does in fact suffer from a defect, or at least a certain percentage of the units do. One defense strategy may be to promptly institute a remediation program that involves providing defect-free replacements for anyone who bought a product that is showing signs of the defect and then seeking to have the class allegations dismissed on mootness or other grounds (more on this possible strategy later). Or perhaps the early case assessment shows that, while certain product lots do indeed have a defect, the unit that the plaintiff purchased is not from one of those lots. In that case, the team might consider asking the court to phase discovery to focus on that key issue—that is, whether plaintiff's product has a defect—so it can be addressed by way of an early motion for summary judgment. Even if the court does not phase discovery, the team will know that it needs to have an expert inspect plaintiff's product as early as possible, which may still allow you to file an early dispositive motion before discovery gets rolling.

In addition, the team will want to develop its class certification defense strategy. What is the factual and legal theory that will be at the core of opposing class certification, or perhaps bringing an early motion to deny class certification? Rather than being reactive and thinking you cannot develop the response to class certification until you know what plaintiff is going to say, develop a proactive certification theory. Why is it that the "common" issues alleged in the complaint are not common? Why is it that any common issues will not predominate? This is where the element-by-element assessment comes in handy. It will help you understand which elements likely cannot be established based on common evidence and where you need to focus your fact gathering and discovery. For example, plaintiff may be seeking to rely on a presumption of materiality or reliance, which your research shows is permissible. In that case, you should be developing the factual record needed to rebut that presumption, often using surveys establishing that materiality and reliance vary based on the experiences of individual class members.

The bottom line is the early case assessment can greatly improve your ability to effectively manage class litigation by allowing you to make informed, proactive strategy decisions, rather than simply respond to the plaintiff's moves.

EARLY RESOLUTION STRATEGY

Given the nature and cost of class action litigation, it is worth considering whether the case can be resolved early in the litigation process or, better yet, before litigation is filed. Some consumer protection and warranty statutes require a plaintiff to send notice before filing a suit for damages.[1] In those jurisdictions, plaintiff's counsel likely will send a demand letter before filing the complaint. Other plaintiffs' lawyers have a practice of sending a demand before filing suit, regardless of whether it is required. Where a company receives this type of notice, it is worth taking the demand seriously, as the defendant has an opportunity to try to dispose of the matter early, cheaply (relatively speaking), and confidentially.

A class action can be settled just like any other lawsuit. The plaintiff and defendant can agree to a payment, and perhaps a change in business practices, in return for a release of any litigation, with the putative class not receiving anything and also not releasing any claims. Where no lawsuit has been filed, this type of "individual settlement" does not require court approval. Where litigation has been filed, some states

---

1. *See, e.g.,* CAL. CIV. CODE § 1782.

require courts to sign off on the deal to ensure that the rights of putative class members are not affected.[2]

In federal court, Rule 23(e) does not require approval of an individual settlement where no class has been certified.[3] Some courts, however, continue to require approval to address whether notice should be provided or if the settlement could prejudice putative class members.[4]

When evaluating whether to consider an individual settlement, a key consideration is the potential exposure. In many class actions, the realistic exposure is well under seven figures, which may not be enough to justify the effort and expense on either side. This is particularly true in cases that involve challenges to food and supplement labeling, where the damages theory generally involves an effort to compute the "price premium" associated with the alleged misrepresentation on the label. Many times, plaintiff's counsel will send a demand letter with the goal of trying to understand the volume of sales potentially at issue. That number, multiplied by an estimated price premium, will allow counsel to estimate a range of potential exposure if the case were litigated on a class basis. Where the exposure is low, plaintiff's counsel often is willing to resolve the matter before filing suit in exchange for a confidential agreement to make a labeling change, along with a payment of attorney's fees (often in the low five figures) and a relatively small amount for the named plaintiff (less than the typical "incentive award" that is part of a class settlement).

The challenge with an individual deal is that it only disposes of the named plaintiff's claims and is not binding on any putative class member. In other words, the settlement avoids or ends the litigation, but does not buy "complete peace." A putative class member could, at any time, send a similar demand letter or file litigation alleging the same claims. On the flip side, the cost of an individual settlement usually is a tiny fraction of a class settlement and generally less than the cost of filing and prevailing on a motion to dismiss. In a sense, the company is in largely the same position after prevailing on a motion to dismiss as

2. *See, e.g.*, CAL. R. CT. RULE 3.770.

3. Stilz v. Glob. Cash Network, Inc., No. 10 CV 1998, 2010 WL 3975588, at *6 (N.D. Ill. Oct. 7, 2010) ("The 2003 amendments to Rule 23(e) changed its language to specify that court approval was required only with respect to a certified class.").

4. Bray v. Simon & Schuster, Inc., No. 4:14-CV-00258-NKL, 2014 WL 2893202, at *2 (W.D. Mo. June 25, 2014) ("some courts have continued to require approval of voluntary, non-prejudicial dismissals sought prior to any ruling on class certification—more specifically, to address whether notice to the putative class is necessary to prevent prejudice").

it is after an individual settlement; either way, putative class members remain free to sue.

One question that often arises is whether the company can obtain an agreement from plaintiff's counsel that they will not sue again on the same theory. Practitioners should look at their own state's ethical standards, but generally this type of proposal is prohibited. Rule 5.6 of the Model Rules of Professional Conduct states that "[a] lawyer shall not participate in *offering or making* . . . (b) an agreement in which a restriction on the lawyer's right to practice is part of the settlement of a client controversy." A settlement that prohibits a lawyer's ability to represent other plaintiffs violates Rule 5.6, as a lawyer is prohibited "from agreeing not to represent other persons in connection with settling a claim on behalf of a client."[5] Similarly, the Restatement (Third) of Law Governing Lawyers, section 13(2) states "[i]n settling a client claim, a lawyer may not offer or enter into an agreement that restricts the right of the lawyer to practice law, including the right to represent or take particular action on behalf of other clients." Echoing this statement, several state bar opinions expressly prohibit a settlement agreement that restricts a lawyer's ability to represent clients in future cases.[6]

In some jurisdictions, a company may be able to retain plaintiff's counsel after resolving the threatened litigation, in which case the lawyer may have a conflict in future cases against the company. But this strategy still carries significant risks and should be carefully evaluated under applicable ethical standards. In most cases, the best a company can do is to obtain a strict confidentiality agreement from the plaintiff and a representation from the plaintiff's lawyer that he has no other clients with similar claims and no present intent to sue.

None of this should be taken to suggest that an individual settlement is appropriate in all class actions. In many cases it doesn't make sense, and many companies are unwilling to consider an individual resolution, thinking it will mark them an easy target. But in situations where it does make sense, an early individual resolution offers many advantages, including avoiding adverse publicity and ending litigation costs.

---

5. MODEL RULES OF PROF'L CONDUCT R. 5.6(b) cmt. 2.

6. ABA Formal Opinion 93-371; Colorado Formal Opinion 92; California Formal Opinion 1988-104; Florida Formal Opinion 04-2; Michigan Opinion CI-1165; New Mexico Opinion 1985-5; New York State Opinion 730; North Carolina Opinion RPC 179.

MOOTING PLAINTIFFS' CLAIMS AND THE CLASS ALLEGATIONS

Another reason to take an early demand letter seriously is that it offers the opportunity to short circuit a class action by mooting the named plaintiff's individual claims and heading off any attempt to sue on behalf of a proposed class.

Pre-Suit Refund and Argue for Dismissal

If a client receives a demand letter, one of the first considerations should be whether to provide a refund to the named plaintiff. The demand letter generally will claim that the plaintiff bought some product or service and was misled, or that the transaction was unlawful in some way. The client may have information regarding the plaintiff's transaction, including what was purchased and paid. Even if the client does not have that information (manufacturers often won't), you can reasonably estimate what the plaintiff paid. Consider refunding the full amount of what the plaintiff paid, including shipping, taxes, and any other charges, *before* a lawsuit is filed. That refund may provide a basis for dismissal.

Several courts have held that a full refund, provided before a lawsuit is filed, negates the plaintiff's injury. Because injury is an element of most consumer protection claims, a plaintiff that receives a full refund may not be able to state a claim. For example, the Ninth Circuit has held, in an unpublished decision, that a pre-filing refund eliminates standing to sue.[7] In *Luman*, plaintiffs filed a false advertising class action. Before filing suit, plaintiffs sent a demand letter requesting a refund, and the defendant credited plaintiff's credit card for the full amount of the purchase. Defendant moved to dismiss, arguing that the refund eliminated plaintiff's standing. The district court agreed, dismissing the case, and the Ninth Circuit affirmed that ruling. "Luman filed his complaint two months after he received a monetary refund from NAC, and therefore no longer met the injury-in-fact requirement for standing at the time

---

7. Luman v. Theismann, 647 F. App'x 804, 806 (9th Cir. 2016).

he filed his complaint."[8] Several district courts have reached the same conclusion.[9]

A related issue is whether a money-back guarantee can help defeat certification or eliminates standing to sue. Some courts have held that a class definition covering individuals who received refunds under a money-back guarantee is overbroad and unascertainable.[10] In another case, the court ruled that the defendant's money-back guarantee defeated a claim for unjust enrichment.[11] Other courts have disagreed. One court held that a money-back guarantee did not defeat predominance because the defendant had records of who received a refund and it would be a "mere mechanical task" to determine who should be excluded from the proposed class.[12] Another court rejected the argument that a money-back guarantee could defeat standing, concluding that such a ruling would render consumer protection laws a "nullity."[13]

8. *Id.* at 806.

9. Friedman v. Dollar Thrifty Auto. Grp., Inc., No. CV12CV02432WYDKMT, 2017 WL 104904, at *8 (D. Colo. Jan. 5, 2017) (granting summary judgment to defendant based on pre-filing refund); Main v. Gateway Genomics, LLC, No. 15CV2945 AJB (WVG), 2016 WL 7626581, at *4 (S.D. Cal. Aug. 1, 2016) (dismissing complaint; "Ms. Main requested and received a full refund of the purchase price of the SneakPeek test on or about November 10, 2015, approximately two months before she filed the original complaint."); Becker v. Skype Inc., No. 5:12-CV-06477-EJD, 2014 WL 556697, at *2 (N.D. Cal. Feb. 10, 2014) (citing "several decisions in which plaintiffs who received a full refund prior to filing suit were found to lack standing"); Amirhamzeh v. Chase Bank USA, N.A., No. CV 13-00527-BRO FFMX, 2014 WL 641705, at *7 (C.D. Cal. Feb. 7, 2014) ("Plaintiff's allegations were mooted by receipt of the pre-litigation refund."); Brandon v. Nat'l R.R. Passenger Corp. Amtrak, No. CV 12-5796 PSG VBKX, 2013 WL 800265, at *5 (C.D. Cal. Mar. 1, 2013) ("Plaintiff contends that the tender did not end the dispute over restitution because she did not cash the check. However, a plaintiff cannot revive a moot claim simply by refusing tender.").

10. Minkler v. Kramer Labs., Inc., No. CV 12-9421-JFW FFMX, 2013 WL 3185552, at *3 (C.D. Cal. Mar. 1, 2013) (granting motion to strike).

11. Demedicis v. CVS Health Corp., No. 16-CV-5973, 2017 WL 569157, at *3 (N.D. Ill. Feb. 13, 2017); *see also* Preira v. Bancorp Bank, 885 F. Supp. 2d 672, 678 (S.D.N.Y. 2012) (availability of refund negated injury).

12. Wiener v. Dannon Co., 255 F.R.D. 658, 670 (C.D. Cal. 2009).

13. Adkins v. Apple Inc., 147 F. Supp. 3d 913, 919 (N.D. Cal. 2014); *see also* Worley v. Avanquest N. Am., Inc., No. C 12-04391 SI, 2013 WL 450388, at *5 (N.D. Cal. Feb. 5, 2013) ("mere fact that defendant offered a 90 day refund does not preclude plaintiff's unfair conduct allegations"); Camasta v. Omaha Steaks Int'l, Inc., No. 12-CV-08285, 2013 WL 4495661, at *6 (N.D. Ill. Aug. 21, 2013) ("A defendant engaging in deceptive or unfair practices should not be allowed to hide behind a refund policy.").

Post-Filing Pickoffs Generally Will Not Work

Once a lawsuit is filed, mooting a class action by offering the named plaintiff full relief is unlikely to be successful, although the law in this area continues to develop. The key recent case is the Supreme Court's decision in *Campbell-Ewald v. Gomez*,[14] where the Court held that an unaccepted Rule 68 offer of judgment did not render a plaintiff's individual claim moot. The Court analyzed the Rule 68 offer under basic contract principles and concluded that a Rule 68 offer "once rejected, had no continuing efficacy"[15] and thus did not moot the claim. Emphasizing that its holding was narrow, the Court explained:

> [w]e need not, and do not, now decide whether the result would be different if a defendant deposits the full amount of the plaintiff's individual claim in an amount payable to the plaintiff, and the court then enters judgment for the plaintiff in that amount.[16]

Following *Campbell-Ewald*, several defendants have tested the hypothetical scenario offered by the Court, with very limited success. For example, in *Bais Yaakov v. Graduation Source, LLC*,[17] the defendant deposited money with the court for the full amount of plaintiff's damages, agreed to an injunction not to violate the Telephone Consumer Protection Act (TCPA), and asked the court to enter judgment. The court denied the request, concluding that the plaintiff still had a live claim and was entitled to try to demonstrate that class certification should be granted.[18]

---

14. Campbell-Ewald v. Gomez, 136 S. Ct. 663 (2016).

15. *Id.* at 671.

16. *Id.* at 672.

17. Bais Yaakov v. Graduation Source, LLC, 167 F. Supp. 3d 582 (S.D.N.Y. 2016).

18. *See also* Heather McCombs, D.P.M., L.L.C. v. Cayan LLC, No. 15 C 10843, 2017 WL 1022013, at *4 (N.D. Ill. Mar. 16, 2017) (where a plaintiff "has made clear its intent to pursue class certification by filing a class complaint and placeholder motion for class certification, tender alone, without entry of judgment by the court in favor of the defendant, is insufficient to moot individual or class claims."); Bell v. Survey Sampling Int'l, LLC, No. 3:15-CV-1666 (MPS), 2017 WL 1013294, at *5 (D. Conn. Mar. 15, 2017) ("cases allowing a defendant to 'pick off' plaintiffs simply by making a tender of complete relief deny plaintiffs a fair opportunity to pursue class claims and are contrary to the spirit of Campbell-Ewald."); Getchman v. Pyramid Consulting, Inc., No. 4:16 CV 1208 CDP, 2017 WL 713034, at *3 (E.D. Mo. Feb. 23, 2017) ("The facts before me indicate that Pyramid made a tender offer of settlement via a check that was subsequently refused and returned by Getchman. This is not materially different than if Pyramid had communicated an offer of settlement that Getchman in turn rejected. In both scenarios, the 'unaccepted [offer]—like any unaccepted contract offer—is a legal nullity, with no operative effect,' and plaintiff is left without satisfaction of either her individual or her class claims.").

The court reached a similar outcome in *South Orange Chiropractic Center, LLC v. Cayan LLC*,[19] but did so using a different rationale. The court held that the plaintiff's individual claim was moot "because Defendant has offered to deposit a check with the court, to satisfy all of Plaintiff's individual claims (and more), and to have the district court enter judgment in Plaintiff's favor."[20] Nevertheless, the court concluded that the defendant's "attempt to moot the request for classwide statutory damages falls within the 'inherently transitory' exception [to the mootness doctrine] . . . because the class issues will likely evade review," and therefore declined to dismiss the case.[21]

The Sixth Circuit addressed this "inherently transitory" exception in *Wilson v. Gordon*.[22] In that case, plaintiffs filed a class action over the failure to process their applications for Medicaid benefits. In response, the defendant entered into an agreement with the named plaintiff under which it enrolled them in Medicaid, the primary relief sought. The trial court nevertheless certified a class action and entered a preliminary injunction on behalf of the class. On appeal, the defendant argued that the case was moot because it had enrolled the named plaintiffs in Medicaid. The Sixth Circuit disagreed, concluding that the "inherently transitory" exception to the mootness doctrine applied. The court found that the "duration of Plaintiffs' claims was tenuous."[23] The defendant could "quickly either hold a hearing on their delayed applications for Medicaid or enroll them" before the district court could reasonably be expected to rule on the class certification motion, thus making the claims "transitory."[24] The court also applied an exception against "picking off" the named plaintiffs in a class action. Although the Supreme Court's *Campbell-Ewald* decision could have but did not address this exception, the *Wilson* court noted that several circuits continued to hold that a defendant should not be permitted to avoid a decision on class

---

19. South Orange Chiropractic Center, LLC v. Cayan LLC, No. 15-13069, 2016 WL 1441791, at *5 (D. Mass. Apr. 12, 2016).
20. *Id.*
21. *Id.* at *6.
22. Wilson v. Gordon, 822 F.3d 934, 944 (6th Cir. 2016).
23. *Id.* at 945.
24. *Id.* at 947.

certification by paying off the named plaintiffs and arguing that the case is moot.[25]

The case law in this area has not all been negative for defendants. For example, in *Leyse v. Lifetime Entm't Servs., LLC,*[26] the Second Circuit affirmed entry of judgment based on an unaccepted Rule 68 offer of judgment. In that case, the district court denied certification and then defendant made a Rule 68 offer of judgment, depositing the full amount of damages and costs recoverable. Plaintiff rejected the offer, but the district court entered judgment anyway. The plaintiff appealed, arguing that *Campbell-Ewald* controlled. The Second Circuit disagreed, holding that the case was outside the holding in *Campbell-Ewald* because the defendant deposited the full amount of the plaintiff's individual claim in an account payable to plaintiff. The court, however, still addressed the denial of class certification, holding that the Rule 68 offer of judgment and tender of complete relief did not make plaintiff's claim moot; it simply allow the court to enter judgment. For that reason, the case appears to have limited usefulness.

The Second Circuit reached a similar conclusion in *Bank v. Alliance Health Networks, LLC,*[27] where the defendant sent plaintiff a check exceeding the amount of his individual claim and the plaintiff cashed it, without ever seeking class certification. The district court then entered judgment on the individual claim and dismissed the rest of the case as moot. On appeal, the Second Circuit affirmed, stating that "where judgment has been entered and where the plaintiff's claims have been satisfied, as they were here when Bank negotiated the check, any individual claims are rendered moot."[28] The court also affirmed the dismissal of the class allegations as moot, explaining that "[s]ince Bank was the sole individual representative for the putative class, once his claim was no longer live, no plaintiff remained in a position to pursue the class claims."[29]

---

25. *See also* Chen v. Allstate Ins. Co., 819 F.3d 1136, 1142 (9th Cir. 2016) (if the "district court were to enter judgment providing complete relief on Pacleb's individual claims for damages and injunctive relief before class certification, fully satisfying those individual claims, Pacleb still would be entitled to seek certification").

26. Leyse v. Lifetime Entm't Servs., LLC, No. 16-1133-CV, 2017 WL 659894, at *3 (2d Cir. Feb. 15, 2017).

27. Bank v. All. Health Networks, LLC, 669 F. App'x 584 (2d Cir. 2016).

28. *Id.* at 585.

29. *Id.* at 586.

In another case involving an accepted Rule 68 offer, the Ninth Circuit held that the plaintiff lacked standing to appeal the denial of certification because he had "no financial interest or other personal interest whatsoever in class certification."[30] The court explained that, "when the plaintiff voluntarily settles his or her individual claims, we have found no case that has held that the 'private attorney general' interest suffices; all cases look to whether the plaintiff has the requisite financial, or otherwise personal, stake in the outcome of the class claims."[31]

The post-*Campbell-Ewald* decision that arguably has gone the farthest on the defense side is *Demmler v. ACH Food Companies, Inc.*[32] In that case, plaintiff sought damages, an order that the product's label be modified, and attorney's fees on behalf of himself and a putative class for the false labeling of barbecue sauce. In response, the defendant sent plaintiff's counsel an unrestricted check for its calculation of the maximum statutory damages and noted that it had already removed the product from the market. Defendant then moved to dismiss or for summary judgment on the basis that the court lacked subject matter jurisdiction due to mootness, which the court granted. The court concluded that it was irrelevant whether plaintiff rejected the check because it was unconditional and amounted to more than the plaintiff could hope to recover in the case, thus taking the case outside of *Campbell-Ewald*. The court also found that there was no evidence that the defendant was attempting to pick off the named plaintiff so as to insulate itself from liability, which the court concluded was necessary for the "pickoff" exception to apply.

From the defense perspective, a few key points can be distilled from these decisions:

- An unaccepted Rule 68 offer of judgment will not moot a plaintiff's individual claims or class allegations.
- Where a defendant unconditionally provides all the relief a plaintiff could hope to recover, that tender may moot the individual claims, but the case law is still developing.
- Tendering complete relief before a plaintiff has a reasonable opportunity to seek class certification is unlikely to result in the dismissal of the class allegations, although there is a glimmer of hope in decisions like *Demmler*.

---

30. Campion v. Old Republic Protection Co., 775 F.3d 1144, 1146–47 (9th Cir. 2014).
31. *Id.*
32. Demmler v. ACH Food Companies, Inc., No. 15-13556-LTS, 2016 WL 4703875, at *5 (D. Mass. June 9, 2016).

- If a plaintiff accepts a Rule 68 offer of judgment, tender, or set-tlement, that acceptance should end the individual claims and eliminate the plaintiff's ability to seek certification.

In the final analysis, the strategy of making a Rule 68 offer for com-plete relief or tendering complete relief remains viable, but only in limited circumstances, primarily where the plaintiff accepts. An unac-cepted Rule 68 offer does provide some strategic advantage in that the plaintiff may be liable for the defendant's post-offer costs if he fails to secure a more favorable recovery and, in certain circumstances, may not be able to recover post-offer attorney fees, even if successful. The strategy is worth considering, but is nowhere near the "silver bullet" that many on the defense side hoped it might be.

Recalls and Other Relief May Limit Class Action Risk

A company that becomes aware of a defect or other problem with one of its products may be able to take steps to limit the risk of class action litigation, at least in certain circumstances. Several courts have held that, where a plaintiff sues based on an allegedly defective or con-taminated product that was recalled, and for which the plaintiff can receive a refund or replacement, the claims are moot. For example, in *Winzler v. Toyota Motor Sales U.S.A., Inc.*,[33] then Judge, now Justice, Gorsuch authored an opinion holding that a voluntary recall overseen by the National Highway Transportation and Safety Administration mooted plaintiff's claims because it promised the class representative "exactly the relief sought in her complaint."[34] Similarly, in *In re Aqua Dots Products Liability Litigation*,[35] the Seventh Circuit rejected certifica-tion in a case where the defendant recalled a defective toy and retailers offered refunds on returns. The court explained that, a "representative who proposes that high transaction costs (notice and attorney fees) be incurred at the class members' expense to obtain a refund that already is on offer is not adequately protecting the class members' interests."[36] Likewise, in *Webb v. Carter's Inc.*,[37] the court denied certification on superiority grounds because the defendant was already offering a

---

33. Winzler v. Toyota Motor Sales U.S.A., Inc., 681 F.3d 1208, 1214–15 (10th Cir. 2012).
34. *Id.* at 1209.
35. *In re* Aqua Dots Products Liab. Litig., 654 F.3d 748, 752 (7th Cir. 2011).
36. *Id.* at 752.
37. Webb v. Carter's Inc., 272 F.R.D. 489, 505 (C.D. Cal. 2011).

refund for the allegedly defective product and reimbursing customers for any medical costs.[38]

This strategy, however, needs to be carefully considered and executed if the goal is to moot class actions. Several decisions have concluded that a recall and refund program that was not well publicized, or did not provide all of the relief that consumers were entitled to, did not moot the case or provide a basis for denying class certification. For example, in *Philips v. Ford Motor Co.*,[39] the court rejected an argument that a recall and refund program made the class action moot for two reasons. The recall program required consumers to submit claims by a certain deadline. The court concluded that it could award relief regardless of any claims deadline. The court also noted that the plaintiffs were seeking to recover the loss in market value due to the defect. The recall and refund program provided no relief for diminished market value, which led the court to conclude that the class action was not moot.

Beware of Catalyst Fees

Offering a voluntary recall and refund is not without risk. In some states, courts are allowed to award attorney fees under a catalyst theory where the plaintiff's lawsuit caused the corrective action. Under California law, for example, a court can award fees to a successful party where, among other things, "a significant benefit, whether pecuniary or nonpecuniary, has been conferred on the general public or a large class of persons."[40] A class action plaintiff is the successful party where (1) the lawsuit was a catalyst motivating the defendants to provide the primary relief sought; (2) that the lawsuit had merit and achieved its catalytic effect by threat of victory, not by nuisance and threat of expense; and (3) the plaintiffs reasonably attempted to settle the litigation prior to filing the lawsuit.[41] Applying this standard, the *MacDonald*

---

38. *See also* Tosh-Surryhne v. Abbott Labs. Inc., 2011 WL 4500880, at *5 (E.D. Cal. Sept. 27, 2011) ("defendant has made a full offer of restitution to plaintiff for the recalled containers of Similac plaintiff alleges she purchased . . . This offer . . . strips this court of jurisdiction"); Vavak v. Abbott Labs., Inc., 2011 WL 10550065, at *3 (C.D. Cal. June 17, 2011) ("Because Abbott offered a full refund to consumers who purchased infant formula from the affected lots, Plaintiff's request for restitution of the monies spent on the product is moot.").

39. Philips v. Ford Motor Co., No. 14-CV-02989-LHK, 2016 WL 693283, at *7 (N.D. Cal. Feb. 22, 2016).

40. CAL. CIV. CODE § 1021.5.

41. MacDonald v. Ford Motor Co., 142 F. Supp. 3d 884, 890–91 (N.D. Cal. 2015).

court awarded more than $800,000 in attorney fees for work on a class action where the defendant initiated a voluntary recall approximately a year after the suit was filed.

Cases like *MacDonald* underscore the importance of the early case assessment. If a real problem exists such that a recall or other corrective action is appropriate, it is far better to know that information and make a decision on initiating the corrective action as early as reasonably possible, *before* significant fees are incurred on both sides.

JURISDICTION/VENUE/ARBITRATION

As any experienced practitioner can attest, jurisdiction, venue, and judicial assignment can make an immense difference in the outcome of a class action. Venue will play a large role in deciding which law applies. Different jurisdictions have different local rules governing class actions. And different judges have different views of class litigation. Some view Rule 23 as a mere procedural device that allows for representative litigation only where the circumstances justify it. Others view class litigation as more of a substantive right. They believe, rightly or wrongly, that certain low-value claims could never be litigated on an individual basis, thus justifying class litigation. Judges also have differing views of motions to dismiss, some viewing it as a critical tool to narrow or eliminate baseless claims, with others convinced it is a delaying tactic that prevents cases from being decided on the merits. Judges also have different tolerances for certain more exotic legal theories, including the rash of "no injury" product defect cases that are now being filed as consumer fraud class actions. In many cases, the venue and how the judge assigned to the case approaches these issues can mean the difference between an early dismissal with prejudice and a certified class action hurtling toward trial.

Evaluating Venue

Because of the importance of venue and because the plaintiff has the advantage of deciding where to file, a central part of defending a class action is evaluating the impact of jurisdiction, venue, and judicial assignment early in the case. The following are a few key considerations:

- What are the key legal issues on which the case will be decided? Has your judge addressed those issues? Is there another potentially available venue where the law on those key issues is better?

- How will your venue handle motions to dismiss and early challenges to the class allegations? Is there another potentially available venue where the standards are more favorable?
- What are the key issues on which class certification will be decided? Is there a different venue with more favorable standards on those issues?
- What are the assigned judge's tendencies in handling motions to dismiss and motions for class certification?
- What options are available for appealing an adverse class certification decision?
- Is there another potentially available venue where the procedural or substantive law will or may be more favorable for your specific case?
- Are there practical reasons to change venue, such as your opponent's unfamiliarity with, or challenges litigating in, a different venue?
- What options are available for securing a more favorable venue, and what are the chances of success?

Keep in mind that, even if successful in changing venue, you generally will not know your new judicial assignment. An educated guess may be possible, but you will not know for sure until the case is transferred and assigned. In some instances, the new judicial assignment could be less favorable, and you will want to keep that risk in mind when making venue decisions. Also consider how the judge assigned to the case may view an effort to change venue. Is the judge eager to streamline his or her docket and thus inclined to agree with your arguments seeking a different venue? Or may the judge view your arguments as signaling weakness or a desire to get out of his or her courtroom? The judge's prior opinions should give you a sense of how the judge is likely to react.

But let's assume you have evaluated all these issues and decided to seek to change venue. What options are available? The following sections discuss the options, as well as some of the key strategic implications.

Options for Changing Venue: Removal

If the case is filed in state court, one of the first considerations should be whether the case can and should be removed to federal court. A full discussion of removal is beyond the scope of this chapter and this subject is covered in more depth in the first section in Chapter 3, Forum Options for Defendants. Three basic options are available: (1) federal question jurisdiction (plaintiff's claims depend on substantial question of federal law); (2) basic diversity jurisdiction (complete diversity between the parties, plus more than $75,000 in controversy, but aggregation of different plaintiff's claims is not permitted); and (3) removal under the Class Action Fairness Act (CAFA) (minimal diversity, plus more than $5 million in controversy and aggregation of claims is permitted, but beware of the exceptions). For class actions, CAFA removal is the most likely option, but do not overlook the others, which still may be useful depending on the case.

The impact of removal can be dramatic. One good example is the impact on a motion to dismiss. In federal court, defense counsel can take advantage of the pleading requirements under *Twombly* and *Iqbal*, but the impact can be even greater in consumer fraud class actions. For example, in California state court, a consumer fraud claim does not have to be pled with specificity,[42] but in federal courts, some jurisdictions require the plaintiff to satisfy Rule 9(b), meaning the he must allege the who, what, when, where, and why of the alleged fraud.[43] In addition, some federal courts have applied the rules governing equitable claims much more stringently than state courts, dismissing consumer fraud claims that are equitable in nature where the plaintiff also seeks damages.[44] In other words, removing to federal court can, in certain cases, provide dismissal arguments that are unavailable in state court.

Removal also can provide advantages at the class certification stage. Although many states have class action procedures that mirror Rule 23, some do not—most notably California. Although the basic class procedures are not dramatically different in California state court, they are different, and federal courts tend to apply the requirements, particularly commonality and predominance, more strictly. Federal courts also

---

42. Morgan v. AT & T Wireless Servs., Inc., 177 Cal. App. 4th 1235, 1256, 99 Cal. Rptr. 3d 768, 785 (2009) ("But AT & T's argument fails to recognize the distinction between common law fraud, which requires allegations of actual falsity and reasonable reliance pleaded with specificity, and the fraudulent prong of the UCL, which does not.").

43. Kearns v. Ford Motor Co., 567 F.3d 1120, 1125 (9th Cir. 2009) ("[W]e have specifically ruled that Rule 9(b)'s heightened pleading standards apply to claims for violations of the CLRA and UCL.").

44. *See, e.g.,* Bird v. First Alert, Inc., No. C 14-3585 PJH, 2014 WL 7248734, at *5 (N.D. Cal. Dec. 19, 2014) ("the court finds that the UCL claims must be dismissed because plaintiff has an adequate remedy at law").

are far clearer about the need to address the merits and resolve factual disputes at the class certification stage.[45] Removing to federal court provides defendants another important option, namely, the right to a discretionary appeal of an adverse class certification decision under Rule 23(f). In California state court, a defendant that loses class certification generally must wait until final judgment before it can appeal certification, whereas the plaintiff has an immediate right of appeal from a denial of class certification under the "death knell" doctrine.[46]

Two points of caution on removal. First, some state courts have expressed a disinclination to certify a nationwide class based on the view that a state has no obligation to take on such a burden, at least where the defendant is not a citizen.[47] Removing a case to federal court would eliminate that consideration and could, in some cases, increase the risk of nationwide certification.

Second, some states prohibit or restrict class actions, and those protections could be lost if the case is removed. Virginia and Mississippi, for example, do not have procedural rules that permit class actions in state court. Other states, like Alabama, South Carolina, and New York, limit class actions in certain types of cases. Removing to federal court could mean that Rule 23 trumps those restrictions. For example, in *Shady Grove Orthopedic Assocs., P.A. v. Allstate Ins. Co.*,[48] the Supreme Court held that a New York law broadly prohibiting class actions in suits seeking penalties or statutory damages conflicted with Rule 23 and was preempted such that it would not apply where a federal court was sitting in diversity. Similarly, in *Lisk v. Lumber One Wood Preserving, LLC*,[49] the court held that Rule 23 trumped an Alabama statute that prohibits class actions for claims under the state's deceptive trade practices act. Other courts have reached different conclusions. In *Fejzulai v.*

---

45. *See, e.g.*, Bias v. Wells Fargo & Co., 312 F.R.D. 528, 535 (N.D. Cal. 2015) ("The Court must resolve factual disputes to the extent necessary to determine whether there was a common pattern and practice that could affect the class as a whole.").

46. *See In re* Baycol Cases I & II, 51 Cal. 4th 751, 757, 248 P.3d 681, 684 (2011) (describing death knell doctrine).

47. *See, e.g.*, J.P. Morgan & Co. v. Superior Court, 113 Cal. App. 4th 195, 221, 6 Cal. Rptr. 3d 214, 234 (2003) ("A court presented with a request to certify a nationwide class may legitimately ask whether it is of benefit to the courts and plaintiffs of this state to do so.").

48. Shady Grove Orthopedic Assocs., P.A. v. Allstate Ins. Co., 559 U.S. 393, 398–401 (2010).

49. Lisk v. Lumber One Wood Preserving, LLC, 792 F.3d 1331, 1336 (11th Cir. 2015).

Sam's W., Inc.,[50] for example, the court held that a South Carolina statute prohibiting class actions under the state's unfair trade practices act was substantive and thus controlled over Rule 23. Similarly, in *Helpling v. Rheem Mfg. Co.*,[51] the court ruled that an Ohio statute restricting when class actions could be filed under state consumer protection law was substantive and had to be enforced. When evaluating removal, practitioners will want to keep these cases in mind.

Challenges to Personal Jurisdiction

One method for influencing venue that often is overlooked in class litigation is a motion challenging personal jurisdiction. Many large companies assume they are subject to class litigation anywhere in the United States and thus forgo opportunities to challenge personal jurisdiction. But recent decisions, including two Supreme Court decisions, give defendants more to say on this issue.

In *Daimler AG v. Bauman*,[52] the Court restricted how district courts can exercise general jurisdiction, essentially limiting it to the state of a defendant's incorporation or primary place of business. In *Walden v. Fiore*,[53] the Court emphasized that specific jurisdiction focuses on a defendant's "suit-related conduct," as opposed to the plaintiff's relationship to the chosen forum. Taken together, *Daimler* and *Walden* give a defendant the ability to seek dismissal of class actions that are not based on its forum-related conduct, as well as claims asserted on behalf of nonresident putative class members.

For example, in *Gullen v. Facebook.com, Inc.*,[54] plaintiff filed a class action alleging that Facebook had unlawfully obtained and stored his biometric information in violation of Illinois law. Plaintiff argued for specific jurisdiction, pointing to Facebook's registration to do business in Illinois, the company's sales and advertising office in Illinois, and that the company allegedly targeted its facial recognition technology to millions of users who were residents of Illinois. The court found these contacts insufficient because the plaintiff had not connected the

---

50. Fejzulai v. Sam's W., Inc., 205 F. Supp. 3d 723, 727 (D.S.C. 2016).
51. Helpling v. Rheem Mfg. Co., No. 1:15-CV-2247-WSD, 2016 WL 1222264, at *13 (N.D. Ga. Mar. 23, 2016).
52. Daimler AG v. Bauman, 134 S. Ct. 746 (2014).
53. Walden v. Fiore, 134 S. Ct. 1115 (2014).
54. Gullen v. Facebook.com, Inc., No. 15 C 7681, 2016 WL 245910, at *1 (N.D. Ill. Jan. 21, 2016).

allegedly wrongful conduct (collecting and storing biometric information) to the company's Illinois contacts. Because Facebook allegedly col-
lected this information from everyone, and not just Illinois residents,
the court held that the company's conduct was not targeted at Illinois
and could not serve as the basis for specific personal jurisdiction. In
other words, the company's broadly applicable practice was *not* sufficient for personal jurisdiction in Illinois because it affected everyone,
not just Illinois residents.

The court reached a similar decision in *Demaria v. Nissan North Am.,
Inc.*,[55] which involved product defect claims filed on behalf of consumers from 16 states. The court held that, under *Daimler*, there was not
general jurisdiction in Illinois over a California and Tennessee entity,
even though the defendants sold cars all over the United States. The
court also held that there was no specific jurisdiction over the claims
asserted by out-of-state residents. "No plaintiff but DeMaria purchased
a car in Illinois or had a repair bill rejected in Illinois, and the FAC
offers no basis to infer that any other plaintiff was affected by [defen-
dants'] Illinois activities."[56]

In *Demedicis v. CVS Health Corp.*,[57] the court used a similar analysis to
dismiss class allegations that sought to assert claims based on other states'
consumer protection laws. Rejecting the argument that defendant's "similar" conduct in other states provided a basis for personal jurisdiction, the
court held that "[p]laintiff has not established personal jurisdiction over
the out-of-state claims as he is the sole connection between Defendants
and Illinois."[58] Likewise, in *Weisblum v. Prophase Labs, Inc.*,[59] the court
dismissed, on personal jurisdiction grounds, California consumer fraud
claims, concluding that the defendant's sales of similar products in New
York did not provide a basis for general or specific jurisdiction in New
York for claims asserted under California law.[60]

---

55. Demaria v. Nissan North Am., Inc., No. 15 C 3321, 2016 WL 374145 (N.D. Ill. Feb.
1, 2016).

56. *Id.* at *8.

57. Demedicis v. CVS Health Corp., No. 16-CV-5973, 2017 WL 569157, at *3 (N.D. Ill.
Feb. 13, 2017).

58. *Id.* at *5.

59. Weisblum v. Prophase Labs, Inc., 88 F. Supp. 3d 283, 290 (S.D.N.Y. 2015).

60. *See also* McDonnell v. Nature's Way Prod., LLC, No. 16 C 5011, 2017 WL 4864910,
at *4 (N.D. Ill. Oct. 26, 2017) (dismissing claims brought on behalf of proposed out-of-state
class members, finding named plaintiff's purchase in the state "cannot provide a basis for
the Court to exercise personal jurisdiction over the claims of nonresidents where [Defen-
dant] has no other connection to this forum").

As noted in Chapter 3, the Supreme Court's decision in *Bristol-Myers Squibb Co. v. Superior Court of California, San Francisco City*,[61] provides further support for a defendant seeking to challenge personal jurisdiction over claims asserted on behalf of nonresident plaintiffs or putative class members. There, the Court held that California courts did not have specific jurisdiction over a drug manufacturer for claims asserted by nonresidents in the absence of in-state conduct that caused the nonresidents' alleged injury. The Court emphasized that "the nonresidents were not prescribed Plavix in California, did not purchase Plavix in California, did not ingest Plavix in California, and were not injured by Plavix in California."[62] And the "mere fact that other plaintiffs were prescribed, obtained, and ingested Plavix in California—and allegedly sustained the same injuries as did the nonresidents—does not allow the State to assert specific jurisdiction over the nonresidents' claims."[63] "What is needed—and what is missing here," the Court explained, "is a connection between the forum and the specific claims at issue."[64] In class actions that include out-of-state plaintiffs or claims asserted on behalf of putative class members in other states, the required causal connection will be tenuous or missing altogether. Defense counsel should consider a motion to dismiss arguing a lack of personal jurisdiction.

Motion to Transfer Venue

Defendants also may have the option of seeking to transfer class litigation to another venue based on a motion to transfer venue under 28 U.S.C. § 1404 or § 1406. Both sections provide for a motion to transfer: § 1404(a) applies where a defendant seeks transfer for the convenience of the parties and witnesses; § 1406(a) applies where the class action was filed in the wrong venue. Again, this subject is covered in more depth in the first section in Chapter 3, Forum Options for Defendants.

From a strategic point of view, the key difference between § 1404 and § 1406 is choice of law. Where a case is transferred because it was filed in the wrong venue, the transferee court will apply the choice of law

---

61. Bristol-Myers Squibb Co. v. Super. Ct. of Cal., San Francisco City, 137 S. Ct. 1773, 1781 (2017).
62. *Id.*
63. *Id.*
64. *Id.*

rules of the state where it sits.[65] The same rule applies where transfer is based on a contractual choice-of-venue provision.[66]

The rule for convenience transfers is different. If a case is transferred under § 1404(a), the transferee court generally must apply the law of transferor.[67] But for federal question cases, the general rule is different: the transferee court generally applies its own circuit's interpretation of federal law.[68] And the transferee court will always apply its procedural law.[69] This means that, for a diversity case, a convenience transfer will change the venue and the procedural rules but not the substantive choice-of-law rules. For a federal question case, a change of venue will change the venue, as well as substantive and procedural law.

Notably, the convenience argument should have especially heavy weight in defending class actions. In considering a § 1404(a) motion, the court will focus primarily on the convenience of the parties and witnesses. Most of the witnesses and much of the evidence will be in the defendant's home state or in a state where it has significant operations, which may help make the showing needed to secure a convenience transfer. In contrast, the plaintiff generally has minimal evidence and few witnesses. In addition, although courts generally give great weight to the plaintiff's choice of venue, many courts hold that, in a class action, a plaintiff's forum choice is given less or minimal weight.[70] Thus, in many class actions, convenience transfer may be a viable strategy.

---

65. Jackson v. W. Telemarketing Corp. Outbound, 245 F.3d 518, 523 (5th Cir. 2001) ("that following a transfer under § 1406(a), the transferee district court should apply its own state law rather than the state law of the transferor district court.").

66. Atl. Marine Const. Co. v. U.S. Dist. Court for W. Dist. of Texas, 134 S. Ct. 568, 583 (2013) ("The court in the contractually selected venue should not apply the law of the transferor venue to which the parties waived their right.").

67. Wu v. Stomber, 750 F.3d 944, 949 (D.C. Cir. 2014) ("A diversity case transferred from one federal forum to another generally retains the state choice-of-law rules of the original forum.").

68. Lanfear v. Home Depot, Inc., 536 F.3d 1217, 1223 (11th Cir. 2008) ("A transferee court is not required to apply the law of the transferor court when, as here, the transferee court interprets federal law.").

69. Anderson v. Aon Corp., 614 F.3d 361, 365 (7th Cir. 2010) ("The procedures of the transferee district govern.").

70. Lou v. Belzberg, 834 F.2d 730, 739 (9th Cir. 1987) ("when an individual brings a derivative suit or represents a class, the named plaintiff's choice of forum is given less weight.").

MDL Transfer

Multi-district litigation (MDL) procedures are covered in Chapter 8, but they can be an important option for securing a more favorable venue. An MDL order has the effect of consolidating several overlapping or duplicative class actions in a single forum for pre-trial proceedings. If one of more class actions is pending in an unfavorable forum or before a challenging judge, an MDL proceeding may allow a defendant to improve its circumstances.

The choice of law implications are similar to a § 1404(a) transfer. In a diversity case, the MDL court will apply the choice of law rules of the transferor courts.[71] For procedural issues and federal question cases, the law of the MDL court controls.[72] This rule can be particularly powerful on class certification issues where, for example, ascertainability is a key defense. If a defendant can secure venue in the Third Circuit or the Fourth Circuit, which apply relatively strict ascertainability requirements,[73] the outcome could be very different than if the class certification motion is decided in a district governed by Ninth Circuit or Seventh Circuit law.[74]

Arbitration

As discussed in more depth in Chapter 3 under Forum Options for Defendants, a motion to compel arbitration can be an especially effective tool for challenging the plaintiff's choice of venue and potentially bringing the case to an early end. The Supreme Court has made clear that the Federal Arbitration Act (FAA) broadly preempts state law rules that disfavor arbitration.[75] Where a class action involves a transaction governed by terms of service or another agreement that requires arbitration on an individual basis, a defendant will want to strongly consider a motion to compel arbitration. In many cases, prevailing on an arbitration motion effectively ends the litigation, as plaintiff's lawyers

---

71. Anschutz Corp. v. Merrill Lynch & Co., 690 F.3d 98, 112 (2d Cir. 2012) ("In multi-district litigation, we apply the choice-of-law rules from the transferor forum—in this case, California—to determine which state law controls.").

72. Menowitz v. Brown, 991 F.2d 36, 40 (2d Cir. 1993) ("We have previously held that a transferee federal court should apply its interpretations of federal law, not the constructions of federal law of the transferor circuit.").

73. Carrera v. Bayer Corp., 727 F.3d 300 (3d Cir. 2013).

74. Briseno v. ConAgra Foods, Inc., 844 F.3d 1121 (9th Cir. 2017).

75. AT&T Mobility LLC v. Concepcion, 563 U.S. 333 (2011).

often believe that the case is not worth pursuing on an individual basis in arbitration. Further, a defendant will normally have an immediate right of appeal for any denial of a motion to compel arbitration.

But there are important strategic issues to consider before making such a motion. First, if the arbitration agreement is silent on whether class arbitration is permitted (as many older contracts do), a defendant could risk a class-wide arbitration—a very risky procedure with very limited appeal rights. Second, in some circumstances, an adverse arbitration ruling may have collateral estoppel effects in future disputes.[76] Third, many courts remain hostile to arbitration and such motions can delay resolution of the action for years. For instance, as discussed more fully in chapter 3, some courts have applied contract law in more stringent ways to avoid arbitration. One recent example is the decision in *Norcia v. Samsung Telecommunications America.,*[77] where the Ninth Circuit rejected long-standing precedent upholding the enforceability of arbitration provisions included with the packaging for consumer products.

Another example of judicial hostility to arbitration is the California Supreme Court's decision in *McGill v. Citibank, N.A.,*[78] which held that a provision requiring arbitration of consumer protection claims seeking injunctive relief on behalf of the general public was invalid and unenforceable under California law. If it stands, the *McGill* decision could have major impacts on consumer litigation, as it appears to allow plaintiffs to file a lawsuit seeking an injunction to stop an unfair or fraudulent business practice without having to certify the case as a class action, and the plaintiff cannot be compelled to arbitrate.

MOTION TO DISMISS STRATEGY

Defense practitioners often debate the wisdom of bringing a motion to dismiss. Some say a motion to dismiss simply "educates" the other side how to fix the complaint. Better to make those arguments on summary judgment or in opposing class certification rather than encourag-

---

76. Cont'l Holdings, Inc. v. Crown Holdings Inc., 672 F.3d 567, 575 (8th Cir. 2012) ("[i]t is settled that the doctrine of res judicata is applicable to arbitration awards and may serve to bar the subsequent relitigation of a single issue or an entire claim.").

77. Norcia v. Samsung Telecommunications Am., LLC, 845 F.3d 1279, 1290 (9th Cir. 2017).

78. McGill v. Citibank, N.A., 2 Cal. 5th 945, 962–63 (2017).

ing plaintiffs to "fix" the complaint at the pleading stage. Others believe motions to dismiss are an invaluable part of defending a putative class action, often narrowing the case or forcing plaintiffs to plead themselves into a theory that has little hope of being certified. These lawyers also believe such a motion can educate the court about the weaknesses in the case and the individuality of each plaintiff's claim. The following sections (1) outline some of the key considerations for and against responding to a class action complaint with a motion to dismiss and (2) discuss some of the core motion to dismiss arguments that should be considered.

Arguments against Filing a Motion to Dismiss

The primary arguments against filing a motion to dismiss are based on efficacy. The idea is that the court is unlikely to provide the desired result—an end to the litigation—thus making a motion to dismiss an inefficient or undesirable option. This argument takes several forms. The motion will educate the plaintiffs how to fix the complaint. Even if the complaint is dismissed, they will appeal. Or worse yet, plaintiff's counsel will find another proposed representative who might have "better" claims.

Defending Class Actions Requires the Long View

The assumption underlying all these arguments is that anything short of an immediate end to the litigation is somehow an undesirable result. In the author's view, the assumption that immediate victory is the only possible advantage from a motion to dismiss is flawed. Defending class actions often requires taking the long view. A series of victories often is required to bring the case to an end or to position the case for a favorable resolution. Yes, it is highly likely the judge will allow leave to amend. But that will require plaintiffs to change their theory or add facts regarding their individual circumstances. The resulting amendments may or may not be subject to a further motion to dismiss, but those additional facts, which were necessary to state a claim, may be demonstrably false (a point that can be raised on an early summary judgment motion) or may create individualized issues that will help defeat certification. And yes, the plaintiffs may appeal or counsel may find a substitute class representative. But either way, the defense has leverage. The trial judge, who would continue to handle the case even after any reversal on appeal, already has shown skepticism toward the case. And a new plaintiff could be a gift, providing a tangible example of the material differences between class members, some of whom may have a claim while others do not.

Other arguments against motions to dismiss have more substance but are more points of caution than reasons not to seek dismissal. One argument is that the motion could result in an adverse ruling on a critical point of law or, worse yet, adverse commentary from the trial judge on the merits of the claim that may be picked up by the press. Another argument is that losing a motion to dismiss creates a "win" for the plaintiffs, and thus momentum, allowing them to proceed to discovery and toward certification.

These are valid points. In any given case, these considerations may lead to the conclusion that a motion to dismiss should not be filed or that certain arguments should not be made. But they are highly judge- and circumstance-specific. A trial judge may have rejected similar arguments in prior cases, making it unwise to raise those arguments until there is an appellate ruling. Or a trial judge may have a peculiar view of motions to dismiss, thinking they are a waste of time or perhaps a delaying tactic. Defense practitioners must be aware of these considerations and take them into account when recommending an appropriate strategy. In many cases, these risks can be mitigated by filing a more carefully crafted dismissal motion, one that does not provide a basis for the court to provide adverse commentary or prematurely reach a critical legal issue. Alternatively, these considerations can help crystalize legal and factual issues that are more amenable to phased discovery and an early summary judgment motion.

Arguments in Favor of Filing a Motion to Dismiss

One of the best reasons to strongly consider filing a motion to dismiss is that it provides an early "win point" that can narrow or eliminate the claims. In any class action, there are four primary points where the defense can prevail: (1) a motion to dismiss, (2) summary judgment, (3) class certification, and (4) trial. Only the first two, motions to dismiss and for summary judgment, involve little or no downside risk for the defense. The other two, class certification and trial, provide a "win point," but also involve significant downside risk, namely, a certified class or adverse verdict. Forgoing a motion to dismiss means that the defense is giving away one half of its no-risk or low-risk win points.

A motion to dismiss also can provide a way to stave off discovery. Although courts may not formally "stay" discovery pending a decision on a motion to dismiss, many judges hold off conducting a formal Rule 16 conference until after ruling on pleading motions. The practical effect often is the same as a discovery stay. Without a Rule 16 conference, initial deadlines to meet and confer under Rule 26(f) are not triggered and the case may sit dormant for months or longer while a dismissal motion remains pending. Even if the plaintiffs press for a Rule 26(f) conference, a motion to dismiss may help the defendant argue for limiting or narrowing discovery until pleading challenges are decided.

Common Dismissal Arguments

Each class action complaint is different. The allegations are different. The applicable law is different. That's part of what makes defending class actions so rewarding. As a procedural mechanism, class action lawsuits affect all types of different businesses and industries and involve numerous substantive legal theories. Each case presents the opportunity to educate yourself (or re-educate yourself) about a substantive legal area or industry. Because each case is different, available motion to dismiss arguments also will differ. The following subsections, however, attempt to summarize common motion to dismiss arguments that often are made in defending class actions, particularly in consumer protection, false advertising, and product defect cases.

Plausibility and Particularity to Illustrate Individual Issues

Defense practitioners are familiar with the plausibility standard that applies in federal court, but this standard often can have special significance in defending class actions. In many cases, plaintiff's counsel prepares a class action complaint that contains few details regarding the named plaintiffs' individual transactions. They do this intentionally to avoid highlighting individualized issues that may pose a problem for class certification. It is therefore incumbent on defense to evaluate whether to test a fact-bare complaint through a motion to dismiss arguing that the allegations do not state a claim.

Two major tools should be considered: (1) the plausibility standards of Rule 12(b)(6), *Twombly* and *Iqbal*, and (2) the particularity requirements of Federal Rule of Civil Procedure 9. To survive a Rule 12(b)(6) motion, a complaint must contain sufficient factual matter, accepted as true, "to state a claim to relief that is plausible on its face."[79] "A claim has facial plausibility when the plaintiff pleads factual content that allows the court to draw the reasonable inference that the defendant is liable for the misconduct alleged."[80]

This plausibility standard provides a critical opportunity for defense counsel, namely the ability to point to alternative explanations. "When considering plausibility, courts must also consider an 'obvious alternative explanation' for defendant's behavior."[81]

> When faced with two possible explanations, only one of which can be true and only one of which results in liability, plaintiffs cannot offer allegations that are merely consistent with their favored explanation but are also consistent with the alternative explanation. Something more is needed, such as facts tending to exclude the possibility that the alternative explanation is true, in order to render plaintiffs' allegations plausible.[82]

Where a class action complaint simply alleges conclusions regarding a defendant's conduct and does not account for alternative explanations, courts have been willing to grant motions to dismiss, sometimes with prejudice.[83] For example, in *G.M. v. Sanofi Pasteur Inc.*,[84] the court relied on the plausibility standard to dismiss a defect claim involving a vaccine, concluding that plaintiff failed to explain or identify the specific defect that caused the alleged injuries. Similarly, in a wage and hour class action alleging misclassification, the court relied on the plausibility standard to require plaintiffs to allege the location where they worked, the department where they worked, the positions held, the job duties actually performed, their work schedules, and the basis for claiming that putative class members working in other locations were similarly situated.[85]

---

79. Bell Atl. Corp. v. Twombly, 550 U.S. 544, 570, 127 S. Ct. 1955, 167 L. Ed. 2d 929 (2007).

80. Ashcroft v. Iqbal, 556 U.S. 662, 678, 129 S. Ct. 1937, 173 L. Ed. 2d 868 (2009).

81. Eclectic Properties E., LLC v. Marcus & Millichap Co., 751 F.3d 990, 996 (9th Cir. 2014).

82. *Id.*

83. *See, e.g.*, Engel v. Novex Biotech LLC, No. 14-CV-03457-MEJ, 2015 WL 846777, at *6 (N.D. Cal. Feb. 25, 2015), *aff'd*, No. 15-15492, 2017 WL 1420347 (9th Cir. Apr. 21, 2017) (requiring plaintiff to allege affirmative evidence, in the form of studies or other facts, showing that advertising claims were false).

84. G.M. v. Sanofi Pasteur Inc., No. CV 14-9549 FMO (ASX), 2016 WL 7638186, at *3 (C.D. Cal. Mar. 22, 2016).

85. Flores v. Starwood Hotels & Resorts Worldwide, Inc., No. SACV141093AGANX, 2015 WL 12912337, at *4 (C.D. Cal. Mar. 16, 2015); *see also* Red v. Kraft Foods, Inc., No. CV 10-1028-GW AGRX, 2012 WL 5504011, at *4 (C.D. Cal. Oct. 25, 2012) (relying on

In some cases, the plausibility standard can be combined with the requirements of Rule 9(b) to seek dismissal. To satisfy this heightened standard, claims sounding in fraud must allege "an account of the 'time, place, and specific content of the false representations as well as the identities of the parties to the misrepresentations.'"[86] The plaintiff also must set forth "what is false or misleading about a statement, and why it is false."[87] This standard applies not just to common law fraud claims, but to any claim that sounds in fraud or is grounded in fraud, including consumer protection and false advertising claims.[88]

These requirements can prove very useful in defending class actions. Again, some complaints are prepared in a way that provides little, if any, detail regarding plaintiffs' individual transactions or how they were deceived. Forcing plaintiffs to provide those details may create avenues to defeat class certification and, in some cases, plaintiffs may be unable to provide the facts necessary to state a claim.

For example, in *Sanford v. MemberWorks, Inc.*,[89] the plaintiffs included a husband and wife who were allegedly deceived by a telephone sales script, but the complaint failed to allege which one was involved in the telephone calls. The Ninth Circuit affirmed dismissal with prejudice under Rule 9(b) because plaintiffs could not identify the party to the alleged misrepresentation.[90] Similarly, in *Davidson v. Apple, Inc.*,[91] the court relied on Rule 9(b) to dismiss a false advertising claim involving an alleged touchscreen defect on a smartphone. The complaint alleged one specific misrepresentation, but failed to allege that any plaintiff was exposed to the representation before purchasing their phones and failed to allege what other statements or advertising plaintiffs relied on. The court concluded that, without these details, plaintiffs could not satisfy Rule 9(b). Although the *Davidson* plaintiffs may be able to supply

---

plausibility standard to conclude that it "strains credulity to imagine that a reasonable consumer will be deceived into thinking a box of crackers is healthful or contains huge amounts of vegetables simply because there are pictures of vegetables and the true phrase 'Made with Real Vegetables' on the box.").

86. Swartz v. KPMG LLP, 476 F.3d 756, 764 (9th Cir. 2007) (internal quotation marks omitted).

87. Swearingen v. Healthy Beverage, LLC, No. 13-CV-04385-EMC, 2017 WL 1650552, at *3 (N.D. Cal. May 2, 2017).

88. Kearns v. Ford Motor Co., 567 F.3d 1120, 1125 (9th Cir. 2009).

89. Sanford v. MemberWorks, Inc., 625 F.3d 550, 558 (9th Cir. 2010).

90. *Id.* at 558.

91. Davidson v. Apple, Inc., No. 16-CV-04942-LHK, 2017 WL 976048, at *8 (N.D. Cal. Mar. 14, 2017).

the required details, doing so may reveal additional reasons for dismissal, including a lack of reliance, or may show that not all putative class members were exposed to the alleged misrepresentation, making certification nearly impossible.[92]

The bottom line here is that motions to dismiss based on a lack of plausibility or particularity can be a powerful tool for defending class litigation. A well-crafted argument can lead to dismissal, or, at a minimum, help expose individualized considerations that defeat certification.

Strategic Requests for Judicial Notice

Many class actions are based on an allegedly common misrepresentation or omission. As odd as it may sound, in many cases, the actual disclosures provided as part of a transaction demonstrate that the allegedly "undisclosed" information was provided or that the alleged "misrepresentation" is far from what the complaint claims. But on a motion to dismiss, the court is limited to the four corners of the complaint and cannot consider extraneous material, right? The answer is not as clear as it may seem. In some class actions, the defendant may be able to rely on provisions that allow the court to take judicial notice of certain facts and documents and use extraneous material to support a motion to dismiss.

The incorporation by reference doctrine permits courts to take into account documents "whose contents are alleged in a complaint and whose authenticity no party questions, but which are not physically attached to the [plaintiff's] pleading."[93] This doctrine also applies to situations

> in which the plaintiff's claim depends on the contents of a document, the defendant attaches the document to its motion to dismiss, and the parties do not dispute the authenticity of the document, even though the plaintiff does not explicitly allege the contents of that document in the complaint.[94]

---

92. *See also* People for the Ethical Treatment of Animals v. Whole Foods Mkt. California, Inc., No. 15-CV-04301 NC, 2016 WL 362229, at *4 (N.D. Cal. Jan. 29, 2016) (dismissing false advertising claim where plaintiffs failed to allege which advertisements they viewed).

93. Knievel v. ESPN, 393 F.3d 1068, 1076 (9th Cir. 2005).

94. *Id.*

The court in *Azoulai v. BMW of N. Am. LLC*,[95] relied on these judicial notice provisions in granting a motion to dismiss. The case involved an allegedly undisclosed defect in vehicle doors. The defendant submitted the owner's manual for the vehicle, asking the court to take judicial notice in connection with a motion to dismiss. The court agreed: "[t]he existence of the contents of the manuals—including, for example, any discussions of the safety of the [vehicle door]—is properly the subject of judicial notice." The court then relied on the warnings in the owner's manual to grant the motion, concluding that the omissions claim failed as a matter of law.[96]

Similarly, in *Baxter v. Intelius, Inc.*,[97] the court took judicial notice of disclosures provided in connection with a consumer transaction, concluding that the actual disclosures contradicted the plaintiff's allegations.[98]

These cases illustrate that, in some cases, defendants may be able to file a motion to dismiss bolstered by material outside the complaint. In any class action alleging omissions or misrepresentations, it is worth considering whether the actual advertising or disclosures may be subject to judicial notice and can be used to defeat plaintiff's allegations.

Challenging Injury Allegations

Over the last several years, there has been an avalanche of class actions that involve little or no actual injury. The defense bar often refers to these cases as "no injury" class actions. They involve technical violation of a federal or state statute. Others allege that a common misrepresentation or defect made the product worth less than advertised. But they do not allege that anyone suffered any physical injury. And many do not even allege that the plaintiff purchased a product manifesting the alleged defect, instead pointing to a "defect" experienced by others and claiming the plaintiff's product is "susceptible" to the same "injury."

The defense bar has responded to the rash of no injury class actions by focusing on the lack of any tangible harm, an argument bolstered by

95. Azoulai v. BMW of N. Am. LLC, No. 16-CV-00589-BLF, 2017 WL 1354781, at *3 (N.D. Cal. Apr. 13, 2017).
96. *Id.* at *9.
97. Baxter v. Intelius, Inc., No. SACV09-1031 AG MLGX, 2010 WL 3791487, at *4 (C.D. Cal. Sept. 16, 2010).
98. *See also* Bird v. First Alert, Inc., No. C 14-3585 PJH, 2015 WL 3750225, at *11 (N.D. Cal. June 15, 2015) ("the information plaintiff claims was omitted was in fact included on the packaging and in the user's manual.").

recent Supreme Court decisions. The Court emphasized the importance of injury in *Spokeo, Inc. v. Robins*,[99] noting that "[t]o establish injury in fact, a plaintiff must show that he or she suffered an invasion of a legally protected interest that is concrete and particularized and actual or imminent, not conjectural or hypothetical." A "concrete" injury is on that is "de facto"; "that is, it must actually exist."[100] The violation of a statutory right is not necessarily sufficient for a "concrete" injury, particularly where a bare procedural violation is alleged.[101] For an injury to be "particularized," it must affect the plaintiff in a personal and individual way.[102] The injury also must not be speculative. The Supreme Court emphasized this point in *Clapper v. Amnesty Int'l USA*,[103] holding that "threatened injury must be certainly impending to constitute injury in fact," and that "[a]llegations of possible future injury" are not sufficient.

In the wake of *Spokeo* and *Clapper*, courts across the country have issued many injury-in-fact decisions, some helpful, some not, and many that are hard to reconcile with one another. In defending any class action, defense counsel will want to analyze the injury allegations in light of the applicable law to assess whether a motion to dismiss based on injury is advisable. One recent decision may prove particularly helpful in defending consumer and privacy class actions.[104] In *Eike*, plaintiffs alleged that defendants' eye drops were unnecessarily large, resulting in wasted drops. Plaintiffs asserted claims for consumer fraud and unfair business practices, claiming that the only reason defendants used oversized eye drops was to increase profits.[105] The district court certified a class, but the Seventh Circuit reversed, holding there was no injury in fact. "One cannot bring a suit in federal court without pleading that one has been injured in some way (physically, financially—whatever) by the defendant."[106]

The fact that a seller does not sell the product that you want, or at the price you'd like to pay, is not an actionable injury; it is just a regret or

---

99. Spokeo, Inc. v. Robins, 136 S. Ct. 1540, 1548, 194 L. Ed. 2d 635 (2016).

100. *Id.* at 1548.

101. *Id.* at 1549–50.

102. *Id.* at 1548.

103. Clapper v. Amnesty Int'l USA, 568 U.S. 398, 133 S. Ct. 1138, 1147, 185 L. Ed. 2d 264 (2013).

104. *See* Eike v. Allergan, Inc., 850 F.3d 315, 316 (7th Cir. 2017).

105. *Id.* at 316–17.

106. *Id.* at 318.

disappointment—which is all we have here, the class having failed to allege an invasion of a legally protected interest.[107]

A word of caution. Although a motion based on *Spokeo* and *Clapper* may appear to be a sound strategic option, these arguments have a downside: winning a motion to dismiss based on standing may result in the case being refiled in or remanded to state court. Consider the recent decision in *Mocek v. Allsaints USA Ltd.*[108] The case involved a federal claim under the Fair and Accurate Credit Transaction Act (FACTA) and was originally filed in state court. Defendant removed based on federal question jurisdiction and then immediately moved to dismiss based on *Spokeo*. Given that the defendant was challenging the court's jurisdiction and plaintiff did not wish to be in federal court, the judge remanded the case based on 28 U.S.C. § 1447(c), concluding that the parties were "aligned in the view" that the court lacked subject-matter jurisdiction.[109] The court also awarded more than $58,000 in attorney fees, concluding that the defendant "tried to have it both ways by asserting, then immediately disavowing, federal jurisdiction."[110]

Other courts have reached the same conclusion as *Mocek*, remanding class actions asserting federal claims based on a lack of Article III standing.[111]

Courts also have remanded cases asserting state law claims based on a lack of standing that were removed under CAFA.[112]

---

107. *Id.; see also* Meyers v. Nicolet Rest. of De Pere, LLC, 843 F.3d 724, 727 (7th Cir. 2016) ("The allegations demonstrate that Meyers did not suffer any harm because of Nicolet's printing of the expiration date on his receipt. Nor has the violation created any appreciable risk of harm. After all, Meyers discovered the violation immediately and nobody else ever saw the non-compliant receipt.").

108. Mocek v. Allsaints USA Ltd., 220 F. Supp. 3d 910, 912 (N.D. Ill. 2016).

109. *Id.* at 913–14.

110. *Id.* at 914.

111. *See, e.g.*, Tyus v. United States Postal Serv., 2016 WL 6108942, at *1 (E.D. Wis. Oct. 19, 2016) (remanding Fair Credit Reporting Act claim after finding plaintiff lacked standing); Hopkins v. Staffing Network Holdings, LLC, 2016 WL 6462095, at *4 (N.D. Ill. Oct. 18, 2016) (remanding FCRA claim based on lack of standing); Schartel v. One Source Technology, LLC, 2016 WL 6024558, at *3 (N.D. Ohio Oct. 14, 2016) (same); Disalvo v. Intellicorp Records, Inc., 2016 WL 5405258, at *5 (N.D. Ohio Sept. 27, 2016) (same); Davis Neurology v. DoctorDirectory.com LLC, 2016 U.S. Dist. Lexis 84391, at *1 (E.D. Ark. June 29, 2016) (sua sponte remand of TCPA claim based on defendant's motion seeking dismissal for lack of standing).

112. *See, e.g.*, Polo v. Innoventions Int'l, LLC, 833 F.3d 1193, 1196 (9th Cir. 2016) ("a removed case in which the plaintiff lacks Article III standing must be remanded to state court"; remanding state consumer protection claim removed under CAFA); Wallace v Conagra Foods Inc., 747 F.3d 1025, 1033 (8th Cir. 2014) (remanding state law consumer

In other words, a defendant can incur the expense of removing a case to federal court and demonstrating that the plaintiff does not have standing, only to have the case end up back in state court and possibly being responsible for the plaintiff's attorney fees as well. Given this risk, defense counsel should consider options for avoiding the result reached in *Mocek*, including the following suggestions:

- **Consider whether state law standing principles provide a better basis for seeking dismissal.** Rather than immediately removing a case to federal court and seeking dismissal for lack of standing, consider whether to remove the case at all. Many states have adopted the same (or more stringent) standing requirements as Article III, and a defendant may be better off making those arguments in state court rather than removing.

- **Think about timing.** If you remove, consider whether it is wise to immediately file a motion arguing that the plaintiff lacks standing. The *Mocek* court appears to have been concerned that the defendant was taking inconsistent positions, arguing for federal jurisdiction, while at the same time claiming the plaintiff did not have standing. Be aware of that risk. It may be better to concede that the allegations of the complaint establish standing and then challenge whether the plaintiff has any actual injury at a later time based on a more developed evidentiary record.

- **Focus on statutory standing.** Not all standing is the same. "Statutory" standing focuses on the merits of the claim, including whether the claim requires proof of injury as a required element. A successful challenge to statutory standing results in dismissal with prejudice, rather than remand or dismissal without prejudice.[113] Therefore, rather than framing arguments in terms of Article III standing, consider focusing on the statutory standing requirements, which may include actual injury, reliance, and causation. The argument may sound like an Article III challenge, but the result should be different.

---

protection claims based on lack of standing); Khan v. Children's Nat'l Health Sys., 188 F. Supp. 3d 524, 534 (D. Md. 2016) (remanding state law claims in data breach class action after finding lack of standing).

113. Maya v. Centex Corp., 658 F.3d 1060, 1067 (9th Cir. 2011) (discussing differences between statutory and Article III standing).

- **Focus on "divestment" of federal question jurisdiction.** For cases removed based on federal question jurisdiction, a defendant has another argument: divestment. In *Advocates for Individuals with Disabilities Found. Inc. v. Russell Enterprises Inc.*,[114] the court faced a situation similar to that in *Mocek*, but declined to remand the federal claim, notwithstanding a lack of standing. The *Russell* case involved claims filed in state court under the Americans with Disabilities Act (ADA). The defendant removed based on federal question jurisdiction and moved to dismiss for lack of standing. In response, the plaintiff filed a motion to remand. Although the court agreed that it lacked subject matter jurisdiction, it declined to remand the ADA claim, concluding that "[p]laintiff is actually arguing that a state's more-lenient standing requirements can divest a federal court of its 28 U.S.C. § 1331 federal question jurisdiction, which Defendant invoked by removing this case to federal court."[115] The court held that it "f[ound] no authority [] that such divestment is possible"[116] and declined to remand the federal claim.

- **Argue that standing relates to justiciability, not jurisdiction.** Not all courts hold that the lack of Article III standing negates jurisdiction. In *St. Louis Heart Ctr., Inc. v. Nomax, Inc.*,[117] for example, the court found that the plaintiff lacked standing, but held that Article III standing is "a part of the concept of justiciability. Where the plaintiff lacks standing, dismissal is appropriate."[118]

- **Consider whether Congress can create a cause of action where plaintiff lacks Article III standing.** For cases that involve federal claims, a defendant also may want to argue that remand would be "futile" because Congress cannot create a cause of action that, whether in state or federal court, runs afoul of Article III. First, a caveat. The Ninth Circuit recently noted that the cases providing a "futility" exception to remand under 28 U.S.C. § 1447(c) "may no longer be good law,"

---

114. Advocates for Individuals with Disabilities Found. Inc. v. Russell Enterprises Inc., 2016 WL 7187931, at *1 (D. Ariz. Dec. 12, 2016).

115. *Id.* at 3.

116. *Id.*

117. *St.* Louis Heart Ctr., Inc. v. Nomax, Inc., No. 4:15-CV-517 RLW, 2017 WL 1064669, at *3 (E.D. Mo. Mar. 20, 2017).

118. *Id.*

although the court declined to decide the issue.[119] Nevertheless, many cases recognize that Congress cannot create a cause
of action that would not satisfy Article III, and it would seem
odd to conclude that a state court could adjudicate a federal
claim that could not be decided in federal court.[120] Therefore,
whether in federal or state court, a defendant should consider
digging into the case law recognizing that Congress cannot
simply do away with Constitutional requirements, including
Article III's injury requirement.

Preemption

Preemption arguments are highly case specific and a full discussion
is beyond the scope of this chapter, but a motion to dismiss based on
preemption is always worth considering. The labels of many products,
particularly foods and beverages, are regulated by federal statute and
many of those statutes include preemption provisions. Where a class
action seeks to impose requirements that are different from the applicable federal statute, they may be preempted.

For example, in *Brower v. Campbell Soup Co.*,[121] plaintiffs challenged
the labeling of a soup product that was subject to the Poultry Products
Inspection Act (PPIA) and the Federal Meat Inspection Act (FMIA).[122]
The label, which stated the product was "healthy," had been approved
by federal regulators. But plaintiffs nevertheless challenged the label
as misleading because the product contained trans fats in unhealthy
amounts. The court held that this claim was preempted because it
sought to "impose additional or different requirements than the PPIA
and FMIA," namely, disclosures regarding trans fats that were not
required by regulators.[123]

---

119. Polo v. Innoventions Int'l, LLC, 833 F.3d 1193 (9th Cir. 2016).

120. *See* Paul J. Katz, *Standing in Good Stead: State Courts, Federal Standing Doctrine, and
the Reverse-Erie Analysis*, 99 Nw. U. L. Rev. 1315 (2005) ("it seems unreasonable that the
Constitution would allow Congress to utilize state courts to enforce statutory directives
where federal courts cannot").

121. Brower v. Campbell Soup Co., No. 316CV01005BENJLB, 2017 WL 1063470, *3
(S.D. Cal. Mar. 21, 2017).

122. *Id.* at *2.

123. *Id.* at *3; *see also* Trazo v. Nestle USA, Inc., No. 5:12-CV-2272 PSG, 2013 WL
4083218, at *8 (N.D. Cal. Aug. 9, 2013), *on reconsideration*, 113 F. Supp. 3d 1047 (N.D. Cal.
2015) ("allowing a jury to weigh in on preapproved USDA labels would surely conflict with the federal regulatory scheme"); Meaunrit v. The Pinnacle Foods Grp., LLC,

Similarly, some courts have relied on regulatory approval to dismiss consumer fraud claims under state law "safe harbor" provisions. For example, in *Pye v. Fifth Generation, Inc.*,[124] the court relied on the Alcohol and Tobacco Tax and Trade Bureau's (TTB) approval of a vodka label to dismiss false advertising claims. Plaintiff claimed the product was misleadingly labeled as "handmade" when in fact it was mass produced. The defendant, however, had received label approval from the TTB, and the court held that this approval provided a safe harbor under state consumer protection law.[125] Although not a preemption decision, decisions like *Pye* demonstrate that regulatory approval of a product or label can provide a powerful defense.

Implied preemption also can provide a useful dismissal argument. For example, in *In re Trader Joe's Tuna Litig.*,[126] the court relied on implied preemption to dismiss state law claims that were based on alleged violations of the FDA's standards for measuring "pressed cake weight." Plaintiffs claimed that defendant's canned tuna was significantly underweight when measured using the appropriate FDA standard and that he was deceived as a result. The court dismissed the claim, explaining that, under principles of implied preemption, "private litigants may not bring a state-law claim against a defendant when the state-law claim is in substance (even if not in form) a claim for violating the [Federal Food Drug and Cosmetics Act]."[127] Because "the theory underlying Plaintiffs' state-law claims depends entirely on an FDA regulation," those claims "are in reality claims violations of an FDA regulation, and therefore, the FDCA prohibits Plaintiffs from bringing them."[128]

No. C 09-04555 CW, 2010 WL 1838715, at *7 (N.D. Cal. May 5, 2010) ("To allow a jury to pass judgment on Defendant's labels, notwithstanding the USDA's approval, would disrupt the federal regulatory scheme.").

124. Pye v. Fifth Generation, Inc., No. 4:14CV493-RH/CAS, 2015 WL 5634600, at *3 (N.D. Fla. Sept. 23, 2015).

125. *Id.* at *4 ("a regulator charged with ensuring that the representations on the Tito's label are not misleading, has approved the use of the terms handmade").

126. *In re* Trader Joe's Tuna Litig., No. 216CV01371ODWAJWX, 2017 WL 2408117, at *2 (C.D. Cal. June 2, 2017).

127. *Id.* at *3.

128. *Id.* at *4; *see also* Loreto v. Procter & Gamble Co., 515 F. App'x 576, 579 (6th Cir. 2013) ("This theory of liability depends entirely upon an FDCA violation—i.e., the only reason Procter & Gamble's products were allegedly 'illegal' was because they failed to comply with FDCA labeling requirements. The theory is impliedly preempted by federal law.").

Challenging Equitable and Injunctive Relief

In recent years, some plaintiff's attorneys have started focusing on arguing for class certification based on Rule 23(b)(2), thus avoiding the rigorous standard required by the predominance and superiority requirements. Because of this trend, defense counsel will want to consider an early challenge to claims seeking injunctive or equitable relief.

For injunctive relief, "to establish standing, plaintiff must allege that he intends to purchase the products at issue in the future."[129]

In addition, courts hold that "there is no right to equitable relief or an equitable remedy when there is an adequate remedy at law."[130] Based on this rule, several courts have barred claims for equitable relief—including claims for violations of California consumer protection statutes—at the motion to dismiss stage where plaintiffs have alleged other claims presenting an adequate remedy at law.[131]

The court in *Bird v. First Alert, Inc.*,[132] applied these two rules to dismiss all of plaintiff's equitable claims in a case involving an alleged safety defect in smoke alarms. Pointing to allegations that the smoke alarms were "defective" and "unsafe," the court held that plaintiff could not plausibly allege that she would purchase the alarms in the

---

129. Rahman v. Mott's LLP, No. CV 13-3482 SI, 2014 WL 325241, at *10 (N.D. Cal. Jan. 29, 2014); *see also In re* 5-hour ENERGY Marketing and Sales Practices Litig., No. MDL 13-2438 PSG, 2014 WL 5311272, at *10–11 (C.D. Cal. Sept. 4, 2014) (dismissing plaintiffs' requests for injunctive relief for failing to allege interest in purchasing defendant's products in the future); Martin v. Tradewinds Beverage Co., No. CV16-9249 PSG (MRWX), 2017 WL 1712533, at *5–6 (C.D. Cal. Apr. 27, 2017) ("because Plaintiff does not allege that she would purchase Defendant's Iced Tea Products again in the future, the requests for injunctive relief associated with Plaintiff's statutory causes of action are dismissed. Moreover, because Defendant removed the 'natural' claims from the Iced Tea Products packaging in October of 2015, Plaintiff cannot plausibly allege that she will, in the future, rely on the 'natural' statement to her detriment.").

130. Duttweiler v. Triumph Motorcycles (Am.) Ltd., 2015 WL 4941780, at *8 (N.D. Cal. Aug. 19, 2015); *see also* Collins v. eMachines, Inc., 202 Cal. App. 4th 249, 260 (2011) (explaining "the general principle of equity that equitable relief (such as restitution) will not be given when the plaintiff's remedies at law are adequate").

131. Munning v. Gap, 2017 WL 733104, at *5 (N.D. Cal. Feb. 24, 2017) (collecting cases); *see also* Nguyen v. Nissan N. Am., Inc., No. 16-CV-05591-LHK, 2017 WL 1330602, at *4 (N.D. Cal. Apr. 11, 2017) ("Plaintiff seeks damages to compensate for 'the exact same' alleged harm 'that forms the basis of' Plaintiff's requests for a restitutionary redesign program and an injunction compelling repair.").

132. Bird v. First Alert, Inc., No. C14-3585 PJH, 2014 WL 7248734, at *5 (N.D. Cal. Dec. 19, 2014).

future and thus did not have standing to seek injunctive relief.[133] And because plaintiff sought actual damages, as well as restitution, the court found that she had an adequate remedy at law, which required dismissal of her equitable claims under California's broad unfair business practices statute.[134] The net effect was a significantly narrower case, with the easiest-to-certify claims dismissed at the pleading stage.

The Ninth Circuit recently weighed in on these issues, holding that

> a previously deceived consumer may have standing to seek an injunction against false advertising or labeling, even though the consumer now knows or suspects that the advertising was false at the time of the original purchase, because the consumer may suffer an "actual and imminent, not conjectural or hypothetical" threat of future harm.[135]

The court explained that, in some cases, "the threat of future harm may be the consumer's plausible allegations that she will be unable to rely on the product's advertising or labeling in the future, and so will not purchase the product although she would like to."[136] In other cases,

> the threat of future harm may be the consumer's plausible allegations that she might purchase the product in the future, despite the fact it was once marred by false advertising or labeling, as she may reasonably, but incorrectly, assume the product was improved.[137]

The *Davidson* decision confirms that to have standing to seek injunctive relief, the plaintiff must plausibly allege a threat of future injury, normally based on an intent to buy the accused product or service in the future. But a plaintiff is not precluded from seeking injunctive relief simply because he or she now is aware that the defendant's advertising is false, at least in the Ninth Circuit. Courts in other jurisdictions may disagree, and the law in this area will continue to develop.

Challenging Claims Based on Products the Plaintiff Did Not Buy

In many class actions, the plaintiff will assert claims based on the products she or he bought, as well as products never purchased. The point,

---

133. *Id.* at *5 ("in a case involving a claim that a product does not work or perform as advertised, where the plaintiff will clearly not purchase the product again, courts have found no risk of future harm and no basis for prospective injunctive relief.").

134. *Id.* ("There is no right to equitable relief or an equitable remedy when there is an adequate remedy at law.").

135. Davidson v. Kimberly-Clark Corp., 889 F.3d 956, 969 (9th Cir. 2018).

136. *Id.* at 969–70.

137. *Id.*

of course, is to try to make the case as large as possible to expand the scope of discovery and increase the leverage on the defendant to settle. To combat this tactic, defense counsel will want to consider asking the court to dismiss claims based on products the plaintiff does not claim to have purchased.

> The majority of the courts that have carefully analyzed the question hold that a plaintiff may have standing to assert claims for unnamed class members based on products he or she did not purchase so long as the products and alleged misrepresentations are substantially similar.[138]

"Products are 'substantially similar' if they contain common ingredients or if the alleged misrepresentations on the labels of the products are identical."[139] "Where product composition is less important, the cases turn on whether the alleged misrepresentations are sufficiently similar across product lines."[140] "Where the alleged misrepresentations or accused products are dissimilar, courts tend to dismiss claims to the extent they are based on products not purchased."[141] Thus, the fundamental question is whether the complaint alleges sufficient similarity between the product the plaintiff purchased and the advertising plaintiff relied on as compared to products the plaintiff did not buy and advertising the plaintiff did not rely on.

In *Oxina v. Lands' End, Inc.*,[142] for example, the court applied this "substantially similar" approach to claims that apparel for sale on defendant's website was improperly marked as "Made in the USA." Plaintiff only claimed to have purchased one item, but sought to include all mislabeled "apparel" on the website as part of the case. Although the alleged representation was the same ("Made in the USA"), the complaint provided no facts regarding the other "apparel," which, in the court's view, "could conceivably encompass hundreds, or even thousands of different types of products, including those presumably made of different materials, and bearing different physical labels than

---

138. Miller v. Ghirardelli Chocolate Co., 912 F. Supp. 2d 861, 869 (N.D. Cal. 2012).

139. Martin v. Tradewinds Beverage Co., No. CV16-9249 PSG (MRWX), 2017 WL 1712533, at *5 (C.D. Cal. Apr. 27, 2017).

140. Miller, 912 F. Supp. 2d at 869.

141. *Id.* at 870; *see also* Coleman-Anacleto v. Samsung Elecs. Am., Inc., No. 16-CV-02941-LHK, 2016 WL 4729302, at *9 (N.D. Cal. Sept. 12, 2016) (the "majority of the courts in this district and elsewhere in California reject the proposition that a plaintiff cannot suffer injury in fact based on products that the plaintiff did not buy.").

142. Oxina v. Lands' End, Inc., No. 14-CV-2577-MMA NLS, 2015 WL 4272058, at *6 (S.D. Cal. June 19, 2015).

the Necktie purchased by Plaintiff."[143] Ultimately, the court dismissed claims as to the unidentified "apparel," ruling that "[w]ithout any factual detail as to which 'apparel' products Plaintiff refers, the Court cannot make a finding that the unpurchased products bear any similarity to Plaintiff's Necktie."[144]

Other courts take a different, bright-line approach, holding that "a named plaintiff in a consumer class action lacks standing to challenge a non-purchased product because there is no injury-in-fact as to that product, even if he purchased a substantially similar product."[145]

Other courts take a third approach, holding that these issues should be addressed at the class certification stage, through the lenses of typicality and commonality. For example, in *Clancy v. The Bromley Tea Co.*,[146] the court held that "[d]eciding at the pleading stage that a plaintiff cannot represent a class who purchased any different products than the plaintiff seems unwarranted, at least on the facts of this case."[147] The court explained that,

> [w]hether products are "sufficiently similar" is an appropriate inquiry, but it does not relate to standing: a plaintiff has no more standing to assert claims relating to a "similar" product he did not buy than he does to assert claims relating to a "dissimilar" product he did not buy.[148]

Seen this way, the court concluded that analyzing the "sufficient similarity" of the products is not a standing inquiry, "but rather an early analysis of the typicality, adequacy, and commonality requirements of Rule 23," which the court found unwarranted.[149]

The bottom line is that defense counsel should always be looking for ways to narrow the case. Depending on the facts alleged and the jurisdiction, a motion to dismiss claims based on products not purchased

---

143. *Id.*
144. *Id.*
145. Garcia v. Kashi Co., 43 F. Supp. 3d 1359, 1393 (S.D. Fla. 2014); Kelly v. Cape Cod Potato Chip Co., 81 F. Supp. 3d 754, 763 (W.D. Mo. 2015) ("the Court agrees that Plaintiff lacks Article III standing as to the varieties of the Chips she did not purchase. Because Plaintiff admittedly did not purchase twelve of the sixteen varieties of the Chips, she was neither personally nor actually harmed as to those twelve varieties."); Ferrari v. Best Buy Co., No. CIV. 14-2956 MJD/FLN, 2015 WL 2242128, at *9 (D. Minn. May 12, 2015) (the "Court concludes that Plaintiff lacks standing to assert claims on behalf of the class for televisions that he did not purchase or advertising that he did not see or rely upon.").
146. Clancy v. The Bromley Tea Co., 308 F.R.D. 564 (N.D. Cal. 2013).
147. *Id.* at 571.
148. *Id.*
149. *Id.*

may be an effective strategy. But, as shown, different courts apply very different standards, and the allegations in the complaint do matter. So it is important to understand how your judge has approached this issue in the past before making these arguments.

MOTION TO STRIKE CLASS ALLEGATIONS

In responding to a class action complaint, defense counsel should consider an early challenge to the class allegations, particularly where a defect is evident from the face of the complaint. From a strategic perspective, a motion to strike, combined with a motion to dismiss, can be an effective "one two" punch. The motion to dismiss demonstrates why plaintiff's individual allegations fail, while the motion to strike explains how the complaint already raises too many individualized issues to justify class treatment. The goal is to create a dilemma for plaintiffs. Adding more factual allegations will only exacerbate the problems for certification, while not adding facts may lead to dismissal.

Legal Basis for Motion to Strike

Although the issue is not free from debate, most courts agree that a defendant can file a motion to strike class allegations. The Supreme Court has expressly recognized that "[s]ometimes the issues are plain enough from the pleadings to determine whether the interests of the absent parties are fairly encompassed within the named plaintiff's claim."[150] And Rule 23(d)(1)(D) of the Federal Rules of Civil Procedure expressly authorizes a motion to strike class allegations by providing for an order "requiring that the pleadings be amended to eliminate allegations about representation of absent persons."

Timing of Motion

Courts, however, are not always willing to decide motions to strike based on the pleadings, instead believing that the certification decision should await discovery. The Eleventh Circuit, for example, has explained that

---

150. Gen. Tel. Co. of Sw. v. Falcon, 457 U.S. 147, 160, 102 S. Ct. 2364, 2372, 72 L. Ed. 2d 740 (1982).

> [w]hile it is sometimes possible to decide the propriety of class certification from the face of the complaint, the Supreme Court has emphasized that class certification is an evidentiary issue, and it may be necessary for the court to probe behind the pleadings before coming to rest on the certification question.[151]

Many other courts have echoed this sentiment, deeming motions to strike "premature."[152]

Motion to Deny Certification

Given some courts' reluctance to strike class allegations on the pleadings, defense counsel should consider an alternative strategy. Rather than moving to strike at the pleading stage, a defendant may elect to conduct focused discovery and then move to deny class certification. In *Vinole v. Countrywide Home Loans, Inc.*,[153] the Ninth Circuit approved this procedure, confirming that a "defendant may move to deny class certification before a plaintiff files a motion to certify a class."[154] Notably, the defendant in *Vinole* participated in discovery for approximately eight months before moving to deny certification, filing the motion before the discovery deadline and several months before the pre-trial motions deadline.[155] How much discovery must take place before moving to deny certification will depend on the case as well as on the plaintiffs' diligence, but a defendant may be well served by aggressively pursuing the discovery needed to defeat certification, while also reasonably cooperating with plaintiffs' discovery demands to avoid charges of delay.

---

151. Herrera v. JFK Med. Ctr. Ltd. P'ship, 648 F. App'x 930, 934 (11th Cir. 2016).

152. *See, e.g.*, Hidalgo v. Johnson & Johnson Consumer Companies, Inc., 148 F. Supp. 3d 285, 292 (S.D.N.Y. 2015) (motion to strike "requires a reviewing court to preemptively terminate the class aspects of litigation, solely on the basis of what is alleged in the complaint, and before plaintiffs are permitted to complete the discovery to which they would otherwise be entitled on questions relevant to class certification. Put differently, motions to strike class allegations are often denied as premature.").

153. Vinole v. Countrywide Home Loans, Inc., 571 F.3d 935, 941 (9th Cir. 2009).

154. *See also* Richardson v. Bledsoe, 829 F.3d 273, 288 (3d Cir. 2016) ("we join the courts of appeals which have held that nothing in the plain language of Rule 23(c)(1)(A) either vests plaintiffs with the exclusive right to put the class certification issue before the district court or prohibits a defendant from seeking early resolution of the class certification question.").

155. Vinole, 571 F.3d at 938–39.

Burden of Proof

The burden of proof on a motion to strike is somewhat unsettled. Some courts hold that "[w]hen the defendant challenges class certification based solely on the allegations in the complaint, the standard is the same as that applied in deciding a motion to dismiss under Rule 12(b)(6)."[156] Other courts have rejected this standard, holding that "[i]t would be error for a court to apply the Rule 12(b)(6) plausibility standard set forth in *Twombly* and *Iqbal* to 'dismiss' class action allegations in a complaint."[157] Instead, these courts apply Rule 23's standards and hold that "the plaintiff has the burden to prove that the requirements set forth in Rule 23 are met," even on a motion to strike.[158]

Grounds for Motion to Strike

Although many motions to strike are denied as premature, courts have granted these motions in a variety of circumstances. The primary arguments that have been successful are summarized in the following subsections.

Standing to Assert Claims under the Laws of Other States

Many class actions attempt to assert claims based on the laws of states for which there is no named representative. A majority of courts to consider this question have concluded that when "a representative plaintiff is lacking for a particular state, all claims based on that state's laws are subject to dismissal."[159] Indeed, "[c]ourts routinely dismiss claims where no plaintiff is alleged to reside in a state whose laws the class seeks to enforce."[160]

---

156. *See, e.g.,* Jimenez v. Allstate Indem. Co., No. 07-CV-14494, 2010 WL 3623176, at *3 (E.D. Mich. Sept. 15, 2010), *on reconsideration in part,* 765 F. Supp. 2d 986 (E.D. Mich. 2011).

157. Cole's Wexford Hotel, Inc. v. UPMC, 127 F. Supp. 3d 387, 404 (W.D. Pa. 2015).

158. *Id.*

159. In re Flash Memory Antitrust Litig., 643 F. Supp. 2d 1133, 1164 (N.D. Cal. 2009).

160. Corcoran v. CVS Health Corp., 169 F. Supp. 3d 970, 990 (N.D. Cal. 2016); *In re* Aftermarket Auto. Lighting Prod. Antitrust Litig., No. 09-MDL-2007-GW-PJW, 2009 WL 9502003, at *6 (C.D. Cal. July 6, 2009) (same); Pardim v. Unilever United States, Inc., 961 F. Supp. 2d 1048, 1061 (N.D. Cal. 2013) ("[w]here . . . a representative plaintiff is lacking for a particular state, all claims based on that state's laws are subject to dismissal."); *see also* Mollicone v. Universal Handicraft, Inc., No. 216CV07322CASMRWX, 2017 WL 440257, at *9 (C.D. Cal. Jan. 30, 2017) ("the court can address the issue of standing before it addresses the issue of class certification"); McGuire v. BMW of N. Am., LLC, No. CIV.A. 13-7356

Variability in Applicable Law

Class action complaints often are drafted to assert claims on behalf of a proposed nationwide class, without specifying the applicable law. Where choice-of-law rules require the application of several different states' laws, courts have been willing to strike nationwide class allegations. For example, in *Pilgrim v. Universal Health Card, LLC*,[161] the Sixth Circuit affirmed a decision striking nationwide class allegation because the applicable choice-of-law rules required the application of the laws of all 50 states and the allegations of the complaint demonstrated variability in defendant's practices.[162]

Fail-Safe Class Definition

Some courts have been willing to strike class allegations where the proposed class definition required a decision on the merits as to each proposed class member.[163] The problem with this type of class definition (sometimes called "fail-safe") is that "a class member either wins, or by virtue of losing, is defined out of the class and is therefore not bound by the judgment."[164]

Thus, in *Zarichny v. Complete Payment Recovery Servs., Inc.*,[165] the court granted a motion to strike class allegations based on a fail-safe

---

JLL, 2014 WL 2566132, at *6 (D.N.J. June 6, 2014) ("This Court agrees that the Plaintiff here lacks standing to assert claims under the laws of the states in which he does not reside, or in which he suffered no injury.").

161. Pilgrim v. Universal Health Card, LLC, 660 F.3d 943, 947 (6th Cir. 2011).

162. *Id.* at 948 ("Even if, as the plaintiffs claim, callers heard identical sales pitches, Internet visitors saw the same website and purchasers received the same fulfillment kit, these similarities establish only that there is some factual overlap, not a predominant factual overlap among the claims and surely not one sufficient to overcome the key defect that the claims must be resolved under different legal standards."); *see also* Rikos v. Procter & Gamble Co., No. 1:11-CV-226, 2012 WL 641946, at *6 (S.D. Ohio Feb. 28, 2012) ("No discovery will change the simple fact that different states have different elements for claims of breach of express warranty, and the Court finds that these variations are material."); *In re* Yasmin & Yaz (Drospirenone) Mktg., 275 F.R.D. 270, 276 (S.D. Ill. 2011) ("because governing choice of law principles require application of the substantive laws of the fifty states and the District of Columbia—laws which vary amongst the jurisdictions—the case cannot be maintained as a nationwide class action").

163. *See, e.g.*, Schilling v. Kenton Cty., Ky., No. CIV.A. 10-143-DLB, 2011 WL 293759, at *6 (E.D. Ky. Jan. 27, 2011) ("Plaintiffs' proposed class definition is fatally flawed because the Court cannot determine its individual members without reviewing the evidence relative to each KCDC inmates' incarceration, which would amount to a merits-based inquiry of each individual's claim.").

164. Mullins v. Direct Digital, LLC, 795 F.3d 654, 660 (7th Cir. 2015).

165. Zarichny v. Complete Payment Recovery Servs., Inc., 80 F. Supp. 3d 610, 625 (E.D. Pa. 2015).

definition in a TCPA case, where the proposed definition required a lack of "prior express consent." Similarly, in *Bell v. Cheswick Generating Station, Genon Power Midwest, L.P.*,[166] the court granted a motion to strike class allegations in a property contamination case where the proposed class definition improperly required a finding of damage caused by an "invasion" by particulates, chemicals, or gases from defendant's power plant.[167]

Other Class Certification Requirements

In some cases, particularly those involving mass torts or personal injury allegations, courts have been willing to strike class allegations based on a lack of typicality or predominance.[168]

In *DuRocher v. National Collegiate Athletic Association*,[169] for example, the court granted a motion to strike class allegations in a case alleging traumatic brain injury caused by inadequate helmets. The court explained that the

> individualized inquiries related to medical causation described by Defendants weigh heavily in favor of striking Plaintiffs' class action allegations and foreshadow a tremendous uphill battle for Plaintiffs to certify a class action based on personal injuries of individual class members.[170]

The court also noted that the "inconsistent laws applicable to the putative members' claims weighs heavily in favor of striking Plaintiffs' current class definition."[171]

Similarly, in *Waters v. Electrolux Home Prod., Inc.*,[172] the court granted a motion to strike, finding a lack of typicality and predominance from

---

166. Bell v. Cheswick Generating Station, Genon Power Midwest, L.P., No. CIV.A. 12-929, 2015 WL 401443, at *4 (W.D. Pa. Jan. 28, 2015).

167. *But see* Van v. Ford Motor Co., No. 14 CV 8708, 2016 WL 1182001, at *8 (N.D. Ill. Mar. 28, 2016) ("The appropriate remedy for alleging a fail-safe class in a complaint is not to strike the class claims, but to refine the class definition.").

168. *See, e.g., In re* Yasmin & Yaz (Drospirenone) Mktg., 275 F.R.D. 270, 276 (S.D. Ill. 2011) ("mass product liability suits are rarely sustainable as class actions"); *see also* Kim v. Shellpoint Partners, LLC, No. 15CV611-LAB (BLM), 2016 WL 1241541, at *8 (S.D. Cal. Mar. 30, 2016) ("Whether a putative subclass member was improperly excessively billed is a highly individualized question, and it is unlikely very many were injured in the way Kim alleges she was."; granting motion to strike).

169. DuRocher v. Nat'l Collegiate Athletic Ass'n, No. 1:13-CV-01570-SEB, 2015 WL 1505675, at *10 (S.D. Ind. Mar. 31, 2015).

170. *Id.* at *10.

171. *Id.*

172. Waters v. Electrolux Home Prod., Inc., No. 5:13CV151, 2016 WL 3926431, at *5 (N.D.W. Va. July 18, 2016).

the face of the complaint. The case involved alleged property damage caused by defective washing machines. The court found that the named plaintiffs were not typical of the proposed classes

> because the proposed class members' substantive claims depend on individual permutations. . . . Each plaintiff must individually prove that he or she experienced personal injuries and/or property damage which was proximately caused by the use of the defendant's products.[173]

The court also held that predominance could not be satisfied because the applicable law would vary and each "class member must individually prove that their washing machine proximately caused damage to their person or particular property."[174]

These cases illustrate that, although a long shot, a motion to strike can be successful in the right case and is worth considering.

ANSWERING THE CLASS ACTION COMPLAINT/AFFIRMATIVE DEFENSES

The answer often receives little attention when discussing strategies for defending class litigation. And perhaps for good reason. As in any lawsuit, defense practitioners should take care to accurately admit and deny the substantive allegations, and, of course, the defendant normally will deny the class allegations. But what else is there to say? The answer lies in affirmative defenses, which should be given careful thought in preparing the answer to a class action complaint.

Consider the decision in *Hofstetter v. Chase Home Financial, LLC*.[175] The case was a financial services class action involving forced-place insurance for home equity lines of credit. After the court certified a class, the defendant discovered that several class members were delinquent in their loan payments and sought to amend the answer to assert defenses for setoff and recoupment. Although the court recognized that these defenses were not relevant to the named plaintiff and did not become relevant until after class certification, the court nevertheless denied the motion to amend, concluding that "defendants were aware of the potential class since the complaint was filed" and that it "is inconceivable

173. *Id.* at *5.
174. *Id.*
175. Hofstetter v. Chase Home Fin., LLC, No. C 10-01313, 2011 WL 2462235, at *1 (N.D. Cal. June 21, 2011).

that defendants did not know that some unnamed members of the class might be delinquent on mortgage payments from the day the complaint was filed."[176] *Hofstetter* underscores the importance of considering and asserting all defenses that may apply to claims asserted on behalf of putative class members. Not doing so runs the risk that the court may not allow those defenses to be asserted post-certification.

Affirmative defenses also can play an important role in defeating class certification, both in terms of showing a lack of commonality and predominance, as well as demonstrating that the named plaintiffs are not adequate representatives or that their claims are atypical. But before addressing how defenses can help defeat certification, we should address a myth commonly repeated by the plaintiffs' bar—namely, that affirmative defenses are "irrelevant" to class certification. That statement or something close to it often finds its way into class certification reply briefs, with the basic message being that a court can ignore defenses.

But the idea that affirmative defenses are irrelevant to class certification is flat wrong. "Because the Rules Enabling Act forbids interpreting Rule 23 to abridge, enlarge or modify any substantive right, a class cannot be certified on the premise that [defendant] will not be entitled to litigate its statutory defenses to individual claims."[177] Thus, where plaintiffs have argued that courts do not need to address defenses as part of the certification analysis, courts have disagreed.[178]

Plaintiffs often cite a passage from *Smilow v. Southwest Bell Mobile Systems*,[179] stating that "courts traditionally have been reluctant to deny class action status under Rule 23(b)(3) simply because affirmative defenses may be available against individual members." This language

---

176. *Id.* at *2.

177. Wal-Mart Stores, Inc. v. Dukes, 564 U.S. 338, 367, 131 S. Ct. 2541, 2561, 180 L. Ed. 2d 374 (2011); Ortiz v. Fibreboard Corp., 527 U.S. 815, 845, 119 S. Ct. 2295, 144 L. Ed. 2d 715, 43 Fed. R. Serv. 3d 691 (1999) ("As we said in *Amchem*, no reading of [Rule 23] can ignore the [Rules Enabling] Act's mandate that rules of procedure shall not abridge, enlarge or modify any substantive right.").

178. Rodney v. Nw. Airlines, Inc., 146 F. App'x 783, 786 (6th Cir. 2005) ("the Advisory Committee Notes to Rule 23(b)(3) advise against class certification where a defendant has a defense to liability that will vary with each individual class member."); Gunnells v. Healthplan Servs., Inc., 348 F.3d 417, 438 (4th Cir. 2003) ("like other considerations, affirmative defenses must be factored into the calculus of whether common issues predominate"); *see also* Lindsey v. Normet, 405 U.S. 56, 66, 92 S. Ct. 862, 870, 31 L. Ed. 2d 36 (1972) ("Due process requires that there be an opportunity to present every available defense.").

179. Smilow v. Southwest Bell Mobile Systems, 323 F.3d 32 (1st Cir. 2003).

continues to be cited to this day,[180] but its import is often misunderstood. In *Smilow*, the court expressly acknowledged that "affirmative defenses should be considered in making class certification decisions," but concluded that the relevant defense (waiver) presented common issues because all class members received the same user guide and invoices that served as the basis for the defense.[181] In other words, the "reluctance" referenced in *Smilow* referred to a situation where an affirmative defense exists but still presents common issues.[182]

But where an affirmative defense does not present a common issue, courts denied certification, either because (1) defenses applicable to the named plaintiffs defeated adequacy or typicality or (2) broadly applicable defenses required individualized inquiries, thus defeating predominance. For example, in *CE Design Limited. v. King Architectural Metals*,[183] the Seventh Circuit rejected certification on adequacy and typicality grounds where the defense of consent applied to the named plaintiffs. The court explained that the

> presence of even an arguable defense peculiar to the named plaintiff or a small subset of the plaintiff class may destroy the required typicality of the class as well as bring into question the adequacy of the named plaintiff's representation.[184]

The "fear is that the named plaintiff will become distracted by the presence of a possible defense applicable only to him so that the representation of the rest of the class will suffer."[185]

The court reached a similar conclusion in *Nghiem v. Dick's Sporting Goods, Inc.*,[186] where the evidence showed that the named plaintiff may have enrolled and unenrolled in the defendant's text marketing program solely to create liability under the TCPA. The court denied certification on adequacy and typicality grounds, explaining that the

---

180. Villanueva v. Liberty Acquisitions Servicing, LLC, No. 3:14-CV-01610-HZ, 2017 WL 1021523, at *6 (D. Or. Jan. 13, 2017).

181. *Id.* at 39.

182. *See* Brinker v. Chicago Title Ins. Co., No. 8:10-CV-1199-T-27AEP, 2012 WL 1081211, at *15 (M.D. Fla. Feb. 9, 2012), *report and recommendation adopted*, No. 8:10-CV-1199-T-27AEP, 2012 WL 1081182 (M.D. Fla. Mar. 30, 2012) (distinguishing *Smilow* on same basis and denying certification where defense presented individualized inquiries).

183. CE Design Ltd. v. King Architectural Metals, 637 F.3d 721 (7th Cir. 2011).

184. *Id.* at 726.

185. *Id.*

186. Nghiem v. Dick's Sporting Goods, Inc., 318 F.R.D. 375, 383 (C.D. Cal. 2016).

Court is convinced that if Nghiem is the class representative, he and his counsel will have to devote most of their time and resources trying to refute Defendants' attacks on his character and his motivations for filing and litigating this lawsuit.[187]

Another good example is the decision in *Payala v. Wipro Techs., Inc.*,[188] which involved wage and hour claims and a defense based on the putative class members' status as exempt employees. Explaining that "[a]ffirmative defenses should be considered in making class certification decisions,"[189] the court reviewed the parties' evidence regarding whether this defense could be adjudicated based on common evidence, concluding that "fact-intensive, individual inquiries will be necessary to determine whether class members are actually performing similar duties, and whether those duties fit within the administrative exemption."[190]

Defense practitioners should be aware that several defenses often raise individualized issues that may be useful in defeating certification. Those defenses include:

- **Voluntary payments doctrine.** This defense generally bars state law claims that seek recovery of payments made with full knowledge of the facts. Because the defense often depends on the individual knowledge of the plaintiff or putative class members, it can provide a basis for defeating certification.[191]

---

187. *Id.*

188. Payala v. Wipro Techs., Inc., No. LACV1504063JAKJPRX, 2016 WL 6094158, at *12 (C.D. Cal. Aug. 23, 2016).

189. *Id.* at *7.

190. *Id.* at *12; *see also* Authors Guild, Inc. v. Google Inc., 721 F.3d 132, 134 (2d Cir. 2013) (reversing certification order issued before adjudication of fair use defense because that analysis "will necessarily inform and perhaps moot our analysis of many class certification issues, including those regarding the commonality of plaintiffs' injuries, the typicality of their claims, and the predominance of common questions of law or fact"); Farrar & Farrar Dairy, Inc. v. Miller-St. Nazianz, Inc., 254 F.R.D. 68, 75 (E.D.N.C. 2008) ("[L]ike other considerations, affirmative defenses must be factored into the calculus of whether common issues predominate.").

191. *See, e.g.,* Newman v. RCN Telecom Servs., Inc., 238 F.R.D. 57, 78 (S.D.N.Y. 2006) (denying certification where plaintiff was aware of allegedly misrepresented download speeds, but continued paying for service); Spagnola v. Chubb Corp., 264 F.R.D. 76, 99 (S.D.N.Y. 2010) ("Ultimately, the Court or the jury will be tasked with the determination, for each individual class member, whether they knew or should have known of the circumstances surrounding the increases in their respective coverages but continued to pay, or whether such payment was the result of a mistake of fact or law relating to their obligation to pay."); Endres v. Wells Fargo Bank, No. C 06-7019 PJH, 2008 WL 344204,

- **Statute of limitations.** A statute of limitations defense can be adjudicated based on common evidence, unless the plaintiffs seek to rely on an exception, such as delayed discovery or concealment. To apply those exceptions, the court must adjudicate whether putative class members exercised reasonable diligence or were on notice of a claim. Those inquiries often involve individualized questions that may defeat predominance.[192]
- **Consent (and/or failure to mitigate).** Consent is a defense to many privacy and statutory consumer protection claims. Where the evidence shows that consent was given in varying ways, or where the effectiveness of consent requires individualized determinations, predominance may be lacking.[193]

---

at *12 (N.D. Cal. Feb. 6, 2008) ("the application of affirmative defenses would require an individualized analysis as to each class member. These include the applicability of the voluntary-payment doctrine, which may bar any claims made by class members who continued to incur and voluntarily pay the overdraft protection fees").

192. *See, e.g.,* Lucas v. Breg, Inc., 212 F. Supp. 3d 950, 971 (S.D. Cal. 2016) ("Under both the discovery rule and the doctrine of fraudulent concealment, the relevant inquiry is whether the plaintiff was on notice—either notice of some wrongdoing in the case of the discovery rule, or notice of the specific cause of action in the case of fraudulent concealment. These determinations are not susceptible to generalized proof. Over the 24-year class period, Defendant Breg has periodically changed the form and content of its instructions and warnings such that putative class members, depending upon when they used the product, may have been on reasonable notice that they had a claim."); Gonzalez v. Corning, 317 F.R.D. 443, 523 (W.D. Pa. 2016) ("Determination of statute of limitations defenses can prevent a finding of predominance.") (collecting cases); Henson v. Fid. Nat. Fin. Inc., 300 F.R.D. 413, 421 (C.D. Cal. 2014) (plaintiff "seeks to rely upon various exceptions to the statute of limitations, such as the discovery rule, equitable tolling, and equitable estoppel. These doctrines are by their very nature fact-intensive and highly individualized. Putative class member No. 1's diligence in unearthing a potential RESPA violation will bear little on putative class member No. 2's actions. With a class that potentially numbers in the tens—if not hundreds—of thousands, the sheer amount of individualized analysis is dizzying.").

193. *See, e.g.,* Connelly v. Hilton Grand Vacations Co., LLC, 294 F.R.D. 574, 578 (S.D. Cal. 2013) ("The Court concludes, however, that HGV has set forth a fairly strong argument that the differing circumstances under which putative class members provided their cell phone numbers to Hilton are, at the very least, relevant to a determination of prior express consent. The context of class members' interactions with Hilton is sufficiently varied to provide dissimilar opportunities for the expression of consent."); Gannon v. Network Tel. Servs., Inc., No. CV 12-9777-RGK PJWX, 2013 WL 2450199, at *2 (C.D. Cal. June 5, 2013), *aff'd,* 628 F. App'x 551 (9th Cir. 2016) ("Plaintiff's class definition would require individual inquiry into whether the potential class members consented to receiving text messages."); Shamblin v. Obama for Am., No. 8:13-CV-2428-T-33TBM, 2015 WL 1909765, at *12 (M.D. Fla. Apr. 27, 2015) ("the evidence necessary to establish Shamblin's claim is not common to both Shamblin and all class members. Individualized inquiries into consent (including where, how, and when) will predominate."); Jamison v. First Credit

- **Superseding or intervening causation.** Causation defenses, including superseding and intervening causation, can help in defeating class certification. These defenses apply to negligence and product defect claims, and may bar breach of warranty claims and some statutory consumer fraud claims as well.[194]

- **Notice.** In many breach of warranty cases and some contract cases, timely notice of breach and a reasonable opportunity to cure are required elements of the claim. A lack of notice may, in some cases, be an individualized defense that helps in defeating certification.[195]

- **Unclean hands.** For cases involving equitable claims (and in some cases breach of contract claims), an unclean hands defense may provide an effective way to challenge typicality or predominance.[196]

- **Setoff/recoupment/counterclaims.** If your defendant has an argument that the class representative is liable (especially in connection with the same transaction), consider including a setoff or recoupment affirmative defense. Such a defense can affect adequacy or typicality. In fact, consider making a counterclaim. The same consideration should be made for the entire class, and such a defense or counterclaim could destroy predominance.

Servs., Inc., 290 F.R.D. 92, 106–07 (N.D. Ill. 2013) ("individualized consent predominate when a defendant sets forth specific evidence showing that a significant percentage of the putative class consented to receiving calls on their cellphone.").

194. *See, e.g.,* Trunzo v. Citi Mortg., No. 2:11-CV-01124, 2014 WL 1317577, at *11 (W.D. Pa. Mar. 31, 2014) ("This critical causation issue [intervening causation] is likely to become a major focus of the litigation," such that "the representative might devote time and effort to the defense at the expense of issues that are common and controlling for the class"); Sergeants Benevolent Ass'n Health & Welfare Fund v. Sanofi-Aventis U.S. LLP, 806 F.3d 71, 97 (2d Cir. 2015) ("we conclude that Plaintiffs are unable to show RICO causation by generalized proof, and we accordingly conclude that the district court did not err in denying Plaintiffs' class-certification motion").

195. *See, e.g., In re* Phenylpropanolamine (PPA) Prod. Liab. Litig., 214 F.R.D. 614, 620 (W.D. Wash. 2003) ("the breach of warranty and unjust enrichment claims could require individualized factual inquiries into issues such as causation, materiality, notice, and/or breach."); *see also* Brown v. Electrolux Home Prod., Inc., 817 F.3d 1225, 1238 (11th Cir. 2016) ("each class member will need to prove that he gave Electrolux pre-suit notice and an opportunity to cure. This showing could require individual proof.").

196. *See, e.g., In re* Grand Theft Auto Video Game Consumer Litig., 251 F.R.D. 139, 157 (S.D.N.Y. 2008) (the equitable defense of unclean hands, which may bar some members' claims for unjust enrichment, also creates individualized issues).

The bottom line is to take affirmative defenses seriously. Contrary to what the plaintiffs' bar often says, defenses are relevant to certification and can be used to defeat certification.

DEVELOPING DEFENSE THEMES AND NARRATIVE

As any persuasion expert will tell you, judges and juries are human, and they process cases, including class actions, through moral foundations and story.[197] Plaintiffs' counsel will frame their case through story, and the decision maker or makers will develop their own story. But far too often, defense counsel presents the case without any moral foundation and without story, framed as a series of technical legal arguments for dismissal, against class certification or for summary judgment. This type of defense can come across as hollow or, worse yet, as trying to escape responsibility for a wrong based on trivialities.

Defense counsel should begin evaluating and developing themes and the defense narrative at the outset of the case, refining them at each stage. What is the case about? Why should the defense win from a moral perspective? Why should the judge or jury care and return a decision for the defense? For lawyers, who are trained in legalistic analysis, answering these questions can be harder than one might think. Many lawyers will reflexively turn to the elements of the claim or the applicable legal standard. Ask a defense lawyer why he should win and you might hear "well, the complaint does not allege a plausible cause of action, so it should be dismissed." That's not a defense theme or narrative; it's a legal argument, and one without any moral foundation.

A good defense theme should be specific to the case, yet resonate with common life experiences and have strong moral grounds. It should be short, simple, and memorable. It should help the judge or jury embrace your position and motivate them to act. The defense theme should then be woven into a defense narrative that has a clear beginning, middle, and end that explains why your client should win.

None of this is easy. At the outset of a case, information may be limited. Defense counsel will have the complaint, perhaps some basic background information, and often little else. The complaint, however, may suggest a defense theme or narrative. Perhaps the timing of plaintiff's individual transaction or lack of prior complaints suggest that the case

---

197. N. Pennington & R. Hastie, *A Cognitive Theory of Juror Decision Making: The Story Model*, 13 Cardozo L. Rev. 519–20 (1991).

is lawyer driven or maybe even a setup. Perhaps the allegations suggest that there is no real harm or that the theory of injury is so implausible that it suggests another defense theme, such as misuse or an overreaching money grab by plaintiff's counsel. The early case assessment, discussed at the beginning of this chapter, can be invaluable in helping develop defense themes and a narrative during the early stages of case.

The need for strong themes and a coherent defense narrative is particularly acute when opposing class certification. Remember that the certification decision is discretionary. And as any experienced class action defense counsel can attest, judges may not decide the merits on class certification, but their view of the merits and the equities can have an enormous impact on the certification decision. In many cases, where the equities appear to weigh in plaintiff's favor, you may see judges relying on principles that favor certification, including the idea that a class can always be decertified later or that, without certification, the case may essentially be dead because the alleged damages are so small or for some other reason. Those considerations often play less of a role where judges view the plaintiff's case as weak.

One helpful tool for developing case themes can be found in moral foundations theory, which was created by a group of social psychologists to explore the idea that humans think about morality using several common foundations, which both unite and divide humans.[198] Those foundations include:

- **Care v. Harm.** We seek protection and oppose harm to ourselves or others.
- **Fairness v. Cheating.** We seek justice based on shared rules and oppose attempts to evade those rules.
- **Loyalty v. Betrayal.** We stand with our own group and oppose threats to the group.
- **Authority v. Subversion.** We expect obedience to legitimate authority and oppose attempts to subvert authority.
- **Sanctity v. Degradation.** We want purity and avoid that which produces disgust.

Defense counsel may be able to apply moral foundations research to hone case themes by analyzing the question of "what is this case about,"

---

198. J. Graham, J. Haidt, S. Koleva, M. Motyl, R. Iyer, S. Wojcik, & P.H. Ditto, *Moral Foundations Theory: The Pragmatic Validity of Moral Pluralism*, 47 ADVANCES IN EXPERIMENTAL SOC. PSYCHOLOGY, 55–130 (2012).

through each of these five foundations. How is the defendant taking care of its customers and society within the context of this case? How is the company acting fairly and justly? Is the company (or more precisely its employees) part of the decision maker's group? How so? How is the company following legal, regulatory, and industry best practices, and are plaintiffs seeking a deviation from those accepted norms? Are the company's motives pure? How so?

After working through these questions, defense counsel should be able to craft themes grounded in common moral foundations. Think about how those themes can be woven into each strategic move in the case, from the motion to change venue, to the motion to dismiss and certainly the opposition to class certification.

5

Class Action Discovery Strategy

Robert J. Herrington and Kathryn Honecker

This chapter addresses discovery in the class action context, covering strategy considerations for plaintiffs and the defense. The chapter also addresses several discovery issues that are unique to class actions. The chapter begins by discussing several important strategic decisions that plaintiffs and defendants often confront when handling discovery in class litigation. The next section covers requests to bifurcate class and merits discovery. We then address when and how plaintiffs can obtain access to a class list at the pre-certification stage, followed by sections addressing communications with putative class members, as well as discovery into communications between putative class members and plaintiffs' counsel. The final sections address discovery as to absent class members, electronically stored information (ESI) considerations, and the recent amendments to Rule 34.

PLAINTIFFS' DISCOVERY STRATEGY

Going into discovery, plaintiffs' counsel must be organized and know what elements they will need to prove for class certification and on the merits. To do this, counsel should prepare a roadmap to guide discovery efforts to establish that (1) the plaintiffs' case is appropriate for class certification under Rule 23, (2) class-wide evidence proves each element of claims asserted, and (3) class-wide evidence negates any potential defenses.[1] To provide the best chance for success, the roadmap should begin by detailing each element of a claim, which may be found in relevant jury instructions, case law, and rules. Once the elements have been identified, counsel should identify any facts they already have established (through pre-filing investigation or otherwise) and any facts the defendants have admitted. Finally, counsel should identify the method(s) of discovery (e.g., interrogatories, requests to admit, depositions, document requests, expert opinions, or third-party discovery) that are best suited to secure the proof needed for any elements that must still be proven. The remainder of this section addresses some considerations and challenges that plaintiffs' counsel may face during this discovery process, and some strategies that may mitigate potential problems.

Consider Seeking Discovery Despite a Motion to Dismiss

Defense counsel commonly attempts to thwart plaintiffs' prospects at class certification by moving to stay discovery pending a decision on their motions to dismiss. But discovery stays are not automatic and may be ripe for abuse.[2] Instead, plaintiffs' counsel should argue that a motion to stay discovery is merely a type of a motion for a protective order that is governed by Rule 26(c), which requires a strong "good cause" showing of undue burden from defendants.[3]

Defense counsel often argue that deferring discovery at the motion to dismiss stage is necessary because (1) their motion may be case

---

1. One such roadmap is a Working Proof Outline. A sample excerpt from a Working Proof Outline is included in the Appendix immediately following this chapter.

2. *See In re* Nexus 6P Prods. Liab. Litig., No. 17-cv-02185, 2017 WL 3581188, at *1 (N.D. Cal. Aug. 18, 2017) ("Had the Federal Rules contemplated that a motion to dismiss under [Rule 12(b)] would stay discovery, the Rules would contain a provision to that effect . . . [and, in] fact, such a notion is directly at odds with the need for expeditious resolution of litigation.") (internal citations omitted). An exception to the general rule applies to securities class actions where discovery stays generally are automatic under the Private Securities Litigation Reform Act. *See* Ave. Cap. Mgmt. II, LP v. Schaden, No. 14-CV-02031, at *2 (D. Colo. Feb. 20, 2015).

3. *See* Fed. R. Civ. P. 26(c); Gray v. First Winthrop Corp., 133 F.R.D. 39, 40 (N.D. Cal. 1990) ("A party seeking a stay of discovery carries the heavy burden of making a 'strong showing' why discovery should be denied.") (quoting Blankenship v. Hearst Corp., 519 F.2d 418, 429 (9th Cir. 1975)).

dispositive, (2) "information disparity" between the parties preju-
dices corporate defendants that bear a larger burden of discovery, and
(3) any delays would not prejudice the plaintiffs' interests for expedient
litigation. As addressed later, these three arguments are often rejected
by federal courts.

Plaintiffs' counsel should remember that some courts will stay discovery only if it appears that the complaint's allegations are frivolous.[4]
As some courts have recognized,

> a stay of the type requested by defendants, where a party asserts that
> dismissal is likely, would require the court to make a preliminary finding
> of the likelihood of success on the motion to dismiss . . . [,] [which] would
> circumvent the procedures for resolution of such a motion.[5]

Thus, instead of seeking protection from hypothetical discovery, some
courts prefer defendants to wait until plaintiffs serve discovery, so the
issues can be addressed in context.[6]

Some federal courts also have rejected defense arguments to stay
discovery based solely on the burden and cost of production.[7] Lastly,
as to defendants' "lack of prejudice to plaintiff" argument, some federal courts have recognized that "there is at least 'a fair possibility'
that Plaintiffs will be harmed by a stay" pending a motion to dismiss.[8] For example, early discovery may be necessary to prevent the

---

4. *See* Galaria v. Nationwide Mut. Ins. Co., No. 2:13-cv-00118, 2013 WL 6578730, at *2
(S.D. Ohio Dec. 16, 2013). Some decisions recognize that a discovery stay is not appropriate unless all plaintiffs' claims "are subject to dismissal 'based on legal determinations
that could not have been altered by any further discovery.'" *Id.* (citing Muzquiz v. W.A.
Foote Mem'l Hosp., 70 F.3d 422, 430 (6th Cir. 1995)); *accord* Torres v. Wendy's Int'l, LLC,
No. 616-cv-210, 2016 WL 7104870, at *3 (M.D. Fla. Nov. 29, 2016) (refusing to grant stay
pending motion to dismiss "although the motion . . . would likely be case dispositive if
granted").

5. *See Gray*, 133 F.R.D. at 40.

6. *See, e.g., id.* Some courts find that a pending motion to dismiss—standing alone—is
insufficient to constitute good cause to support a stay of discovery. *See* Rosario v. Star-
bucks Corp., No. 2:16-cv-01951, 2017 WL 4122569, at *1 (W.D. Wash. Sept. 18, 2017).

7. *See, e.g., Torres*, 2016 WL 7104870, at *3. For example, in *Torres*, the defendant-cor-
poration moved to stay discovery pending the court's resolution of its motion to dismiss
a data breach class action, arguing, in effect, that a stay was appropriate because it would
otherwise be forced to "devot[e] significant resources to discovery that may never need to
be taken." *Id.* at *2. The *Torres* court, however, was unconvinced, noting that "[t]he burden argued by Defendant is that of most any large company saddled with a class action
complaint." *Id.* at *3.

8. *In re* Galena Biopharma, Inc. Derivative Litig., 83 F. Supp. 3d 1033, 1043 (D. Or.
2015).

spoliation of evidence, inform and assist the parties in meeting document preservation obligations, which remain regardless of whether a stay is imposed, and help the parties determine what evidence is relevant to the claims and defenses.[9] Further, plaintiffs' counsel may argue that the relevant and pertinent information is likely in the defendants' control, thus making early discovery necessary for plaintiffs to properly frame their class action complaint.[10] Plaintiffs' counsel can also point to defendants' motions to dismiss to identify factual issues that could be resolved by early discovery. The granting of a stay, thus, may prejudice the plaintiffs by hindering their ability to prepare their case while simultaneously delaying the case.

Accordingly, plaintiffs' counsel should consider challenging attempts to stay discovery by holding defendants to their burden of demonstrating that discovery will create an undue burden.[11] Counsel also should consider obtaining necessary and relevant information by sending early document requests under Rule 34. Frank discussions with opposing counsel regarding the scope and type of discovery needed and available may alleviate the need for costly litigation regarding a discovery stay. Further, many of the concerns and issues related to a stay of discovery will likely be addressed at the case management stage, or, alternatively, counsel should raise those during the case management conference should the court fail to do so.

Merits/Class Bifurcation

Plaintiffs' counsel should also be wary of attempts to bifurcate discovery between class certification issues and merits issues. Although bifurcation may help plaintiffs narrow their discovery efforts and potentially expedite certification, some defendants tend to have a very narrow view of what discovery is relevant to class certification and err on the side of withholding information that is relevant to class issues if the requested discovery also covers a merits issue. Bifurcation, while noble in theory, frequently leads to costly discovery disputes over whether a piece or category of discovery goes toward class certification or the merits, which can delay proceedings and waste resources. As cautioned by the leading treatise on class action litigation:

---

9. *See Galaria*, 2013 WL 6578730, at *3.
10. *See id.*
11. *See, e.g., Torres*, 2016 WL 7104870, at *3.

> [T]he defense [often] objects to all of [plaintiffs'] discovery demands claim-
> ing all are "merits discovery." As a result . . . the court [will have to]
> immerse itself in the discovery process and rule on each demand, declaring
> it "merits" or "class issues" discovery. In any event, the expected economies
> of discovery bifurcation are rarely achieved.[12]

Not surprisingly, many courts have observed that "bifurcated discovery 'belies the principles of judicial economy,'" and can result in significant duplication of effort and expense to the parties.[13] One opinion from the Northern District of Illinois, rejecting a defendant's request to bifurcate discovery, exemplifies these problems. In *In re Groupon, Inc. Securities Litigation*, the district court assessed three factors in determining whether bifurcated discovery was appropriate: (1) expediency, (2) economy, and (3) severability.[14] Concerning expediency, the *Groupon* court rejected defendant's argument that "highly burdensome merits discovery [will] . . . despite the parties' best efforts, [cause] a delay in the parties' submission of their briefs on the class certification issue . . . ."[15] Instead, the court noted that, but for the exceptional case where merits discovery would entail the review of millions of additional documents, the expediency factor favored concurrent class and merits discovery.[16] Next, in considering the economy factor, the court noted that bifurcating discovery can increase the costs of litigation due to disputes over discovery classification and the duplication of efforts and expenses.[17] Finally, the severability factor also failed to support bifurcation, as the *Groupon* court held that class-and-merits discovery was not severable because the court's analysis of certification issues "will have some overlap [with merits issues] and bifurcation will not create efficiencies."[18]

The *Groupon* court's opinion aligns with today's trend in federal courts against bifurcation, because "some overlap between certification

---

12. NEWBERG ON CLASS ACTIONS § 9:44 n.4 (4th ed. 2012).
13. *See, e.g., In re Rail Freight Fuel Surcharge Antitrust Litig.*, 258 F.R.D. 167, 174 (D.D.C. 2009).
14. No. 12-C-2450, 2014 WL 12746902, at *1 (N.D. Ill. Feb. 24, 2014).
15. *Id.* at *2.
16. *Id.*
17. *Id.* at *3–4.
18. *Id.* at *4.

and merits discovery" is inevitable.[19] Indeed, the Supreme Court has clarified that a district court's class certification inquiry is *required* to reach into the merits of the action.[20] A more detailed discussion on the current federal trend against bifurcation follows in a later section.

Notwithstanding the current trend, however, it may be better practice for plaintiffs' counsel to plan for potential bifurcation issues early on to avoid the pitfalls of long discovery battles or duplicative costs. Defense counsel may argue for a "soft" bifurcation, prioritizing certain discovery or leaving selected issues for later merits discovery (such as a class list). Plaintiffs' counsel should focus discovery on the essential elements of Rule 23 and quickly identify the type of discovery necessary to achieve certification and plan for any potential issues. Counsel also should work with defense counsel to tailor the scope of discovery, which often is more cost efficient than discovery litigation. As reflected by the 2015 Amendments to the Federal Rules of Civil Procedure, federal courts have become more involved with case management and proactive in the discovery process to reduce costly discovery disputes and will focus on proportionality, including alternative means of discovery.[21]

How to Maximize Pre-certification Discovery

To ensure that counsel timely obtains the necessary discovery for the certification motion, counsel must identify early on the type of proof that the parties are expected to present, and tailor the discovery requests to discovering evidence to establish each element of Rule 23. One way to go about this is to review your roadmap or working proof outline to identify any evidence gaps in the case where more discovery is needed, while assessing potential areas of weaknesses that the defense may

---

19. *Wal-Mart Stores, Inc. v. Dukes*, 564 U.S. 338, 351 (2011); *see also* Frieri v. Sysco Corp., No. 316-cv-01432, 2017 WL 2908777, at *4 (S.D. Cal. July 7, 2017) (allowing limited merits discovery pre-certification); Talavera v. Sun Maid Growers of California, No. 115-cv-00842, 2017 WL 495635, at *4 (E.D. Cal. Feb. 6, 2017) (commenting that bifurcation goes against judicial economy).

20. *See* Comcast Corp. v. Behrend, 569 U.S. 27, 35 (2013).

21. *See, e.g.*, Fed. R. Civ. P. 1 (imposing on the court a duty to make litigation as efficient and inexpensive as possible); *In re* Semgroup Energy Partners, L.P., Sec. Litig., No. 08-md-1989, 2010 WL 5376262, at *3 (N.D. Okla. Dec. 21, 2010) (noting that a case management schedule that prioritized class certification as opposed to bifurcation "will, to a considerable extent, alleviate defendants' concerns about extensive and costly discovery").

target.[22] Counsel should think critically about which discovery devices are most appropriate for obtaining the missing information or meeting potential defenses, as well as the order in which the discovery devices should be served.

For example, affidavits, declarations, or even reasonable estimates in briefs may be sufficient to establish the approximate size of the class. But, in some cases, numerosity may be seriously disputed. In those situations, requests for admission and interrogatories may be effective to ascertain the number of potential class members in the proposed class. Alternatively, a carefully targeted request for internal documents—for example, sales records in a consumer fraud action or personnel records in a wage and hour action—may also be effective.

As another example, plaintiffs sometimes lack information on the common core of facts, or how defendant's conduct impacted the class in the same way, as necessary to establish commonality. Strategic use of interrogatories and targeted depositions may be indispensable to determine what common evidence exists that will help establish the common core of facts, and that the putative class members suffered a common injury. Counsel can use the information gleaned from an initial round of discovery to propound carefully targeted supplemental discovery requests to collect those forms of class-wide proof. For example, consider requesting document destruction policies early, as they can often provide the exact names of documents relevant to the claims.

Depending on the type of case, expert opinion may be required to demonstrate that defendant's alleged misconduct affected the entire class and that damages can be determined on a class-wide basis. If an expert is required, counsel should consider identifying the necessary experts and preparing them early on. Consulting experts who are not expected to testify at trial are generally shielded from discovery and may be invaluable in helping draft complaints and create targeted discovery. Be careful, however, to review the case law in your district about whether pleading information learned from consulting experts in your complaint may result in a potential waiver of the consultant's protection. Courts handle the timing of testifying expert discovery related to class certification differently. Some allow depositions, others do not. Some allow rebuttal reports, and others do not. And some require expert reports to be exchanged before the class certification briefing they support, and others

---

22. *See, e.g.,* the Appendix immediately following this chapter.

do not. As such, check your judge's preference when drafting your case management order. A full discussion of the use of experts during class certification can be found in Chapter 11.

> Expert opinion may be required to demonstrate that defendant's alleged misconduct affected the entire class and that damages can be determined on a class-wide basis.

Counsel should apply the same line of thinking to potential weaknesses in the plaintiffs' case to avoid being caught by surprise at the motion for certification stage—after class discovery has closed. For example, one of the defense's main objectives during class certification is to identify potential differences between putative class members and the named plaintiff to defeat typicality or commonality.

In a consumer fraud action where misrepresentations concerning multiple products are alleged, defendants may argue that a proposed named plaintiff who has not purchased or been injured by each line of products complained of is atypical of the putative class. But such a blanket rule is inconsistent with many cases and therefore discovery is proper to make a complete record. For instance, some courts have considered whether "the type of claim and consumer injury is substantially similar as between the purchased and unpurchased products."[23] For discovery purposes, counsel should tailor their discovery to uncover information supporting their contention that the proposed named plaintiff and putative class members suffered an injury or injuries that were substantially similar.

Another popular area of attack at the certification stage is the named plaintiffs' adequacy. Defense counsel will likely argue there that the proposed class members' interests may differ from those of the named representatives for a variety of reasons. For example, defendants frequently argue that, if different state law must be applied to different class members, a proposed named plaintiff in one state would be

---

23. Ang v. Bimbo Bakeries USA, Inc., No. 13-CV-01196, 2014 WL 1024182, at *8 (N.D. Cal. Mar. 13, 2014); *accord* Kurtz v. Kimberly-Clark Corp., 321 F.R.D. 482, 535 (E.D.N.Y. 2017) (finding the "fact that all the representations on [a defendant's] products are substantially similar is sufficient" to establish typicality—even if the named plaintiff did not purchase each and every product at issue).

inadequate to represent class members subject to different legal standards for relief in other states.[24]

Also, in mass tort actions, defendants may argue that those with present injuries have different interests than those who have been exposed to the tortious conduct but have not yet manifested injury—or suffered a less severe injury.[25] If a plaintiff is seeking to apply the state laws of the state where the corporate defendant is headquartered, plaintiffs' counsel should carefully review the applicable choice-of-law rules and request discovery to support application of that state's laws to similarly situated consumers who live in other states. Alternatively, counsel can submit a trial plan to identify distinct claims or other issues that may demand separate representation through subclasses and explain how those will be presented at trial. Trial plans are covered in Chapter 10.

As to discovery strategies regarding the plaintiffs' adequacy, counsel must be diligent and act proactively instead of reactively. Because adequacy discovery is generally unilaterally propounded by the defense against the plaintiff and his or her counsel, it may be tempting for counsel to focus on the other elements of Rule 23. But an attack based on adequacy can have real teeth, and courts have denied certification on adequacy grounds many times.[26] Counsel should therefore be wary of potential adequacy challenges that the defense may raise, and the type and form of discovery defense counsel may seek to support its challenge. Only then will counsel be able to strategically and effectively mount the appropriate response and safeguards. Note, however, the difference between an established adequacy problem and a speculative one, as the latter is usually insufficient to defeat adequacy.

Taken together, the preceding examples demonstrate the level of attention, detail, and care that counsel must undertake during pre-certification discovery. By strategically planning for potential problems early on—as opposed to reacting to discovery issues as they arise—counsel can

---

24. *But see* Spencer v. Hartford Fin. Servs. Grp., Inc., 256 F.R.D. 284, 293 (D. Conn. 2009) (holding "that the potential for varying standards of proof under state law does not defeat adequacy.").

25. *In re* Chinese-Manufactured Drywall Prod. Liab. Litig., No. MDL 2047, 2017 WL 1421627, at *17 (E.D. La. Apr. 21, 2017) (commenting that toxic torts with delayed manifestations of injury may create individualized issues).

26. *See, e.g.,* Hooper v. City of Seattle, No. C17-77RSM, 2017 WL 4410029, at *7 (W.D. Wash. Oct. 4, 2017) (denying certification due to conflict of interest between proposed named plaintiffs and putative class members).

ensure efficient discovery concerning certification without missing crucial information.

How Much Pre-certification Discovery to Propound—Be Targeted

To maximize efficiency, counsel should resist the temptation to simply ask for as much discovery as possible. Rather, critically think about what pre-certification discovery is needed and propound carefully targeted requests to that effect. Understandably, the urge to propound broad discovery requests may be strong given the frequent asymmetry of information in class actions. Counsel, thus, may want to ask for as much as possible to bridge the information gap as soon as possible. Although it may seem counterintuitive, counsel should resist this urge because propounding broad discovery requests early on may backfire and entangle counsel in either reviewing an overwhelming amount of irrelevant discovery or engaging in costly discovery litigation.

For example, propounding broad discovery may not necessarily result in any relevant or pertinent information. Instead, defendants are more likely to push back against broad discovery and may simply withhold information based on the objections. Common objections include that the requests are an improper fishing expedition and impose undue burden, coupled with references to the asymmetry in information. Plaintiffs' counsel may become entangled in time-consuming meet-and-confers or discovery motions, fighting over the relevancy of certain categories of, or specific, documents. Also, broad discovery requests may create a risk of fighting peripheral discovery battles on issues or documents not necessarily pertinent to the case. Many courts have, at best, a profound disdain for discovery disputes. Counsel, therefore, may have difficulty explaining to a skeptical judge why the broad discovery is necessary.

This is not to say that counsel may not craft voluminous discovery requests. To the contrary, due to the asymmetry of information, voluminous discovery requests may be necessary in cases involving corporate defendants. But there is a difference between a large number of broad discovery requests and a significant number of targeted discovery requests. By critically thinking about what discovery is needed—for example, the quantity and form of discovery necessary for certification—and crafting carefully targeted requests, counsel will have a reasonable explanation ready for the judge regarding why such discovery is needed if discovery disputes arise. For example, consider shortening the relevant time period for certain requests and only seek information covering a longer period when necessary. Further, by having carefully targeted requests, counsel will make it more difficult for defendants to object.

As an additional consideration, asking for too much ESI discovery could be dangerous because, as discussed later, it may trigger cost shifting.[27] Even without cost shifting, plaintiffs' counsel will need to pay to host the ESI received from defendants, which is often charged by the volume of data.

How to Conduct Efficient Pre-certification Depositions

Similar to other pre-certification discovery, plaintiffs' counsel should show restraint and carefully consider which witnesses are necessary for class certification issues, and not simply depose all witnesses with potentially relevant information.[28] As a general rule of thumb, counsel should identify and limit the number of deponents to ten witnesses in accordance with Rule 30(a).[29] Although there are always exceptions to the general rule, abiding by this limit helps counsel think critically about the necessity of each witness deposed, which, in turn, may result in more efficient depositions. Plaintiffs' counsel also should have the elements of each of the claims in mind, as well as which witnesses are necessary for each element to achieve certification.

As a starting point, plaintiffs' counsel should identify who may have relevant information regarding the claims. If the defendant is a corporate defendant, then identifying which executives or departments may have been the decision-making body that promulgated the allegedly harmful policies or conduct is important, as is identifying topics to designate in a Rule 30(b)(6) deposition notice. For example, if the policymaker's identity is unknown, asking the corporation to designate someone to testify about the creation or implementation of the policy

---

27. *See* Zubulake v. UBS Warburg, LLC, 217 F.R.D. 309, 318–20, 324 (S.D.N.Y. 2003).
28. *See, e.g., In re* Benicar (Olmesartan) Prods. Liab. Litig., No. 15-2606, 2016 WL 5817262, at *7 (D.N.J. Oct. 4, 2016) (denying motion to compel witnesses as not proportional to needs of the case after requesting party had already conducted 38 fact witness depositions).
29. *See* FED. R. CIV. P. 30(a)(2)(A)(i)–(ii).

should reveal the individual's identity, even if the company does not designate that person to testify. If you have been conservative with the number of deposition notices, you can issue a notice to the policymaker as an individual.[30]

In addition, counsel should place themselves in the shoes of the defense and think about whose declarations are most likely to be proffered against certification. Doing so will not only help counsel ensure that all pertinent individuals are deposed, but also that any individual or entity with relevant information has been identified and considered. Then, after all relevant witnesses have been identified, counsel should determine whether the potential deponents have information that pertains to certification, merits, or both. Since time may be of the essence at the pre-certification stage, counsel may want to prioritize witnesses needed for certification. Thinking about these issues strategically will help counsel determine whether a particular person should be deposed or not. Before noticing any depositions, it is a good practice, and sometimes required by local rules, to discuss deposition dates with opposing counsel.

> Counsel should place themselves in the shoes of the defense and think about whose declarations are most likely to be proffered.

Rule 30(b)(6) depositions are almost always taken in a putative class action. Remember that a Rule 30(b)(6) designated witness may be asked to testify on any topic, not simply those identified in your deposition notice. Whether they are binding on the corporation will ultimately depend on the individuals' role with the company and the scope of the notice. An objection can be made for the record, but the deponent generally needs to answer the question.

A defendant may also designate multiple witnesses to testify about the various topics identified in plaintiffs' Rule 30(b)(6) deposition notice. Each designated witness must be adequately prepared to testify on behalf of the company and generally may be deposed for up to seven hours.[31] As one court explained, the burden of preparing a

---

30. Remember that officers and other high-level employees may not need to be subpoenaed and can be deposed by serving a notice of deposition on the corporate defendant. Lower level employees may need to be subpoenaed and paid a witness fee.

31. FED. R. CIV. P. 30(b)(6), Advisory Notes for the 2000 Amendment ("For purposes of this durational limit, the deposition of each person designated under Rule 30(b)(6) should be considered a separate deposition.").

witness is simply the cost of being allowed to take advantage of the corporate form:

> Rule 30(b)(6) explicitly requires [defendant] to have persons testify on its behalf as to all matters known or reasonably available to it and, therefore, implicitly requires such persons to review all matters known or reasonably available to it in preparation for the Rule 30(b)(6) deposition. This interpretation is necessary in order to make the deposition a meaningful one and to prevent the "sandbagging" of an opponent by conducting a half-hearted inquiry before the deposition but a thorough and vigorous one before the trial. This would totally defeat the purpose of the discovery process. The Court understands that preparing for a Rule 30(b)(6) deposition can be burdensome. However, this is merely the result of the concomitant obligation from the privilege of being able to use the corporate form in order to conduct business.[32]

Also, remember that defendants might not designate the person(s) with the most or best knowledge of the topic, or even someone who has been adequately prepared, as required by the rule, so be certain to question the witnesses about their review of the deposition notice's subjects and who else may have more knowledge. Such testimony may later help support a request that the defendant produce another witness or your request for an additional deposition to depose an individual who was specifically identified to make up for a defendant's failure to comply with its duty to adequately prepare a witness.

Shifting Discovery Costs

Counsel also should be wary of the costs associated with broad discovery requests to avoid being potentially saddled with the defendant's costs of production. The greater the production, the more likely corporate defendants are to object and request that plaintiffs pay for the discovery sought (cost shifting), which is permissible under Rule 26.[33]

For example, in *Boeynaems v. LA Fitness International, Inc.*, the court shifted the costs of pre-certification discovery to the plaintiff in a class action based on the defendant's alleged significant discovery costs

---

32. *United States v. Taylor,* 166 F.R.D. 356, 362 (M.D.N.C.), *aff'd,* 166 F.R.D. 367 (M.D.N.C. 1996).

33. *See* Fed. R. Civ. P. 26(b)(2)(C). Although cost shifting is uncommon in class actions, there is always the potential risk. *See, e.g.,* Schweinfurth v. Motorola, Inc., C.A. No. 05–0024, 2008 WL 4449081, at *2 (N.D. Ohio Sept. 30, 2008) (ordering cost sharing for one million pages of paper discovery).

and the asymmetry of discoverable information between the parties.[34] Interestingly, the *Boeynaems* court hinted that its decision to shift costs turned on the plaintiffs' *counsel's* financial ability to bear the costs of discovery.[35] From the plaintiffs' perspective, the *Boeynaems* decision effectively stands as an outlier case, and, while often cited by the defense, the weight of legal authority remains against pre-certification discovery cost shifting (and is discussed later in the chapter from the defense perspective).[36] Federal courts generally recognize that corporate defendants can better shoulder the costs of discovery and, therefore, have no need for cost sharing—while forcing discovery cost sharing upon class action plaintiffs seeking small monetary damages would effectively deter the bringing of meritorious class action claims.[37]

Importantly, discovery cost shifting is not exclusively a defense-friendly device. Plaintiffs also may, under certain situations, utilize cost shifting to their advantage and have the defense share in the costs of production. For example, in *Wiginton v. CB Richard Ellis, Inc.*, the plaintiff-employees in a sexual harassment class action successfully moved the court to have their employer share in the costs of searching through the employees' backup files and servers.[38] And, more recently, a district court expressed frustration at the defendants for refusing to accept a discovery cost-shifting proposal from plaintiffs' counsel.[39] Additionally, cost sharing may be appropriate in situations where the parties both seek access to information not within the custody of any party—for example, through third-party subpoenas. Accordingly, plaintiffs' counsel should not think of discovery cost shifting solely as a defense option, but should use it offensively where available—even if the asymmetry of information is high.

As an additional consideration, the recent proliferation and increased importance of ESI have played important roles in discovery cost shifting

---

34. 285 F.R.D. 331, 334–37 (E.D. Pa. 2012).

35. *Id.* at 335 ("Plaintiffs are represented by [a] very successful and well-regarded Philadelphia firm . . . [that] has the financial ability to make investment in discovery.").

36. *See, e.g., In re* Checking Account Overdraft Litig., No. 09-md-02036, 2010 WL 3361127, at *3 (S.D. Fla. Aug. 23, 2010).

37. *See id.*

38. 229 F.R.D. 568, 577 (N.D. Ill. 2004).

39. *See* Davis v. E. Idaho Health Servs., No. 16-00193, 2017 WL 1737723, at *5 (D. Idaho May 3, 2016).

by creating an exception to the general rule against cost shifting.[40] Some courts appear to favor discovery cost shifting in situations where the volume of ESI requested is high, and the ESI is either in an inaccessible format or must be recreated.[41] Additional implications of ESI on discovery are discussed in more detail in a later section.

The current trend in many federal jurisdictions is to encourage *cooperation* between the parties and leave any discovery cost-shifting disputes out of the courtroom.[42] Some jurisdictions have gone as far as implementing local rules, model stipulations, and standing orders that require parties to take affirmative steps to work together to make discovery a more efficient, inexpensive, and cooperative experience.[43] Although the defense is unlikely to easily agree to any cost-sharing agreements requested by plaintiffs, plaintiffs' counsel should consider whether cost sharing or cost shifting is appropriate and meet-and-confer with defense counsel before seeking the court's assistance.

DEFENSE DISCOVERY STRATEGY

For defendants facing class litigation, the discovery process presents unique challenges, the principal one being that discovery generally is asymmetrical. The defendant has hundreds of thousands of pages of potentially relevant documents and several witnesses with relevant knowledge, while the named plaintiff often has very little. Some class action plaintiffs try to leverage this asymmetry by serving very broad discovery requests, with the goal of convincing the defendant that it

---

40. *See, e.g.,* U.S. *ex rel.* Carter v. Bridgepoint Educ., Inc., 305 F.R.D. 225, 237–38 (S.D. Cal. 2015) ("It was the modern proliferation and prevalence of ESI . . . that prompted the courts to reconsider their disinclination to authorize cost shifting.").

41. *See, e.g.,* Juster Acquisition Co., LLC v. N. Hudson Sewerage Auth., No. CIV.A. 12-3427, 2013 WL 541972, at *3 (D.N.J. Feb. 11, 2013) (denying defendant's request for cost shifting but commenting that an opposite holding may be appropriate if the discovery sought inaccessible ESI).

42. *See* FED. R. CIV. P. 1.

43. *See, e.g.,* Nevro Corp. v. Boston Sci. Corp., No. 16-06830, 2017 WL 2687806, at *3 (N.D. Cal. June 22, 2017) (noting that "Paragraph 11 of the Model ESI Order 'encourages the parties to confer on a process to test the efficacy of the search terms'"); Tadayon v. Greyhound Lines, Inc., No. CIV. 10-1326, 2012 WL 2048257, at *6 (D.D.C. June 6, 2012) ("The filing of forty-page discovery motions . . . will cease and will now be replaced by a new regimen in which the parties, without surrendering any of their rights, must make genuine efforts to engage in the cooperative discovery regimen contemplated by the *Sedona Conference Cooperation Proclamation*.").

will cost less to settle. This section discusses several strategies defendants may wish to consider to more effectively address these challenges.

Stay Pending Motion to Dismiss

Defense counsel should consider seeking a discovery stay while a motion to dismiss is pending. A stay is not automatic, except in certain securities class actions, and courts generally evaluate stay requests by analyzing the equities. Factors include: (1) plaintiffs' interests in proceeding expeditiously with the civil action and the potential prejudice to plaintiff of a delay; (2) the burden on the defendants; (3) the convenience to the court; (4) the interests of persons not parties to the civil litigation; and (5) the public interest.[44] Some courts also engage in a preliminary analysis of the motion to dismiss to determine the likelihood of success.[45] Other courts focus on whether the motion will dispose of the entire case, or at least the portion of the case on which discovery is sought.[46]

Regardless of the formulation, defendants facing class litigation often will be able to make compelling arguments for at least a short stay. Class discovery often is wide-ranging and costly.[47] Some courts have recognized that a defendant should not be subjected to those costs if the claims ultimately are dismissed or significantly narrowed.[48] Defendants should argue that waiting a few months while dispositive motions are decided will not cause any real harm to the plaintiff, thus tipping the equities in defendant's favor.

---

44. *In re* Broiler Chicken Grower Litig., No. 6:17-CV-00033-RJS, 2017 WL 3841912, at *3 (E.D. Okla. Sept. 1, 2017).

45. *See* Hong Leong Fin. Ltd. (Singapore) v. Pinnacle Performance Ltd., 297 F.R.D. 69, 72 (S.D.N.Y. 2013) ("[W]e follow the courts that have required a motion for a stay be supported by 'substantial arguments for dismissal.'").

46. *In re* Nexus 6p Prod. Liab. Litig., No. 17-CV-02185-BLF, 2017 WL 3581188, at *1 (N.D. Cal. Aug. 18, 2017) ("[A] pending motion must be potentially dispositive of the entire case, or at least dispositive on the issue at which discovery is directed.").

47. *See* Grosvenor v. Qwest Commc'ns Int'l, Inc., No. 09–cv–02848–WDM–KMT, 2010 WL 1413108, at *1 (D. Colo. Apr. 1, 2010) ("[W]hile the ordinary burdens associated with litigating a case do not constitute an undue burden, the breadth of class action discovery implicated in this case if a stay were not granted would be a significantly elevated burden on Defendants.").

48. *See, e.g.*, Valverde v. Xclusive Staffing, Inc., No. 16-CV-00671-RM-MJW, 2016 WL 8737774, at *2 (D. Colo. Nov. 4, 2016) ("[T]he Court recognizes that Plaintiffs have an interest in proceeding expeditiously while also recognizing that there is certainly a burden on Defendants if a stay is not put in place because they may be forced to conduct discovery which may not otherwise be necessary.").

In some jurisdictions, a formal stay motion may be unnecessary. Discovery generally cannot begin until the parties hold a Rule 26(f) conference, and that conference often does not occur until shortly before a Rule 16 scheduling conference with the court. Some judges do not set a Rule 16 conference until after the hearing on the motion to dismiss, which has the practical effect of staying discovery. In some cases, plaintiffs' counsel attempts to "speed up the process" by demanding a Rule 26(f) meeting before one is required. Handling those requesting requires defense counsel to balance the defendant's legitimate interests in not being subjected to premature discovery with the need not to be seen as stalling or obstructing the case. Plaintiffs sometimes will tip their hand by serving early document requests under Rule 34. If those requests are very broad or will be costly to respond to, they may provide defense counsel with tangible examples of the burden associated with class discovery and serve as a basis for moving to stay discovery pending a decision on the motion to dismiss.

Merits/Class Bifurcation

If a court declines a stay, defense counsel will want to consider asking the court to place limits on pre-certification discovery. Up until 2011, it was common to "bifurcate" class discovery from merits discovery and such a request was a staple of defending class litigation. Bifurcating discovery still occurs. But for defense counsel, seeking to bifurcate discovery now involves balancing important strategic considerations, including the potential that bifurcation could foreclose certain arguments or evidence at the class certification stage.

In 2011, the Supreme Court emphasized that trial courts must undertake a "rigorous analysis" of each Rule 23 requirement—an analysis that frequently "will entail some overlap with the merits of the plaintiffs' underlying claim."[49] In 2013, the Supreme Court emphasized this point again, criticizing the lower court's "refus[al] to entertain arguments against respondents' damages model that bore on the propriety of class certification, simply because those arguments would also be pertinent to the merits determination."[50] After these decisions, defense counsel should think long and hard about whether to seek to bifurcate merits and class discovery and, if so, where to draw the line between

---

49. Wal-Mart Stores, Inc. v. Dukes, 564 U.S. 338, 351 (2011).
50. Comcast Corp. v. Behrend, 569 U.S. 27, 34 (2013).

"merits" and "certification."[51] As courts have recognized, the "merits/ certification distinction is not always clear," because the facts that are relevant to the class determination frequently overlap with the facts that are relevant to the merits of the case.[52] If a defendant wants to draw a hard line and refuse discovery on an issue because it relates to the "merits," counsel should consider whether that position may later foreclose certain arguments when opposing class certification. Plaintiffs' counsel may well argue that such a refusal should preclude the defendant from later claiming that the issue is relevant to certification. After all, if discovery was improper because of an issue related to the "merits," how can the same issue preclude certification, particularly where the plaintiff was denied discovery?

> Defense counsel should think long and hard about whether to seek to bifurcate and, if so, where to draw the line between "merits" and "certification."

The risk of taking a hard line on bifurcation can be seen in *Zurn Pex Plumbing Product Liability Litigation*, where the defendant successfully bifurcated discovery between certification and the merits, but later sought to preclude expert testimony offered to support certification.[53] The Eighth Circuit sided with the plaintiffs, explaining that it "was after all *Zurn* which sought bifurcated discovery which resulted in a limited record at the class certification stage, preventing the kind of full and conclusive *Daubert* inquiry *Zurn* later requested."[54]

Rather than insisting on bifurcation, defendants may be better off taking a more measured approach. Plaintiffs' counsel often will agree with the idea that pre-certification discovery should "focus" on certification issues and may be willing to limit requests to issues that fairly go to Rule 23's requirements. Working with opposing counsel to tailor discovery often is less costly (and less risky) than litigating what constitutes "merits" versus "certification" discovery.

---

51. *See* Chen-Oster v. Goldman, Sachs & Co., 285 F.R.D. 294, 299 (S.D.N.Y. 2012) ("[C]ases subsequent to *Dukes* emphasize the importance of adjudicating a class motion only after class-related discovery is complete, discovery that often overlaps substantially with the merits.").
52. Shaw v. Experian Info. Sols., Inc., 306 F.R.D. 293, 297 (S.D. Cal. 2015).
53. *In re* Zurn Pex Plumbing Prod. Liab. Litig., 644 F.3d 604, 612–13 (8th Cir. 2011).
54. *Id.*

Other Ways to Limit Pre-certification Discovery

Aside from seeking to bifurcate discovery, defense counsel should consider other avenues for limiting discovery. One oft-overlooked option is the case management plan. In some cases, defendants may be able to identify a handful of threshold issues that require only limited discovery but are case dispositive. In consumer fraud actions, the case may turn on whether the plaintiff was actually injured, whether the plaintiff saw and relied on the alleged misrepresentation, or whether the plaintiffs' product exhibited the alleged defect. In wage and hour class actions, the case may turn on whether the plaintiff was properly classified as exempt or an independent contractor. Antitrust class actions may turn on whether the plaintiff can establish antitrust injury. The point is that defense counsel may be able to identify a dispositive threshold issue, one that will require only limited discovery. With that issue, the defendant can ask the court to craft a case management plan under which the dispositive issue is addressed first, before expensive class-wide discovery begins. If the defendant can prevail on that issue, there may never be a need to conduct class discovery.

> In some cases, defendants may be able to identify a handful of threshold issues that require only limited discovery but are case dispositive.

The decision in *In re Bayer Healthcare & Merial Ltd. Flea Control Product Marketing & Sales Practices Litigation*, provides a good example of how a case management plan can help avoid expensive class discovery.[55] The case involved flea-and-tick products for pets, with plaintiffs alleging that the advertising was false and misleading. Plaintiffs claimed that, contrary to the advertising, the product did not disperse over an animal's entire body.[56] At the case management conference, the court adopted an evidentiary plan that required defendants to produce the evidence supporting the advertising claim (i.e., that the product did disperse over the animal's entire body) and giving plaintiffs the chance to refute that evidence, while staying other discovery.[57] Once that process was complete, defendants moved for summary judgment, which the court granted. On appeal, the Sixth Circuit affirmed. Defense counsel should look for similarly creative strategies for focusing discovery on the issues that truly matter.

---

55. 752 F.3d 1065, 1072 (6th Cir. 2014).
56. *Id.* at 1068.
57. *Id.* at 1069–70.

Shifting Discovery Costs

Defense counsel also should consider whether to ask plaintiffs to share the cost of pre-certification discovery in the appropriate case. Although there are conflicting decisions, Federal Rule of Civil Procedure 26(b)(2)(C) provides authority for shifting costs as part of the enforcement of proportionality limits. Among the factors the court may consider in enforcing proportionality limits are (1) the specificity of the discovery requests; (2) the likelihood of discovering critical information; (3) the purposes for which the responding party maintains the requested data; (4) the relative benefit to the parties of obtaining the information; (5) the total cost associated with the production; (6) the relative ability of each party to control costs and its incentive to do so; and (7) the resources available to each party.[58] Cost shifting, however, is not the rule, and, in some jurisdictions, courts will consider cost shifting only for discovery requests that seek inaccessible data.[59] Still, in some jurisdictions, cost shifting can be an effective tool for reducing the cost and burden of discovery in class litigation.

One of the most defense-friendly decisions on cost shifting is *Boeynaems v. LA Fitness Int'l, LLC*, mentioned earlier in the plaintiffs' perspective section.[60] In *Boeynaems*, plaintiffs filed a putative class action alleging deceptive trade practices by a fitness club. The defendant provided extensive pre-certification discovery, at its own cost, but plaintiffs were requesting additional materials that could cost hundreds of thousands of dollars to review.[61] After reviewing the additional discovery sought, the court ruled that

> where (1) class certification is pending, and (2) the plaintiffs have asked for very extensive discovery, compliance with which will be very expensive, that absent compelling equitable circumstances to the contrary, the plaintiffs should pay for the discovery they seek.[62]

In reaching this ruling, the court noted that discovery in class actions is often asymmetrical and emphasized that "discovery burdens should

---

58. *F.D.I.C. v. Brudnicki*, 291 F.R.D. 669, 676–77 (N.D. Fla. 2013).

59. S. ex rel. Guardiola v. Renown Health, No. 3:12-CV-00295-LRH, 2015 WL 5056726, at *9 (D. Nev. Aug. 25, 2015) ("many federal courts, including this district and most courts in this circuit to have specifically considered the issue, have held that cost shifting is appropriate only when the ESI is not reasonably accessible").

60. 285 F.R.D. 331, 334–41 (E.D. Pa. 2012).

61. *Id.* at 340–41.

62. *Id.* at 341.

not force either party to succumb to a settlement that is based on the costs of litigation rather than the merits of the case."[63] Although similar decisions are few and far between, *Boeynaems* provides a solid roadmap for cost shifting in the appropriate case.[64]

Offensive Discovery

For defendants facing class litigation, the discovery process does not have to be solely about playing defense. Defense counsel should consider aggressively exploring the plaintiffs' claims, as well as their background, both through formal discovery requests and informal investigation. In many cases, a background investigation can uncover facts that may disqualify the plaintiff from serving as a class representative, including serious criminal convictions, bankruptcies, and overly close connections to plaintiffs' counsel. Look to see if the plaintiff is overly litigious or has served as the named representative multiple times for the same firm. Evaluate the plaintiffs' social media postings to determine if he has posted about the case or the defendant, or engaged in conduct that may be disqualifying.

Background investigation can uncover enormously helpful information. In one recent case, defense counsel determined that the named plaintiff had a suspended driver's license. During deposition, plaintiff claimed to have arrived at the deposition by bus, but was unable to produce a ticket or receipt. During the lunch break, defense counsel monitored the plaintiffs' Twitter feed, which was publicly available, and identified a post where the plaintiff complained about a parking ticket received during the morning's deposition session. After lunch, defense counsel presented the Twitter post as an exhibit, and the plaintiff admitted to lying. The case was dismissed a few days later.

Formal discovery also can be helpful. Insist that the plaintiff produce all documents and communications related to their claims or dealings with the defendant and follow up if there are gaps in the production. It is surprising how often plaintiffs neglect to take reasonable steps to preserve relevant evidence. In one recent case, the plaintiff filed a class

---

63. *Id.* at 342.

64. *See also* Schweinfurth v. Motorola, Inc., No. 1:05CV0024, 2008 WL 4449081, at *2 (N.D. Ohio Sept. 30, 2008) ("Because it does not pertain to phones used by named Plaintiffs and because of the delay in Plaintiffs moving for discovery, the Court has some concerns that such discovery could be used as a weapon to compel settlement," requiring plaintiffs to pay half the cost of production).

action claiming that the defendant's product (a consumer electronics product) contained a latent defect. When asked to produce the product for inspection, the plaintiff was unable to do so because he had discarded it. At deposition, plaintiff admitted he discarded the device *after* filing the lawsuit, leaving no way to test the allegations in the complaint. Again, the case was dismissed shortly after that admission.

When conducting discovery, be sure not to overlook basic issues, including whether the plaintiff actually purchased the product at issue. In one case, discovery showed that the plaintiff, who claimed she was misled based on the product label, actually had not bought the product. Rather, the plaintiffs' husband made the purchase and did so for reasons that had nothing to do with the label. In another case, the plaintiff testified at deposition that she purchased the product at a specific retail location near her home, providing a remarkably detailed account of the transaction. But the plaintiff had one problem. The defendant could prove that its product (an alcoholic beverage) had never been sold at that location because it did not have a liquor license.

Defense counsel also should consider serving discovery requiring plaintiffs to explain their plan for trying the case should it be certified and how each Rule 23 element is satisfied.[65] See Chapter 10, Trial Plans.

PRE-CERTIFICATION ACCESS TO CLASS LIST

In class litigation, plaintiffs often serve discovery requests that seek the names and contact information for all putative class members, or a list of individuals who have complained about a product feature or defect, or a list of current and former employees (in wage and hour cases). These requests for class lists often are one of the most hotly litigated discovery issues in a case. From the plaintiffs' perspective, these lists identify the class she is seeking to represent. These individuals are percipient witnesses, who may have evidence needed to satisfy Rule 23 or the merits of the case. From the defense perspective, a class list has

---

65. *See* Vega v. T-Mobile USA, Inc., 564 F.3d 1256, 1279 (11th Cir. 2009) ("[T]he proposal of a workable trial plan will often go a long way toward demonstrating that manageability concerns do not excessively undermine the superiority of the class action vehicle. Moreover, there is a direct correlation between the importance of a realistic, clear, detailed, and specific trial plan and the magnitude of the manageability problems a putative class action presents. We therefore recommend that district courts make it a usual practice to direct plaintiffs to present feasible trial plans, which should include proposed jury instructions, as early as practicable when seeking class certification.").

nothing to do with proper discovery. If the case is going to be certified, it cannot be based on individualized testimony or evidence from putative class members. And, class lists sometimes are misused to troll for more plaintiffs and other cases.

> Requests for class lists often are one of the most hotly litigated discovery issues.

In 1978, the Supreme Court acknowledged that there is no absolute bar on discovery of putative class member names and addresses.[66] Plaintiffs, however, often cite *Oppenheimer Fund, Inc. v. Sanders*, for the opposite conclusion, namely, that discovery of putative class member contact information generally is permissible. But that interpretation ignores the Court's holding. The *Oppenheimer Fund* decision addressed whether Rule 23(d) or the discovery rules governed the process of compiling a class list for purposes of sending class notice. The Supreme Court held that Rule 23(d) applied, that plaintiffs generally must bear the burden of compiling the list and that it was an abuse of discretion to require defendants to pay third-party costs incurred to create the list.[67] In reaching this conclusion, the Court noted that discovery of class member contact information may be appropriate in certain cases, but concluded that it was not appropriate in that case.[68]

Courts have adopted a wide range of approaches to deciding whether "class list" discovery is permissible. Some courts say that, in class actions, "the disclosure of names, addresses, and telephone numbers is commonly allowed . . . ."[69] Other courts say that discovery of "class members' identities prior to class certification is not favored where plaintiffs' attorneys may be seeking the information to solicit new clients, rather than to establish the propriety of certification."[70]

---

66. Oppenheimer Fund, Inc. v. Sanders, 437 U.S. 340, 354 (1978) ("We do not hold that class members' names and addresses never can be obtained under the discovery rules. There may be instances where this information could be relevant to issues that arise under Rule 23, or where a party has reason to believe that communication with some members of the class could yield information bearing on these or other issues.").

67. *Id.*

68. *Id.* at 354.

69. Shaw v. Experian Info. Sols., Inc., 306 F.R.D. 293, 301 (S.D. Cal. 2015).

70. Hankinson v. Class Action R.T.G. Furniture Corp., No. 15-81139-CIV, 2016 WL 1182768, at *2 (S.D. Fla. Mar. 28, 2016).

In some jurisdictions, courts require a plaintiff seeking contact information to first establish a prima facie basis for class certification.[71] Other decisions focus on whether the plaintiff can show a good faith need for contact information to evaluate or establish the propriety of certification.[72] In some cases, a defendant may be able to avoid producing contact information by not contesting one or more elements of Rule 23, such as numerosity.[73] Some courts, however, "have recognized that the identities of putative class members may be relevant in investigating and analyzing issues related to commonality."[74] Thus, the defendant seeking to avoid producing contact information, and the plaintiff seeking its production, should evaluate the extent to which class member contact information will be relevant to demonstrating commonality and predominance.

As part of this analysis, a defendant should think about how it intends to defend against class certification. If the defendant intends to submit declarations from putative class members to oppose certification, it should pause before taking a hardline position on refusing to produce class member contact information. A court may take a dim view of class member declarations if the defendant refused to provide at least some access to information regarding class members' identities.[75] In evaluating whether to require production of contact information,

---

71. Maes v. JP Morgan Chase, No. 12CV782, 2013 WL 811839, at *1 (S.D. Cal. Mar. 5, 2013) ("Plaintiff carries the burden of making either a prima facie showing that the requirements of Fed. R. Civ. P. 23(a) to maintain a class action have been met or that discovery is likely to produce substantiation of the class allegations.").

72. Stebbins v. S&P Oyster Co., No. 3:16CV00992, 2017 WL 1246334, at *3 (D. Conn. Apr. 3, 2017); Godson v. Eltman, Eltman & Cooper, PC, No. 11-CV-0764, 2013 WL 4832715, at *2 (W.D.N.Y. Sept. 11, 2013) ("As the Court finds no basis to believe that communication with members of the class would assist the Court in determining the appropriateness of certifying a class action, plaintiffs' motion to compel disclosure of the names and addresses of putative class members is denied.").

73. See Swelnis v. Universal Fid. L.P., No. 2:13-CV-104, 2014 WL 1571323, at *3 (N.D. Ind. Apr. 17, 2014) ("The Court concludes that there isn't any reason to think that this information would help Plaintiff establish numerosity.").

74. Mervyn v. Atlas Van Lines, Inc., No. 13 C 3587, 2015 WL 12826474, at *3 (N.D. Ill. Oct. 23, 2015).

75. See Artis v. Deere & Co., 276 F.R.D. 348, 353 (N.D. Cal. 2011) ("As a general rule, before class certification has taken place, all parties are entitled to equal access to persons who potentially have an interest in or relevant knowledge of the subject of the action, but who are not yet parties."); In re Facebook Privacy Litig., No. 5:10-CV-02389-RMW, 2015 WL 3640518, at *2 (N.D. Cal. June 11, 2015) ("Facebook cannot on the one hand seek to deny Plaintiff access to the putative class members as irrelevant to class certification discovery and then on the other hand conduct its own discovery of those very individuals.").

courts also weigh putative class members' privacy rights,[76] balancing the plaintiffs' need against the relevant privacy interests.[77] The trial court also must "expressly identify any potential abuses of the class action procedure that may be created if the discovery is permitted, and weigh the danger of such abuses against the rights of the parties under the circumstances."[78] Courts sometimes resolve these issues by entering a protective order or requiring the parties to provide notice to putative class members and allow them to opt out of having their information produced.[79] Even in cases where putative class member contact information is discoverable because it is relevant to Rule 23, a sampling, rather than a full list, is sometimes considered sufficient.[80] As noted next, courts also may impose restrictions on the parties' communications with putative class members to prevent abuse if class lists are produced.[81]

COMMUNICATION WITH PUTATIVE CLASS MEMBERS

Regardless of whether you represent plaintiffs or defendants, you likely will have an interest in communicating with putative class members.

---

76. Dowell v. Griffin, 275 F.R.D. 613, 617 (S.D. Cal. 2011); Artis v. Deere & Co., 276 F.R.D. 348, 352–53 (N.D. Cal. 2011).

77. *See Artis*, 276 F.R.D. at 352–53 ("Even when discovery of private information is found directly relevant to the issues of ongoing litigation, it will not be automatically allowed; there must then be a 'careful balancing' of the 'compelling public need' for discovery against the 'fundamental right of privacy.'").

78. Adkins v. Apple Inc., No. 14-CV-01619, 2014 WL 4618411, at *5 (N.D. Cal. Sept. 15, 2014).

79. Edward v. Genuine Title, LLC, No. CV-14-0081, 2015 WL 8915564, at *8 (D. Md. Dec. 15, 2015) ("[T]his Court will not suspend Plaintiffs' discovery rights or restrict Plaintiffs' future contact with potential class members, but will enter a Confidentiality Order governing the discovery of sensitive third-party personal and financial information."); Aldapa v. Fowler Packing Co. Inc., 310 F.R.D. 583, 588 (E.D. Cal. 2015) ("[C]ourts have adopted the *Belaire* opt out procedure in employment class actions.").

80. *See, e.g.*, McLaughlin on Class Actions § 11:1 (13th ed.); Johnson v. Bankers Life & Cas. Co., No. 13-CV-144-WMC, 2013 WL 5442374, at *2 (W.D. Wis. Sept. 30, 2013) (requiring that defendant select 50 customers in a random fashion agreed upon by the parties).

81. *See* Velasquez-Monterrosa v. Mi Casita Restaurants, No. 5:14-CV-448, 2015 WL 1964400, at *8 (E.D.N.C. May 1, 2015) ("At the same time, production of the contact information sought in Interrogatory No. 3 presents the risk of recruitment of class members outside the bounds of court supervision and, at this point, unjustified intrusion on the employees' privacy."); Fejzulai v. Sam's W., Inc., No. CV 6:14-3601, 2016 WL 7497235, at *7 (D.S.C. Sept. 20, 2016) (limiting production of class member information, restricting contact to written communications and requiring disclosure to the opposing party).

Plaintiffs' counsel wants to verify their clients' claims and may be looking to add additional plaintiffs to their complaints. Defense counsel need to build a defense to those claims and class certification, and may be seeking to settle with individuals before a class is certified. Defendants may also need to continue normal business with putative class members or may also be concerned about the impact on their customer relationships. But whether counsel can engage in such communications with putative class members will depend on several factors, including the law and ethical rules where the case is pending, whether a class has already been certified, whether counsel represents the plaintiff or defendant, and whether the communication is being made for a proper purpose.

Many of these issues stem from concerns about violating Model Rule of Professional Conduct 4.2, which prohibits counsel from engaging in ex parte communications with represented parties. In the context of a class action, the question is: At what point are putative class members represented by plaintiffs' counsel? Although the question has been answered, it has not been answered uniformly by all courts. A handful of jurisdictions have held that putative class members are represented by plaintiffs' counsel as soon as the complaint is filed, which means that defense counsel cannot engage in ex parte communications with putative class members in those jurisdictions.[82] However, the majority of jurisdictions disagree, holding instead that putative class members are unrepresented before class certification.[83] This means plaintiffs and defense counsel both would be seeking to communicate with someone who is not their client.[84]

---

82. Dondore v. NGK Metals Corp., 152 F. Supp. 2d 662, 666 (E.D. Pa. 2001); Corll v. Edward D. Jones & Co., 646 N.E.2d 721 (Ind. Ct. App. 1995); Rankin v. Bd. of Educ., 174 F.R.D. 695, 697–98 (D. Kan. 1997); Pollar v. Judson Steel Corp., No. 82-cv-6833, 1984 WL 161273, at *2 (N.D. Cal. Feb. 3, 1984); Impervious Paint Indus. Inc. v. Ashland Oil, 508 F. Supp. 720, 723 (W.D. Ky. 1981) (from the time the complaint is filed "the implication is unavoidable that defendants' counsel must treat plaintiff class members as represented by counsel").

83. See Castaneda v. Burger King Corp., No. C 08-4262, 2009 WL 2382688, at *4 (N.D. Cal. July 31, 2009) (collecting cases and treatises finding same); see RESTATEMENT (THIRD) OF LAW GOVERNING LAWYERS § 99 cmt. 1 (2000) ("[A]ccording to the majority of decisions, once the proceeding has been certified as a class action the members of the class are considered clients of the lawyer for the class.").

84. Some states, such as California, allow defendants to subpoena a limited number of putative class member depositions. National Solar Equip. Owners' Assn. v. Gumman Corp., 235 Cal. App. 3d 1273, 1283 (1991). Written discovery from putative class members is generally not permitted. Id. at 1282.

In majority jurisdictions, counsel for both parties therefore must take care not to violate Model Rule 4.3's prohibition against providing legal advice to unrepresented persons when speaking with putative class members. Additionally, plaintiffs' counsel must remember that their communications with putative class members aimed at encouraging participation in the class or service as a class representative are governed by their state's ethical rules regarding soliciting clients.[85]

Nevertheless, communications by both parties are generally permitted before class certification. In *Gulf Oil Co. v. Bernard*,[86] the Supreme Court held that a district court could not limit plaintiffs' counsel's ability to communicate with the putative class members absent a "clear record and specific findings that reflect a weighing of the need for a limitation [on communications] and the potential interference with the rights of the parties."[87] *Gulf Oil's* holding has been extended to allow similar communications with putative class members by defense counsel, and it is generally understood that, in interpreting their powers under Rule 23, a court "must not interfere with any party's ability to communicate freely with putative class members,"[88] because for class action purposes "both parties need to be able to communicate with putative members . . . to engage in discovery regarding issues relevant to class certification—from the earliest stages of class litigation."[89]

Accordingly, provided the defendant has not refused to identify class members, as discussed earlier, defense counsel can generally communicate with putative class members before class certification to establish defenses to certification motions or the merits of plaintiffs' claims. For example, in a consumer fraud case, defense counsel may want to speak with other consumers to see if they also relied on certain representations in the same manner as the named plaintiff, which could relate to whether individual issues of law or fact predominate under Rule 23(b)(3) or whether the named plaintiffs' reliance was reasonable. In most cases, neither the parties nor their counsel are required to obtain prior

---

85. *See, e.g.*, MODEL RULE OF PROF'L CONDUCT R. 7.3.

86. 452 U.S. 89, 102 (1988).

87. *Id.*

88. Williams v. Chartwell Fin. Servs., Ltd., 204 F.3d 748, 759 (7th Cir. 2000).

89. Austen v. Catterton Partners V, LP, 831 F. Supp. 2d 559, 567 (D. Conn. 2011); *accord* Coleman v. Jenny Craig, Inc., No. 11-CV-1301, 2013 WL 2896884, at *7 (S.D. Cal. June 12, 2013); Wiegele v. FedEx Ground Package Sys., No. 06–CV01330, 2007 WL 628041 (S.D. Cal. Feb. 8, 2007) (holding as a general rule that before certification, all parties are entitled to equal access to putative class members who potentially have an interest in or relevant knowledge of the subject of the action).

judicial approval before communicating with putative class members unless needed to prevent serious misconduct.[90] However, counsel must be careful not to abuse its ability to communicate with putative members, as that ability can be taken away.

Although court restrictions on communications between counsel and members of a putative class may invoke First Amendment concerns in certain cases, "a district court has both the duty and the broad authority to exercise control over a class action and to enter appropriate orders governing the conduct of counsel and parties."[91] A communication with putative class members will be considered improper and a protective order granted if the court finds a clear record that it "threatens the proper functioning of the [class] litigation."[92] However, any protective order granted must further, rather than hinder, the policies of and purpose of Rule 23 and be "carefully drawn . . . to limit[] speech as little as possible."[93]

Such a threat is often shown where the communication coerces putative class members from participating in the litigation, contains misleading or confusing statements, seeks to undermine cooperation or confidence in class counsel, or fails to provide the putative class members with sufficient information to fairly evaluate a settlement offer.[94] Notably, oral communications with putative class members have been

---

90. Salgado v. O'Lakes, No. 1:13-CV-0798-LJO-SMS, 2014 WL 7272784, at *10 (E.D. Cal. Dec. 18, 2014); *Castanada*, 2009 WL 2382688, at *5; Moreno v. Autozone, Inc., No. C-05-4432 MJJ EMC, 2007 WL 2288165, at *1 (N.D. Cal. Aug. 3, 2007).

91. *Gulf Oil*, 452 U.S. at 100; *see* Recinos-Recinos v. Express Forestry, Inc., No. 05-cv-1355, 2006 WL 197030, at *9 (E.D. La. Jan. 24, 2006) (distinguishing between cases invoking First Amendment concerns, such as racial discrimination, and less protected commercial speech cases, such as an employment or commercial case).

92. Cox Nuclear Med. v. Gold Cup Coffee Servs., Inc., 214 F.R.D. 696, 697–98 (S.D. Ala. 2003) (collecting cases); *Jeld-Wen, Inc.*, 250 F.R.D. at 561; *Hampton Hardware, Inc.*, 156 F.R.D. at 632.

93. *Gulf Oil*, 452 U.S. at 102.

94. *See id.* at 101 ("An order limiting communications between parties and potential class members should be based on a clear record and specific findings that reflect a weighing of the need for a limitation and the potential interference with the rights of the parties."); *In re* Southeastern Milk Antitrust Litig., No. 2:08-md-1000, 2009 WL 3747130, at *3 (E.D. Tenn. Nov. 3, 2009) (prohibiting communication where absence of specific information made communication misleading); Lee v. Am. Airlines, Inc., No. 3:01-CV-1179P, 2002 WL 226347, at *2 (N.D. Tex. Feb. 12, 2002) (allowing communication where there was no clear evidence of abusive or unethical communications; explaining that "the mere possibility of abuses does not justify routine adoption of communication bans"); Recinos-Recinos v. Express Forestry, Inc., No. 05-cv-1355, 2006 WL 197030, at *9 (issuing protective order where evidence demonstrated "a campaign designed to threaten, intimidate and coerce plaintiffs, opt-in plaintiffs and potential class members to capitulate and withdraw their pending claims was in fact perpetrated").

found to be very susceptible to abuse and "wont to produce distorted statements on the one hand and the coercion of susceptible individuals on the other."[95] To satisfy this standard, the "threat" must have occurred or be likely to occur, and not be merely speculative.[96] For example, in *Southeastern Milk Antitrust Litigation*, the defendants requested the court's review and approval of a communication conveying a proposed settlement offer to putative class members. The district court prohibited the proposed settlement communication, finding it to be "confusing at best, and misleading at worst," because putative class members lacked sufficient information to fairly evaluate the offer in that a protective order shielded important documents from their view.[97]

Accordingly, despite the general guideline permitting communications with putative class members, federal courts recognize that direct communications with putative class members can lead to abuse, and counsel should think carefully about whether to have such communications, the timing of such communications, the content of such communications (for instance, disclosing the lawsuit and class counsel's contact information, if a release or declaration is sought), and whether to communicate orally or in writing.

The discretion to limit communications with putative class members resides with the district courts, and this supervisory authority exists even before a class is certified.[98] A showing of actual harm is not always necessary.[99] While district courts often differ in the degree of potential harm required to justify the granting of an order, they generally agree that communications that are misleading, coercive, or have a "chilling

---

95. Kleiner v. First National Bank of Atlanta, 751 F.2d 1193, 1206 (11th Cir. 1985) (citing Ohralik v. Ohio State Bar Ass'n, 436 U.S. 447, 457 (1978)); *accord Recinos-Recinos*, 2006 WL 197030, at *9 (issuing protective order to stop oral communications with putative class members, despite defendant's production of self-serving declaration from speaker that he did not believe his communications were threatening); *Hernandez*, 2015 WL 7176352, at *5–6; *Austen*, 831 F. Supp. at 567 (quoting MANUAL FOR COMPLEX LITIGATION § 21.12, at 248 (4th ed. 2004) ("Direct communications with class members . . . whether by plaintiffs or defendants, can lead to abuse.")).

96. *Gulf Oil*, 452 U.S. at 104; *Cox Nuclear Med.*, 214 F.R.D. at 697 n.3.

97. *In re* Southeastern Milk Antitrust Litig., No. 2:08-md-1000, 2009 WL 3747130, at *2 (E.D. Tenn. Nov. 3, 2009).

98. *See, e.g., In re* Initial Public Offering Sec. Litig., 499 F. Supp. 2d 415, 418 n.13 (S.D.N.Y. 2007); Piper v. RGIS Inventory Specialists, Inc., No. C–07–32, 2007 WL 1690887, at *7 (N.D. Cal. June 11, 2007); Ralph Oldsmobile Inc. v. Gen. Motors Corp., No. 99 Civ. 4567, 2001 WL 1035132, at *2 (S.D.N.Y. Sept. 7, 2001).

99. *See, e.g., In re* School Asbestos Litig., 842 F.2d 671, 683 (3d Cir. 1988); Hampton Hardware, Inc. v. Cotter & Co., 156 F.R.D. 630, 633 (N.D. Tex. 1994).

effect" on the litigation against putative class members should be limited.[100] Recent district court opinions also have not strayed in the interpretation or application of the *Gulf Oil* exception.[101]

Counsel must also remember that communications with putative class members before certification may be discoverable by the opposing party, depending on the applicable privilege and confidentiality rules governing the action.[102] Once the class is certified, all the rules change. Defense counsel's ability to communicate with absent class members ex parte disappears per Rule 4.2, while class counsel's ability to communicate with absent class members and provide legal advice expands, as they then may be considered class counsel's clients.

DISCOVERY CONCERNING COMMUNICATIONS BETWEEN PLAINTIFFS' COUNSEL AND PUTATIVE CLASS MEMBERS

Communications between class counsel and putative class members may not be discoverable, as they may constitute privileged

---

100. *See, e.g., Hernandez*, 2015 WL 7176352, at *14 (holding defense settlement solicitations against putative class members without providing adequate notice to be misleading); Wright v. Adventures Rolling Cross Country, Inc., No. C–12–982, 2012 WL 2239797, at *5 (N.D. Cal. June 15, 2012) (limiting communications after defendants contacts with potential class members "chilled" participation); Urtubia v. B.A. Victory Corp., 857 F. Supp. 2d 476, 485 (S.D.N.Y. 2012) (limiting defendants' contact with potential class members where employment relationship placed defendant in a position to exercise "strong coercion"); *Jeld-Wen, Inc.*, 250 F.R.D. at 561 (recognizing unilateral communications between a party and putative class members have high potential for coercion); Jones v. Casey's Gen. Stores, 517 F. Supp. 2d 1080, 1088 (S.D. Iowa 2007) (limiting communications with putative class members with potential to mislead); Wiginton v. Ellis, No. 02 C 6832, 2003 WL 22232907, at *2 (N.D. Ill. 2003) (noting communications that seek to discourage participation in class action to be misleading).

101. *See, e.g.,* Chime v. Peak Sec. Plus, Inc., No. 13-cv-470, 2016 WL 3440593, at *3 (E.D.N.Y. June 20, 2016) (noting that [a] protective order restricting communication "should be based on a clear record and specific findings); Talavera v. Leprino Foods Co., No. 1:15-cv-105, 2016 WL 880550, at *5 (E.D. Cal. Mar. 8, 2016); Cheverez v. Plains all Am. Pipeline, LP, No. 15-cv-4113, 2016 WL 861107, at *3 (C.D. Cal. Mar. 3, 2016) (granting limiting order because defendants' advertisements were likely to result in abuse of the class action process).

102. For example, in class actions where jurisdiction for state-law claims is based on CAFA, privilege and confidentiality issues are governed by the forum state's law, not federal law.

attorney-client communications.[103] This is true even if the attorney was never hired.[104] Indeed, for the last 20 years, class actions often include plaintiffs' counsel advertising their cases on the Internet in hopes of finding additional plaintiffs or increasing class participation.[105] When potential class members contact plaintiffs' counsel independently or in response to solicitations (e.g., by submitting online forms or questionnaires or e-mailing or calling plaintiffs' counsel) courts often find that they were seeking confidential legal advice that is protected from discovery, even when the solicitation or questionnaire explicitly disclaimed confidentiality.[106]

Counsel should remember, however, that in CAFA and other diversity actions based on state law causes of action, whether a communication is privileged depends on how the attorney-client privilege is defined under the state's law that also governs the substantive issues.[107] Despite potential variances in state law, the privilege's application usually requires a confidential communication with a client or potential client seeking legal advice. Because a solicitation letter or advertisement is neither a communication from a client seeking legal advice nor an attorney's response to a request for legal advice, they are usually not found to be privileged communications.[108]

A few courts have also analyzed whether solicitation letters may nonetheless qualify as protected attorney-work product under Rule 26(b)(3). Where the solicitation failed to contain counsel's mental

---

103. Although federal courts have not issued many opinions discussing whether a defendant is entitled to discovery into communications made between counsel and putative class members following the 2015 amendment to the Federal Rules of Civil Procedure, their general approach on this issue remain fairly consistent to before the amendments. *See* Barton v. Smithkline Beecham, 410 F.3d 1104, 1109–11 (9th Cir. 2005); Fangman v. Genuine Title, LLC, No. CV RDB-14-0081, 2016 WL 3362538, at *4 (D. Md. June 17, 2016); *Jones*, 250 F.R.D. at 563.

104. *Fangman*, 2016 WL 3362538, at *4; *In re* Grand Jury Proceedings Under Seal, 947 F.2d 1188, 1190 (4th Cir. Va. 1991) (citing United States v. Dennis, 843 F.2d 652, 656 (2d Cir. 1988)).

105. *Barton*, 410 F.3d at 1109–11 (recognizing common use of Internet advertising in 2005).

106. *Id.* (applying California's attorney-client privilege).

107. *See, e.g., id.*

108. *Fangman*, 2016 WL 3362538, at *3 (quoting Petry v. Prosperity Mortgage Co., No. WMN-08-1642 (Gauvey, J.) (D. Md. Aug. 13, 2010) (ECF No. 157) (determining that "solicitation letters are not privileged because an attorney-client relationship had not yet been established.")); E.E.O.C. v. CRST Van Expedited, Inc., No. C07-0095, 2009 WL 136025, at *3–5 (N.D. Iowa Jan. 20, 2009); Baker v. Gen. Motors Corp., 209 F.3d 1051, 1054 (8th Cir. 2000).

impressions or legal theories, at least a few district courts have found them to only qualify as "ordinary work product," which, while protected from discovery, is discoverable if the defendant establishes that it cannot obtain substantially equivalent materials by other means.[109] Discovery may be permitted, for example, if the court finds that counsel's representations in the solicitations are relevant to the class member's credibility. Accordingly, in drafting any such solicitations, plaintiffs' counsel would be prudent to do so under the assumption that it may be discoverable and later used as an exhibit in the action. Nevertheless, discovery of solicitation letters remains the exception to the general rule that communications between plaintiffs' counsel and putative class members are privileged.

DISCOVERY AGAINST ABSENT CLASS MEMBERS

"Discovery from absent members of the putative class is not the norm."[110] Traditionally, absent class member discovery is "rarely permitted because absent members are not 'parties' to the action."[111] Some courts refuse to permit any type of discovery on absent class members before certification.[112]

Other courts take a more flexible approach, allowing discovery where: "(1) the information sought is not designed to take undue advantage of class members or reduce the size of the class; (2) the discovery is necessary; (3) responding to the discovery requests would not require the assistance of counsel; and (4) the discovery seeks information not already known by the proponent."[113] Most courts agree, however, that "[d]eposing absent class members requires greater justification than written discovery."[114] Most courts now follow a flexible approach that

---

109. *CRST Van Expedited*, 2009 WL 136025, at *3–5; *Fangman*, 2016 WL 3362538, at *3; EEOC v. Pioneer Hotel, Inc., Case No. 2:11-cv-01588, 2014 WL 4987418 (D. Nev. Oct. 6, 2014).

110. McLaughlin, *supra* note 80, § 3:9.

111. Stinson v. City of New York, No. 10 CIV. 4228, 2015 WL 8675360, at *1 (S.D.N.Y. Dec. 11, 2015).

112. Carlin v. DairyAmerica, Inc., No. 109CV00430, 2017 WL 4410107, at *4 (E.D. Cal. Oct. 4, 2017) ("This Court declines to adopt a rule permitting discovery upon 'absent' class members.").

113. Taylor v. Shippers Transp. Express, Inc., No. CV132092, 2014 WL 12561080, at *2 (C.D. Cal. Apr. 30, 2014).

114. *See* Discovery from Class Members, Ann. Manual Complex Lit. § 21.41 (4th ed.).

permits, in the first instance, written interrogatories and document requests to be propounded to absent class members where the information requested is important and the discovery is not designed to harass class members or used as a device to persuade them not to participate in the class."[115] "If the responses to documentary discovery suggest a need for additional information, courts may authorize depositions of certain class members."[116]

The decision in *Arredondo v. Delano Farms Co.* illustrates the type of showing that may warrant discovery from absent class members.[117] The case involved a certified class alleging off-the-clock work. The defendant sought to depose approximately 200 absent class members, representing less than 1 percent of the overall class, as part of a pilot study they intended to use to refute plaintiffs' representative evidence on liability. Concluding that "[d]efendants have made a persuasive case that it is necessary for them to conduct the discovery at this juncture and that such discovery is relevant to the reliability of sampling and the statistical study to be used to establish liability," the court allowed the 200 depositions of absent class members.[118] Courts also are more willing to allow absent class member discovery where those individuals injected themselves into the case, are identified as witnesses, or previously were named plaintiffs.[119] Defense counsel, however, should be

---

115. McLaughlin, *supra* note 80, § 3:9.

116. *Id.*

117. No. 1:09-CV-01247, 2014 WL 5106401, at *6 (E.D. Cal. Oct. 10, 2014).

118. *Id.; see also* Indergit v. Rite Aid Corp., No. 08CIV9361, 2015 WL 7736533, at *2 (S.D.N.Y. Nov. 30, 2015), *objections overruled*, No. 08-CV-9361, 2016 WL 236248 (S.D.N.Y. Jan. 20, 2016) (allowing absent class member depositions regarding job duties in misclassification case).

119. Antoninetti v. Chipotle, Inc., No. 06CV2671, 2011 WL 2003292, at *1 (S.D. Cal. May 23, 2011) ("Although Courts do not usually allow discovery from absent class members, the rules pertaining to such discovery are flexible, especially where the proposed deponents have been identified as potential witnesses or have otherwise 'injected' themselves into the litigation."); Makaeff v. Trump Univ., LLC, No. 10-CV-0940, 2013 WL 990918, at *6 (S.D. Cal. Mar. 12, 2013) ("[A] court in this judicial district noted that federal courts in California allow discovery of absent potential class members when they are identified as witnesses, or submit declarations, or are represented by the plaintiffs' counsel"); Johnson v. Ford Motor Co., No. 3:13-CV-06529, 2015 WL 3540802, at *3 (S.D.W. Va. June 4, 2015) ("[T]hese four individuals were previously named parties, who affirmatively interjected themselves into the prosecution of the claims and maintained their representative roles until opting for voluntary dismissals").

hesitant to seek sanctions against absent class members, as some courts view doing so as evidence of bad faith and a reason to deny discovery.[120]

ESI CONSIDERATIONS

Virtually every class action will involve the preservation and production of electronically stored information (ESI). While ESI is also an issue in non-class actions, the amount of ESI a defendant must preserve in those cases is naturally more limited by the fact that the claims and defenses at issue are restricted to those of the named plaintiffs. In contrast, the amount of ESI in class actions is magnified by the number of putative class members. Because of this, ESI is a common topic of disagreement, with several interests and duties at play:

- **Duty to preserve evidence.** Once litigation is foreseeable, the company is under a legal duty to preserve (i.e., identify, locate, and maintain) information that may be potentially relevant to the litigation, even though any certification of a class may still be years in the future.
- **Duty of diligence.** Counsel has an ethical duty of zealous representation, which may include plaintiffs' counsel advocating to ensure that the company fully complies with its preservation duty so that documents necessary to prove the class members' claims are not inadvertently destroyed pursuant to the company's document destruction policies.
- **Duty of cooperation.** The parties, their counsel, and the court share a duty under Rule 1 to ensure an "inexpensive determination" of the action,[121] which a company may find difficult in some cases, depending on the cost to retain all potentially relevant records and accompanying metadata (the data behind the data) for each potential class member throughout the pendency of the case. Any excessive burden or expense must be measured in light of Rule 26(b)(2)(C)'s proportionality standard.

---

120. *See* Cox v. Am. Cast Iron Pipe Co., 784 F.2d 1546, 1556–57 (11th Cir. 1986) ("[W]e decline to approve the use of the discovery sanction of dismissal against passive class members in a class action suit even to the extent that it may be permitted"); *Arredondo*, 2014 WL 5106401, at *10 ("Defendants assured the Court that they will not seek to remove absent class members from the action for failure to appear at depositions.").

121. Fed. R. Civ. P. 1.

Because of these clashing interests, counsel often disagree as to the proper scope of the defendant's duty to preserve such records. If ESI or its metadata is important to proving the substantive claims, plaintiffs' counsel should raise the issue with defense counsel during the Rule 26(f) conference.

To assist with this preservation of ESI discussion, the parties should be prepared to discuss the following four issues related to the location of potential ESI.

1. **Custodians.** The people (including their names, titles, and relation to the litigation) most likely to have discoverable ESI in their possession, custody, or control, as well as the type of information under their control.
2. **Non-custodial data sources.** The non-human locations where data is stored, such as network or shared drives, servers, etc., that are likely to contain discoverable ESI.
3. **Third-party data sources.** Sources operated by third parties that are likely to have discoverable ESI, such as third-party e-mail accounts, mobile device providers, cloud storage, etc.
4. **Inaccessible data.** Sources that are likely to contain discoverable ESI, but which cannot be reasonable accessed under Rule 26(b)(2)(C)(i).

With this information in mind, the parties should try to reach agreement on the date range, sources, and metadata fields that need to be preserved. If the parties cannot agree, they can set forth their competing positions in their Joint Rule 26(f) Statement for the court to address at the Rule 16 Case Management Conference. It is critical that this issue be resolved early—before any records are destroyed or defendants incur additional costs to unnecessarily preserve evidence.

This duty to preserve ESI does not only apply to the defendant, however. A named plaintiff has a duty to preserve evidence as well. For the named plaintiff, such ESI may include e-mails, social media posts and pages, text messages, chats, online postings, computer files and documents, voicemail messages, and digital photographs. At the time they are retained, plaintiffs' counsel should educate their clients both orally and in writing (e.g., in the retention agreement) about their duty to preserve such evidence. This message should include a clear warning not to delete or otherwise alter any postings or photos already existing on social media websites, like Facebook. The client's deletion of information, however, does not delete the information from the social media platform's servers and can still be accessed by defendants through a subpoena to the platform. However, plaintiffs' counsel may advise their clients to change their privacy settings and to not share additional photos or posts on social media from that point forward.

In addition to discussing the scope of the parties' duty to preserve ESI evidence at the Rule 26(f) conference, counsel should discuss implementing an ESI protocol to govern the production of such evidence in the case. Early resolution of this issue is best to ensure that producing parties are not faced with having to later reproduce documents in a usable format. Many courts have standard ESI protocols drafted and posted to their websites that the parties can adopt or use as samples in drafting their own protocol.[122]

If a model ESI protocol is unavailable in the forum, counsel should work together to establish a universal ESI protocol that is agreeable to all sides and covers all productions. Instead of requiring an all native file form with all metadata preserved or TIFF images with corresponding load files, counsel's ESI production specs may agree to accept other forms of production and limit the categories of metadata that may be sought.

ESI should never be produced, however, as PDFs without load files, unless the requesting party has agreed, because such files lack the original metadata, are reviewable only as individual files, and lack full text, which is required to run searches on the documents' text for target information. Courts have repeatedly upheld ESI requests that call for TIFF files with a corresponding load file containing some of the identified metadata fields and extracted text (for instance, the transmittal information for e-mails).[123] Indeed, as the *Aguilar* court recognized, there is no longer a presumption against the production of metadata, especially in light of *"the need to produce reasonably accessible metadata that will enable the receiving party to have the same access, search, and display the information as the producing party. . . ."*[124] Relying on the

---

122. For example, the Northern District of California has ESI guidelines, a checklist, standing order, and model ESI protocol available on its website at http://www.cand .uscourts.gov/eDiscoveryGuidelines.

123. *See, e.g.*, Wilson v. Conair Corp., 1:14-CV-00894, 2015 WL 1994270, at *4 (E.D. Cal. Apr. 30, 2015) (ordering the defendant to produce discovery in TIFF format with associated metadata).

124. Aguilar v. Immigration & Customs Enf't Div. of U.S. Dep't of Homeland Sec., 255 F.R.D. 350, 356 (S.D.N.Y. 2008) (emphasis original) (quoting *Sedona Principles 2d*, Principle 12).

commentary to the *Sedona Principles 2nd*, the *Aguilar* court explained the practical benefits of producing documents with load files, not just images:

> [A] production in static image form, such as TIFF or PDF, can be Bates numbered and redacted, but entails the loss of metadata and involves significant processing time. *Id.* The commentary notes that in "an effort to replicate the usefulness of native files while retaining the advantages of static productions, image format productions typically are accompanied by 'load files,' which are ancillary files that may contain textual content and relevant system metadata." *Id.* One marked disadvantage of this format is that the production involves significant costs; it also does not work well for spreadsheets and databases.
>
> Weighing the advantages and disadvantages of different forms of production, the Conference concluded that even if native files are requested, it is sufficient to produce memoranda, emails, and electronic records in PDF or TIFF format accompanied by a load file containing searchable text and selected metadata. *Id.* Cmt. 12b Illus. i. The Conference explained that this "satisfies the goals of Principle 12 because the production is in usable form, e.g., electronically searchable and paired with essential metadata."[125]

Accordingly, counsel should meet and confer until they have reached an agreement to produce documents in a reasonably usable form, which generally will mean that the documents are accompanied by load files containing both sufficient metadata and extracted full text.[126] With this said, not all metadata is created equal and production of full metadata (for instance, the substance of changes in a Word document) can often await a showing of need for a particular document. Likewise, production of native files is not common except for particular file types (for instance, spreadsheets are sometimes produced in a native format). If counsel are unable to reach an agreement, they may consider submitting to the court a draft ESI protocol that contains agreed upon provisions as well as each sides' proposal for provisions upon which agreement could not be reached, and ask the court to select the final version of each contested provision.

As the requesting party, counsel must ensure to either have an ESI protocol in place before issuing discovery or provide instructions as to how the responding party is to produce ESI. For example, in *Aguilar*

---

125. *Aguilar*, 255 F.R.D. at 356–57.
126. *See, e.g., id.* at 353 ("*A typical request might be to produce Word documents in TIFF format with a load file containing the relevant system metadata.*") (italics original).

the court rejected the plaintiffs' request for metadata because it came after the defendant had nearly completed collecting the responsive documents.[127]

If counsel have not agreed upon an ESI protocol, they should be careful to address the production of ESI in their document requests to ensure they receive the type of information they need when the documents are first produced or, at least, open the door for the producing party to address the issue before production. For example, if certain metadata fields are crucial to your case, counsel would want to request that the documents be processed in a form that provides those metadata fields.

Federal Rule of Civil Procedure 34(b) "permits the requesting party to designate the form or forms in which it wants electronically stored information produced."[128] And Rule 34(a)(1)(A) allows a party to request "the responding party to translate electronic data into a 'reasonably usable form.'"[129] While the needs of the case may dictate the form of production to request in your instructions, the following are just two examples of instructions addressing the form of production required for ESI.

Sample A

Documents that comprise electronically stored information shall be produced in native file format to the extent that such native files are in a directly obtainable medium. Documents that comprise electronically stored information that does not exist in a directly obtainable medium shall be translated into a reasonably usable form that preserves all metadata for such documents.

Sample B

Documents that comprise electronically stored information shall be produced as Group IV Single-Page TIFF files (minimum 300 DPI) with multi-page text files, and Concordance .dat and Opticon .opt load files, and photographs produced in response to these requests shall include all metadata.

The responding party has no obligation to produce non-ESI, such as paper or tangible evidence, according to these instructions. However, once a requesting party has specifically identified the form of production required for ESI, the burden is on the responding/producing party

---

127. 255 F.R.D. at 353.
128. Fed. R. Civ. P. 34(b), Advisory Notes to 2006 Amendment.
129. D'Onofrio v. SFX Sports Group, Inc., 247 F.R.D. 43, 47 (D.D.C. 2008).

to timely object to the instruction and show why the information, such as metadata, should not be produced.[130] And, as required by the 2015 Rule Amendments, any such objection is required to be "stated with specificity" and "state whether any responsive materials are being withheld on the basis of that objection."[131] Indeed, as one court relying upon the *Sedona Principles* explained,

> [t]he burden to object to the disclosure of metadata is appropriately placed on the party ordered to produce its electronic documents as they are ordinarily maintained because that party already has access to the metadata and is in the best position to determine whether producing it is objectionable.[132]

It further explained that "[p]lacing the burden on the producing party is further supported by the fact that metadata is an inherent part of an electronic document, and its removal ordinarily requires an affirmative act by the producing party that alters the electronic document."[133] ESI issues such as which metadata fields to produce, therefore, must be addressed by the parties, either through agreement and cooperation or through a timely and specific objection to a document requests' demand for a particular format or scope.

ROLLING PRODUCTIONS

Although not unique to class litigation, both plaintiffs' counsel and defense counsel should be cognizant of the 2015 Amendments to Rule 34, particularly those requiring that (1) objections be stated with

---

130. *See The Sedona Principles, Second Edition: Best Practices Recommendations and Principles for Addressing Electronic Document Production*, cmt. 12.a. (Sedona Conference Working Group Series 2007) (*Sedona Principles, Second Edition, 2007*) (citing Williams v. Sprint/United Mgmt. Co., 230 F.R.D. 640, 652 (D. Kan. 2005) ("The initial burden with regard to the disclosure of the metadata would therefore be placed on the party to whom the request or order to produce is directed.")); *accord* FED. R. CIV. P. 34, Advisory Committee Notes, 2006 Amendments ("In the written response to the production requests that Rule 34 requires, the responding party must state the form it intends to use for producing electronically stored information if the requesting party does not specify a form or if the responding party objects to a form that the requesting party specifies."); *Aguilar*, 255 F.R.D. at 355 (explaining that the requesting party is entitled to specify the form of production, including the production of metadata in a load file, and it is the responding party's burden to object).

131. FED. R. CIV. P. 34, Advisory Committee Notes, 2015 Amendments.

132. Williams v. Sprint/United Mgmt. Co., 230 F.R.D. 640, 652 (D. Kan. 2005) (relying upon *Sedona Principles* 12.a.). Courts have found the *Sedona Principles* instructive with respect to electronic discovery issues. *See, e.g., Aguilar*, 255 F.R.D. at 355.

133. *Id.*

specificity, (2) the response state if documents are being withheld on the basis of an objection, and (3) documents be produced by a specific date:

- **Rule 34(b)(2)(B).** For each item or category, the response must either state that inspection and related activities will be permitted as requested or state with specificity the grounds for objecting to the request, including the reasons. The responding party may state that it will produce copies of documents or of electronically stored information instead of permitting inspection. The production must then be completed no later than the time for inspection specified in the request or another reasonable time specified in the response.
- **Rule 34(b)(2)(C).** An objection must state whether any responsive materials are being withheld on the basis of that objection. An objection to part of a request must specify the part and permit inspection of the rest.

The advisory notes explain that "production must be completed either by the time for inspection specified in the request or by another reasonable time specifically identified in the response. When it is necessary to make the production in stages the response should specify the beginning and end dates of the production."[134] The advisory notes also state that it is acceptable to indicate whether materials have been withheld by stating "the limits that have controlled the search for responsive and relevant materials."[135]

Courts are enforcing these requirements. For example, in *Moser v. Holland*, the defendant's objections were boilerplate, and the court ruled that "[g]eneral boilerplate objections are inappropriate and unpersuasive. The recent amendments to Rule 34 make this particularly clear."[136] Similarly, in *Grodzitsky v. America Honda Motor Co.*, the court emphasized that amendments to Rule 34 "place a burden on the parties to ensure that a reasonable and complete search is conducted and that all responsive material is either produced, or that it is withheld under a proper objection."[137] The court also required that the defendant submit a "declaration signed under penalty of perjury by a corporate officer or

134. FED. R. CIV. P. 34, Advisory Notes for the 2015 Amendment.
135. *Id.*
136. No. 2:14-CV-02188, 2016 WL 426670, at *3 (E.D. Cal. Feb. 4, 2016).
137. No. CV121142, 2017 WL 2616917, at *3 (C.D. Cal. June 13, 2017).

director attesting that it is not withholding any information on the basis of its general objection . . . ."[138]

Another court recently issued a "wake up call" to counsel, expressly stating that responses to discovery requests must:

- State grounds for objections with specificity;
- State in the objection whether any responsive materials are being withheld on the basis of that objection; and
- Specify the time for production and, if a rolling production, when production will begin and when it will be concluded.[139]

The court continued,

> [f]rom now on in cases before this Court, any discovery response that does not comply with Rule 34's requirement to state objections with specificity (and to clearly indicate whether responsive material is being withheld on the basis of objection) will be deemed a waiver of all objections (except as to privilege).[140]

Counsel defending or prosecuting class litigation would be well advised to heed these admonitions.

CONCLUSION

Both plaintiffs and defendants should carefully map out the discovery they need to make their eventual arguments under Rule 23's factors for class certification. Nevertheless, neither side is served by overbroad discovery or unnecessarily narrow discovery responses that will create needless discovery fights. Failure to carefully plan discovery can leave either side with a failure of proof. It is the plaintiffs' burden to show evidence—not merely legal argument to demonstrate that all of Rule 23's elements have been met. Likewise, the defendant cannot merely make hypothetical arguments about predominance, but should come forth with evidence to demonstrate real variations in the class.

---

138. *Id.* at *5.

139. Fischer v. Forrest, No. 14CIV1304, 2017 WL 773694, at *1 (S.D.N.Y. Feb. 28, 2017) (bullet list in original).

140. *Id.* at *3.

Appendix

Sample Working Proof Outline

In May 2017, Skyline Organic, a well-known dairy company, faced a storm of negative publicity in the wake of an investigative report. Although inspectors, who Skyline hired and directly paid, had certified its products as organic for years, a *Washington-Post Gazette* story detailed how the company allegedly failed to meet U.S. Department of Agriculture standards. Federal regulations require organic dairies to permit their cows to graze every day over the course of the growing season, meaning they must be grass-fed and not enclosed in barns. The *Post-Gazette* made occasional visits to the dairy complex in California and hired a satellite imagery firm, and it found that no more than 10 percent of Skyline's cattle was ever outside grazing.

The day after the story broke, Charlie Utter, who regularly purchased Skyline 2% organic milk, became incensed that he had been funding what he viewed as animal cruelty. Expecting that many other consumers felt the same way, he contacted a class action attorney. The attorney filed a complaint in the Northern District of California that alleged violations of California's Unfair Competition Law, Consumer Legal Remedies Act, and False Advertising Law. Because the dairy farm was located in California along with Skyline's headquarters, the attorney sought to certify a nationwide class. Several months after the complaint's filing, Skyline moved to dismiss Charlie Utter's claims involving whole milk, skim milk, and 1% milk because Mr. Utter had only bought 2% milk. The court found that Mr. Utter had standing to bring claims on behalf of these products' purchasers because the claims were all substantially similar. Discovery is currently ongoing, and Mr. Utter's class certification motion is due in two months. Before drafting the Class Action Complaint, Mr. Utter's attorneys reviewed their working proof outline detailing each element required for the causes of action being considered. In preparation for class certification briefing, Mr. Utter's attorneys began including evidence that supports Mr. Utter's claims, which will provide an easy reference point and illustrate where additional discovery is needed. Following is an excerpt from the working proof outline that involves Rule 23(a).

RULE 23(A)

a) The class is sufficiently numerous because at least 10,000 consumers were injured.[1]

Fact	Supporting Evidence	Additional Evidence Needed
The challenged milk products were sold on the open market for three years.	Johnson Dep. at 76:16-19. Williams Dep. at 34:8-12.	
Defendant admits that at least 10,000 people purchased the product in question.	Def.'s Resp. to Pl.'s Req. for Admis., Set 2, No. 24.	

---

1. A 40-member class is generally sufficiently numerous to satisfy Federal Rule of Civil Procedure 23(a)(1). *Villalpando v. Excel Direct Inc.*, 303 F.R.D. 588, 605-06 (N.D. Cal. 2014); *In re Facebook, Inc., PPC Adver. Litig.*, 282 F.R.D. 446, 452 (N.D. Cal. 2012).

b) Commonality is satisfied because common questions will drive the case's resolution.[2]

Fact	Supporting Evidence	Additional Evidence Needed
The complaint raises a number of common questions, including (1) whether Skyline permitted its cows to graze daily over the course of the growing season; (2) whether federal regulations require such daily grazing; and (3) whether violating such federal regulations is likely to mislead a reasonable consumer, in addition to (4) the extent of the price premium attributable to Skyline's false/misleading claims.	Compl., ¶ 63.	
These common questions are likely to drive the case's resolution because "California has created what amounts to a conclusive presumption that when a defendant puts out tainted bait and a person sees it and bites, the defendant has caused an injury; restitution is the remedy."	*Pulaski & Middleman, LLC v. Google, Inc.*, 802 F.3d 979, 986 (9th Cir. 2015) (citing *Stearns v. Ticketmaster Corp.*, 655 F.3d 1013, 1020 (9th Cir. 2011)).	

---

2. "[E]ven a single common question will do." *Wal–Mart Stores, Inc. v. Dukes*, 131 S.Ct. 2541, 2556 (2011). Common questions must, however, "resolve an issue that is central to the validity of each . . . claim[ ] in one stroke." *Id.* at 2551. The common questions must, therefore, "generate common answers apt to drive the resolution of the litigation." *Id.*

Plaintiff is typical because his claims are reasonably coextensive with those of the putative class members, and no unique defenses affect his claims.[3]

Fact	Supporting Evidence	Additional Evidence Needed
Plaintiff, like each putative class member, purchased Skyline "organic" milk that was not actually organic, and he paid more for the product than it would have cost had it been accurately labeled and advertised.	Utter Dep. at 42:4-7. UTTER0000032 (receipt showing purchase). Maverick Expert Rep. at 35 (stating that 20% price premium resulted from misleading claims).	
Plaintiff would not have purchased Skyline's milk but-for the company's claim that it was organic, and he is not subject to any other unique defenses such as unclean hands, estoppel, or an arbitration agreement.	See Utter Dep. at 52:13-17 (stating that plaintiff would not have bought Skyline's milk if he knew Skyline's cows did not have the grazing time required by federal regulations).	
The 2% milk purchased by plaintiff is substantially similar to the whole milk, 1% milk, and skim milk products that are also at issue.	Doc. 32 at 12.	Expert Opinion Testing

3. "[C]laims are 'typical' if they are reasonably coextensive with those of absent class members; they need not be substantially identical." *Hanlon*, 150 F.3d at 1020. "The test of typicality is whether other members have the same or similar injury, whether the action is based on conduct which is not unique to the named plaintiffs, and whether other class members have been injured by the same course of conduct." *Hanon v. Dataproducts Corp.*, 976 F.2d 497, 508 (9th Cir. 1992)).

Plaintiff and his counsel are adequate representatives, as they would vigorously prosecute this action, and no conflicts will prevent them from doing so.[4]

Fact	Supporting Evidence	Additional Evidence Needed
No conflicts of interest will prevent plaintiff or his counsel from effectively representing the putative class.	Smith Declaration, ¶ 12 (stating that no conflicts of interest exist between counsel and the putative class). Utter Dep. at 23:3-8.	
This action has been vigorously prosecuted by plaintiff and his counsel.	Smith Declaration explaining work done to date and attaching Firm Resume.	

---

4. "To determine whether named plaintiffs will adequately represent a class, courts must resolve two questions: (1) do the named plaintiffs and their counsel have any conflicts of interest with other class members and (2) will the named plaintiffs and their counsel prosecute the action vigorously on behalf of the class?" *Ellis v. Costco Wholesale Corp.*, 657 F.3d 970, 985 (9th Cir. 2011).

6

Summary Judgment Strategy

Gregory C. Cook and Steven C. Corhern

It may seem odd to talk about summary judgment—a decision that usually comes toward the end of the litigation—in a book regarding class certification—a decision that is supposed to come at the beginning. Strategic litigators will recognize, however, that filing an early summary judgment motion can be a powerful weapon for class action defendants and sometimes plaintiffs. For example, a defendant may be able to dismiss the named plaintiff and stop the litigation cold. Even if the motion fails, it may highlight individualized factual issues that will help defeat predominance at class certification, or eliminate certain important claims that might support class certification. Further, there may be good reason for a defendant to file the motion at the same time as filing a response to a motion for class certification. While plaintiffs file early summary judgment motions less often, there are certain limited situations where one can be very effective. This chapter addresses the relationship between class certification and summary judgment, outlines the strategic considerations for defendants and plaintiffs, and offers some examples of these strategies in practice.

HISTORY OF THE RELATIONSHIP BETWEEN CLASS CERTIFICATION AND SUMMARY JUDGMENT

Since the federal rules were adopted in 1938, Rule 23 has undergone several amendments bearing on its relationship with summary judgment. Federal Rule of Civil Procedure 56 has long permitted a defending party to move for summary judgment "at any time," with or without supporting affidavits.[1] But the Federal Rules of Civil Procedure were silent on whether summary judgment should (or even could) be decided before class certification. In 1964, the drafters of the federal rules recommended changing the language of Rule 23 to provide that class certification should be decided "[a]s soon as practicable after the commencement *and before the decision on the merits* of an action brought as a class action."[2] The italicized language was ultimately disapproved but the remaining language was adopted. Based on the deletion of the italicized language, many believed that the committee did not want to constrain a district court's discretion to decide class certification before summary judgment.

Ten years later, the U.S. Supreme Court appeared to contradict this position in *Eisen v. Carlisle & Jacquelin*. In that case, the Court held that neither "the language or history of Rule 23 . . . gives a court any authority to conduct a preliminary inquiry into the merits of a suit in order to determine whether it may be maintained as a class action."[3] This statement was intended to divorce the decision on the merits from the decision on class certification, but it is easy to see how some believed this statement required class certification to come before a decision on summary judgment. The Supreme Court further complicated the matter a few years later when it decided *General Telephone Co. of the Southwest v. Falcon*. In that case, the Court explained that "sometimes it may be necessary for the [district] court to probe behind the pleadings before coming to rest on the certification question."[4] Further, the Court clearly stated "any . . . class [action] may only be certified if the trial court is

---

1. *See* Fed. R. Civ. P. 56 cmt. 1946 amendment.
2. Committee on Rules of Practice and Procedure of the Judicial Conference of the United States, *Preliminary Draft of Proposed Amendments to Rules of Civil Procedure for the United States District Courts*, 34 F.R.D. 325, 386 (1964) (emphasis added).
3. 417 U.S. 156, 177–78 (1974).
4. Gen. Tel. Co. of Sw. v. Falcon, 457 U.S. 147, 160 (1982).

satisfied, after a rigorous analysis, that the prerequisites of Rule 23(a) have been satisfied."[5]

In the wake of *Eisen* and *Falcon*, courts sometimes struggled to apply both decisions consistently. Those that interpreted *Eisen* as precluding any inquiry on the merits before deciding class certification were particularly troubled by considering a summary judgment motion before class certification. Often, these courts decided certification on the pleadings (before any discovery had occurred) with little more than a cursory analysis of the elements of the cause of action or the plaintiffs' ability to prove that the Rule 23 requirements were satisfied.

By the late 1990s, most courts agreed that summary judgment could be considered before class certification. Most courts also permitted discovery on at least the matter of class certification and also required plaintiffs to prove the Rule 23 requirements with evidence. However, parties and courts sometimes disagreed about what the "as soon as practicable" language required, as it did appear to be in tension with delaying a decision on certification until after substantial discovery. In 2003, the drafters addressed this tension by replacing the "as soon as practicable after commencement of an action"[6] language with "at an early practicable time."[7] In making this change, the drafters "recognize[ed] that there may be many valid reasons justifying the deferral of the initial certification decision, including that the opposing party may prefer to win dismissal or summary judgment as to the individual plaintiffs."[8] They also explained that:

> Although an evaluation of the probable outcome on the merits is not properly part of the certification decision, discovery in aid of the certification decision often includes information required to identify the nature of the issues that actually will be presented at trial. In this sense it is appropriate to conduct controlled discovery into the "merits," limited to those aspects relevant to making the certification decision on an informed basis.[9]

Thus, the 2003 change to Rule 23 left little doubt that it was appropriate to allow discovery *before* the decision on class certification. While the drafters stated that they were merely adopting current practice,

---

5. *Id.*

6. *See* FED. R. CIV. P. 23 advisory committee's cmt. to 2003 Amendments.

7. FED. R. CIV. P. 23(c)(1).

8. 7AA CHARLES A. WRIGHT & ARTHUR R. MILLER, FEDERAL PRACTICE & PROCEDURE Civ. § 1785.3 (3d ed. 2016).

9. *See* FED. R. CIV. P. 23 advisory committee's cmt. to 2003 Amendments.

the change certainly clarified lingering doubts about the relationship between summary judgment and class certification.

If any doubts remained after 2003, they were eliminated in 2011 when the Supreme Court decided *Wal-mart Stores, Inc. v. Dukes*. In that case, the Court clearly and unequivocally stated that "Rule 23 does not set forth a mere pleading standard" and that a district court must conduct a "rigorous analysis" of the Rule 23 factors before certifying a class.[10] The Court continued, "Frequently [the] 'rigorous analysis' will entail some overlap with the merits of the plaintiff's underlying claim. That cannot be helped. The class determination generally involves considerations that are enmeshed in the factual and legal issues comprising the plaintiff's cause of action."[11] Thus, *Wal-mart* stands for the proposition that a federal district court must base its certification decision on evidence, not mere allegations, and the failure to do so can be reversible error. Federal court defendants, therefore, can expect to conduct substantial pre-certification discovery. *Wal-mart*, of course, does not apply to any state law versions of Rule 23. Many states nonetheless require their courts to base certification decisions on evidence rather than the pleadings.

CLASS CERTIFICATION OR SUMMARY JUDGMENT: WHICH *SHOULD* COME FIRST?

While the 2003 amendment to Rule 23 and *Wal-mart* address whether summary judgment *can* come before class certification, neither addressed which decision *should* come first. As in so many areas of law, the answer is "it depends."

The vast majority of courts (if not all courts) have held that a district court has discretion to decide whether to address summary judgment before addressing class certification.[12] For example, in *Thompson v. County of Medina, Ohio*, the Sixth Circuit held that: "[The case law]

---

10. Wal-Mart Stores, Inc. v. Dukes, 564 U.S. 338, 351–52 (2011).

11. *Id.* (internal alterations, quotation marks, and citations omitted).

12. *See, e.g.*, Powers v. Credit Mgmt. Servs., Inc., 776 F.3d 567, 571 n.1 (8th Cir. 2015); Telfair v. First Union Mortg. Corp., 216 F.3d 1333, 1343 (11th Cir. 2000); Schweizer v. Trans Union Corp., 136 F.3d 233, 239 (2d Cir. 1998); Thompson v. Cnty. of Medina, Ohio, 29 F.3d 238, 241 (6th Cir. 1994); Wright v. Schock, 742 F.2d 541, 543–44 (9th Cir. 1984); Project Release v. Prevost, 722 F.2d 960, 963 & n.2 (2d Cir. 1983); Pharo v. Smith, 621 F.2d 656, 663–64 (5th Cir. 1980); Acker v. Provident Nat'l Bank, 512 F.2d 729, 732 n.5 (3d Cir. 1975).

do[es] not establish a broad rule that in all cases the determination of the propriety of a class action must precede any consideration on the merits."[13] Similarly, in *Schweizer v. Trans Union Corp.*, the Second Circuit explained that:

> There is nothing in Rule 23 which precludes the court from examining the merits of the plaintiff's claims on a proper Rule 12 motion to dismiss or a Rule 56 motion for summary judgment simply because such a motion precedes resolution of the issue of class certification.[14]

In the Ninth Circuit, the rule is that a district court "has discretion to rule on a motion for summary judgment before it decides the certification issue" whenever "it is more practicable to do so and where the parties will not suffer *significant* prejudice."[15] This language is strong and requires not just prejudice but significant prejudice before a judge loses her discretion to decide in which order to address certification and summary judgment.

The Seventh Circuit, on the other hand, has taken the position that a decision on certification should usually come before a decision on summary judgment.[16] As the court recently explained:

> Normally the issue of certification should be resolved first, because if a class is certified this sets the stage for a settlement and if certification is denied the suit is likely to be abandoned, as the stakes of the named plaintiffs usually are too small to justify the expense of suit, though that may not be true in this case.[17]

---

13. *See* 29 F.3d at 241.

14. *See* 136 F.3d at 239 (internal quotation marks and citation omitted).

15. *See Wright*, 742 F.2d at 543–44 (emphasis added).

16. Thomas v. City of Peoria, 580 F.3d 633, 635 (7th Cir. 2009) ("First ruling on the merits of the federal claims, and then denying class certification on the basis of that ruling, puts the cart before the horse, as we have emphasized in previous cases. Among other objections to that way of proceeding, it deprives the defendants of the benefit of res judicata should they be sued by other members of the class. But as is also all too common, the defendants in this case defend the denial of certification—perversely, because they are rightly confident that the plaintiff's claim, and therefore the claims of the other class members, have no merit, so that if the class had been certified the judgment for the defendants would spare them further suits by members of the class.") (internal citations omitted); Bertrand ex rel. Bertrand v. Maram, 495 F.3d 452, 454–56 (7th Cir. 2007) ("[T]he district court bypassed [the certification decision], ruled on the merits almost two years after the suit had been filed, and then insisted that the class does not matter. 'Early' is a plastic term that affords latitude to district judges in case management, but 'never' is not within any plausible understanding of "early.").

17. Thomas v. UBS AG, 706 F.3d 846, 849 (7th Cir. 2013).

But even this certification-first preference does not prohibit a pre-certification summary judgment motion. After all,

> deciding whether to certify a class can take a long time. Rule 23(c)(1) (A) requires that the decision be made at "an early practicable time," but early is often not practicable. So when as in this case the suit can quickly be shown to be groundless, it may make sense for the district court to skip certification and proceed directly to the merits.[18]

A class action guide published by the Federal Judicial Center states that federal judges have discretion in this area but takes the position that it is often more efficient—and therefore preferable—to address summary judgment before class certification.

> Given the flexibility in the rules, the most efficient practice is to rule on motions to dismiss or for summary judgment before addressing class certification.
>
> Determining whether a proposed class meets Rule 23 certification requirements demands a rigorous analysis. You have discretion to decide on both the extent of discovery and whether or not to hold a hearing to determine whether the requirements have been met. You need to make factual and legal determinations with respect to the requirements of Rule 23.
>
> Ruling on class certification may prove to be unnecessary. The most important actions you can take to promote settlement are to rule on dispositive motions and then, if necessary, rule on class certification.[19]

The principle rationale for addressing summary judgment first is avoiding the enormous costs associated with class litigation. If limited discovery shows that the class representative's claims fail as a matter of law, then the class action cannot proceed—at least not without a different class representative. Allowing the court to enter summary judgment on that plaintiff's claim early in the litigation will conserve the resources of the parties and the court.

The principle rationale for deciding certification first is the problem of "one-way intervention"—where putative class members wait on the sidelines to see if the particular plaintiff will prevail before deciding to participate in the litigation. By waiting, these plaintiffs can avoid being bound by an unfavorable judgment but take full advantage of one that

---

18. *Id.*

19. Barbara J. Rothstein & Thomas E. Willging, *Managing Class Action Litigation: A Pocket Guide for Judges*, Federal Judicial Center (2010), *available at* https://www.fjc.gov /sites/default/files/2012/ClassGd3.pdf.

goes in their favor.[20] By deciding class certification first, some jurists argue that defendants ensure that they will not have to relitigate the same issues again and again. In the trenches of class litigation, however, most defendants would disagree that having a class certified is ever beneficial. In practice, many judges (especially in federal court) will grant defendants considerable leeway regarding which decision the court should address first.

Despite the Seventh Circuit's position, Judge Posner's decision in *Cowen v. Bank United of Texas, FSB* (a decision issued before the 2003 change to Rule 23) succinctly explained the calculus many defendants may go through in deciding to move for summary judgment before a decision on class certification:

> The bank elected to move for summary judgment before the district judge decided whether to certify the suit as a class action. This is a recognized tactic, and does not seem to us improper. It is true that Rule 23(c)(1) of the civil rules requires certification as soon as practicable, which will usually be before the case is ripe for summary judgment. But "usually" is not "always," and "practicable" allows for wiggle room. Class actions are expensive to defend. One way to try to knock one off at low cost is to seek summary judgment before the suit is certified as a class action. A decision that the claim of the named plaintiffs lacks merit ordinarily, though not invariably, . . . disqualifies the named plaintiffs as proper class representatives. The effect is to moot the question whether to certify the suit as a class action unless the lawyers for the class manage to find another representative. They could not here because the ground on which the district court threw out the plaintiff's claims would apply equally to any other member of the class. After granting the defendant's motion for summary judgment, therefore, and since (as was predictable, given the district judge's ground) no one stepped forward to pick up the spear dropped by the named plaintiffs, the judge denied the motion for class certification.
>
> When the procedure that we have just described is followed, the defendant loses the preclusive effect on subsequent suits against him of class certification but saves the added expense of defending a class action and may be content to oppose the members of the class one by one, as it were, by moving for summary judgment, every time he is sued, before the judge presiding over the suit decides whether to certify it as a class action. If we reverse, the plaintiffs will be able to renew their motion for class

---

20. *See* WILLIAM B. RUBENSTEIN, NEWBERG ON CLASS ACTIONS § 7:8 (5th ed. 2017).

certification; that is no doubt why they appealed the adverse judgment in this ostensibly trivial case.[21]

As Judge Posner points out, defendants may find it less costly to defend cases "one by one," attacking the merits of the class representative's claims on its particular facts rather than facts common to the class.

Another reason given for deciding certification before summary judgment is that it allows the parties to determine what is at stake for purposes of settlement or before devoting substantial resources toward defending the matter. Again, if the class representative's claims fail on the merits, then the defendant can bring the litigation to an end quickly before conducting expensive discovery directed toward the merits. Similarly, if a defendant will be unable to defeat the litigation by picking off the class representative, it may be willing to pay more to settle the dispute.

Courts have not articulated a standardized or consistent test for determining whether class certification or summary judgment should be addressed first. In *Thornton v. Mercantile Stores Company, Inc.*, the court discussed three factors that weighed in favor of deciding summary judgment before class certification: (1) sufficient doubt regarding the likelihood of success on the merits of plaintiffs' claims, (2) where inefficiency would result from deciding certification first, and (3) where neither plaintiffs nor members of the putative class would be prejudiced.[22] The court relied on the defendant's willingness to assume the risk that any judgment would not be res judicata as to the other members of the class. As the court explained: "Where the defendant seeks summary judgment knowing of the possibility that other plaintiffs will enter the case and not be bound thereby, it is not for the plaintiffs or the court to deter them from assuming that risk."[23]

Other courts have appeared to base their decision solely on whether the defendant is willing to run that risk. In *Kim v. Commandant, Defense Language Institute, Foreign Language Center*, the district court held that it was appropriate to decide summary judgment before certification because "the defendant [had] assume[d] the risk that summary

---

21. Cowen v. Bank United of Texas, FSB, 70 F.3d 937, 941–42 (7th Cir. 1995) (internal citations omitted).

22. 13 F. Supp. 2d 1282, 1289 (M.D. Ala. 1998).

23. *Id.*

judgment in his favor will only have stare decisis effect on the members of the putative class."[24]

The federal court in *Adair v. Johnston* is one example of a court deciding class certification before summary judgment.[25] That case involved claims against a life insurance company under ERISA. The court decided that the proposed class was not ascertainable because it was not adequately defined and denied the motion for class certification. Then, turning to the defendant's motion for summary judgment, the court concluded the claim failed on the merits. Importantly, there were two defendants that had not moved for summary judgment and against whom claims remained pending. Thus, deciding class certification first made sense because the summary judgment motion did not dispose of the entire lawsuit. The court was going to have to address class certification no matter the decision on summary judgment. On the other hand, the court could just as easily have decided certification and summary judgment in reverse (especially if the summary judgment eliminated claims for which certification was possible).

As mentioned earlier, the court will usually defer to the parties regarding the timing of the class certification and summary judgment decisions. Perhaps surprisingly, it is not uncommon for the parties to agree on which matter the judge should address first. For example, in *Ray v. Judicial Correction Services*, the defendants moved for summary judgment a few weeks before the plaintiffs filed their certification motion. At a hearing, the plaintiffs affirmatively requested that the court address the summary judgment issue first. The court

> agree[d] that this is the appropriate order of operations and recognizes that the legal landscape of this case may be different after its ruling on the dispositive motions. This change in landscape could significantly affect the arguments for class certification and the proposed class definition.[26]

However, rather than merely holding the motion for class certification in abeyance until it has resolved the summary judgment motions, the court administratively terminated the motion with leave to refile at a later date.

Ray illustrates two points that deserve further discussion. First, the parties vigorously disagreed about the standards for liability. The court

---

24. 772 F.2d 521, 524 (9th Cir. 1985).
25. 221 F.R.D. 573, 576–77 (M.D. Ala. 2004).
26. *See* Order of October 16, 2016, *Ray v. Judicial Correction Services, et al.*, No. 12-2819-RDP (N.D. Ala.), ECF No. 496.

correctly recognized that this disagreement would impact the class certification analysis. The answers to these questions were critical to the question of whether the plaintiffs could prove their claims with common evidence.

Second, the court's decision to terminate the class certification motion—rather than holding it in abeyance—reveals an opportunity for gamesmanship. Normally, the court can simply hold the certification motion in abeyance. In *Ray*, the court elected to administratively terminate the certification motion because it concluded that its decision on summary judgment might impact the plaintiffs' arguments in favor of certification. The effect of this decision is that the plaintiffs had an opportunity to rebrief the class certification had the court not granted summary judgment for the municipal defendant. Having already seen the defendants' opposition, the plaintiffs would have had an opportunity to shore up their weaker arguments.

The takeaway is that defendants should avoid making a weak summary judgment motion when the plaintiff's motion for class certification is already pending. If the court denies summary judgment, it may terminate the plaintiff's motion and give them another chance to rebrief the issues. Further, if the plaintiff has filed a weak motion for certification, then the defendant should consider delaying the filing of a summary judgment motion to ensure that the plaintiff will not have an opportunity to rebrief the issues.

STRATEGIC CONSIDERATIONS: DEFENDANTS

For defendants, there are three possible benefits to an early motion for summary judgment. First, a defendant can remove the class representative because his or her individual claim fails on the merits. Assuming that no other plaintiff steps forward to represent the class, the lawsuit will be over. Second, to survive summary judgment, the plaintiff may need to highlight issues that will be individualized and fact dependent. If so, then the plaintiff will achieve only a pyrrhic victory, one that all but ensures defeat at class certification. Third, an early summary judgment motion may allow the defendant to defeat certain claims and, thereby, narrow the size or scope of the class as well as discovery. Fourth, a summary judgment motion may eliminate the only claims that might be certifiable.

The primary disadvantage is that the summary judgment decision will not be binding on putative class members. For cases that are likely to see numerous copycat lawsuits, knocking off an individual plaintiff will be a meaningless victory for the defendant, as other plaintiffs will just file suit in different courts and in front of different judges. The costs of defending each of these lawsuits may rival or exceed the costs of litigating the class action in a single court. Further, the new lawsuit might be in a less favorable forum or might be in front of a less favorable judge. Thus, defendants should carefully consider whether they want to defeat the named plaintiff, especially if they are in a good forum with a good judge.

Another potential disadvantage is that a defendant could lose the summary judgment argument. Losing a summary judgment motion, of course, will seldom result in a judgment being entered, but it can remove the uncertainty regarding the issues raised. As a result, the settlement value of the case may increase substantially, especially if these uncertain issues were central to the defense's position. Along the same lines, if the defendant loses early on, the court may be unwilling to entertain a subsequent summary judgment motion later in the case (even if it is brought on different issues).

Finally, because the defendant is moving for summary judgment before discovery is complete, you may lose summary judgment *because* discovery is not complete. Defendants should carefully consider the personality of their judge along with the facts available to them in deciding whether an early motion for summary judgment makes sense.

Perhaps the most appealing time for a defendant to file a summary judgment motion is in reply to the class certification motion. This focuses the court on the need for element by element review for the claim of each class member at the very time the court is considering certification. Moving at that time may also demonstrate adequacy problems with the named plaintiff, allow the defendant the last word in the briefing, and provide additional pages to explain the problems with the claims.

Advantages to Defendant	Disadvantages to Defendant
• Could eliminate named plaintiff's claim and therefore the entire action • May highlight individual nature of key issues to court • May defeat key claims or narrow remaining claims or scope of class	• Will not be binding on class members • May need to defend new claims (or claims from new plaintiffs) in new, less favorable forum • May lose summary judgment argument thus increasing settlement value • Might lose summary judgment if discovery is not complete

WHAT ISSUES ARE OFTEN RAISED IN PRE-CERTIFICATION MOTIONS FOR SUMMARY JUDGMENT?

The archetypal pre-certification summary judgment motion attacks the named plaintiff's standing to bring a claim. In perhaps all but a few situations, the named plaintiff must have standing to bring a claim on behalf of the class, which means they must have suffered the same injury as the rest of the class. As one federal court has explained, a "plaintiff cannot include class action allegations in a complaint and expect to be relieved of personally meeting the requirements of constitutional standing, even if the persons described in the class definition would have standing themselves to sue."[27] Moreover, standing must be analyzed claim by claim. Thus, it is possible that the plaintiff may have standing as to one claim but not another.

For example, in *Griffin v. Dugger*, the plaintiff sued his employer for using disciplinary procedures and promotion criteria that discriminated against him on account of his race. Because the plaintiff had been disciplined and denied a promotion, he had standing to assert those claims on behalf of a class. But the plaintiff also challenged an entry-level exam required by his employer. Because the plaintiff had already been hired, he could not show an injury as a result of that exam. Accordingly, the Eleventh Circuit held that the plaintiff "lacked constitutional standing to assert a testing claim [directed to that exam]" and therefore, "the district court erred when it permitted [him] to raise the testing claim on behalf of himself and on behalf of others."[28]

Other issues that are possible arguments for eliminating the named plaintiff include:

- Statute of limitations
- Failure to exhaust administrative remedies
- Res judicata
- Real party in interest
- Waiver
- Capacity
- Failure to provide pre-suit notice
- Voluntary payment rule

---

27. Griffin v. Dugger, 823 F.2d 1476, 1483 (11th Cir. 1987).
28. *Id.* at 1484.

- Judicial estoppel
- Unclean hands
- Assumption of the risk
- Release
- Accord and satisfaction

The second potential benefit of moving for summary judgment early is highlighting a potential flaw in the plaintiff's arguments for class certification. So, any element of a plaintiff's claim that is likely to require individualized inquiry may be a good candidate for summary judgment. To illustrate, the Eleventh Circuit recently held that a TCPA plaintiff can partially revoke consent for calls to his or her cell phone. Specifically, the plaintiff told the defendant not to call her while she was at work (or between the hours of 8 a.m. and 5 p.m.).[29] In an appropriate case, a defendant might move for summary judgment on the issue of consent. The plaintiff must then marshal evidence to show that consent was revoked. Undoubtedly, this evidence will be individualized and will likely involve reviewing the transcript from the plaintiff's conversations with the defendant. Even if the defendant loses on the motion for summary judgment, the plaintiff will have demonstrated that the issue of consent is likely to be an individualized issue. At class certification, the defendant can then point to consent as a tangible exercise that must be required for each and every plaintiff to determine liability.

Another issue that might be ideal for this approach is the reasonableness of certain charges or expenses. Often, contracts allow businesses to add a "reasonable" fee or charge for fuel costs. Plaintiffs often argue that the charges selected are not reasonable. If there is no standardized method for determining the increase, an individualized issue would be presented on the issue of reasonableness of each instance of the fee. Similarly, a claim for breach of warranty may fail unless the plaintiff provided pre-suit notice of the defect and an opportunity to cure. If there is serious doubt that the plaintiff actually compiled with this requirement, a defendant could move for summary judgment to highlight the individualized analysis necessary to determine liability.

Other issues that may be suitable for this approach include: assumption of the risk, waiver, estoppel, voluntary payment, failure to exhaust, and the application of equitable tolling or the discovery rule.

---

29. Schweitzer v. Comenity Bank, No. 16-10498, 2017 WL 3429381 (11th Cir. Aug. 10, 2017).

The third and final potential benefit of summary judgment is that it may allow a defendant to narrow the scope of the case. For example, if the complaint alleges fraud and breach of contract, a defendant might move for summary judgment on the fraud claim to eliminate it from the case.[30] Discovery related to a fraud claim is generally much broader than discovery targeted to a single contract. Additionally, if there is a factual dispute about when a cause of action accrued for purposes of the statute of limitations, a defendant might move for summary judgment on that issue to narrow the scope of the putative class.

Of course, there is an issue of timing. Moving for summary judgment for the purposes of narrowing discovery makes little sense if the discovery has already occurred. For that reason, defendants may want to be aggressive in deposing the plaintiff early in the case to learn if there are any issues that are ripe for summary judgment. If there are clear-cut issues that can be decided from evidence outside the four corners of the complaint, a defendant may want to move for summary judgment shortly after filing its answer. Again, each case is different and each client's needs are different. However, in appropriate circumstances, a defendant should consider filing an early motion for summary judgment to knock out particular claims or issues. Even if the motion is filed simultaneously with the motion for class certification, the defendant may succeed in narrowing the scope of the class being considered.[31]

PLAINTIFF'S STRATEGY CONSIDERATIONS

Plaintiffs rarely move for summary judgment before class certification. Indeed, the general consensus is that plaintiffs *should not* move for summary judgment. However, there are some extraordinary situations where a targeted summary judgment motion makes strategic sense. First, if the plaintiff seeks only or primarily injunctive relief, then courts are generally less concerned about the potential effect on absent class members. Second, a limited motion for summary judgment may increase pressure on the defendant to settle the case. Third, there may

---

30. *See, e.g, Jamieson v. Vatterott Educ. Centers, Inc.*, 259 F.R.D. 520, 543 (D. Kan. 2009).

31. *Id.* at 525–26 ("After examining the issues involved, the court concludes it is appropriate to address the pending motion for summary judgment prior to the motion for class certification."); *Ray*, 2017 WL 660842, at *2 (explaining that the court administrative terminated the plaintiff's motion for class certification pending a determination on the motion for summary judgment).

be an affirmative defense that might be appropriate for summary judgment. If these issues can be resolved quickly so as to streamline the case for trial or class certification, then it might make sense for a plaintiffs' counsel to expend time and resources on a motion for summary judgment.

But, even if the resolution of the issue is not in doubt, a plaintiff may not want to expend the time and resources moving for summary judgment. It will create additional work for the court and will rarely be case dispositive. Further, it will likely consume considerable resources to gather the evidence and brief the motion. Third, facts on critical issues are rarely undisputed. Thus, the plaintiff will rarely benefit from moving for summary judgment. Fourth, even if the facts are undisputed, the plaintiff may be able to obtain a concession with considerably less effort—a request for admission, an interrogatory, a stipulation, etc.

WHAT EXTRAORDINARY CIRCUMSTANCES MAY WARRANT A PLAINTIFF'S MOTION FOR SUMMARY JUDGMENT?

As discussed earlier, a principle concern surrounding pre-certification motions for summary judgment is the problem of "one-way intervention." This concern effectively disappears in class actions brought under Rule 23(b)(2) because the absent class members have no right to opt out of the court's determination. As the Sixth Circuit recently explained,

> The rule against one-way intervention prevents potential plaintiffs from awaiting merits rulings in a class action before deciding whether to intervene in that class action. . . . [W]e find no support for applying the prohibition on one-way intervention to Rule 23(b)(2) class certifications, in which class members may not opt out and therefore make no decision about whether to intervene.[32]

Plaintiffs might also move for summary judgment on an affirmative defense or a counterclaim. Unlike liability, the defendant bears the burden of proof on affirmative defenses or claims. Thus, it makes sense that the plaintiff would be the party moving for summary judgment. If the defendant fails to put forth substantial evidence supporting it,

---

32. Gooch v. Life Inv'rs Ins. Co. of Am., 672 F.3d 402, 432–33 (6th Cir. 2012) (citing Paxton v. Union Nat'l Bank, 688 F.2d 552, 558–59 (8th Cir. 1982)).

courts will strike their affirmative defenses.[33] Likewise, obtaining summary judgment on a counterclaim eliminates a defendant's opportunity to argue that the counterclaim will involve individualized inquiry—thus, decreasing the likelihood that the court will deny class certification on that basis.

Another situation where a motion for summary judgment may make sense is when the defense relies on an unqualified or unreliable expert. Assuming the expert's testimony is critical, the plaintiff should consider moving to exclude the expert and simultaneously moving for summary judgment. Even if neither motion is successful, the fact they are pending may give the plaintiff leverage in settlement negotiations.

WHAT CAN PLAINTIFF'S COUNSEL DO TO AVOID THE LIKELIHOOD OF AN EARLY SUMMARY JUDGMENT MOTION BY DEFENDANTS?

Because an early motion for summary judgment is often undesirable for plaintiffs, plaintiffs' counsel should always consider strategies to avoid them. At the outset, plaintiffs' counsel should bring suit with multiple plaintiffs and assert all potentially viable theories of relief. This strategy makes it less likely that a defendant can defeat the lawsuit by knocking out the class representative. It will also make the briefing more difficult because the defendant must spill ink addressing each claim and plaintiff. On the other hand, this strategy could backfire if the named plaintiffs' claims are not sufficiently similar. To avoid this problem, plaintiffs' counsel should carefully interview and examine each putative class representative's individual circumstances to identify and address potential pitfalls to class certification before the lawsuit is ever filed.

Plaintiffs' counsel should push to complete as much discovery as possible before the summary judgment motion is filed. A principle justification for early summary judgment motions is that they will conserve the resources of the parties and the court. These efficiencies largely disappear if discovery is nearing completion by the time the summary judgment motion is filed. Additionally, discovery may give the defendants additional grounds for opposing a pre-certification motion for

---

33. *See* Myers v. Harold, No. 15 C 7418, 2017 WL 3642110, at *15 (N.D. Ill. Aug. 24, 2017).

summary judgment. Of course, if there are multiple plaintiffs, discovery will almost certainly take longer before the defendant can be in a position to move for summary judgment.

CONCLUSION

It is now well-settled that a court may decide summary judgment before class certification. It is also well settled that a district court has discretion to decide which decision it will address first. For defendants, the benefits of moving for summary judgment before class certification are substantial. For plaintiffs, moving for summary judgment is rarely a wise decision, but it can make strategic sense to increase settlement leverage or to simplify the issues to be tried.

Class Certification Strategy

Catha Worthman and Andrew J. McGuinness

ppellate courts typically employ an abuse of discretion standard when reviewing a trial court decision on class certification. This practice might tempt some to conclude that class certification is entrusted to the trial court's discretion. Not so:

> By its terms [Rule 23] creates a categorical rule entitling a plaintiff whose suit meets the specified criteria to pursue his claim as a class action.
>
> . . .
>
> [Rule 23] says that if the prescribed preconditions are satisfied "[a] class action *may be maintained*" (emphasis added)—not *"a class action may be permitted."* Courts do not maintain actions; litigants do. The discretion suggested by Rule 23's "may" is discretion residing in the plaintiff: He may bring his claim in a class action if he wishes.[1]

To be sure, weighing the factors that govern certification under Rule 23 or its state court counterparts (discussed later in the chapter) involves matters of judgment, and in that sense can be viewed as "discretionary." From a strategic point of view, even experienced class practitioners find it very difficult to predict whether a particular case

---

1. Shady Grove Orthopedic Assoc. v. Allstate Ins. Co., 559 U.S. 393, 398–400 (2010).

will be certified, since the same judge may reach different "correct" results on seemingly similar facts. Counsel must be certain their clients understand this inherent unpredictability.

Despite this element of unpredictability, class certification is nonetheless governed by highly developed (albeit evolving) standards. It is important when developing a class certification strategy to understand the nature of the exercise: to persuade the district court (and build a record for later review) establishing that the plaintiff has either met or failed to meet the requirements that would entitle her to represent a particular class.

CLASS CERTIFICATION BASICS

Most class certification motions are won or lost on the evidentiary record. Certification is not an exercise in theory and abstract legal argument. While the law governs, the party who has marshaled the most compelling record frequently comes out ahead.

Plaintiff's Strategy

The certification motion is the pivotal moment in the class action. Before the court rules on the motion, the case is just a proposed class action. Afterwards, if the plaintiff prevails, the case proceeds on behalf of a certified class, and plaintiff's counsel has become class counsel, with all of the attendant rights, responsibilities, and increased leverage that entails. Not surprisingly, settlement discussions often revolve around the filing or resolution of the certification motion.

The motion must persuade the court that it should certify a proposed class under Federal Rule of Civil Procedure 23, or the equivalent state court rule. Plaintiffs bear the burden of proof in establishing that the Rule 23(a) prerequisites for certification are satisfied. Because several of these determinations involve judgments by the court that border on discretionary rulings, the plaintiff should endeavor to demonstrate that the case at bar readily satisfies Rule 23. This is not necessarily an easy task—but the plaintiff should make it look as easy as possible. The central goal for the motion is to show the court that this is the sort of case that makes sense for class treatment, because it will lead to efficient and fair resolution of the issues at stake, without undue complication. The motion should emphasize common, overarching issues that affect the class as a whole, while demonstrating that the court is well-positioned to resolve them on a class-wide basis.

The text of Rule 23 is the place to start when formulating the strategy for certification. First, the plaintiff must show that the four elements of Rule 23(a) are met, including numerosity, commonality, typicality, and adequacy—all discussed in more detail later in the chapter. Additionally, the class must fulfill the requirements of at least one of Rule 23(b)'s subsections.

How to approach the motion varies depending on what type of class the plaintiff is attempting to certify—(b)(1), (b)(2), (b)(3), or a combination. Rule 23(b)(1) applies to cases where class members or the defendant might suffer adverse effects if the issues were resolved in separate actions, rather than on a class-wide basis. Such classes are often used where a common interest is held in shared property, or where there is a common trust or employee benefits plan. Rule 23(b)(2) applies to cases seeking injunctive and declaratory relief and are common in civil rights cases. Rule 23(b)(3) is intended for cases where class issues predominate over individual issues, as where individual damages are at issue as in wage and hour, consumer, securities, and antitrust class actions.

Regardless of the type of class involved, the goal of the opening motion remains the same: to show the court how simple and straightforward it would be to act on a class-wide basis. To keep it simple, most opening motions begin with a fact section that emphasizes common facts that bind the class together. The legal argument can be readily organized according to the rule's elements, beginning with the subsections of Rule 23(a), followed by any applicable subsections of Rule 23(b), and concluding by showing class counsel's adequacy under Rule 23(g). If plaintiff's counsel is proposing "issue certification" under Rule 23(c)(4), that is often proposed as an alternative at the end of the motion.

A significant strategy concern is what evidence to include and emphasize. The nature and amount of evidence to include in the opening motion will vary depending on the type of case. If plaintiff's counsel has the strategy for the certification motion in mind from the outset of the case, then class certification issues will have guided pre-filing investigation, selection of the class representative(s), and the preparation of the complaint, as well as shaped pre-certification discovery. Plaintiff's counsel should use that discovery and any early motion practice to focus on the key documents and testimony that best show why class treatment is appropriate.

In most cases the motion will rely on defendants' documents and often on Rule 30(b)(6) testimony that illustrate the class-wide policies or practices being challenged. Plaintiffs should focus their argument on defendant's conduct as the unifying theme of their motion to certify.

Choices that must be made include whether to provide class member declarations, and whether to provide expert reports. Class member declarations may be useful to demonstrate common practices that contradict written policies—for example, declarations would likely be helpful where a class of workers seeks to show that they were forced to work off-the-clock without pay in contravention of an official policy, a challenging type of class action. In other cases, declarations can be helpful to illustrate the common nature of the harms suffered and demonstrate broad interest on the part of the class. On the other hand, in other cases providing declarations may not be necessary and their use risks raising potential individual issues.[2]

Similarly, expert reports at class certification are essential for some types of cases (as where statistical evidence is required to establish a class-wide violation), and entirely superfluous in others. Particularly in antitrust, product defect, and (increasingly) securities cases, and infrequently in some consumer cases (e.g., where the governing law requires analysis of consumer understanding of an allegedly misleading representation, or consideration of whether a "reasonable" consumer would have relied on the representation), expert witness testimony at the class certification phase may be important.

Where appropriate, expert testimony can bear on certification in two distinct ways: (1) an expert opinion that defendant's conduct violates a legal standard may substantiate a finding of predominance in a Rule 23(b)(3) damages class action; and (2) an expert opinion can help demonstrate that a common methodology exists to determine whether a defendant's conduct violated a legal standard as to a particular group of consumers over a distinct class period (e.g., economic testimony in

---

2. For similar reasons, class counsel should weigh the disadvantages of multiple named class representatives (if available)—whose individual testimony, at deposition, may help defendant's argument against typicality or predominance—against the advantages of multiple named plaintiffs, such as demonstrating to the court that the case has importance to real people, and as a hedge against one or more representatives dropping out or having her claims defeated on the merits. See section titled "How Many Class Representatives?" in Chapter 2, Investigating and Filing a Class Action.

antitrust cases). For a more detailed discussion of expert issues in class actions, please refer to Chapter 11.

Plaintiff's counsel will also have to decide how much to frontload the evidence and what, if anything, to save for the reply. The opening motion need only satisfy the plaintiff's burden of initially satisfying the Rule 23 criteria. Less is often more. By anticipating defenses, plaintiff's counsel can determine what evidence can most effectively be saved for the reply and where it may be helpful to cut an expected opposition off ahead of time. For example, a plaintiff may wish to lay out a roadmap for the court as to how damages will be determined, to show that the case is eminently manageable as a class action, thereby anticipating a defendant's likely argument that individualized damage issues thwart certification.

Figuring out what evidence to include in the opening motion and how to defeat anticipated defenses is a matter of reading the class certification decisions in the relevant area of law and learning what the courts cite as sufficient evidence to justify class treatment in that area. Of course, being familiar with the recent and most often-cited class certification decisions is also a minimum requirement for formulating an effective overall strategy for the motion. Judges may be familiar with recent Supreme Court or other appellate decisions on "hot" class action topics, so class counsel should anticipate that the court may want class counsel to address such cases that may be perceived as being potentially relevant to the case at hand.

Finally, although the rule and interpretive case law are the foundations of a class certification strategy, a good class certification motion does more than show how the rule's requirements are met. Even though merits are not technically relevant except to the extent necessary to demonstrate why certification is appropriate, the motion should demonstrate the strengths of the plaintiff's case on the merits. As discussed in more detail later in the chapter in the section titled "Interplay between Merits and Class Certification," at least in a (b)(3) class action, "superiority" is an element; demonstrating that the case has merit and that hundreds or thousands of class members will effectively go without relief if the court denies certification will go a long way toward establishing this element. The motion and brief should also paint a picture of the scope of relief needed to resolve the case and show the other side that plaintiff's counsel is willing and able to try the case on a class-wide basis if no resolution is reached.

Finally, depending upon the case and perhaps local custom and practice, consider developing and submitting a detailed trial plan. This can be an effective means to demonstrate manageability, and to allay any concerns the court may have about how the case will be tried if it certifies a class. For a more detailed discussion of trial plans (and examples) see Chapter 10.

While customizing the argument and submissions to your particular case are key, don't ignore the thousands of publicly filed class certification motions available on PACER written by accomplished and nationally and regionally distinguished class counsel. These can be great idea generators and templates for a strong brief in support.

Defense Strategy

While there are certain common strategies to defending against a class action, the first point bearing emphasis is this: *a defense strategy must be tailored to the particulars of each case.* Chief among the factors to consider:

- What is the potential exposure?
  - How strong/weak are the theories of liability?
  - What is the prospect for certification?
  - What range of damages is realistic?
- What are the reputations and resources of class counsel?
- What are the client's resources?
  - Is insurance available (e.g., D & O in securities fraud action)? Conditions? Limits?
- What is the experience and reputation of the district court? Of the appellate court?

Consider also that often technical expertise—for example, of an engineering, scientific, or legal nature—outside of the typical skill set of a class action litigator is necessary. Marshal those resources early on.

Putting aside case-specific considerations, here is what might be called a "generic" defense strategy blueprint:

- File a motion to dismiss to attack any claims that are legally insufficient as pleaded;
- Argue to stay or limit discovery while the motion to dismiss is being briefed and decided;
- Consider early individual or class settlement consistent with client goals;

- Seek to contain discovery after a motion to dismiss is denied, since the disproportionate costs of discovery will fall on your client, except where broader discovery (e.g., of third parties) can illuminate individual issues and help defeat predominance in a (b)(3) class;
- Consider bifurcation of discovery (e.g., discovery as to only the class certification issue or prioritizing class discovery) as a way to achieve the preceding goal—although this practice has become far less common in recent years due to a desire to speed up complex cases and the interjection of more "merits" elements into the certification decision;
- Oppose class certification, and consider asking for an evidentiary hearing (e.g., as in an antitrust case, where testimony from expert economists may be critical);
- File a Rule 23(f) petition with the circuit clerk within 14 days of the entry of an order certifying a class seeking review of the decision; and seek a stay in the district and (if necessary) appellate courts pending review;
- File a motion for summary judgment if there is arguably no genuine issue of material fact as to one or more elements of plaintiffs' claims;
- If summary judgment is not a viable option or is unsuccessful, consider seriously negotiating a class-wide settlement;
- Barring successful motion practice or a settlement, consider filing a motion to decertify, or to narrow, the class;
- Try the case;
- Appeal an adverse judgment.

Not to belabor the point, but each of the preceding points must carefully be evaluated and adapted to the needs of the case at hand.[3]

From a strictly strategic perspective, developing superior expert testimony (and challenging the admissibility of any inadequate expert

---

3. To illustrate the point, in a case where each claim is substantial, and liability turns on a technical issue likely to be determined in a battle of competing experts, a defendant might propose pre-certification that each side take a limited number of depositions, including experts, followed by a defendant's summary judgment motion. (Plaintiff would not seek summary judgment prior to class certification.) If successful, the defendant might thereby avoid disclosing the identities of individual putative class members who might otherwise be solicited to bring individual suits even if class certification were denied. Strategy is situation specific.

opinions proffered by plaintiffs) can reap tremendous benefits. The best experts may be (and often are) expensive. Defense counsel should candidly discuss with the client its exposure to develop a realistic and appropriate litigation budget. The economics of the class action bar and the dynamics of multi-firm plaintiffs' groups are such that plaintiffs often have a harder time raising sufficient funds to hire the best experts. Particularly in light of plaintiffs' burden of proof and the increased scrutiny of class experts in recent years, this creates an opportunity for the defendant willing to devote the resources necessary to develop more compelling expert testimony than the other side can muster.

A key consideration in any complex or high-exposure litigation, including class actions, is building a record for appellate review. Partly for this reason, defendants frequently press for an evidentiary hearing at class certification, including expert testimony. In addition to under-scoring the importance of the certification decision to the trial judge, the record adduced at this hearing may be critical in any Rule 23(f) inter-locutory appeal from class certification. Similarly, once at trial, defense counsel will want to adduce as much evidence as permitted to demon-strate to an appellate court (or even to the trial court, post-trial[4]) that the class should be decertified.

INTERPLAY BETWEEN MERITS AND CLASS CERTIFICATION

There are two ways the merits of a case might impact a decision whether to certify a class under Rule 23 (and comparable state class action rules).

First, judges are people, too. Of course, these are *procedural* rules— ostensibly ones that operate independently from the merits of the case. Valid claims often do not meet the requirements for class certification, and meritless ones are just as often readily certifiable as class actions. But most experienced class action litigators see the wall between sub-stance and procedure as somewhat permeable when it comes to class procedure. In other words, the stronger the claim, the more likely it is to be certified (all else being equal)—particularly in a situation where denial of certification will, for economic reasons, effectively forestall the

---

4. In *Mazzei v. The Money Store*, 829 F.3d 260, 269 (2d Cir. 2016), the Second Circuit held that a trial court can decertify a class even after a jury returns a verdict in its favor.

prosecution of any individual claims. In simple terms, the judge must be persuaded that a real wrong is (or is not) at the core of the case.

This is not just a rule of equity, or "judicial realism" (though it is partly that); it has a basis in Rule 23(b)(3)'s "superiority" requirement for damages class actions. This rule directs the court to consider "the class members' interests in individually controlling the prosecution or defense of separate actions" in making a superiority calculation. If the prosecution of separate claims is not economically feasible in light of modest individual damages, there is effectively no interest in "individually controlling" such separate actions.[5] The Supreme Court has also recognized that "the [1966] Advisory Committee had dominantly in mind vindication of 'the rights of groups of people who individually would be without effective strength to bring their opponents into court at all.'"[6]

A second interplay has gotten far more attention in recent case law: the extent to which the court should evaluate whether plaintiffs' proffered method of proving a common issue on a class-wide basis—such as "impact" (whether a given class member suffered antitrust injury based on defendant's alleged wrongful conduct)—*actually does so*. If this determination requires the court to evaluate the merits of the claim, the question becomes to what extent may it do so?

The answer is now clear: a court may reach the merits only to the extent necessary to determine whether the party seeking certification (typically the plaintiff) has actually met her burden of satisfying the Rule 23 prerequisites. The Supreme Court explained this definitively in *Amgen Inc. v. Connecticut Retirement Plans and Trust Funds*.[7] Perhaps the lead pre-*Amgen* case applying this rule is the Third Circuit case *In re Hydrogen Peroxide Antitrust Litigation*.[8]

The practice point to be taken from these cases is this: in a (b)(3) damages class action, class counsel (*and* defense counsel) must devote substantial effort not just to *proposing* (or criticizing) a plan for proving

---

5. *See* FED. R. CIV. P. 23, 1966 Advisory Committee Notes to subdivision (b)(3).

6. Amchem Products, Inc. v. Windsor, 521 U.S. 591, 671 (1997) ("The policy at the very core of the class action mechanism is to overcome the problem that small recoveries do not provide the incentive for any individual to bring a solo action prosecuting his or her rights. A class action solves this problem by aggregating the relatively paltry potential recoveries into something worth someone's (usually an attorney's) labor.") (citing Mace v. Van Ru Credit Corp., 109 F. 3d 338, 344 (7th Cir. 1997)).

7. 568 U.S. 455, 464–65 (2013).

8. 552 F.3d 305 (3d Cir. 2008).

required elements on a class-wide basis, but must also persuade the district court at the certification phase that common proofs will *actually* permit the jury to do so. If the defense can disprove the efficacy of the proposed proofs or methodology—even if such challenge overlaps with the merits in some respect—then the district court may conclude either that common issues do not predominate or that the proposed class action would be unmanageable, and deny certification.

MOTIONS TO DENY CLASS CERTIFICATION OR TO STRIKE CLASS ALLEGATIONS

A number of courts have permitted defendants to file a motion to strike a complaint's class allegations or to deny certification even before the plaintiff files a motion to certify.[9] Whether or not to allow such a motion is within the court's discretion.[10]

Whether to *file* such a motion is a matter of defense counsel's judgment. Such motions are disfavored.[11] A number of courts have held that the burden is on a defendant filing such a motion to demonstrate that plaintiffs will be unable to establish the Rule 23 requirements for

---

9. FED. R. CIV. P. 23(c)(1)(A) has been relied upon for these motions. See 7AA CHARLES ALLEN WRIGHT ET AL., FEDERAL PRACTICE AND PROCEDURE § 1785 (3d ed. 2018); Pilgrim v. Universal Health Card, 660 F.3d 943, 949 (6th Cir. 2011) (affirming an order striking class allegations for a putative nationwide class because the forum state's choice of law rule would require the application of 50 state consumer protection laws); Vinole v. Countrywide Home Loans, Inc., 571 F.3d 935, 941–44 (9th Cir. 2009) (affirming an order denying class certification of a wage and hour case lacking predominance); Cook County College Teachers Union, Local 1600 v. Byrd, 456 F.2d 882, 884–85 (7th Cir. 1972) (affirming an order to dismiss the class action because none of Rule 23(a)'s requirements were met).

10. The local rules of two district courts, the District of Columbia and the Northern District of Ohio expressly allow motions to strike class allegations. D.D.C. L. CIV. R. 23.1(b); N.D. Ohio L.R. 23.1(c). Under the local rules of other federal courts, a plaintiff can attempt to prevent an early motion to deny certification by addressing it in the Rule 16 scheduling conference. If necessary, the plaintiff can discuss why a defense motion should not be allowed in the case management conference. The plaintiff will fare best where there are specific and plausible class action allegations in the complaint, and where there are solid arguments that class treatment is at least somewhat likely to be appropriate.

11. *In re* Apple, AT&T iPad Unlimited Data Plan Litig., No. C1002553 RMW, 2012 WL 2428248, at *2 (N.D. Cal. June 26, 2012) (citing Thorpe v. Abbott Labs., Inc., 534 F. Supp. 2d 1120, 1125 (N.D. Cal. 2008)). A study of federal decisions in California over a year-and-a-half period showed that courts denied 17 out of 18 motions to strike class allegations. Scott Kaiser et al., *Strategies for Moving To Strike Class Allegations*, LAW360, (Sept. 4, 2012), https://www.law360.com/articles/374582/strategies-for-moving-to-strike-class-allegations.

class certification.[12] The motion is most attractive where defendant faces unusually expensive discovery or other defense costs and the class allegations—or the likelihood of plaintiff successfully establishing the Rule 23 prerequisites—are very weak.[13] Particularly when filed before significant class discovery has occurred, an ill-considered and failed motion to strike class allegations could annoy the court, waste time and resources, and possibly even incline the trial judge more favorably toward certification on a full record.[14]

Defendants are most likely to succeed in bringing a motion to deny certification where there has been sufficient time for discovery that has not identified a basis for class treatment, and where the plaintiff has pleaded an overly broad class or made class action allegations with insufficient specificity or factual support.[15]

CLASS DEFINITION AND ASCERTAINABILITY

In addition to the explicit requirements of Rule 23, some federal courts have found an "implicit" requirement for class certification: that the proposed class be "ascertainable."[16] Historically this has been understood

---

12. *See, e.g.*, Green v. Liberty Ins. Corp., No. 15-10434, 2016 WL 1259110, at *2 (E.D. Mich. Mar. 30, 2016) (citing Bell Atlantic Corp. v. Twombly, 550 U.S. 554, 555 (2007) and Ashcroft v. Iqbal, 556 U.S. 662, 679 (2009)); see also Bessette v. Avco Fin. Servs., Inc., 279 B.R. 442, 451 (D.R.I. 2002) (noting that where the question "is not whether the class should be certified, but whether the class allegations in the complaint should be stricken . . . the burden is not on the party seeking class certification, rather, as the nonmoving party, all reasonable inferences must be construed in [the plaintiff's] favor"); *but see* Blihovde v. St. Croix Cnty., Wis., 219 F.R.D. 607, 613–14 (W.D. Wis. 2003) (holding that the burden remains on party seeking certification).

13. *See, e.g.*, John v. Nat'l Sec. Fire & Cas. Co., 501 F.3d 443, 445 (5th Cir. 2007) (identifying the standard as whether "it is facially apparent from the pleadings that there is no ascertainable class"); *see also* Lindsay Transmission v. Office Depot, Inc., No. 4:12-CV-221 2013 WL 275568 at *4 (E.D. Mo. Jan. 24, 2013) (granting motion to strike class allegations for "fail safe" class).

14. *See, e.g.*, Mills v. Foremost Ins. Co., 511 F.3d 1300, 1309 (11th Cir. 2008) (reversing determination that claims were not appropriate for class treatment on motion to dismiss as premature).

15. *See Vinole,* 571 F.3d at 943 (affirming an order denying certification in a case where there had been "significant discovery," and Plaintiff's counsel "did not intend to propound any additional discovery . . . regarding the propriety of class certification").

16. Some courts also refer to standing as a second "implicit" requirement for class actions. However, standing in federal court is a requirement in all cases—class or individual actions—and so is not addressed here, other than to note that that is the standing of the *named plaintiffs only* that matters for establishing a "case or controversy" sufficient to give a federal court jurisdiction under Article III of the Constitution. O'Shea v.

to require that a person's membership in a proposed class be determinable (1) by objective criteria, (2) that can be applied independently of a determination of the defendant's liability for the claimed wrong.

Objectivity

In some relatively recent court decisions, the first of these two criteria, objectivity, has blossomed into a somewhat aggressive offshoot based on "administrative feasibility." To illustrate this development, consider an individual (non-class) lawsuit in which a consumer claims under a state consumer protection statute that she was deceived by the labeling on the package of a retail product. Even if she had not retained a receipt for that purchase, the question of whether or not she had purchased the product would not be considered anything other than an "objective" issue of fact. She either purchased the product or she did not. She could take the witness stand at trial and testify that she purchased it, perhaps offer some salient details surrounding her purchase, and be subject to cross-examination by defense counsel. The fact finder would decide whether, based upon the admissible evidence, she had purchased the product.

Under the traditional view, this same analysis holds in the context of a class action. Because the question whether a given putative class member has purchased the offending product is an objective one, the class is ascertainable. If, after certification, the claim was dismissed under Rule 12(b)(6) for failing to state a claim, or under Rule 56 on summary judgment, or after trial, each member of the class would be bound by the adverse result. A subsequent lawsuit (individual or class) by a class member who had not validly opted out of the prior class lawsuit would be dismissed on grounds of res judicata.

But what if the lawsuit is successful, either in generating a settlement or on the merits at trial? In the former case (settlement), the parties will typically negotiate a fund set at a percentage of the defendant's potential *aggregate* liability. Since not all absent class members will testify at trial (which is more or less the point of a class trial in the first place), how will each class member's purchase of the product—and thus her

---

Littleton, 414 U.S. 488, 494 (1974) ("[I]f none of the named plaintiffs purporting to represent a class establishes the requisite of a case or controversy with the defendants, none may seek relief on behalf of himself or any other member of the class.").

status as a class member—be determined? This has been the focus of the ascertainability debate over the past few years.

Where the parties negotiate a settlement, the defendant will have agreed to a claims process—usually involving some sort of attestation, short of sworn affidavits, that the class member purchased the product—thereby obviating any due process concerns from the defendant's perspective.

If there is no settlement, many courts have accepted the prospect of a claims procedure short of "mini-trials" for each class member— for example, sworn affidavits or declarations subject to penalty of perjury—as a way for each class member to prove up her claim and entitlement to relief. In such situations, defendants may claim that their due process rights are infringed upon by the lack of opportunity to cross examine each class member.[17] If the court deems the argument to be sufficiently serious, it might deny certification for lack of manageability or lack of predominance; actually order "mini-trials" under a procedure designed to be workable and preserve due process rights; or instead certify an issue class under Rule 23(c)(4) to establish whether the defendant is liable, thereby permitting individual class members to use a favorable verdict on liability in separate individual actions that would focus on causation and perhaps damages.

It is the second scenario—the prospect of a class trial—that has prompted some courts (including prominently the Third Circuit's *Carrera v. Bayer* decision) to require not only that the class be objectively defined in the traditional sense, but also that it be administratively feasible to determine class membership though class-wide proofs at a class trial.[18]

The *Carrera* decision is controversial. A number of other circuit courts of appeals have either rejected or declined to follow its ascertainability

---

17. This argument is stronger where there is no acceptable methodology for calculating aggregate damages because the opportunity to cross-examine class members could (at least theoretically) alter defendant's overall exposure. By contrast, if aggregate damages can be calculated then defendant arguably has no real interest in determining the precise allocation of those damages. Relatedly, a recent concurring opinion in a wages class action upholding an award of aggregate damages suggests that it may be an open question whether a class can include uninjured members. Tyson Foods, Inc. v. Bouaphakeo, 136 S. Ct. 1036, 1050 (2016).

18. *See* Carrera v. Bayer Corp., 727 F.3d 300, 305 (3d Cir. 2013).

holding.[19] Even a later Third Circuit panel appears to have softened its earlier holding in *Carrera*.[20] Until clarified by the Supreme Court or a rule change, class litigators should consult the current ascertainability case law in the applicable jurisdiction.

Independence (Avoiding the "Fail-Safe" Class)

The second element of the traditional test for ascertainability—that the criteria for class membership cannot depend on the defendant's liability—is much more settled. This element is designed to avoid so-called fail-safe classes. The following is an example of a fail-safe class:

> All customers of ABC brokerage who purchased XYZ Corp. options between the period of January 1, 2016, and December 31, 2016, to whom the broker breached its fiduciary duty.

The problem with this class is that one cannot determine whether an individual customer of ABC brokerage is a member or not until there is a decision on the merits of the claim. If the judge or jury decides that there was no breach of fiduciary duty as to a given absent putative class member, then by definition that person is not a member of the class as defined, and not bound by the judgment. He or she could bring an individual claim the very next day. By contrast, if a breach of fiduciary duty is found, then he or she is a member of the class and the defendant is bound by the judgment. This lack of mutuality of the binding effect of the judgment in the class action is inherently unfair—whether or not the proposed class would raise predominance or other obstacles under Rule 23.

In contrast, the following class definition is ascertainable:

> All customers of ABC brokerage who purchased XYZ Corp. options between the period of January 1, 2016, and December 31, 2016.

The difference is the omission of the last clause. Perhaps plaintiff's theory is that the options were inherently unsuitable, or that the brokerage failed to disclose a conflict of interest it had in promoting the options. Win, lose, or draw, *all* parties (including absent class members) will be bound by the judgment.

---

19. Mullins v. Direct Digital, 795 F.3d 654, 665 (7th Cir. 2015); Sandusky Wellness Ctr., LLC, v. Medtox Sci., Inc., 821 F.3d 992, 995–96 (8th Cir. 2016); Rikos v. Procter & Gamble Co., 799 F.3d 497, 525 (6th Cir. 2015); Briseno v. ConAgra Foods, Inc., 844 F.3d 1121, 1127 (9th Cir. 2017). In *Briseno*, the Ninth Circuit noted that it had not identified an "ascertainability" requirement as such, but in any event rejected application of an "administratively feasible" proof requirement for the class. 844 F.3d at 1124 n.3 & n.4.

20. *See* Byrd v. Aaron's Inc., 784 F.3d 154, 170 (3d Cir. 2015).

ESTABLISHING AND CHALLENGING NUMEROSITY

Numerosity is the least controverted class prerequisite and has been found in cases with as few as two dozen or so putative class members. There are still decisions, however, where numerosity is central to the denial of class certification. While it is uncommon for this denial to be based on the simple lack of numerosity, sometimes it is a result of the plaintiff's failure adequately to *demonstrate* numerosity, which cannot be presumed. Accordingly, the worst thing a plaintiff can do is to ignore or only pay lip service to this element.

The driving consideration regarding numerosity is whether there are so many class members that aggregation of their claims in a single case through joinder would be "impracticable."[21] This inquiry depends to some extent on the particulars of a given case. There might be little difficulty in joining twenty-five employees at a single job site who are complaining about a single practice or policy, while joining twenty-five consumers from around a state or wider geographic region to a complaint about a product or consumer transaction might be deemed impracticable.

ESTABLISHING AND CHALLENGING COMMONALITY

The Rule 23(a)(2) requirement for commonality is particularly important in the injunctive/equitable claims context, such as in the employment arena. The test for commonality has become more demanding since the Supreme Court's 2011 decision in *Wal-Mart Stores, Inc. v. Dukes*.[22] In *Wal-Mart*, a suit challenging sex discrimination in pay and promotions, the Court reversed certification for a proposed nationwide class of about one and a half million current and former female employees.[23] Its decision turned on its holding that there was no commonality under Rule 23(a)(2).

Class certification attorneys now know by heart the core precepts the Supreme Court set forth in *Wal-Mart*, repeating a standard first articulated by the Court in *General Telephone Co. v. Falcon*.[24] First, the trial court may certify the class only if it determines, "after a rigorous analysis,

---

21. FED. R. CIV. P. 23(a)(1).
22. 564 U.S. 338, 349–50 (2011); cf. 1 H. NEWBERG & A. CONTE, NEWBERG ON CLASS ACTIONS § 3.10 (3d ed. 1992) (stating the previously held widespread view that the commonality requirement "is easily met").
23. *Wal-Mart*, 564 U.S. at 342.
24. 457 U.S. 147, 159 (1982).

that the prerequisites of Rule 23(a) have been satisfied."[25] Specific to commonality, the proponent of certification must identify "a common contention of such a nature that it is capable of classwide resolution."[26] It is not enough to show a common question or multiple common questions, "even in droves."[27] Rather, the plaintiff must show "the capacity of a classwide proceeding to generate common *answers* apt to drive the resolution of the litigation."[28] In short, a common contention is one that "will resolve an issue that is central to the validity of each one of the claims in one stroke."[29]

Defense briefs opposing class certification often cite heavily to *Wal-Mart* to argue that the issues presented are too individualized for class treatment. Indeed, in a widely cited dissent, Justice Ginsburg argued that the Supreme Court has now effectively conflated commonality with the more demanding standard for predominance.[30] However, the *Wal-Mart* majority itself said it was not raising the standard for commonality under Rule 23(a)(2)—recognizing that even a single common issue meets this prerequisite.[31] Rather, the Court, applying the familiar *Falcon* "rigorous analysis" approach, found that there was no common issue across a nationwide class where defendant used a decentralized, store-level discretionary policy for hiring and promotion decisions.[32]

Some hailed *Wal-Mart* as the death-knell of class actions, and it has certainly posed new challenges for plaintiff's attorneys, particularly in large-scale civil rights litigation. But courts continue to certify cases that focus on a truly common policy or practice. *Wal-Mart* is frequently distinguished based on the huge size and vast geographic scope of its proposed class, and the discretionary decision making at issue in that case. As the Supreme Court itself noted in *Wal-Mart*, it was "one of the most expansive class actions ever,"[33] in which the plaintiffs wanted to "sue

---

25. *Id.*

26. *Wal-Mart*, 564 U.S. at 350.

27. *Id.*

28. *Id.* at 389–90 (emphasis in original, quoting Richard Nagareda, *Class Certification in the Age of Aggregate Proof*, 84 N.Y.U. L. Rev. 97, 132 (2009)).

29. *Id.* at 350.

30. *Wal-Mart*, 564 U.S. at 368 (Ginsburg, J., dissenting) (stating that "the Court imports into the Rule 23(a) determination concerns properly addressed in a Rule 23(b)(3) assessment").

31. 564 U.S. at 359.

32. *Id.* at 353.

33. *Id.* at 342.

about literally millions of employment decisions at once."[34] "Without some glue holding the alleged *reasons* for all those decisions together," the Court held, there was no commonality where it was "impossible to say that examination of all the class members' claims for relief will produce a common answer to the crucial question *why was I disfavored.*"[35]

In contrast to the claims of the "unprecedented nationwide class" in *Wal-Mart*,[36] commonality may be relatively easy to show where plaintiffs are challenging an official policy or well-documented practice that applies uniformly to a proposed class, particularly a class that is narrowly defined. Such a case is, as the Ninth Circuit has stated, "the classic case for treatment as a class action: that is, the commonality linking the class members is the dispositive question in the lawsuit."[37]

To succeed on commonality after *Wal-Mart* it is more important than ever that the plaintiff's strategy begin with the simple step of identifying similar decisions and citing the same arguments and types of evidence that have prevailed in those cases. Courts have continued to find commonality, for example, in wage and hour cases challenging unlawful provisions uniformly applied; consumer cases where proof of liability arises from a common event or uniform product defect; and securities fraud, antitrust, and other cases involving a single course of conduct or action by the defendant.

Courts have continued to certify some civil rights cases involving the discriminatory exercise of subjective discretion.[38] As the Court in *Wal-Mart* explained, "giving discretion to lower-level supervisors can be the basis of Title VII liability under a disparate impact theory," because "a common mode of exercising discretion that pervades the entire company" can constitute "a general policy."[39] But the plaintiff should be prepared to withstand a thorough analysis about exactly how the exercise of discretion presents a common question subject to a common

---

34. *Id.* at 352.
35. *Wal-Mart*, 564 U.S. at 352 (emphasis in original).
36. Brown v. Nucor Corp., 785 F.3d 895, 900 (4th Cir. 2015).
37. Evon v. Law Offices of Sidney Mickell, 688 F.3d 1015, 1030 (9th Cir. 2012).
38. *Compare, e.g.,* Bolden v. Walsh Construction Co., 688 F.3d 893, 896–97 (7th Cir. 2012) (denying certification where the court found there was a policy of discretion), *with* Parra v. Bashas', 291 F.R.D. 360, 376 (D. Ariz. 2013) (certifying a class challenging a two-tier wage scale).
39. *Wal-Mart*, 564 U.S. at 355, 356.

answer related to liability. [40] As the Fourth Circuit described in *Scott v. Family Dollar Stores, Inc.*,[41] commonality can exist in a discretion-based case where "the exercise of discretion is tied to a specific employment practice," and the "subjective practice at issue affected the class in a uniform manner."[42] For example, the Seventh Circuit in *McReynolds v. Merrill Lynch*, found commonality where plaintiffs sued based on a company-wide framework that, by policy, allowed brokers to select their own teams and then distributed accounts based on revenues earned by the teams. The plaintiffs alleged that the teams operated like "little fraternities," as Judge Posner's opinion termed them, and that racial exclusion and lower earnings for non-white broker teams resulted.[43] Likewise, in *Ellis v. Costco Wholesale Corp.*, the Northern District of California upheld certification in a gender discrimination case involving the biased exercise of discretion.[44] In finding commonality as to the plaintiff's claims, the court cited evidence not only of a "tap on the shoulder" selection system for promotion, but also of other company-wide policies within which the discretion operated.[45] Contrast *Ellis* with *Davis v. Cintas Corp.*, where the Sixth Circuit held there was no commonality in a case alleging that subjective decisions made by managers favored males because of a "common white male business culture."[46]

For the non–employment discrimination attorney, there are two lessons from the discretion cases with regard to commonality. First is the need to define the common policies or practices at issue with clarity and specificity. Second is the need to support the existence and nature of those policies and practices with evidence sufficient to withstand the court's rigorous analysis. Consider, as well, the interplay between the merits and class certification discussed earlier in the section titled "Interplay between Merits and Class Certification."

---

40. For a thorough analysis of the impact of *Wal-Mart* on class certification decisions in civil rights cases, see Katherine E. Lamm, *Work in Progress: Civil Rights Class Actions After Wal-Mart v. Dukes*, 50 HARV. C.R.-C.L. L. REV. 153 (2015).

41. 733 F.3d 105, 113 (4th Cir. 2013).

42. *Id.* (quoting Elizabeth Tippett, *Robbing a Barren Vault: the Implications of Dukes v. Wal-Mart for Cases Challenging Subjective Employment Practices*, 29 HOFSTRA LAB. & EMP. L.J. 433, 446 (2012)).

43. McReynolds v. Merrill Lynch, Pierce, Fenner & Smith, Inc., 672 F.3d 482, 489 (7th Cir. 2012).

44. 285 F.R.D. 492, 510 (N.D. Cal. 2012).

45. *Id.* at 511, 521, 531.

46. Davis v. Cintas Corp., 717 F.3d 476, 489 (6th Cir. 2013).

In summary, from the perspective of defense counsel, *Wal-Mart* supports greater scrutiny of the commonality prerequisite and provides a platform upon which to urge the trial court to reject certification of overbroad classes. In particular, defendants gain traction after *Wal-Mart* by criticizing the plaintiff's ambiguous arguments about discretion; by emphasizing the individual concerns of diverse class members; and by focusing on any elements of the claim for which the merits and commonality are intertwined.

For plaintiff's counsel, *Wal-Mart* raises the level of scrutiny for the commonality requirement, particularly in the employment context. The cases that will fare best are those that identify a common policy, practice, conduct, or product defect, and cite rigorously developed evidence including, where necessary, expert testimony and analysis.

ESTABLISHING AND CHALLENGING TYPICALITY

As goes the claim of the named plaintiff, so go the claims of the absent class members.[47] This statement encapsulates the ideal of perfect "typicality" under Rule 23(a)(3). As an ideal it is perhaps seldom achieved, but, nonetheless, it is the measure against which a proposed class is measured.

The case law, of course, is a bit more nuanced than the ideal. A class representative's claim need not be a carbon copy of each and every absent class member's claim in order to meet the typicality prerequisite. Typicality is met if the class members' claims are "fairly encompassed by the named plaintiffs' claims."[48] But the more differences—the less typical the representative's claims—the less cohesive the class and the weaker the argument for class certification.

The observation is frequently made that there is overlap among the prerequisites of adequacy, typicality, and even commonality, but it is useful to focus on the core goal of typicality: cohesion. Among other goals, a principal goal of Rule 23 and aggregate litigation generally is efficiency. If the class representative's claims are perfectly typical (and the other prerequisites of Rule 23 satisfied), then there can be no real objection—either by absent class members or defendants—to permitting that representative to stand in for all other class members who do not opt out (in a Rule 23(b)(3) action). All available defenses would

---

47. Sprague v. Gen. Motors Corp., 133 F.3d 388, 399 (6th Cir. 1998) (en banc).
48. *Id.* (quoting *In re* Am. Med. Sys., 75 F.3d 1069, 1082 (6th Cir. 1996)).

apply to that one plaintiff's claim; each burden placed by substantive or evidentiary rules applies to her claim; and trying one single claim is undoubtedly more efficient than trying dozens, hundreds, or thousands of them.

But the less typical the named plaintiff(s)' claims are, the more cohesion breaks down and the more difficult it is to achieve a trial that efficiently and fairly resolves the class claims in a single proceeding. This is true whether or not there are any meaningful conflicts between the named plaintiff and absent class members (the province of the adequacy prerequisite). This is true even if there are a number of common issues (the product's defect; the defendant's negligence or knowledge; etc.). This is true even if, in the aggregate, common issues outweigh individual ones (the predominance requirement in a (b)(3) class).

What makes for typicality, or lack thereof, depends on the circumstances of each case. Were class members sold a uniform product alleged to have consistently failed in the same way? Were defendant's warranty disclaimers uniform? In a fair debt collection case, were class members all sent form letters alleged to have violated applicable law? In a securities fraud case, are defendants alleged to have failed to disclose the same material facts relevant to a stock's value in a defined period? In an indirect-purchaser antitrust case, did the named plaintiff(s) purchase through a distribution channel that operates with a measure of consistency across class members?

Alternatively, are the named plaintiffs subject to unique defenses—such as a statute of limitations defense that does not apply to absent class members, or a release, consent, or ratification? Is there a credible unclean hands defense to an equitable claim? Under the applicable legal standard, is materiality of a representation a class member-specific inquiry? Was the named plaintiff using the product in an unusual or atypical way? In these instances, the party opposing certification will have a stronger argument that the movant has failed to demonstrate typicality.

Beyond the efficiency goals discussed earlier, typicality invokes due process concerns as to both absent class members and defendants.[49] A class representative who is subject to unique defenses may taint the claims of numerous absent class members who would not be subject to

---

49. The Supreme Court has stated:

The adequacy-of-representation requirement "tends to merge" with the commonality and typicality criteria of Rule 23(a), which "serve as guideposts for determining

that defense. Alternatively, if many absent class members' claims would be subject to defenses that vary among them, their claims are not typical even if the class representatives are not subject to those defenses. In this situation, the defendant will argue that certification will thwart its due process right to mount a defense to each class member's claims.

Note that the groundwork for an effective typicality argument is laid in class discovery. Plaintiffs should aggressively pursue evidence of company policies or business practices that apply to the bulk of the proposed class. Defendants, on the other hand, should pursue evidence that class representatives' claims are not typical. This occasionally requires third-party discovery (as in antitrust cases) and sometimes discovery of absent class members. Courts frequently require defendants to obtain leave of court to depose absent class members and may impose limits on such depositions to avoid harassment.

ESTABLISHING AND CHALLENGING ADEQUACY

Adequacy has two elements: (1) adequacy of the named plaintiff(s) and (2) adequacy of counsel.

With respect to the named plaintiff, the court will ask whether the individual is sufficiently informed and engaged to afford some assurance that class counsel is actually accountable to the client. A second, and potentially more serious, consideration is whether there is any conflict of interest between the named plaintiff(s) and absent class members.

Cases in which the class representative has been held not to be adequate include:

- Where the class representative is not a member of the proposed class (this happens more often than one might suppose)[50]
- Where the class representative is a relative or employee of class counsel[51]

---

whether . . . maintenance of a class action is economical and whether the named plaintiff's claim and the class claims are so interrelated that the interests of the class members will be fairly and adequately protected in their absence."

Amchem Prods. v. Windsor, 521 U.S. 591, 626 n.20 (quoting *Falcon*, 457 U.S. at 157).

50. *See, e.g.*, Foster v. Ctr. Twp. of LaPorte Cnty., 798 F.2d 237, 244 (7th Cir. 1986) ("It is, of course, axiomatic that the named representative of a class must be a member of that class.").

51. *See, e.g.*, Susman v. Lincoln American Corp. (7th Cir. 1977) 561 F.2d 86, 90–91 (collecting cases).

- Where the class representative has a tangible conflict of interest with other class members[52]
- Where the class representative displays (e.g., at deposition) a near-total lack of attention or ambivalence to the case, or imprudence regarding the underlying transaction[53]

This list is not exhaustive. Counsel should be most attentive to the conflicts issue, which is the most frequent basis for a finding of inadequacy.

A prominent example of the conflict problem was presented in *Amchem*, where the Supreme Court addressed a challenge to a proposed nationwide asbestos settlement class for future claimants.[54] Nine class representatives sought to represent a unified class of individuals (without subclasses) that had been exposed to asbestos, including both individuals who had manifested symptoms and individuals who had not yet manifested symptoms. The Supreme Court held these nine representatives inadequate based on the inherent conflicts among the class between these two subgroups—those with present symptoms, who would favor higher up-front payouts, and those without symptoms, who would favor interest-adjusted payouts (which the settlement did not provide) and more liberal back-end opt-out opportunities.

The *Amchem* decision does not mean that a proposed class cannot encompass claimants with varying claims based on defendants' alleged misconduct. In order to meet the adequacy of representation prerequisite, however, class members with divergent interests must at minimum be designated by discrete subclasses.[55] Depending upon the depth of the conflict, separate class counsel might need to be appointed for subclasses as well.[56]

---

52. *See, e.g.*, Amchem Prods, 521 at 625–26.

53. *See, e.g.*, Hoving v. Lawyers Title Ins. Co., 256 F.R.D. 555, 565–66 (E.D. Mich. 2009) (Lawson, J.).

54. 521 U.S. at 625–28.

55. Where subclasses are proposed, each subclass must have a class representative and individually satisfy the elements of Rule 23. *See* FED. R. CIV. P. 23(c)(5) ("When appropriate, a class may be divided into subclasses that are each treated as a class under this rule.").

56. *See, e.g.*, *In re* Payment Card Interchange Fee & Merch. Disc. Antitrust Litig., 827 F.3d 223, 233–34 (2d Cir. 2016) (reversing $7.5 billion class settlement based on inadequacy where certain members of class not separately represented had interests antagonistic to the rest of the class); *see also* Valley Drug Co. v. Geneva Pharms., 350 F.3d 1181, 1189 (11th Cir. 2003) (rejecting class certification where conflict was "fundamental").

The second element of adequacy—adequacy of counsel—is less frequently litigated. The test is whether class counsel has the experience and ability to effectively prosecute the claims of the proposed class; can muster the resources necessary to advance the litigation; and demonstrates through her conduct that she is proceeding appropriately with the case.[57] In addition, class counsel must be free of conflicts in her representation of the various members of the class or subclass whose interests she is designated to advocate.

It is worth noting that, absent tangible grounds for doing so, some courts are leery of defense counsel making adequacy arguments. A court may quite naturally question the earnestness of the defendant's professed concern for whether the named plaintiffs or their counsel are adequate—rather than simply seeking to defeat class certification for strategic purposes. Adequacy challenges coming from objectors to a proposed settlement may be given more credence (all else being equal) for this reason. Defendants nevertheless *do* have an important—perhaps even compelling—interest in the adequacy issue: one of the limited grounds for challenging the res judicata effect of a class settlement is a claim that absent class members' due process rights were not protected due to inadequacy of representation.[58]

INJUNCTIVE RELIEF AND LIMITED FUND CLASSES

Rule 23(b)(2) applies where injunctive or declaratory relief could suffice to redress a class-wide injury. Civil rights class cases are often pleaded under Rule 23(b)(2), but (b)(2) cases also arise in other areas of law, including consumer, environmental, antitrust, and employee benefits actions. The Supreme Court has written that

> [t]he key to the (b)(2) class is the "indivisible nature of the injunctive or declaratory remedy warranted—the notion that the conduct is such that it can be enjoined or declared unlawful only as to all of the class members or as to none of them."[59]

The cohesion inherent in a (b)(2) class raises several strategy issues that are relevant for both the proponent and opponent of class certification.

---

57. *See generally* Ballan v. Upjohn Co., 159 F.R.D. 473, 486–88 (W.D. Mich. 1994) (Hillman, J.).

58. *See, e.g.* State v. Homeside Lending, Inc., 826 A.2d 997, 1019 (Vt. 2003).

59. *Wal-Mart*, 564 U.S. at 360 (2011) (quoting Nagareda, *supra* note 28, at 132).

Plaintiff's Strategy

The first strategy question is why a plaintiff would bring a class action when the case can be won with a single injunction or declaration striking down an illegal law or policy, without the possible delay and complexity of class certification. Sometimes, the right choice is to eschew class certification, as where the affected group is small and identifiable, or where there is a need for quick resolution.

Certification can offer distinct advantages, however—and may even be required—where a particularly broad remedy is being sought. First, proceeding with class certification may better define for the court the scope of relief needed, improving the likelihood that the court will issue an appropriate expansive injunction, perhaps one reaching beyond an individual worksite to encompass an entire company, or beyond a small geographic region to encompass a larger one. Second, where the group's "members are incapable of specific enumeration," the (b)(2) class is particularly appropriate, as the Federal Rules Advisory Committee Notes explain.[60] Thus, a (b)(2) class provides advantages for the plaintiff class where it may not be able to satisfy the implied requirement of definiteness or ascertainability that some courts have read into Rule 23.[61] Third, where there is a risk of mootness for any one plaintiff, the class action device protects the class's claims. Pre-certification, the court has discretion to certify a class notwithstanding mootness as to an individual plaintiff for inherently transitory claims that nonetheless continue to affect a broader group of people.[62] Post-certification, where a claim is "capable of repetition yet evad[es] review," a post-certification case should not become moot so long as the challenged conduct continues to threaten the class.[63] In short, the (b)(2) class can offer multiple procedural and practical advantages, particularly where larger classes are involved.

Another strategy question is whether to pursue (b)(2) or another form of certification. The (b)(2) class—like the (b)(1) class—is mandatory, while the (b)(3) class is not. In addition to requiring that the plaintiff demonstrate predominance and superiority, Rule 23(b)(3) also requires

---

60. FED. R. CIV. P. Advisory Committee Notes to Amended Rule 23(b)(2) (1966).

61. *See, e.g.*, Floyd v. City of New York, 283 F.R.D. 153, 161–62 (S.D.N.Y. 2012) (citing WILLIAM B. RUBENSTEIN ET AL., NEWBERG ON CLASS ACTIONS § 3:7 (5th ed. 2011) (stating "it is not clear that the implied requirement of definiteness should apply to Rule 23(b)(2) class actions at all.").

62. Deposit Guar. Nat'l Bank v. Roper, 445 U.S. 326, 343–44 (1980).

63. Franks v. Bowman Transp. Co., 424 U.S. 747, 753–55 (1976).

notice followed by an opportunity for putative class members to withdraw from or "opt out" of the class. The lack of opt-out rights would seem to afford advantages to the plaintiff seeking certification, but a (b)(2) class can't be chosen without sufficient justification.[64] As discussed earlier, certification under (b)(2) is limited to discrete circumstances and types of cases. Citing due process considerations, the Supreme Court has held that (b)(2) may be inappropriate for claims seeking money damages that are more than "incidental to the injunctive or declaratory relief":[65] Claims seeking to recover individualized money damages for class members are candidates for certification only under Rule 23(b)(3).

The limitations thus imposed upon (b)(2) classes by the Supreme Court do not mean that (b)(2) is inapplicable in any case that seeks monetary relief for the class. Until the Supreme Court weighs in again, practitioners will want to check their circuit's law as to how the lines have been drawn between class actions considered to seek only "incidental" monetary relief that are potentially subject to certification under (b)(2), and those seeking individualized money damages that will require notice and opt-out options under (b)(3).

In the Seventh Circuit case of *Johnson v. Meriter Health Services Employee Retirement Plan*,[66] Judge Posner explained the difference as follows: monetary relief can be awarded under (b)(2) where "the calculation of monetary relief will be mechanical, formulaic, a task not for the trier of fact but for a computer program," in contrast to individualized awards of relief under (b)(3) where "awards [are] based on evidence specific to particular class members."[67]

The *Meriter* opinion also highlights a pragmatic option where the remedies sought in a class action overlap between (b)(2) and (b)(3): a hybrid class or divided certification.[68] In such a case, the plaintiff may seek (b)(2) certification first, and pursue injunctive or declaratory relief, followed by a (b)(3) proceeding to award monetary damages if appropriate. As the court explained, in such a case, "[o]nce declaratory relief

---

64. The court may still order notice in a (b)(2) class, but the differences are that (1) such notice is not mandatory but discretionary on the part of the court and (2) the remedy for a class member who objects is to intervene in the action, not withdraw from the class.

65. *Wal-Mart*, 564 U.S. at 360.

66. 702 F.3d 364, 370 (7th Cir. 2012).

67. *Id*. at 370.

68. *See id*. at 371.

is ordered, all that is left is a determination of monetary relief, and that is the type of proceeding for which (b)(3) is designed."[69]

Where the liability determinations for declaratory relief and damages are inextricably intertwined, *Meriter* states that under the Seventh Amendment a party may demand that damages claims be tried first to a jury.[70] But in that instance, the court may nonetheless be able to proceed under (b)(2) while ordering a notice and opt-out procedure to satisfy due process requirements. Note, as well, that where the underlying claims are equitable and no jury trial rights arise (as was the case in *Meriter* under the Employee Retirement Income Security Act), or where all parties consent to a bench trial, the court would be free to manage the case in whatever order or sequence seems most practical.

Plaintiffs should also not overlook the possibility of seeking certification under Rule 23(b)(1)(A) or (b)(1)(B). As under (b)(2), a (b)(1) class is appropriate where there is an inherent reason for treating the case on a class-wide basis, rather than through multiple individual suits. Specifically, courts will certify a (b)(1)(A) class where different outcomes in multiple cases would result in "incompatible standards of conduct" for a defendant, or where an individual judgment, "while not technically concluding [the claims] of the other members, might do so as a practical matter."[71]

Examples of cases appropriate for certification under (b)(1)(A) include bond or riparian rights cases, employee benefits cases, and the hybrid relief cases discussed earlier, where monetary relief may be sought along with both equitable or declaratory relief. Rule 23(b)(1)(B) cases are limited fund cases, where many claimants are seeking relief against a single fund unlikely to provide complete relief as to all of them.

Why would a plaintiff consider certification under (b)(1) rather than (b)(2)? In addition to the ability to obtain a damage award in a limited fund case, other reasons may include adherence to precedent in a particular circuit (as in ERISA cases), or to highlight the inherent cohesion of the class's claims.

For the plaintiff, the advantages of proceeding under (b)(2) or (b)(1), even on a hybrid basis, are not just in achieving coherent relief for the class, but also in emphasizing for the court how and why the class

---

69. *Id.*

70. *Id.*

71. Fed. R. Civ. P. Advisory Committee Notes to Amended Rule 23 (1966).

should be treated as a group, and therefore merits certification. Defining a plan for the court that offers the option of divided certification if necessary or explaining how computation of monetary relief will be merely "mechanical" or "formulaic," provides the court with a ready-made trial plan, which can inspire the court's confidence that certification is appropriate.

Defense Strategy

All of the strategy issues for plaintiffs in evaluating whether and how to proceed under (b)(2), alone or on a hybrid basis, suggest possible class opposition arguments for the defense. That is, the defense may be able to attack the appropriateness of certification based on the lack of internal cohesion (lack of Rule 23(a) commonality) of the class, by arguing that liability actually requires adjudication on an individual basis. Likewise, the defense can attack class certification under (b)(2) by attempting to demonstrate that any demands for monetary relief are really "individualized monetary claims,"[72] which require meeting the more difficult (b)(3) elements. Additionally, a defendant resisting (b)(2) certification may want to attack the request for injunctive relief on traditional grounds for defeating injunctive claims. For instance, if a defendant can persuasively argue at the certification stage that money damages provide an adequate remedy for each putative class member, then it may be able to paint the request for certification of a (b)(2) class as tantamount to an attempted "end run" around the additional certification requirements and due process safeguards of a (b)(3) class, including the requirement that plaintiffs demonstrate predominance, that they notify all class members and provide for opt outs, and that they demonstrate superiority.

DAMAGES CLASSES
Establishing and Challenging Predominance

Notwithstanding the recent attention post-*Wal-Mart* to Rule 23(a)(2) commonality and the implied ascertainability requirement, the dominate factor determining whether a damages class is certified remains Rule 23(b)(3)'s predominance requirement. Class counsel must critically

---

72. *Wal-Mart*, 564 U.S. at 362.

assess this element more than any other from the outset; defense counsel will mark most of their victories in defeating class certification as notches on their predominance belts.

Short of good briefing, class counsel's best bet to establish predominance comes at the case conception/class definition phase—with perhaps one stand-out exception in antitrust class actions, where development of compelling expert testimony (usually an economist) can go a long way toward establishing predominance. In a products case, for example, class counsel can shape the class to cover a limited number or range of products, produced over a limited time frame, or only at particular factories. The broader the scope of the claims, the greater the opportunity for defendant to develop a solid factual record demonstrating lack of predominance. Of course, class counsel should pay equal attention during class discovery to developing a thorough evidentiary record in all areas touching upon contested issues, beyond just expert opinions, to support a finding of predominance at the certification hearing.

The dilemma of predominance, viewed from the plaintiff's perspective, pits a desire to exploit practical benefits that are often inherent in a broader class definition—such as improved leverage or maximizing the opportunity to compensate the greatest number of injured class members—against the goal of constructing a tightly defined class that can actually be certified. The question is one of balance and judgment.

In this context, a few generalizations might be helpful:

- It is easier to narrow a broad class (as defined in the complaint) than to expand a narrow one (e.g., in the class certification brief or at the class hearing);
- The scope of the class set forth in the complaint will impact the scope of class discovery and also the tolling of individual claims under *American Pipe*;[73]
- Different substantive areas (e.g., antitrust; securities fraud) may have more favorable case law regarding the weight attributed to defendant's conduct (e.g., the existence of a collusive agreement or material nondisclosure), which could affect the scope of the proposed class (e.g., product lines, geographic, or temporal). In other words, research your particular puddle before you leap into it; and

---

73. Am. Pipe Constr. Co. v. Utah, 414 U.S. 538, 558 n.29 (1974); *see* China Agritech, Inc. v. Resh, No. 17–432 2018 WL 2767565, at *3 (U.S. June 10, 2018).

- Do not bite off more than you can chew. A plainly overbroad class may sour the court on the certification question well before you get to the motion or hearing.

From the defense perspective, few classes are as chock full of common issues as plaintiffs portray in the class complaint. Depending on the case and the amount at stake, defendants frequently do well to spend a significant amount of their case budget on defeating predominance. Since so little information is normally available from class representatives, assembling the evidence and expert testimony to *prove* that individual issues predominate frequently requires a major look inward and to third parties. This is where effective client management—both by outside and inside counsel—to marshal the necessary resources is key. Subpoenaing of non-parties (e.g., in an antitrust case, to demonstrate that alleged overcharges were not passed on through all avenues of product distribution and retail) can prove invaluable.

There are few common issues which, on close examination, cannot colorably be argued to present individual issues. Collusive agreement? Well, for how long? For what markets? Among which of the defendants? And in antitrust cases in particular, the question of whether the plaintiffs' model for demonstrating "impact" (antitrust injury, typically in the form of higher prices) was experienced by all or almost all class members over the class period is a predominance issue. In civil rights cases, is the discriminatory behavior or the disparate impact common across departments, actors, and class members, or are there individual reasons that would justify each employment decision?

While the point is perhaps obvious, it is worth making: it is class counsel's job to propose the class definition and establish its compliance with the predominance requirement; it is defense counsel's job to demonstrate why that proposed class does not present a predominance of common issues; and it is the court's job to evaluate the arguments and record presented in order to answer that question. Everyone is shooting at the same target, drawn by class counsel. In this, defense counsel should resist any inclination to speculate whether some other more narrowly drawn class might meet the requirements of Rule 23. That way lies a slippery slope.

A Word about Experts

In most class actions, the named plaintiffs are individuals with a relative lack of sophistication who may have a genuine but limited financial or other interest in the case. As an evidentiary matter, for purposes of a contested class certification hearing (and later at trial), these individuals will often have little to offer on issues of commonality or predominance. Depending upon the facts of the case, their testimony may even present a risk (from a plaintiff perspective) or an opportunity (from a defense one) of highlighting a lack of typicality or a preponderance of individual issues.

Contrast this with a plaintiff's expert. His or her testimony—to the extent admissible and probative—will by definition be "common evidence," helping to underscore the predominance of common issues. A class expert will virtually always help keep the focus on the defendant's conduct: another common issue. Compared to lay witnesses with limited sophistication and engagement, the expert presents a unique opportunity for class counsel to put plaintiff's best foot forward.[74]

Of course, as alluded to earlier, the expert offers the defendant an equally important opportunity to defeat certification, often by demonstrating through testing actual data that issues plaintiffs seek to portray as common are in actuality individual issues. Where a plaintiff's (or even a defendant's)[75] expert is vulnerable under the standards governing Federal Rule of Evidence 702, a strong *Daubert*[76] motion can be an important part of a party's class certification strategy.[77] Over the last two decades class certification has frequently become a "battle of the experts."

All of which is to underscore the importance of experts from a strategic perspective. A good place to start is Chapter 11 of this book on class action experts.

---

74. Plaintiffs will also benefit to the extent that their experts are able to present "representative evidence" consistent with the standards set forth in *Bouaphakeo*, 136 S. Ct. at 1046.

75. For an example of an ultimately successful plaintiff's *Daubert* challenge of a defense expert, see Messner v. Northshore Univ. Health Sys, 669 F.3d 802, 811–14 (7th Cir. 2012).

76. Daubert v. Merrell Dow Pharms., Inc., 509 U.S. 579, 587 (1993).

77. The Supreme Court's decisions in *Wal-Mart*, 564 U.S. at 354, and Comcast Corp. v. Behrend, 569 U.S. 27, 31 (2013), have underscored the potential importance of *Daubert* motions in the class certification context. But knee-jerk *Daubert* motions—like any other canned tactic—can do a party more harm than good, by tilting the trial court toward the view of the opposing expert whose testimony the court finds admissible on such a challenge. However, even if unsuccessful in the trial court a strong *Daubert* challenge is likely necessary to preserve error on appeal. *See Bouaphakeo*, 136 S. Ct. at 1044.

Establishing and Challenging Superiority

Superiority is an aspect of class certification that has drawn little attention from the courts, but for which parties must prepare. Rule 23(b)(3) sets forth a number of factors relevant to the court's required determination that "a class action is superior to other available methods for fairly and efficiently adjudicating the controversy." These include:

- the class members' interests in individually controlling the prosecution or defense of separate actions;
- the extent and nature of any litigation concerning the controversy already begun by or against class members;
- the desirability of concentrating the litigation of the claims in the particular forum; and
- the likely difficulties in managing a class action.

In sum, the rule directs that the court weigh the costs and benefits of the class device in a case brought under Rule 23(b)(3).[78]

Do not ignore the issues posed by superiority or give them short shrift. On the plaintiff's side, arguing superiority can be a great opportunity to illustrate why "classwide litigation of common issues will reduce litigation costs and promote greater efficiency."[79] On the defense side, the superiority factors provide an opportunity to argue to the trial court why a class action will be unwieldy and unmanageable, overwhelming the court and perhaps even failing to result in a meaningful determination on the merits. Efficiencies of litigation and managing complex actions are of great concern to the courts, as they have made explicit in many class action decisions.[80] As Judge Posner observed when suggesting a discrimination class could be certified on an issue basis under Rule 23(c)(4) (discussed later), "[t]he only issue at this stage is whether the plaintiffs' claim of disparate impact is most efficiently determined on a class-wide basis rather than in 700 individual lawsuits."[81]

The fourth superiority factor, manageability, has become a hot button issue for class action litigants. Following *Comcast* and *Amgen*, the courts have reaffirmed that individual damages issues cannot thwart

---

78. *See* WRIGHT ET AL., *supra* note 9, § 1780.
79. Valentino v. Carter-Wallace, Inc., 97 F.3d 1227, 1234 (9th Cir. 1996).
80. "[E]fficiency and economy of litigation . . . is a principal purpose" of Rule 23. *China Agritech*, 2018 WL 2767525, at *6 (quoting *Am. Pipe*, 414 U.S. at 553).
81. *McReynolds*, 672 F.3d at 491.

certification.[82] But the plaintiff still bears the burden of showing that the case is manageable as a class action. Often, the best way to do that is to submit a trial plan that clearly shows the court how plaintiffs plan to manage a class trial, including determining liability and damages. In some cases, a trial plan can be briefly described in a few paragraphs at the end of a brief. In other cases, especially where plaintiffs are aware of particular concerns about manageability (e.g., where large numbers of individual proceedings may in fact be required, or they anticipate a dispute about statistical sampling), plaintiffs may instead submit an entirely separate document as a proposed trial plan.[83] Courts are increasing looking for trial plans as a part of the motion to certify. Plaintiffs will also want to emphasize that the court has broad discretion to manage the trial.

Defendants can attempt to undermine superiority by using some of their anti-predominance arguments, underscoring a theme that the issues presented are in fact individual, myriad, and complex. For example, in an indirect purchaser antitrust case, the defendant might argue that individual retailers who purchased through wholesalers (direct purchasers) that passed on all of the alleged collusive overcharge have an interest in separately suing the manufacturers, rather than being lumped together with retailers who purchased from wholesalers who absorbed the overcharge entirely (resulting in zero damages through those distribution channels).

In the past, appellate courts only rarely discuss superiority, but a couple of recent decisions suggest this may be changing. In *Mullins v. Direct Digital*, the Seventh Circuit came out heavily in favor of class certification, as compared to multiple individual actions, emphasizing that Rule 23(b)(3)'s "superiority requirement . . . is comparative: the court must assess efficiency with an eye toward 'other available methods.'"[84] The Seventh Circuit quoted favorably the Wright & Miller *Federal Practice & Procedure* treatise's admonition that

> a decision against class-action treatment should be rendered only when the ministerial efforts simply will not produce corresponding efficiencies. In no event should the court use the possibility of becoming involved with the

82. *Bouaphakeo*, 136 S. Ct. at 1045.
83. See Chapter 10, "Trial Plans."
84. *Mullins*, 795 F.3d at 664.

administration of a complex lawsuit as a justification for evading the responsibilities imposed by Rule 23.[85]

Further, the court continued, "refusing to certify on manageability grounds alone should be the last resort."[86] The court cited a number of arguments that plaintiffs will want to raise as to superiority, including that

a district judge has discretion to (and we think normally should) wait and see how serious the problem may turn out to be after settlement or judgment, when much more may be known about available records, response rates, and other relevant factors.[87]

The court pointed out that decertification can be done later "if a problem is truly insoluble," and held that before decertifying or refusing to certify a class, the trial court should evaluate whether the options proposed in Rules 23(c) and (d) would be of assistance, such as use of "a special master, representative trials, or other means" to manage individual issues.[88]

Defendants, however, have some superiority cases in their arsenal to cite (at least in ERISA breach of fiduciary duty cases). The Sixth Circuit, in *Pipefitters Local 636 Insurance Fund v. Blue Cross Blue Shield of Michigan*, noted that "[g]iven the huge amount of judicial resources expended by class actions, particular care in their issuance is required."[89] The court reversed certification on superiority grounds under (b)(3) because, it reasoned, determining fiduciary status for the defendants in this particular ERISA breach of fiduciary duty case would require "looking at the contract terms and funding arrangements of 550 to 875 class members."[90] The court observed that individual damages awards were not so small that individual class members would be precluded from seeking relief in independent litigation. Finally, the court considered testimony offered by the commissioner of financial and insurance regulation that a class action would lead to Blue Cross Blue Shield being forced to stop collecting more than $100 million dollars annually, and

---

85. *Id.* at 663 (quoting 7AA CHARLES A. WRIGHT ET AL., FEDERAL PRACTICE & PROCEDURE § 1760 (3d ed. 2008)).

86. *Id.* at 664.

87. *Id.*

88. *Id.*

89. Pipefitters Local 636 Ins. Fund v. Blue Cross Blue Shield of Michigan, 654 F.3d 618, 630 (6th Cir. 2011).

90. *Id.* at 631–32.

to charge higher premiums to others, including the elderly.[91] The court concluded by allowing the case to proceed on an individual basis, with the common issue still being decided but not affecting others not before the court.

ISSUE CERTIFICATION—RULE 23(C)(4)

Rule 23(c)(4) provides that "[w]hen appropriate, an action may be brought or maintained as a class action with respect to particular issues." In an early case, the Fifth Circuit noted: "A district court cannot manufacture predominance through the nimble use of subdivision (c)(4)."[92] But, in recent years, the prevailing view has broken the other way, concluding that certification of one or more discrete issues will advance the litigation.[93]

A number of courts have been persuaded by the American Law Institute's Principles of Aggregate Litigation regarding the question of issue classes. Under those principles, a given issue can be certified for class treatment if that issue will "materially advance the resolution of multiple civil claims by addressing the core of the dispute in a manner superior to other realistic procedural alternatives, so as to generate significant judicial efficiencies."[94] A number of appellate decisions have

---

91. *Id.* at 632.

92. Castano v. Am. Tobacco Co., 84 F.3d 734, 745 n.21 (5th Cir. 1996).

93. *In re* Deepwater Horizon, 739 F.3d 790, 804 (5th Cir. 2014); *In re* IKO Roofing Shingle Prods. Liab. Litig., 2014 WL 2958615, at *4 (7th Cir. 2014); *McReynolds*, 672 F.3d at 491; *In re* Nassau County Strip Search Cases, 461 F.3d 219 (2d Cir. 2006) ("[W]e hold that . . . a court may employ rule 23(c)(4)(A) to certify a class as to an issue regardless of whether the claim as a whole satisfies the predominance test."); Bolin v. Sears, Roebuck & Co., 231 F.3d 970, 976 (5th Cir. 2000) ("Rule 23(c)(4) explicitly recognizes the flexibility that courts need in class certification by allowing certification 'with respect to particular issues' and division of the class into subclasses."). The Sixth Circuit recently surveyed the various approaches of circuit courts to this question in Martin v. Behr Dayton Thermal Prods., 896 F.3d 405, 2018 U.S. App. LEXIS 19441 (6th Cir. 2018) (adopting "broad view").

94. ALI, Aggregate Litigation § 2.02 Principles for the Aggregate Treatment of Common Issues (2009). The full text of § 2.02(a) provides:

> The court should exercise discretion to authorize aggregate treatment of a common issue by way of a class action if the court determines that resolution of the common issue would:
>
> > materially advance the resolution of multiple civil claims by addressing the core of the dispute in a manner superior to other realistic procedural alternatives, so as to generate significant judicial efficiencies;

authorized issue classes in the consumer and employment context.[95] This argument is also covered in Chapter 10 on trial plans.

Issue classes raise a number of strategic considerations for both class and defense counsel. Key to plaintiffs' counsel are:

- Which issues can be identified and proven in isolation so as to actually further the goals of the litigation?
- If class counsel proposes, in the alternative, an issue-only class, will this encourage the trial judge to certify that limited class in lieu of a full Rule 23(b)(3) class?
- Would an issue class certification (alone, or after prevailing on the issue at trial) provide the leverage necessary to negotiate a class settlement in the interests of the class?
- What comes after an issue trial?
- How would counsel be compensated for their time and efforts if there is no "common fund" created by the successful issue trial?

Given these questions, the use of a trial plan in connection with any proposed issue class could be particularly helpful.

Among the key considerations for defendants facing an issue class proposed by plaintiffs or perhaps by the court are:

- What would the expense and disruption of an issue trial be (e.g., to determine liability, or defect, misrepresentation, etc.), and how would that compare with full certification?
- What would be the negative/positive public relations consequences of a finding of liability or non-liability in an issue trial?
- Would a bifurcated approach—whereby liability is determined on a class basis, followed by individual or subgroup damages procedures—substantially contain the financial exposure of the defendant? and

---

     conform to the general principles for aggregate proceedings in §§ 1.03-1.05; and not compromise the fairness of procedures for resolving any remaining issues presented by such claims.

See also id. §§ 2.02(b)–(e); 2.03–2.09.

95. *See, e.g.,* Butler v. Sears, Roebuck & Co., 727 F.3d 796, 801 (7th Cir. 2013) (Posner, J.) (consumer product claim); McReynolds v. Merrill Lynch, Pierce, Fenner & Smith, Inc., 672 F.3d 482, 492 (7th Cir. 2012) (Posner, J.) (employment discrimination); Glazer v. Whirlpool Corp., 722 F.3d 838, 860 (6th Cir. 2013) (consumer product claim).

- Would defendant's settlement posture improve or substantially deteriorate if plaintiffs were to prevail at the issue trial?

Most of the defendant's considerations will arise only after certification of an issue class. In other words, barring an early settlement strategy, most defendants will oppose any class certification—full or limited to one or more issues. Accordingly, these considerations will mostly be relevant to whether to pursue a global settlement in lieu of an issue trial.

In the final analysis, issue classes may become a second best option for both plaintiffs and defendants. Plaintiffs will continue to push for class certification encompassing all issues within the claims. Defendants will continue to resist same (up until they desire a class settlement). But if plaintiffs cannot establish predominance in a full Rule 23(b)(3) class, an issue class (for example, as to liability, or a product defect) will frequently give plaintiffs substantial leverage. And defendants will likely prefer these classes to full class certification, since they place additional hurdles for class counsel in achieving class-wide relief, thereby potentially reducing the case's value, at least in the short run.

APPOINTMENT OF CLASS COUNSEL

The court's supervisory responsibilities in a class action include the selection and appointment of class counsel. When moving for class certification, plaintiff's counsel must also file a motion for appointment as class counsel under Rule 23(g). The criteria set forth in Rule 23(g) provide some factors that the court must consider, while also granting the court broad discretion in its appointment-making authority.

The court must consider factors relevant to counsel's experience and resources, including the work counsel has done identifying and investigating the claims in the action, counsel's knowledge of applicable law, experience in handling the particular type of claims—and class actions more generally—as well as the resources that counsel can and will commit to the case.[96]

The court is permitted to "further consider any other matter pertinent to counsel's ability to fairly and adequately represent the interests of the class."[97] While the court is granted discretion here, it is mandatory

---

96. Fed. R. Civ. P. 23(g)(1)(A).
97. Fed. R. Civ. P. 23(g)(1)(B).

that class counsel "fairly and adequately represent the interests of the class."[98] This means that the court will consider conflicts of interest if any are raised, such as situations where counsel would favor a set of existing clients or named plaintiffs over the class members as a whole, or where a law firm represents a party in another matter with interests adverse to the class. But speculative or hypothetical conflicts of interest will not defeat adequacy. Counsel should anticipate any arguments that might be made as to a potential conflict of interest and conduct a careful analysis, and then cure any problems (e.g., securing separate class counsel for a subclass, if necessary).

To support the motion for appointment, it is routine to submit a declaration that sets forth counsel's qualifications, experience, investigation, and work on the case to date, and the ability to finance the litigation. Would-be class counsel must conduct an honest self-assessment here, and bring in co-counsel if necessary, well before the actual motion will be filed.

Where substantial resources will be required to litigate a case, commonly more than one set of counsel will be involved. The Federal Judicial Counsel Class Action Pocket Guide (FJC Guide) suggests that where multiple class counsel are involved and have "agree[d] to divide the labor, expenses and fees," the court "may want to review those agreements (which will be subject to disclosure upon settlement in any event)" in order to "safeguard the interests of the class to prevent unnecessary litigation and overstaffing."[99] This is more likely to occur in higher-profile cases, but courts have been known to appoint some but not all of the applicants for class counsel, even where multiple class counsel apply cooperatively.

Where multiple counsel are competing to represent a class, the court will select lead counsel. The court is required to select "the applicant best able to represent the interests of the class,"[100] which does not provide much specificity. The advisory notes state that the court should consider the strengths of proposed class counsel based on the factors enumerated in the rule—such as counsel's experience in handling class actions, other types of litigation, and the types of claims asserted in the action—and opines that counsel's relationship to the lead plaintiffs

---

98. FED. R. CIV. P. 23(g)(4).

99. BARBARA J. ROTHSTEIN & THOMAS E. WILLGING, MANAGING CLASS ACTION LITI-GATION: A POCKET GUIDE FOR JUDGES (3d ed. 2010), Federal Judicial Center, 5.

100. FED. R. CIV. PROC. 23(g)(2).

may also be relevant. In securities class actions, the Private Securities Litigation Reform Act directs the judge to employ a special procedure for selecting "the most adequate" lead plaintiff (often the plaintiff with most sizeable claims) who, in turn, has the right to select and retain class counsel, subject to court approval.[101]

A limited number of courts have experimented with competitive bidding to select lead counsel. This process has been criticized because bidding based on lowering fees or costs may not be the most appropriate way to select class counsel in many circumstances, as where the evolution of the litigation is difficult to predict and/or where additional resources may be required. As the FJC Manual notes, a Third Circuit Task Force concluded that competitive bidding "should be an exception to the rule that qualified counsel can be selected either by private ordering or by judicial selection of qualified counsel."[102]

Counsel may sometimes wish to move to be appointed interim counsel to act on behalf of the class before moving for class certification.[103] This may be desirable, for example, where motions or settlement discussions will occur before certification, or where reasons for coordination among multiple counsel require it.

Defense counsel rarely weigh in on issues relating to appointment of class counsel. They may raise issues relating to conflicts if they are aware of them, but where defense counsel supports appointment of one set of counsel over another, the court may become suspicious that collusion has occurred or that defense counsel is selecting proposed counsel for the class that is least likely to be effective. If there is a substantial basis for challenging class counsel's adequacy, however, and a colorable chance of defeating certification on this basis, defense counsel should consider opposing the certification on adequacy grounds.

Attorney fees and costs should be reasonable and recorded contemporaneously. The court has the authority to "order potential class counsel to provide information on any subject pertinent to the appointment and to propose terms for attorney's fees and costs," as well as to include provisions in its appointment order about the award of attorney fees or costs.[104] The FJC Guide advises judges that they may want to

---

101. 15 U.S.C.A. § 78u-4(a)(3)(B).
102. FJC Guide at 8 (quoting Third Circuit Task Force, *Report on Selection of Counsel*, 74 Temp. L. Rev. 689, 741 (2001)).
103. Fed. R. Civ. P. 23(g).
104. Fed. R. Civ. P. 23(g)(1)(C)–(E).

"make clear to counsel at the outset the content and form of records . . . require[d] to support applications for awards of fees and expenses or for a lodestar cross-check."[105] Class counsel should keep careful time and expense records in every case. The court will very likely scrutinize the reasonableness of fees and costs, whether at settlement or after a trial.

Although very often only a detailed summary is required, courts are increasingly asking for detailed records. Keep records as though a court will scrutinize them later. Enter time contemporaneously and make your entries as specific and detailed as necessary to make evident that the time was worthwhile.

And it probably goes without saying, but do not bill excessive costs that are not consistent with class counsel's fiduciary duty to the class. An expensive bottle of wine may go well with a celebratory dinner at a Michelin-starred restaurant, but do not bill it to the case. A good rule of thumb is not to bill anything you would not want reported in the *New York Times*.

APPELLATE STRATEGY

While it is difficult to generalize about appellate strategy, a central issue for both class counsel and defense counsel for any appeal of a certification decision is the state of the record. The more compelling a record that exists either supporting or demonstrating the impropriety of certification, the stronger the hand of either the proponent or opponent of certification. Of course, this record must be built in advance (or at) the class certification hearing and trial.

Rule 23(f), providing for discretionary interlocutory appeal of a grant or denial of certification, has been around long enough that most circuits have developed standards for evaluating petitions under the rule. Tailor a Rule 23(f) petition accordingly. Note that the deadline for filing the petition is very short: 14 days after entry of the certification order. While some courts have held that this deadline is not strictly "jurisdictional,"[106] it nonetheless "is well-established that Rule 23(f)'s

---

105. FJC Guide at 22.
106. *See* Lambert v. Nutraceutical Corp., 870 F.3d 1170, 1177 (9th Cir. 2017) (14-day limit was subject to equitable tolling based upon a motion to reconsider), *cert. granted*, No. 17-1094 (Feb. 1, 2018).

fourteen day filing requirement is a rigid and 'inflexible' restriction."[107] Generally, two Rule 23(f) petition themes gain the most traction: (1) that the district court's ruling appears to ignore the standards set forth in recent comparable Supreme Court or circuit decisions, and the consequence of the district court's certification decision will be devastating to the complaining party; or (2) that the certification decision raises issues that have been insufficiently analyzed by circuit precedent, and whose clarification would assist all district courts in the circuit and thereby advance the law.[108] To maximize the chances of getting the petition granted, counsel should focus on one or two key issues, and not try to attack every finding by the district court.

The familiar standard for review of a certification decision is "abuse of discretion." This should be taken with a grain of salt, both for the reasons stated at the start of this chapter (based on the Supreme Court's *Shady Grove* decision), and because appellate courts are sensitive to the "do or die" nature of the certification decision. In addition, the familiar "rigorous analysis" requirement for a district court's certification decision lends itself to a more searching inquiry.

CONCLUSION

Class certification requires both plaintiff and defendant to present evidence to satisfy the elements of Rule 23 or to demonstrate concretely why the elements are not met. Practitioners should begin each case by carefully planning how they will argue each element of Rule 23 and should keep those elements foremost in mind at each stage leading up to the certification motion and hearing.

---

107. Fleischman v. Albany Med. Ctr., 639 F.3d 28, 31 (2d Cir. 2011) (quoting Coco v. Inc. Vill. of Belle Terre, N.Y., 448 F.3d 490, 491–92 (2d Cir. 2006)).

108. While Rule 23(f) petitions are most frequently filed by defendants seeking interlocutory review of a grant of certification, plaintiffs have successful employed the rule as well. *See, e.g.*, Messner v. Northshore Univ. Health System, 669 F.3d 802, 826 (7th Cir. 2012) (reversing denial of certification in antitrust case).

8

Managing Multiple Class and Enforcement Actions

Gregory C. Cook and Daniel R. Karon

What happens when there is not just one class action filed, but several or even dozens across multiple jurisdictions? To avoid procedural chaos, the federal courts have a procedure known as multi-district litigation (MDL) that can be used to consolidate cases for pre-trial proceedings. To successfully navigate this often unpredictable process, practitioners must master the procedure and strategy of managing multiple class actions both within and outside the MDL process.

In this chapter, we cover the risks and advantages of consolidating multiple class actions. First, we discuss the MDL process—covering both procedure and strategy. Next, we explore the mechanics of consolidated proceedings, including case management orders, steering committees, and consolidated complaints, including analyzing which plaintiffs to include in the consolidated complaint and what law to apply—among many other topics—providing both the strategic perspective of both plaintiff and defense counsel. Finally, this chapter addresses what happens *after* MDL (remand of actions from the consolidated proceeding); how to handle competing state cases (or, if consolidation is denied, how to handle competing federal actions); how to navigate reverse auctions; and how to deal with pending, parallel criminal investigations.

MDL CONSOLIDATION

The Judicial Panel on Multi-district Litigation (the MDL Panel), established by the multi-district venue statute, 28 U.S.C. § 1407, is authorized to transfer multi-district civil actions to a single district court for *pre-trial* proceedings. Its purpose is to streamline the entire pre-trial process by eliminating duplication in discovery and other pre-trial proceedings.[1] Pursuant to its authority under § 1407, the MDL Panel decides (1) whether to transfer, (2) to which court and judge to transfer, and (3) how long the cases should stay. On the latter point, as discussed later, there is continuing debate over when, how, and whether to remand sections back to their originating court. As a practical matter, very few transferred actions are ever remanded.

Section 1407 provides a series of factors for the panel to consider when determining whether to transfer an action: there must be (1) multiple civil actions (2) "involving one or more common questions of fact" that (3) are "pending in different districts," and (4) transfer must promote judicial efficiency, economy, and fairness (as discussed later).

There are essentially two ways to initiate a transfer: (1) the MDL Panel itself may initiate this proceeding, or (2) a party to one of the actions may file a motion with the clerk of the district court in which the action is pending. With a few unique exceptions, any civil action may be transferred. These exceptions include antitrust actions by the United States,[2] injunction actions by the Securities and Exchange Commission,[3] and mass actions removed pursuant to the Class Action Fairness Act (CAFA) *unless* the majority of plaintiffs consent.[4]

Strategic Concerns

Filing an MDL consolidation motion is a calculated gamble. The MDL Panel's authority is strikingly large and can drastically change the

---

1. There is one exception to the "pretrial only" rule: *Parens patriae* antitrust actions brought by states under 15 U.S. C. § 15c(a)1 may be transferred for both pretrial and trial. 28 U.S.C. §1407(h).
2. 28 U.S.C. § 1407(g).
3. 15 U.S.C. § 78u(g).
4. 28 U.S.C. § 1332(d)(11)(C).

posture of an existing case—even one that has been pending for a considerable period. Transfers occur quickly and frequently. There is no express deadline for filing such a motion. A consolidation motion can functionally be case dispositive, and should therefore be taken very seriously.

There can be substantial advantages to consolidation. It commonly can reduce discovery costs for all parties. Without consolidation, it may be very difficult to coordinate deposition schedules with multiple actions in multiple jurisdictions. Courts may have different time lines and scheduling requirements. Judges can disagree over discovery decisions. Producing witnesses once for deposition for a discrete period of time, eliminating duplicative and conflicting hearings, and complying with one protocol for document production can combine to provide substantial cost savings.[5]

Section 1407(b) provides extraordinary discovery powers to the transferee judge, including the power to exercise the authority/jurisdiction of a federal judge in any district, even if not physically present in such district. Thus, for example, a judge overseeing MDL litigation can exercise supervisory power over depositions in other districts including compelling third-party attendance there.

Advantages to Consolidation	Disadvantages to Consolidation
• Reduces discovery costs	• Loss of control
• Reduces difficulties in coordinating depositions between actions and risk of duplicative deposition	• Judge unable to spend time on issues individual to a particular case
• Reduces problems from different discovery deadlines and scheduling orders	• MDL Panel rules on consolidation very quickly with little opportunity for input by litigants; briefing schedule very short
• Reduces problem of judges disagreeing about discovery disputes	• Very limited (nonexistent?) appeal rights for consolidation decision
• Reduces problem of conflicting and duplicative hearings	• MDL Panel may transfer case to any district with no limitations based on personal jurisdiction, venue or forum selection clause

---

5. See Manual for Complex Litigation Fourth (Federal Judicial Center, 2004) (after consolidation, court can appoint lead and liaison counsel, require shared discovery, and case management plans, etc.) (hereinafter *Manual*).

Advantages to Consolidation	Disadvantages to Consolidation
• Produce documents once pursuant to single protocol	• Case becomes well-known, prompting filing of copycat cases (some of which may have little merit)
• Power of judge to adjudicate discovery disputes nationally, even if different districts	• Choice of law can change if circuits have varying interpretations of federal law
• Normally judge experienced and capable, vetted by MDL Panel and normally consents before transfer	• Harder to settle individual cases
• Defendants deal with single plaintiff steering committee	
• Tag along transfers	
• Remands for trial are required but rare in practice	

Purposeful and intentional selection of a judge is another critical consideration. Typically, the MDL Panel selects transferee judges who are experienced, capable, and willing to serve. This is a major advantage to all parties. It is generally understood that the MDL Panel will discuss actions with the transferee judge (and sometimes with other judges—for instance, the chief judge in a particular district) before ruling to ensure that he or she has sufficient time and interest to handle the matter.

From a defense perspective, consolidation can facilitate settlement. If a matter is serious, it can be much easier to reach a global resolution with a plaintiff steering committee in a consolidated matter.

Another advantage following from a consolidation order is that future actions can be transferred with the mere filing of a tag-along notice with the panel (subject to the right of the new party to object and be heard—an objection which rarely succeeds). In fact, Panel Rules 7.2(I) and 7.5(e) impose a duty on parties (and their counsel) promptly to notify the MDL Panel of any potential tag-along action in which that party is named (or in which its counsel appears).

This tag-along procedure has substantial benefits in cost savings to all parties. Normally, the transferee judge's case management plan will include provisions for handling such tag-along actions, including that (1) rulings on common issues—such as rulings regarding a statute of limitations—shall be deemed to have been made in the tag-along action and (2) discovery already taken shall be usable in the tag-along cases.

However, consolidation also comes with certain risks and disadvantages. All parties risk losing control of the litigation. First, the MDL Panel has been known, on occasion, to transfer cases over the objections of even the majority of parties. The MDL Panel's orders typically do not provide substantive explanations for consolidation (although the panel tends to provide more explanation if consolidation is denied). In addition, some lawyers believe that the panel is biased towards consolidation. Further, the MDL Panel's power is large and virtually unreviewable, as discussed later.

The MDL Panel may transfer to "any" federal district court. Thus, normal considerations relating to choice of forum do not limit the MDL Panel, including (for example) personal jurisdiction, venue, and forum selection clauses.[6] Transfer decisions are not always predictable and can result in transfer to a venue that most parties *oppose—or even to a venue that no party has suggested.*

The transferee judge will likely appoint a steering committee of plaintiff counsel (and sometimes defense counsel). Virtually every decision thereafter will need to be coordinated among that group—leaving very little control to individual plaintiffs or defendants (for instance, when depositions will begin, in what format electronic data will be produced, where depositions will be convened, the order of depositions, and even when dispositive motions might be heard).

Individual litigants have very little opportunity to distinguish themselves, particularly where there is a large number of consolidated cases. Some defendants may have unique case-dispositive defenses (for instance, personal jurisdiction motions) that will be ignored for years because of the complexity and size of the consolidated cases.

The most common example of the "lost in the shuffle" problem are motions to remand to state court. Plaintiffs can be left without a ruling for long periods, since the transferor court can stay (formally or informally) its action during the pendency of the consolidation motion—and the transferee court will often deal with the common issues (the "big picture" items) before reaching the individual issues, like remand.

The transferor court does retain jurisdiction during the pendency of the remand motion, and the rules of the panel expressly provide that a pending consolidation motion "does not affect or suspend orders or pretrial proceedings in the district court in which the action is

---

6. *E.g., In re* FMC Corp. Patent Litig., 422 F. Supp. 1163, 1165 (J.P.M.L. 1976).

pending."[7] While the MDL Panel handles consolidation requests very quickly, it is common for approximately two months to pass between the filing of the motion and the ruling by the panel.

Nevertheless, many transferor courts will stay an action pending the panel's consolidation decision (including staying decisions on remand motions).[8] Such a stay makes sense when a pending motion raises issues likely to be raised in other cases—and thus promotes efficiency for all. For example, there would be little purpose in entering a scheduling order while a conditional order of transfer is pending. Likewise, the transferor court will normally carefully consider whether any discovery is necessary while the MDL Panel considers the consolidation motion (factoring in such things as the maturity of the action, any current scheduling order, local rules on discovery, and the like).

The MDL Panel has a policy that it generally will not delay a transfer decision merely because a remand motion is pending. The MDL Panel has on rare occasions delayed ruling on transfer to permit the court in which the case has been pending to decide critical, fully briefed and argued remand motions. Far more often, however, the panel allows such motions to be addressed by the transferee judge. In fact, the pendency of motions raising common questions can itself be an additional justification for transfer.[9]

The risk of being "lost in the shuffle" can also arise before the MDL Panel itself. Parties often get squeezed and receive little if any time to argue their unique perspective that consolidation is not required for *their* particular case. For instance, it not uncommon for a party in a large, complex case to be awarded three minutes (or less) at oral argument to present its position. Worse, the MDL Panel commonly rejects arguments against transfer based upon the assertion that a party has unique defenses or issues.[10]

Other problems can arise if the transferee court decides to revisit rulings from the transferor courts. A transfer under § 1407 becomes

---

7. J.P.M.L.R.P. 1.5; *In re* Four Seasons Sec. Laws Litig., 362 F. Supp. 574, 575 n.2 (J.P.M.L. 1973).

8. Moore v. Wyeth-Ayerst Labs., 236 F. Supp. 2d 509, 510–11 (D. Md. 2002) (observing that the MDL transferee judge had faced multiple motions to remand cases removed from state courts).

9. See, e.g., In re Ivy, 901 F.2d 7, 9 (2d Cir. 1990).

10. *E.g. In re* Starlink Corn Prods. Liab. Litig., 152 F. Supp. 2d 1378, 1380 (J.P.M.L. 2001) (rejecting the argument by a class of farmers against consolidation based on significant differences between their interests and the interests of a class of consumers).

effective when the order granting the transfer is filed in the office of the clerk of the transferee court. At that point, the transferee court has exclusive jurisdiction. Unless changed, the transferor court's orders remain in effect.[11] Nonetheless the transferee judge may revisit and potentially modify any prior order of a transferor court.[12] If there have been inconsistent rulings by different transferor courts, such review may become a necessity. As a consequence, transfer may in fact lead to rebriefing of motions or redoing of discovery.

Consolidating cases can also slow down the litigation substantially in comparison to an individual case. It takes time to assemble a steering committee, propose and obtain approval for a case management order, and plan discovery. Hearings typically last longer and are often more difficult to schedule in consolidated actions. Further, for individual litigants, costs can go up—because their counsel may have to travel to hearings in another venue, wade through piles of pleadings filed by other parties, endure protracted hearings and hearing dockets, and perhaps sit through depositions that are largely irrelevant to their particular case. These problems can be mitigated by the appointment of lead counsel, thereby reducing the need for all lawyers routinely to travel to the transferee district, but this may be an imperfect solution.

From a defense perspective, the quality of opposing counsel often improves after consolidation. Frequently, the most experienced and competent plaintiff counsel are appointed to the steering committee. While it is possible that some of these lawyers might have been involved in scattered lawsuits, they essentially become lead counsel in all cases. Further, consolidation results in far better resource and information sharing among plaintiff counsel, which generally works to the detriment of defense counsel.

Another potential downside for defendants is that consolidating the case may enhance its significance and spawn other lawsuits. Other plaintiff counsel are more likely to take notice of a matter that has been consolidated, particularly those who monitor the MDL docket. Moreover, consolidation can at times be perceived as a marker that a matter is truly serious. In other words, counsel may view a consolidation order as somehow indicating that the panel believes that the claims are significant and may have merit. Some lawyers have even argued that certain

---

11. *See In re* Master Key Antitrust Litig., 320 F. Supp. 1404 (J.P.M.L. 1971).

12. *See, e.g., In re* Upjohn Co. Antibiotic Cleocin Prods. Liab. Litig., 664 F.2d 114 (6th Cir. 1981).

transferee judges view transfer orders as an assignment from the panel to resolve the matters—not simply to manage the cases and remand for trial—and perceive the transferee court as better leveraged to impose undue pressure on defendants to settle meritless cases.

Consolidation can also impact choice of law analysis. While claims based upon state law should not be affected, issues under federal law may be governed by the transferee court's precedent (which can, of course, vary among circuits). Some courts make a further distinction between substantive law and procedure. The transferor district's law is applied to substantive issues and the transferee's law to procedural issues. Some courts make a distinction regarding statutes of limitations.[13] This choice of law issue can become even more complicated if the case is ultimately remanded to the transferor court. For instance, the transferee court might deny summary judgment based upon substantive law applicable in that circuit and then remand for trial to the transferor court where a party might file another motion for summary judgment (or file a Rule 50 motion during trial) that would then be decided under the original circuit's law.

Discovery can also become more invasive for a defendant in a consolidated matter. Typically a transferee judge will take broader discovery requests more seriously.

Similar problems can arise with settlement. Prior to consolidation, defense counsel might be able to settle individually with particular plaintiffs or their counsel. After consolidation, it becomes difficult, as a practical matter, to settle out individual cases.

Recently, some defense lawyers have expressed concerns that MDL actions have put defendants at a disadvantage. Their comments illustrate the potential negatives to defendants from some consolidations. The Lawyers for Civil Justice (LCJ) submitted a Request for Rulemaking to the Advisory Committee on Civil Rules on August 10, 2017. The LCJ argued that consolidated actions now make up 45 percent of the federal docket; that the Federal Rules of Civil Procedure do not provide practical procedures in MDL actions; and that courts are now improvising procedures, resulting in a lack of uniformity and predictability. The petition argued that "there is no pretrial testing of claims because the existing FRCP mechanisms for doing so are not practical

---

13. *See, e.g., In re* MTBE Products Liability Litig., 241 F.R.D. 185 (S.D.N.Y. 2007) (discussing conflicting cases); *In re* United Mine Workers of America Employee Ben. Plans Litig., 854 F. Supp. 914 (D.D.C. 1994) (discussing conflict in statute of limitations cases).

at a large scale," and that a large number of plaintiffs added via master complaints have no real claim, but help to prop up the plaintiff count to give increased leverage to plaintiff counsel. Further, "very, very few MDL cases get the benefit of appellant review" because of the large number of plaintiffs, and many "MDL courts hold 'bellwether trials' without obtaining the willing consent of the parties."[14]

In sum, consolidation is a powerful tool that should be used with caution. If it is sought or granted, all parties must re-examine their approach to the litigation and attempt to take full advantage of the efficiencies of the consolidation and alter their normal approach of single party litigation.

The Mechanics of MDL Consolidation

The MDL Panel is composed of seven district judges appointed by the Chief Justice. The MDL Panel has its own procedural rules, and enforces those rules strictly, especially deadlines. The rules are not lengthy and should be read very carefully. They provide that, within twenty days of the filing of a motion to transfer, all parties may file a response, and a failure to do so will be treated as acquiescence. There is a five-day time limit for a reply. Briefs are limited to twenty pages. The matter is then typically placed on the hearing docket, which occurs on a roughly monthly basis. The official office of the MDL Panel is located in Washington, DC, but the MDL Panel holds hearings around the country (with location changing each month).

The hearing docket is normally crowded and practitioners should arrive early in the morning for argument because of the panel's penchant for last minute orders, including changes in schedules and time allocations for speakers. There are often meetings on the "sidelines" of the hearings among counsel. Vendors (such as class action notice companies) even sponsor events the evening before the hearing for counsel. Such interactions provide counsel with an additional opportunity to coordinate positions among parties and jockey for position on any subsequent steering committee.

Appeals of the MDL Panel's decision are strictly limited and are only available under extraordinary writ (28 U.S.C. § 1651) to the Court of Appeal with jurisdiction over the district in which the hearing of the

---

14. http://www.uscourts.gov/sites/default/files/17-cv-rrrrr-suggestion_lcj_0.pdf.

MDL Panel occurred. We are unaware of a single decision reversing the MDL Panel.

As noted earlier, if an "MDL" has already been established, new matters may be transferred with no action by the MDL Panel upon the filing of a "tag along" notice. The clerk of the MDL Panel will make the transfer unless there is an objection within 15 days. An objector will then be given 15 days to file a brief, or his objection is automatically deemed withdrawn.

Procedural Concerns

By statute, the MDL Panel considers three factors in deciding whether to consolidate: (1) whether there are one or more common questions of fact; (2) whether the transfer is for the convenience of all of the parties involved; and (3) whether the transfer will promote judicial efficiency, economy, and fairness.

Common Questions of Fact

In order for a motion to transfer to prevail, the MDL Panel must find the common questions of fact to be "sufficient." The MDL Panel, which has a great deal of discretion, often interprets "common questions of fact" broadly. For instance, cases do not need to have identical parties or facts; instead, they must only involve "common" questions.[15]

Number and Complexity of Questions

Some decisions of the MDL Panel appear to weigh common issues against individual issues to determine which predominate.[16] The more complex the common questions, the more likely the transfer. The degree of complexity of the common questions becomes particularly important if the transfer request involves a small number of cases. *The most commonly cited reason for denial of consolidation is the lack of sufficiently numerous or complex common questions of fact.*

---

15. *See In re* General Motors Class E Stock Buyout Sec. Litig., 696 F. Supp. 1546, 1546–47 (J.P.M.L. 1988).

16. *See, e.g., In re* Rely Tampon Prods. Liab. Litig., 533 F. Supp. 1346, 1347 (J.P.M.L. 1982) (transfer denied because panel "not persuaded that the common questions of fact will predominate"); *In re* Sears, Roebuck & Co. Employment Practices Litig., 487 F. Supp. 1362, 1364 (J.P.M.L. 1980) (transfer denied for five discrimination cases where "individual rather than common factual questions predominate").

On occasion, the MDL Panel appears to have considered whether common questions of *law* exist, but generally the MDL Panel sticks to the statutory language, which contemplates analysis only of common questions of *"fact."*[17] Notably, the MDL Panel has recently indicated that if the consolidated action would involve the laws of many different states, it might not be appropriate for consolidation.[18]

Convenience of Parties and Witnesses

Though often given the least amount of weight, the MDL Panel must look to see whether transfer of the actions will be for the convenience of *all* of the parties (thus, the panel looks at the overall savings and convenience to the system rather than individual parties). If the other two requirements are met, then the court will likely not reject a motion to transfer simply because it is inconvenient for some of the parties. If the actions are pending in adjacent federal districts, the panel has sometimes denied consolidation, finding that the ready availability of cooperative management mitigates against formal centralization.[19]

Judicial Efficiency

The most important factor that the MDL Panel must weigh is whether the transfer will promote the just and efficient conduct of the actions. Efficiency factors often cited in support of transfer are the avoidance of duplication of discovery, prevention of inconsistent pre-trial rulings, and the conservation of both human and financial resources on the part of both the parties and the judiciary.

The MDL Panel has sometimes denied motions to transfer where there were alternative means available for coordination of discovery and avoidance of duplication. The Manual for Complex Litigation (Fourth) § 20.14 lists a number of these alternatives, including special assignment of a judge to multiple actions; coordination between the courts to designate a lead case; joint hearings and conferences and

---

17. *E.g., In re* Nat'l Ass'n for the Advancement of Multijurisdictional Practice Litig., MDL No. 2568, 52 F. Supp. 3d 1377 (J.P.M.L. Oct. 9, 2014).

18. *In re* DirecTV, Inc. Fair Labor Standards Act (FLSA) and Wage and Hour Litig., MDL No. 2594, 84 F. Supp. 3d 1373 (J.P.M.L. Feb. 6, 2015); *In re* Narconon Drug Rehabilitation Marketing, Sales Practices and Prods. Liab. Litig., MDL No. 2598, 84 F. Supp. 3d 1367 (J.P.M.L. Feb. 5, 2015).

19. *E.g., In re* Unitrin, Inc. Ins. Sales Practices Litig., 217 F. Supp. 2d 1371, 1372 (J.P.M.L. 2002).

orders; joint appointments of special masters or experts; cross-filing of discovery; and even stays of some litigation. These are discussed in more detail later in the chapter.

Significant Drop in Number of MDLs—Why?

The attitude of the MDL Panel has changed noticeably over the last several years, making it far less likely that a motion to consolidate will be granted than in prior years. For instance, the number of pending MDLs were only 244 at the end of 2016, compared to 271 at the end of 2015, and 290 at the end of 2014. Likewise, the percentage of petitions that have been granted have dropped from over 80 percent in 2008 to just 47 percent in 2016 (compared to 50 percent in 2015 and 64 percent in 2014).[20]

One change that may be driving these numbers is the renewed interest of the MDL Panel in alternatives to consolidation. For instance, when there are pending venue motions under 28 U.S.C. § 1404, the panel will sometimes deny the motion or request that the parties withdraw their motion. The MDL Panel has reasoned that if a § 1404 motion were granted, "that would moot the issue of centralization."[21] Indeed, the panel recently wrote that "where 'a reasonable prospect' exists that the resolution of a Section 1404 motion or motions could eliminate the multidistrict character of litigation, transfer under Section 1404 is preferable to centralization." Likewise, in denying consolidation, the MDL Panel often appears deferential to "voluntary cooperation and coordination" and "information coordination and cooperative efforts" where applicable.[22] Further, the panel has recently treated multiple actions pending in a federal district as if they were a single action, again emphasizing the

---

20. *See generally* Alan Rothman, *And Now a Word from the Panel: A Year of Vanishing MDLs,* Law360 (Jan. 24, 2017), https://www.law360.com/articles/884302/and-now-a-word-from-the-panel-a-year-of-vanishing-mdls. Mr. Rothman authors a periodic column on the MDL for Law360 throughout the year and is an invaluable resource on trends in the panel's decisions. *See also* Alan Rothman, *And Now a Word from the Panel: 2015 JPML Practice Trends,* Law360 (Jan. 26, 2016), https://www.law360.com/articles/749702/and-now-a-word-from-the-panel-2015-jpml-practice-trends; Alan Rothman, *And Now a Word From the Panel: 2014 JPML Practice Trends,* Law360 (Jan. 27, 2015), https://www.law360.com/articles/615718/and-now-a-word-from-the-panel-2014-jpml-practice-trends.

21. *In re* 3M Company Lava Ultimate Prods. Liab. Litig., MDL No. 2727, 222 F. Supp. 3d 1347 (J.P.M.L. Aug. 5, 2016).

22. *In re* Petrobras Securities Litig., MDL No. 2728, 222 F. Supp. 3d 1345 (J.M.P.L. Aug. 5, 2016); *In re* 3M Company Lava Ultimate Prod. Liab. Litig., 222 F. Supp. 3d 1347.

need for parties and judges to work cooperatively to provide an alternative to invoking formal consolidation under § 1407.[23]

Do Enough Cases Exist to Require an MDL?

It is impossible to provide a magic number for consolidation. For instance, if there is a strong likelihood that additional actions will be filed, the existing number of actions is less important. However, the mere potential for additional actions is insufficient to justify MDL coordination. Likewise, if the common questions are very important and overlap significantly, a smaller number of actions will justify consolidation. As a general proposition, "those advocating transfer bear a heavy burden of persuasion when there are only a few actions, particularly those involving the same parties and counsel."[24] With all of that said, five separate actions would generally present a credible argument for consolidation (assuming the other factors are sufficiently met) while two actions are unlikely to be consolidated.

What Type of Actions Are Being Consolidated?

The type of action may influence whether a petition to consolidate is granted. Examples of the types of actions that have satisfied this test in the past include antitrust, securities, mass tort (particularly single-incident), patent, copyright, trademark, and product liability actions. Today, product liability actions constitute approximately 20 percent of the current roster of MDLs.[25] However, the panel normally disfavors product liability consolidations if multiple products are involved.[26] Sales and marketing actions were the second most common new MDL in 2016 and 2015; data breach actions (a new category for MDLs) were third; and antitrust actions were fourth.

---

23. *E.g., In re* Petrobras Securities Litig., 222 F. Supp. 3d 1345. In fact, the MDL Panel has written that "centralization under Section 1407 should be the last solution after considered review of all other options." *In re* Nutek Baby Wipes Prods. Liab. Litig., 96 F. Supp. 3d 1373 (Apr. 2, 2015).

24. *Manual*, ¶ 20.131.

25. *See generally, infra* n.20.

26. *But see In re* 100 percent Grated Parmesan Cheese Mktg. & Sales Practices Litig., MDL No. 2705, 201 F. Supp. 3d 1375 (June 2, 2016) (granting consolidation but stating the general rule).

Where to Encourage Centralization and Transfer?

The MDL Panel may transfer an action to "any" district.[27] The court and judge to handle a consolidated case can often be the primary drive in a party's decision to request consolidation, or even to remove to federal court. The issue of where (and to which judge) the cases will be assigned often occupies a sizeable portion of the briefs before the panel, and can monopolize the entire oral argument time.

The panel considers a number of factors in making these decisions, judicial efficiencies are again given considerable weight. The availability of an experienced and capable judge familiar with the litigation is one of the more important factors in selecting a transferee forum. The MDL Panel often transfers cases to a judge that is already involved in one of the consolidated cases; however, it has transferred cases to experienced judges who have had no currently pending cases. While transfers have traditionally been made to judges with past MDL experience, the MDL Panel has also begun assigning at least some matters to judges without MDL experience (perhaps to balance caseload).[28] However, as noted earlier, it is generally understood that the MDL Panel discusses the transfers with the judges involved and with the chief judges of the involved districts in their effort to find the best forum and the right judge, and is unlikely to transfer a case to a judge who does not want it.

The panel will often send cases to locations near the defendant's headquarters or to a district near the main concentration of plaintiffs or witnesses.[29] This location of the defendant's corporate headquarters has recently been emphasized by the MDL Panel.[30]

---

27. 28 U.S.C. § 1407(a); *see also In re* New York City Mun. Sec. Litig., 572 F.2d 49, 51 (2d Cir. 1978).

28. *E.g., In re* 21st Century Oncology Customer Data Security Breach Litig., MDL No. 2737, 214 F. Supp. 3d 1357 (J.P.M.L. Oct. 6, 2016).

29. *See, e.g., In re* Factor VIII or IX Concentrate Blood Prods., 853 F. Supp. 454, 455 (J.P.M.L. 1993) (parties' principal place of business); *In re* Air Crash Disaster Near Coolidge, 362 F. Supp. 572, 573 (J.P.M.L. 1973) (location of documents necessary to action); *In re* Rio Hair Naturalizer Prods. Liab. Litig., 904 F. Supp. 1407–08 (J.P.M.L. 1995) (centrally located between the parties and the witnesses); *In re* Regents of the Univ. of Cal., 964 F.2d 1128, 1136 (Fed. Cir. 1992) (district in which the earliest actions were filed); *In re* Republic National-Realty Equities Sec. Litig., 382 F. Supp. 1403, 1406–07 (J.P.M.L. 1974) (district in which the largest number of cases are pending or the most comprehensive case); *In re* American Continental Corp./Lincoln Sav. & Loan Sec. Litig., 130 F.R.D. 475, 476 (J.P.M.L. 1990) (district in which a bankruptcy action involving the defendant is pending).

30. *E.g., In re* Daily Fantasy Sports Litig., MDL No. 2677, 158 F. Supp. 3d 1375 (J.P.M.L. Feb. 4, 2016); *In re* Sprouts Farmers Market, Inc. Employee Data Security Breach, MDL No. 2731, 232 F. Supp. 3d 1348 (J.P.M.L. Oct. 6, 2016).

Other factors the MDL Panel will consider include where the largest number of cases are pending, where discovery has already occurred, whether there is an emotional connection with a particular forum (for instance, the BP oil spill off the Louisiana coast), and where cases have progressed the furthest.[31]

Administrative concerns are also relevant. For instance, docket conditions are normally relevant, as is whether venue would be proper (although this is not a disqualifying test).[32]

Although not common, the MDL Panel will sometimes select a district and division with no clear connection to the existing case and facts, and sometimes will assign a judge to sit specially in the transferee district on an intra-circuit or even inter-circuit assignment.

How to Best Present the Argument for a Favorable Venue?

In arguing for a particular forum, parties often compare the pending case data for the competing forums (for instance, number of cases, number of MDLs, number of civil cases per judge, number of judicial vacancies, and the like). Parties also cite facts related to forum convenience, such as accessibility by air, the number of hotel rooms, and courtroom sizes and technology.

Such quantitative data is relevant, but can quickly become mind numbing. As noted earlier, the most important factor to the panel appears to be the availability of capable, experienced judges who are willing to accept the cases and have sufficient time to devote to them. It is difficult to predict how to best present such information to the panel. One possible option would be to cite to transcripts or other orders of the trial judge indicating a receptive attitude and attention to detail in the action. It is useful to warn the proposed trial judge of any impending MDL motion so that the judge will not be surprised by such a motion, and will be prepared when panel members call to discuss the potential assignment.

---

31. *E.g., In re* Johnson & Johnson Talcum Powder Prods. Mktg., Sales Practices and Prods. Liab. Litig., MDL No. 2738, 220 F. Supp. 3d 1356 (J.P.M.L. Oct. 4, 2016).
32. *See, e.g., In re* Yart Processing Patent Validity Litig., 341 F. Supp. 376 (J.P.M.L. 1972).

What If All (or Some) of the Cases Are Already in the Correct Forum and Need Consolidation?

In rare circumstances, multiple actions will all be pending in one district, but before different judges. This can happen, for example, if there is a forum selection clause in the applicable contract. The local rules of many districts authorize transfer of related cases filed before different judges in the same district to a single judge. For example, one local rule defines related cases as those in which "a substantial saving of judicial resources is likely to result" by assigning them to the same judge "because of the similarity of facts and legal issues or because the cases arise from the same transactions or events."[33] Normally, such local rules provide that the cases will be transferred to the first-filed judge, subject to the authority of the chief judge or the agreement among the judges to some other result.[34] Once transferred to a single judge, the cases can be consolidated under Rule 42(a).

When Is the Best Time to File the MDL Motion?

In general, it is best to file a consolidation motion under § 1407 earlier, rather than later. The reason is simple: the cost savings from combined discovery and motion practice will be lost if the motion is delayed. Further, the longer the delay, the more likely that some portion of the discovery or motion practice might need to be redone in the consolidated matter. For these reasons, the panel sometimes rejects consolidation because the motion is filed too late and will therefore not promote judicial economy and may even delay the progress of cases approaching trial.[35]

---

33. U.S. Dist. Ct. R. 50.3(1)(a) (E.D.N.Y Westlaw, current as of Sept. 1, 2015); *cf.* U.S. Dist. Ct. R. 40.1(b)(3)(A) (E.D. Pa. Westlaw, current as of Dec. 1, 2015) (defining a related case as one that "relates to property included in another suit, or involves the same issue of fact or grows out of the same transaction as another suit").

34. U.S. Dist. Ct. R. 50.3(e) (E.D.N.Y. 2014).

35. *E.g., In re* Asbestos Sch. Prods. Liab. Litig., 606 F. Supp. 713, 714 (J.P.M.L. 1985) (denying motion to transfer based on several factors including the fact that several "actions [were] scheduled for trial within the next six months"); *In re* Propulsid Prods. Liab. Litig., No. 1355, 2000 U.S. Dist. LEXIS 11651, at *3–*4 (J.P.M.L. Aug. 7, 2000). Note, however, that the panel rarely grants a second motion to transfer, so it is preferable to wait until there is a critical mass of cases. *In re* Plavix Marketing, Sales Practices and Prods. Liab. Litig. (No.II), MDL No. 2418, 923 F. Supp. 2d 1376, 1378 (J.P.M.L. 2013) (second transfer motions granted "only rarely" and "where a significant change in circumstances has occurred" such as with the number or geographic scope of relevant case filings).

HOW TO CONDUCT THE ACTIONS AFTER CONSOLIDATION

Determining Leadership and Working Protocols

After MDL consolidation and transfer, two projects lie ahead: case organization and plaintiffs' case leadership. Case organization means implementing an initial case protocol, including: (1) an initial case-management order that describes motion dates, procedures, and counsel roles; and (2) an electronically stored information (ESI) protocol that governs the storage, searching, and production of electronic data.[36]

Before the case can move forward productively, plaintiffs' case leadership must be decided.[37] The case leadership determination can differ depending on the nature of the case, meaning whether the case is *public* or *proprietary*. Public cases are cases that are no secret to the plaintiffs' bar, such as cases stemming from guilty pleas, indictments, or amnesty agreements. Investigations by DOJ or FTC described in the news media or revealed in a company's corporate filings can put the plaintiffs' bar on notice of a potential case. Of course, the *strength* of the public information affects the zeal with which the plaintiffs' bar will mobilize. At one extreme are actions where amnesty agreements have occurred. At the other extreme are mere government investigations sometimes only intimating a lawsuit.

Proprietary cases, on the other hand, spring from investigations of counsel. Typically, these cases take time to develop, often with the aid of expensive economists or other experts to validate counsel's class and liability theories. Sometimes, different groups of counsel are independently investigating the same case opportunity, and sometimes a case is truly proprietary, with only one lawyer or group of lawyers recognizing and understanding the possibility. Of course, even a truly proprietary case may not prevent other lawyers from jumping on the bandwagon, claiming that they have been investigating the case themselves for months or even years.

If multiple lawyers are involved, plaintiffs' case leadership must be decided, whether the case development has been public or proprietary.

---

36. *See Manual,* at § 21.11 ("Initial case-management orders in a class action guide the parties in presenting the judge with the information necessary to make the certification decision and permit the orderly and efficient development of the case.").

37. *See Manual,* at § 22.62 ("Organization of Counsel—Early organization of the counsel who have filed the various cases transferred or consolidated for pretrial purposes is a critical case-management task.").

Plaintiffs' lawyers are reluctant to fight openly over leadership before the court, because it can create a first impression that the plaintiffs' lawyers are greedy and unwilling to cooperate. Nonetheless, sometimes the court *must* decide leadership, whether presented with competing leadership panels, through competitive bidding, or otherwise.[38]

Smart plaintiffs' lawyers work hard to avoid bringing leadership issues to the court and instead favor *private ordering*. Private ordering involves plaintiffs' lawyers arranging leadership among themselves and proposing a leadership structure to the court. Rarely are all plaintiffs' counsel happy with the outcome, but most will agree that the outcome is better than involving the court.

The court will also schedule a case-management conference, as required by Federal Rule 16(b)(1). In anticipation of this conference, Rule 26(f)(1) requires the "parties [to] confer as soon as practicable—and in any event at least 21 days before [the Rule 16(b)] scheduling conference." During this meeting, the parties should strive to agree on as many discovery dates and protocols as they can. It is far better for all parties if the court can simply enter some version of the parties' negotiated case-management order. In particular, this negotiated document should set forth a case calendar and other obligations, such as an ESI protocol, the identity and responsibilities of lead counsel, liaison counsel, and the executive committee (if any), the need to submit contemporaneous time-and-expense records to liaison counsel, and the like. An example ESI protocol is available at http://www.cand.uscourts.gov/eDiscoveryGuidelines.

If leadership is *not* resolved through private ordering and instead must be resolved by motion, defense counsel might be uncomfortable talking to *any* set of lawyers, since they will not know with whom to discuss scheduling and ESI issues. As a result, those discussions might have to wait.

This discomfort can be even more disruptive for the plaintiffs' side when, in the midst of competition for and uncertainty over case leadership, one lawyer or a group of lawyers appoints itself spokesperson for plaintiffs, then negotiates plaintiffs' discovery-scheduling and ESI

---

38. *See Manual,* at § 22.62 ("Where several counsel are competing to be lead counsel or to serve on a key liaison committee, the court should establish a procedure for attorneys to present their qualifications, including their experience in managing complex litigation and knowledge of the subject matter, their efforts in researching and investigating the claims before the court, and the resources that they can contribute to the litigation.").

positions with defense counsel. When such uncertainty exists, defense counsel can either accept the self-appointed representative or resist, explaining that until plaintiffs speak with a single voice, defendants are unwilling to negotiate. Defense counsel should consider the reputation of the emerging plaintiffs' counsel, defense counsel's personal relationship with plaintiffs' counsel, the likelihood that the emerging plaintiffs' group will prevail, and the lawsuit's demand for speed and efficiency.

As for the ESI protocol, negotiating it is not for the faint of heart. Although electronic discovery dominates our practice, the rules governing electronic discovery still elude many lawyers. For this reason, the best approach is for both sides to have a lawyer skilled in electronic discovery negotiate the ESI protocol.

Filing the Consolidated Amended Complaint

Consolidation and transfer invariably results in combining multiple complaints (sometimes 100 or more).[39] This means that multiple plaintiffs, represented by multiple plaintiffs' firms (who are not lead counsel), are uncomfortably living together before one federal judge.

To lend some sanity and organization to this process, a common approach is for the plaintiffs to file a consolidated amended complaint, or *CAC*. This complaint combines all (or many) of the individual transferred complaints into a single "master complaint" that can have the effect of giving defendants a single target on which to focus and the transferee judge a complaint that arguably cannot be given full effect by any individual transferor court, ultimately resulting in a trial in the transferee judge's court.[40] If the consolidated actions do not have the same defendants, filing a consolidated complaint may be difficult (for instance, some actions may have named particular local individuals in an effort to defeat removal or because local agents assisted in the alleged wrong in one geographic area).

It can be challenging (and controversial) for plaintiffs' counsel to decide which plaintiffs to include in the CAC. Naturally, all plaintiffs'

---

39. *See, e.g., In re* TFT–LCD (Flat Panel) Antitrust Litig., Nos. M 07–1827, C 09–5840, 2010 WL 2610641, at *1 (June 28, 2010) (describing the panel's "transfer order consolidating pretrial proceedings for a number of actions").

40. *Cf., In re* Refrigerant Compressors Antitrust Litig., 731 F.3d 586, 589 (6th Cir. 2013) ("Some federal appellate courts have concluded that, after the cases are consolidated, they retain their separate identities, others that they always merge, and still others that they sometimes merge and sometimes remain.").

lawyers involved in the case want *their* clients to be named in the CAC, especially plaintiffs' lawyers who are not part of case leadership and have no relationship with the case leaders. Having one's client included in the CAC is often the only way for such counsel to stay involved in what might be a meaningful case. Nevertheless, it can never be relationships or eagerness that controls the plaintiff-naming effort for the CAC. Instead, the CAC must include the plaintiffs with the strongest claims and damages, and who will make the best presentation, even if this means lead counsel's clients are not included.

As for plaintiffs who do not make it into the CAC, they simply have individual cases in the MDL court, which they can opt out at the appropriate time. Alternatively, if appropriate they can participate as class members. Importantly, and unlike traditional opt-out plaintiffs, the unnamed MDL plaintiffs' cases do not get aggressively litigated. Rather, they are tacitly stayed by agreement, since pursuing them would often be wasteful. Of course, these clients can always dismiss their complaints, since they have been essentially rendered absent class members by the process.

Plaintiffs' counsel should carefully vet plaintiffs for inclusion in a CAC on the basis of plaintiffs' *residency*. After all, if a lawsuit is premised on violation of state law, it is normally best practice for plaintiffs' counsel to include plaintiffs from as many states as possible, expecting that the consumers' residency will largely drive the law that will control the plaintiffs' claims, (for instance, consumer-antitrust or consumer fraud-deceptive trade claims). Likewise, effort should be made to include plaintiffs from the more populous states, such as California, Florida, New Jersey, New York, Ohio, Pennsylvania, and Texas.

Such vetting should help ensure that plaintiffs included in the CAC have solid claims (i.e., real grievances and quantifiable damages).

Plaintiffs' legal theory must also be accounted for when deciding which states are most material. For instance, Pennsylvania does not have an antitrust statute, so it would be worthless for plaintiffs' counsel to include a Pennsylvania plaintiff in a consumer-antitrust case. Of course, where a federal question exists—like in cases alleging direct-purchaser antitrust claims or violations of federal securities laws—none of the forgoing state-law considerations are relevant, and a single plaintiff's claim can cover the entire country.

When a complaint alleges state law claims, the challenge for plaintiffs' counsel is to allege the broadest class possible. This can be achieved by making a state law claim resemble a federal law claim—namely, trying to cover all 50 states through use of a single law. State laws differ to varying degrees. Most states' common law as to contracts is similar (if not largely identical). On the other hand, states' consumer fraud laws can vary considerably, but even there, similar state laws may be grouped together.[41]

Critical when considering choice of law is to appreciate the Supreme Court's holding in *Klaxon Co. v. Stentor Manufacturing Co.*[42] that the forum court's conflicts (or choice-of-law) jurisprudence will control.[43] With this in mind, plaintiffs' counsel must work to ensure that venue exists in a federal judicial circuit (or district) that still respects the choice-of-law principles advanced by the Supreme Court in *Philips Petroleum Co. v. Shutts.*[44]

In *Shutts,* the Court explained (or suggested, depending on your interpretation) that applying a single state's substantive law was permissible in a multistate case so long as one of two circumstances was presented: *either* no conflict exists in the first place,[45] in which case no problem exists applying a single state's substantive law; *or* application of a single state's substantive law is shown to be consistent with due process.[46]

Demonstrating compliance with due process requirements may include proof that defendant's alleged scheme was at least partially hatched, implemented, concealed, advertised, marketed, or profited from in the state whose law plaintiffs' counsel seeks to apply. If

---

41. *See, e.g.,* Telectonics Pacing Sys., Inc., Accufix Atrial "J" Leads Prods. Liab. Litig., 172 F.R.D. 271, 291 (S.D. Ohio 1997) ("[I]f the elements of the cause of action are the same and the legal standards on 'important/meaningful/significant/pivotal' issues are substantial similar the state laws can be grouped for purposes of class certification.").

42. Klaxon Co. v. Stentor Manufacturing Co., 313 U.S. 487 (1941).

43. *Id.* at 496 ("The conflict of laws rules to be applied by the federal court in Delaware must conform to those prevailing in Delaware's state courts. Otherwise the accident of diversity of citizenship would constantly disturb equal administration of justice in coordinate state and federal courts sitting side by side.").

44. Philips Petroleum Co. v. Shutts, 472 U.S. 797 (1985).

45. *Id.* at 815 ("There can be no injury in applying Kansas law if it is not in conflict with that of any other jurisdiction connected to this suit.").

46. *Id.* at 818 ("[F]or a State's substantive law to be selected in a constitutionally permissible manner, that State must have a significant contact or significant aggregation of contacts, creating state interests, such that choice of its law is neither arbitrary nor fundamentally unfair.") (quoting Allstate Ins. Co. v. Hauge, 499 U.S. 302, 312–13 (1981) (quotation marks omitted)).

defendant's customers have a claim, it stands to reason that they would expect the law of that defendant's home state to control.[47]

Although not adopting a wholesale *Shutts* discussion, in *AU Optronics*, the Ninth Circuit recently applied California's Cartwright Antitrust Act nationwide, allowing claims by consumers in states that did not even have antitrust statutes (like Pennsylvania, mentioned earlier).[48] The court described California's interest in protecting nonresidents from misbehaviors committed by misbehaving California corporate citizens, and concluded that due process was not offended by applying California law nationwide.[49]

If the circuit or district does not embrace this reading of *Shutts* (or at least its theme), it will be considerably more difficult for plaintiffs to convince a court to apply a single state's law extraterritorially. And unless plaintiffs' claim sounds in contract, which is less subject to conflicts among states,[50] plaintiffs' counsel must hope to achieve a similar result through one of the following alternatives.

Suing in 50 states under 50 states' substantive laws. One alternative is to bring 50 (or however many) class action lawsuits. Another option is to allege state law claims on behalf of 50 (or however many) states' class members in a single class action lawsuit. Both approaches require considerable resources and legwork, and plaintiffs' counsel should examine whether such legwork is feasible, particularly in light of the risk of overwhelming the court.[51]

Plaintiffs' counsel must balance the benefit of achieving national coverage versus the risk of leaving some states' claims unfiled. While bringing claims for class members in all 50 states (whether by way of

---

47. *Id.* at 821.

48. AT&T Mobility LLC v. AU Optronics Corp. Am., Inc., 707 F.3d 1106, 1113 (9th Cir. 2014) ("[W]e hold in this case that the Cartwright Act can be lawfully applied without violating a defendant's due process rights when more than a de minimis amount of that defendant's alleged conspiratorial activity leading to the sale of price-fixed goods to plaintiffs took place in California. Such a defendant cannot reasonably complain that the application of California law is arbitrary or unfair when its alleged conspiracy took place, at least in part, in California.").

49. *Id.*

50. *See, e.g.,* Klay v. Humana Corp., 382 F.3d 1241 1261 (11th Cir. 2004) ("A breach is a breach is a breach, whether you are on the sunny shores of California or enjoying a sweet autumn breeze in New Jersey.").

51. *See, e.g., In re* Bridgestone/Firestone, Inc., 288 F.3d 1012, 1018–21 (7th Cir. 2002) (decertifying nationwide class action alleging claims for breach of express and implied warranties "[b]ecause these claims must be adjudicated under the law of so many jurisdictions, a single nationwide class is not manageable.").

50 initially separate lawsuits or by one master complaint) might deter unwelcomed attorneys from horning in on plaintiffs' case, such peace of mind is meaningless if the court ultimately dismisses the case for lack of manageability.[52]

Pursuing Exemplar-State Class Actions

Suing on behalf of class members in a discrete number of states—*exemplar states*—is another alternative to prosecuting multiple cases or one mega-case, and can address the potential management difficulties associated with overly ambitious pleading. Using this strategy, plaintiff counsel might file suit for residents of four or five states, carefully choosing enough states to represent the various differences in state laws across the country.[53]

If plaintiffs' counsel take the exemplar route, they must include class representatives from enough states to effectively litigate their case, focusing on states with good state law and robust populations. Doing so allows the exemplar case to remain small enough to avoid manageability issues, yet big enough to coax a global settlement should the opportunity arise.[54]

That said, attorneys can immediately access all federal class action cases through electronic databases like PACER, CourtLink, CaseStream, or CourtEXPRESS. Suing with only exemplar states leaves plaintiffs' counsel vulnerable to competition based on overlapping class actions. Plaintiffs' counsel bringing exemplar state class action cases must therefore negotiate and consolidate their leadership position early to fend off likely leadership attacks. If they don't, they must prepare to argue and win inevitable lead counsel fights by demonstrating their extensive (if true) pre-suit investigation, their lawsuit's innovative or proprietary nature, and other factors justifying their placement in the lead, or at least a co-lead, counsel position.

---

52. *See* FED. R. CIV. P. 23(b)(3)(D) (When deciding whether a class action is superior to other ways to resolve a controversy, the court may consider "the difficulties likely to be encountered in the management of a class action.").

53. *See e.g.*, *In re* New Motor Vehicles Canadian Export Antitrust Litig., 235 F.R.D. 127, 148 (D. Me. 2006) (certifying six exemplar states out of many alleged).

54. *See, e.g.*, Sullivan v. D.B. Inv., Inc., 667 F.3d 273, 303–04 (3d Cir. 2011) ("Because we are presented with a settlement class certification . . . we simply need not inquire whether the varying state treatments of indirect purchaser damage claims at issue would present the type of 'insuperable obstacles' or 'intractable management problems' pertinent to certification of a litigation class.").

If individual state subclasses are created, the complaint will need a subclass representative from each included state. Some complaints attempt to avoid this necessity by lumping similar states together in a limited number of aggregated subclasses (for instance, placing ten states within a particular subclass for indirect purchaser antitrust claims and arguing that the elements of such claims are common among those ten states). This approach typically requires an appendix to the class brief charting the elements of the claims for each such state with citations to case law or statutes. While this may work, it introduces a whole new set of arguments for defendants at class certification regarding the existence, materiality, and predominance of variations between the law of the various states within that subclass.

A related concern is whether to include multiple class representatives for each subclass. Including more than one class representative provides a "belt-and-suspenders" approach to defeating any adequacy (and typicality) concerns. For instance, defendants may attempt to attack a particular class representative as beyond the statute of limitations or as not properly within the class definition. Alternatively, defendants may attack the standing of the putative class representative—for instance, do they have Article III standing (injury) and statutory standing? Class representatives may also need to withdraw for reasons unrelated to the litigation.

On the other hand, including multiple class representatives provides the opportunity for defendants to compare testimony and thereby try to demonstrate variations in the class (for instance, one class representative testifies that they relied upon the alleged deceptive label and another testifies that they did not). This risk can be reduced with thorough vetting and deposition preparation.

Bristol-Myers Squibb Co. v. Superior Court of California's Effect on Consolidated Lawsuits

In June 2017, the U.S. Supreme Court decided *Bristol-Myers Squibb Co. v. Superior Court of California*.[55] The case involved hundreds of people from 33 states, including California, who sought compensation for injuries related to Bristol-Myers' drug Plavix. Though Bristol-Myers had considerable California contacts, the non-Californians' claims had little to do with California. For instance, Bristol-Myers neither developed nor

---

55. Bristol-Myers Squibb Co. v. Superior Court of California, 137 S. Ct. 1773 (2017).

manufactured Plavix in California. What's more, nothing existed to suggest that non-Californians' injuries were related to Bristol-Myer's California marketing, promotion, or distribution of Plavix. Instead, the only way non-Californians' claims related to California was that Bristol-Myers' advertising and distribution efforts that reached them also reached Californians.

The California Supreme Court held that Bristol-Myers' substantial California contacts allowed California courts to exercise specific jurisdiction over the non-Californians' claims even though the relation between non-Californians' claims and Bristol-Myers' California activities was slight. The Supreme Court disagreed, observing the California court's failure to "identif[y] any adequate link between the State and the nonresidents' claims"[56] and ruling that the California court lacked specific jurisdiction to entertain the non-Californians' claims.

The Court did not believe its ruling posed a practical problem for mass-tort plaintiffs, explaining that its ruling

> does not prevent the California and other out-of-state plaintiffs from joining together in a consolidated action in the States that have general jurisdiction over [a defendant.] Alternatively, the plaintiffs who are residents of a particular State—for example, the 92 plaintiffs from Texas and the 71 from Ohio—could probably sue together in their home States.[57]

Perhaps more practically, plaintiffs' attorneys interested in consolidating multiple states' claims should consider filing their cases in the defendant's home jurisdiction. Often that state will now be the only state court forum that can entertain a consolidated nationwide lawsuit. Obviously, if jurisdiction in federal court exists and enough cases are in suit to encourage an MDL, plaintiffs should consider consolidation (at least for pre-trial purposes) via an MDL Panel centralization-and-transfer order.

REMAND AND TRIAL

Section 1407(a) states that "[e]ach action so transferred *shall be remanded* by the panel at or before the conclusion of such pre-trial proceedings to the district from which it was transferred." Nevertheless, very few actions are ever remanded. Many actions are settled or terminated in

---

56. *Id.* at 1781.
57. *Id.* at 1783.

the transferee court. Occasionally, transferee courts (or the parties themselves) may decide that the action should stay in the transferee court where experience has been developed. However, the Supreme Court has made clear that the remand provision is generally mandatory. In *Lexecon, Inc. v. Milberg Weiss Bershad Hynes & Lerach*,[58] the Supreme Court reversed where the transferee court had transferred actions to itself for trial under 28 U.S.C. § 1404(a), writing that § 1407(a) "uncondition[ally]" commands the panel to remand, at the end of pre-trial proceedings, each action transferred by the panel that has not been terminated in the transferee district.

There remains considerable debate over whether there are methods for the transferee court to retain matters for trial despite the language of § 1407 and *Lexecon*. The Manual on Complex Litigation explains several possible methods:

- Prior to recommending remand, the transferee court could conduct a bellwether trial of a centralized action or actions originally filed in the transferee district, the results of which (1) may, upon the consent of parties to constituent actions not filed in the transferee district, be binding on those parties and actions, or (2) may otherwise promote settlement in the remaining actions.
- Soon after transfer, the plaintiffs in an action transferred for pre-trial from another district may seek or be encouraged (1) to dismiss their action and refile the action in the transferee district, provided venue lies there, and the defendant(s) agree, if the ruling can only be accomplished in conjunction with a tolling of the statute of limitations or a waiver of venue objections, or (2) to file an amended complaint asserting venue in the transferee district, or (3) to otherwise consent to remain in the transferee district for trial.
- After an action has been remanded to the originating transferor court at the end of § 1407 pre-trial proceedings, the transferor court could transfer the action, pursuant to 28 U.S.C. § 1404 or § 1406, back to the transferee court for trial by the transferee judge.
- The transferee judge could seek an intercircuit or intracircuit assignment pursuant to 28 U.S.C. § 292 or § 294 and follow a

---

58. Lexecon, Inc. v. Milberg Weiss Bershad Hynes & Lerach, 523 U.S. 26 (1998).

remanded action, presiding over the trial of that action in that originating district.[59]

Of course, if a putative class action is certified in the transferee court and reaches judgment, any resolution of the remaining actions may be determined based upon res judicata or collateral estoppel, perhaps making remand irrelevant.

Because transferee courts do not typically provide ongoing status reports to transferor courts, it is the best practice for the transferee court to provide a pre-trial order upon remand that fully explains the proceedings, summarizes important rulings, and outlines any remaining issues for discovery and trial.[60]

After remand, the transferor judge has the power to modify rulings by the transferee judge, subject to any comity and "law of the case" considerations, but it is exceptionally rare that the transferor judge will change such rulings absent a significant change of circumstances or governing law.

Despite the forgoing, at the end of the day, it is the MDL Panel (not the transferee court) that determines when and how remand should occur.[61] Even so, the panel will normally look to the transferee judge to suggest when remand should occur.[62] It is very unlikely that a remand motion by an individual party would be granted by the panel. The time and method of remand varies significantly among actions, depending upon the particular needs of the actions and the preferences of the transferee judge.

One recurring issue is whether to remand before considering summary judgment. If the basis of the summary judgment motion is an issue that relates to only a limited number of cases (or rests on application of the transferor court's conflicts-of-law or substantive law rules), remand may be appropriate.[63] On the other hand, if the summary

---

59. *Manual,* at § 20.132.

60. *See In re* Diet Drugs Prods. Liab. Litig., MDL No. 1203, 2001 WL 497313 (E.D. Pa. May 9, 2001).

61. *See In re Roberts,* 178 F.3d 181 (3d Cir. 1999); J.P.M.L. R.P. 7.6(c).

62. *In re IBM Peripheral EDP Devices Antitrust Litig.,* 407 F. Supp. 254, 256 (J.P.M.L. 1976).

63. *See In re* Orthopedic Bone Screw Prods. Liab. Litig., MDL No. 1014, 1997 WL 109595, at *2 (E.D. Pa. Mar. 7, 1997) (ruling on motions for partial summary judgment would not advance the litigation and would serve no useful purpose); *see also* Francis E. McGovern, *Judicial Centralization and Devolution in Mass Torts,* 95 Mich. L. Rev. 2077 (1997) (*citing In re* Silicone Gel Breast Implants Prods. Liab. Litig., 887 F. Supp. 1455 (N.D. Ala. 1995)).

judgment motion involves issues common to all of the consolidated cases, there is a better argument that the transferee judge is in the best position to rule.[64]

Another recurring dispute is whether the MDL Panel can transfer (or remand) particular claims. Section 1407(a) authorizes the panel to transfer only "civil actions," not claims; however, § 1407(a) also empowers the panel to accomplish "partial" transfer by (1) transferring an entire action to the transferee district, and (2) simultaneously remanding to the transferor court any claims for which transfer was not deemed appropriate, such as cross-claims, counterclaims, or third-party claims. Nevertheless, the panel has rejected most requests to exclude portions of a case from transfer.[65]

The panel is much more receptive to requests by the transferee judge to remand particular claims in particular actions, since the transferee judge will have far more information about the details of the litigation.[66]

COORDINATION AMONG ACTIONS WHEN MDL IS NOT AVAILABLE

Sometimes similar class actions are filed in both state and federal courts. Sometimes the state cases are not removable by defendants.[67] Why would plaintiff counsel want to file in state court when consolidation might be available in federal court? The reasons are many. In some state courts, broader discovery is allowed than in federal court. Some state courts may be perceived to be more plaintiff friendly. Plaintiffs' counsel might have a long-standing relationship with the judge. Some states do not require jury verdicts to be unanimous, which federal courts do. Potentially even more important, plaintiffs' counsel will be in

---

64. *See, e.g., In re* Norplant Contraceptive Prods. Liab. Litig., 215 F. Supp. 2d 795, 810, 835 (E.D. Tex. 2002) (granting summary judgment terminating "nearly all remaining non-settling Plaintiffs and their claims in the Norplant multidistrict litigation proceedings" based in part on the common-law application of the learned intermediary doctrine).

65. *But see In re* Hotel Tel. Charge Antitrust Litig., 341 F. Supp. 771 (J.P.M.L. 1972); *cf. In re* Midwest Milk Monopolization Litig., 386 F. Supp. 1401 (J.P.M.L. 1975).

66. *See, e.g., In re* Collins, 233 F.3d 809 (3d Cir. 2000), *cert. denied sub nom.* Collins v. Mac-Millan Bloedel, Inc., 532 U.S. 1066 (2001) (upholding severance of punitive damage claims by the transferee court in actions where the rest of the claims were suggested for remand); *In re* Patenaude, 210 F.3d 135, 143 (3d Cir. 2000).

67. *See generally* GREGORY C. COOK, THE CLASS ACTION FAIRNESS ACT: LAW AND STRATEGY (2013).

control of their case—rather than being lost in the crowd of plaintiffs' counsel in an MDL proceeding in federal court.

The downside—and it is substantial—is that plaintiffs' counsel will likely need to limit their class to one state. But, even a single state limitation may not prevent removal. In fact, even a limitation of a specific dollar figure recovery should not ordinarily prevent removal.[68] Although a complete discussion of CAFA jurisdiction is beyond this book (but see Chapter 3), if the damages exceed \$5 million and it is a class action with at least minimal diversity, the action is likely to be removable.

Some plaintiffs' counsel have sued in a handful of states, sought broad discovery, threatened to sue in other states, located additional plaintiffs through discovery, and then brought additional new single state suits. Apart from the risk of removal, this strategy risks losing the claims of many potential class members, because a suit for a class of citizens of one state will not toll the statute of limitations for non-class members located in another state.[69]

If state class actions are filed, it is almost certain that defendants will attempt to remove to federal court where consolidation is easier through the MDL procedure and predictability is likely higher. Of course, removal may not be successful—or consolidation may fail before the MDL Panel. In either circumstance, the parties should strongly consider whether to attempt informal coordination among the actions. This should be easier if all cases are in federal court. The Manual on Complex Litigation (Fourth) section 20.14 provides a menu of options that is very helpful, particularly if all actions are in federal court. Some of these include (1) the special assignment of a single judge under 28 U.S.C. §§ 292–294, (2) the designation of one case as the "lead case" (giving the rulings in the lead case presumptive effect in the other actions), (3) the joint appointment of a special master, or (4) appointment of common lead counsel (or the appointment of liaison counsel). Other options listed by the Manual on Complex Litigation include:

- **Joint conferences and orders.** All judges may attend joint hearings or conferences, in person or by telephone. Federal Rule of Civil Procedure 77(b) requires consent of the parties for trials

---

68. Standard Fire Ins. Co. v. Knowles, 568 U.S. 588, 133 S. Ct. 1345, 185 L. Ed. 2d 43981 (2013).

69. American Pipe & Constr. Co. v. Utah, 414 U.S. 538 (1974).

or hearings to be conducted outside the district; consent is not required for other proceedings, such as conferences. . . .

- **Avoiding duplicative discovery.** Judges should encourage techniques that coordinate discovery and avoid duplication, . . . Filing or cross-filing deposition notices, interrogatories, and requests for production in related cases will make the product of discovery usable in all cases and avoid duplicative activity. Relevant discovery already completed should ordinarily be made available to litigants in the other cases. If the material is subject to a protective order, the court usually may accommodate legitimate privacy interests by amending the order to include the new litigants within the order's restrictions, and the party seeking the discovery may be required to bear a portion of the cost incurred in initially obtaining the information. Document production should be coordinated and joint depositories established. The resolution of discovery disputes can also be coordinated to some degree (e.g., by referring them to a single magistrate judge or special master).

Yet another option is a stay of some or all of the related actions. (See Chapter 3 in this book for more on this subject.) Such a stay is far more likely if all of the parties jointly request the stay. However, there is substantial federal case law regarding such stays.

If some of the cases are in state court, coordination is still a viable option, particularly if the state court judge is willing to assist. There are many examples of successful state and federal coordination of related actions.[70] Of course, coordination takes effort and time.[71] Moreover, the federal courts (including the MDL Panel) have no power over the state courts except in extreme and very rare circumstances. Coordination

---

70. *See generally* William W. Schwarzer et al., *Judicial Federalism in Action: Coordination of Litigation in State and Federal Courts*, 78 VA. L. REV. 1689 (1992) (discussing a study of 11 notable instances of state–federal coordination in litigation arising from (1) 1972 Federal Everglades air crash, (2) 1977 Beverly Hills Supper Club fire, (3) 1979 Chicago air crash, (4) 1980 MGM Grand Hotel fire, (5) 1981 Hyatt skywalk cases, (6) 1986 technical equities fraud, (7) 1987 L'Ambience Plaza collapse, (8) 1989 Exxon Valdez oil spill, (9) 1989 Sioux City air crash, (10) Ohio asbestos litigation, and (11) Brooklyn Navy Yard asbestos litigation).

71. *See* Francis E. McGovern, *Rethinking Cooperation Among Judges in Mass Tort Litigation*, 44 UCLA L. REV. 1851, 1858 (1997) (hereinafter McGovern, *Rethinking Cooperation*) ("[P]laintiffs' attorneys rush to their favorite judges and demand draconian procedures to pressure defendants to make block settlements . . . Defendants seek the opposite—delay is their nirvana.").

is far easier when counsel for some or all of the parties in the related actions are the same. This may be a reason to include counsel who also have pending state actions or the steering committee for a federal MDL action. It might also be possible to create a judicial advisory committee among the judges who have pending, related actions. Coordination is particularly important if the actions are identical or have substantially overlapping class definitions.

The location of state court actions can also be a factor in the decision of the MDL Panel on where to locate any consolidated federal action. To facilitate coordination, the court should require—as a part of any standard CMO—that all counsel be required to disclose any related or similar actions pending in other courts.

The specific steps for state and federal coordination can include:

1. Coordination of the timing of class certification hearings and decisions (and perhaps even joint hearings)
2. Joint hearings on other motions and possibly coordinated briefing with supplements for variations in the applicable laws
3. A stay (formally or informally) of some actions to allow the court with the most cases to reach the class certification or merits issues first to avoid confusion and conflicting results
4. Appointment of a special master (or court-appointed expert) to assist all courts with discovery or other matters
5. Exchange of case management orders, pleadings, and discovery protocols among courts

Of course, coordinated discovery can produce the greatest benefits. The Manual explains the options for such coordination, noting that specific elements of discovery coordination have included:

- creating joint federal–state, plaintiff–defendant document depositories, accessible to attorneys in all states;
- ordering coordinated document production and arrangements for electronic discovery;
- ordering discovery materials from prior state and federal cases to be included in the document depository;
- scheduling and cross-noticing joint federal–state depositions;
- designating state-conducted depositions as official MDL depositions;
- enjoining attorneys conducting federal discovery from objecting to use of that discovery in state courts on the grounds that it originated in federal court;

- adopting standard interrogatories developed by state judges for litigation in their cases; and
- coordinating rulings on discovery disputes, such as the assertion of privilege, and using parallel orders to promote uniformity to the extent possible.

Perhaps the most important (and dangerous) issue with multiple actions pending in different forums is settlement. With a class action, a defendant could settle with a particular plaintiff and seek approval for a class-wide settlement. Should the court grant approval, all class members who fail to opt out of a Rule 23(b)(3) class will be bound and res judicata (as well as the release in the settlement) will bar their claims. A competing, uncertified class action in a different forum may be able to continue—but as an individual case rather than a class action, perhaps leaving counsel in the second action without a viable case and without a source for any attorney fees. If defendants seek the best settlement from competing cases, some have termed the procedure a "reverse auction."[72] Of course, the mere existence of competing class actions does not mean that a particular settlement was not the best result for all of the parties involved. In every case, court approval is required, as is providing notice and an opportunity to be heard.

PARALLEL GOVERNMENT ENFORCEMENT ACTIONS
Advantages and Disadvantages

For plaintiffs, a parallel government enforcement action can provide both a significant source of information and a significant pressure on the defendant to settle. However, managing civil litigation with the concurrent enforcement action can be difficult, and can create major delays in the civil action. To facilitate coordination, related criminal/ enforcement and civil actions would be best assigned to the same judge.

For defendants, an overriding issue may be Fifth Amendment concerns where the government action has criminal connotations. Further, defendants will likely be far more concerned about the government enforcement action than the civil action, and thus will want to avoid

---

72. *E.g.*, Reynolds v. Beneficial Nat'l Bank, 288 F.3d 277, 280–85 (7th Cir. 2002); *In re* Checking Account Overdraft Litig., 859 F. Supp. 2d 1313 (S.D. Fla. 2012) (enjoining settlement of later filed federal class action because of concerns over reverse auction (among others) and using the All Writs Act and the First-to-File rule as its basis).

providing discovery in the civil action that can be used in the criminal/ enforcement action.

Criminal Issues and Fifth Amendment Concerns

Witnesses may claim the Fifth Amendment privilege against self-incrimination in a civil action, especially if examined prior to the conclusion of criminal proceedings. Even when the criminal matter ends, testimony still may not be available.[73] Simply producing paper or electronic evidence in a civil proceeding can sometimes have a detrimental effect in a parallel criminal matter (for instance, the civil production may include adverse or exculpatory evidence to which the prosecution would not be entitled under Federal Rule of Criminal Procedure 16).

Stays

Defendants typically seek a stay of civil matters while related criminal proceedings are pending. The criminal proceeding ordinarily has first priority, both because of the short pre-trial period allowed under the Speedy Trial Act, and because of the potential impact of a conviction. If a conviction occurs, it may be admissible in the civil case as substantive evidence of the essential elements of the offense under Federal Rule of Evidence 803(22), or as impeachment evidence under Federal Rule of Evidence 609.

However, a general stay of all pre-trial activities in the civil litigation is not usual, since it may be possible to conduct major portions of the civil case discovery before completion of the criminal proceedings.[74]

CONCLUSION

Managing multiple class actions (or enforcement actions) is exceptionally challenging, and there is no "one size fits all" answer. In fact, the answer will be different for each matter and is constantly changing. The best advice is to keep an open mind for new solutions and work cooperatively with opposing (and co-counsel). In the end, cooperation will almost always produce the right result.

---

73. *See* Pillsbury Co. v. Conboy, 459 U.S. 248 (1983) (witness compelled by grant of "use immunity" to give testimony to grand jury does not waive right to claim Fifth Amendment in subsequent civil litigation).

74. *See, e.g.,* Landis v. N. Am. Co., 299 U.S. 248, 254–55 (1936); Texaco, Inc. v. Borda, 383 F.2d 607 (3d Cir. 1967).

9

Class Action Settlement

Jason B. Tompkins and Christopher K. Friedman

Had this chapter been written ten years ago, far fewer pages would have been sufficient to cover the major issues surrounding the settlement of class actions. Today, an entire book could be written on the subject. Until recently, judges took seriously the mantra that "courts favor the settlement of class action lawsuits." That truism is now being challenged in significant ways. Many judges who, in the past, would have rubber-stamped a class settlement now apply a more rigorous standard of judicial review. This newfound scrutiny may be due to the combination of negative media coverage of class action attorney fees, or appellate courts' increasing willingness to overturn settlement approvals. In addition to more rigorous judicial scrutiny, the rise of professional objectors threatens to scuttle otherwise legitimate settlements. While most class action settlements are ultimately approved, judicial approval is never guaranteed. This increased scrutiny is most notable in federal courts. In contrast, some state courts, due to their often overloaded dockets, may apply a less exacting standard of scrutiny to proposed settlements.

For both plaintiffs and defendants, every step in the litigation process should be taken with the possibility of settlement in mind. Consequently, practitioners must understand and appreciate the substantive and procedural complexities that protect the interests of absent class members because these can be traps for the unwary.[1]

Settling a non-class action lawsuit is relatively simple. Once the parties resolve their differences, they can terminate the lawsuit by filing a joint stipulation of dismissal, signed by all parties.[2] If the parties resolve their differences before the defendant responds to the plaintiff's complaint, then the plaintiff can simply file a notice of dismissal with no involvement by the defendant.[3] Generally, the only time that a court becomes involved in a non-class action settlement is when the parties request that the court enter an order consistent with the settlement. Otherwise, the parties are in total control of the substance and procedure underlying the agreement.

Conversely, settlement on a class-action basis is subject to court supervision, and the court acts as a fiduciary for absent class members. The procedures for voluntary dismissal and settlement of class actions, which incorporate Federal Rules of Civil Procedure 41(a)(1) and 23(e), as well as the settlement provisions of the Class Action Fairness Act (CAFA), require rigorous court supervision: extensive briefing, multiple hearings, notice to the class, and, ultimately, a final stamp of approval by the court. These procedures are geared toward safeguarding absent class members, and ensuring that class action defendants are protected from the danger of re-litigating the same issues. In addition, unlike traditional litigation, the named plaintiffs are ordinarily not the final decision makers regarding the acceptance of a settlement offer. And always lurking around the corner of any settlement is the specter of objectors aiming to scuttle arduously negotiated settlement proposals. It is fair to say that in many class actions, the settlement has become one of the most contentious and vigorously litigated phases of the case. Moreover, the contents of the actual settlement agreements are more complicated in class actions. Monetary terms often take the form of complex mathematical equations designed to approximate the value of thousands—sometimes millions—of potential claims. Some class actions include an injunctive component to proscribe future conduct, as well as a mechanism to monitor compliance. In addition, monetary

---

1. *See, e.g., In re* Nat'l Football League Players Concussion Injury Litig., 775 F.3d 570, 581 (3d Cir. 2014); Ehrheart v. Verizon Wireless, 609 F.3d 590, 593 (3d Cir. 2010); *In re* Cathode Ray Tube (CRT) Antitrust Litig., MDL No. 1917, 2016 WL 721680, at *10 n.17 (N.D. Cal. Jan. 28, 2016).

2. FED. R. CIV. P. 41(a)(1)(A)(ii).

3. FED. R. CIV. P. 41(a)(1)(A)(i).

class action settlements require notice to class members (and sometimes also to governmental officials) that can be time consuming and expensive. Taken together, class action negotiation and settlement can be very complicated, and counsel for plaintiffs and defendants must take great care to ensure that the process and substance of the agreement is proper.

This chapter addresses the basics of these substantive and procedural rules, focusing especially on potential points of conflict between class action plaintiffs and defendants that might arise during the process of settlement, and—perhaps more importantly—potential red flags in settlement agreements that could threaten to undermine a deal before it leaves the judge's desk.

Setting Proper Expectations

Class action negotiation and settlement is very different than the settlement process in traditional litigation, both for plaintiffs and defendants. One of the chief differences is that the named plaintiffs are not the sole decision makers regarding negotiation tactics, or whether to ultimately accept a settlement offer. As a practical matter, on the plaintiffs' side, class counsel typically make the decisions regarding negotiation.

For defense counsel and their clients, this fact changes the negotiation dynamics significantly. Many negotiation tactics that might work in traditional litigation will not be effective in the class action context. For instance, the strategy of offering an amount of money that is well below the value of a claim, but that might be tempting to an individual plaintiff, will generally not work. In the class action context, defense counsel may be negotiating with lawyers who have a good understanding of the value of the underlying claims, and who may not be tempted by a quick, but undervalued settlement.

JUDICIAL REVIEW OF CLASS ACTION SETTLEMENTS
Scope of Rule 23(e)

Under Rule 23(e), a class action cannot be "settled, voluntarily dismissed, or compromised" without the court's approval.[4] The language of the rule only requires court approval for certified classes. In other words, under the federal rule, the parties can dismiss an action that has not yet been certified as a class, or where class certification has been

---

4. Fed. R. Civ. P. 23(e).

denied. The purpose of this rule (as well as the details for class action notice requirements) is to protect absent class members' due process rights. The class action gives absent class members a vehicle to seek vindication of their rights when they have claims that are not worth pursuing individually. However, when their claims are aggregated, class members necessarily sacrifice their ability to direct the course of the litigation and, absent this rule, many class members might have legal claims disposed of without their knowledge. The court approval requirement for settlements places the judge in the role of fiduciary for absent class members.

Prior to 2003, Rule 23(e)(1)(A) applied to the dismissal of a "class action." Accordingly, under the old rule, some jurisdictions applied the requirements of Rule 23(e) to putative (uncertified) classes, reasoning that absent putative class members might be prejudiced by pre-certification settlement or voluntary dismissal.[5] However, in 2003, the Advisory Committee on the Rules of Civil Procedure clarified this ambiguity by amending Rule 23(e) to apply specifically to "certified class[es]."[6] Despite this clarification, a handful of federal courts have reserved the right to require "appropriate notice" to putative class members, and "may consider whether . . . the proposed settlement and dismissal are tainted by collusion or will prejudice absent putative members with a reasonable 'reliance' expectation of the maintenance of the action for the protection of their interests."[7] One of these courts considered the potential prejudice suffered by putative class members when a statute of limitations period is nearing its end.[8] Also note that

---

5. *See* McLaughlin on Class Actions § 6:1. The 2003 revisions attempted to clarify this ambiguity by making reference to a "certified class."

6. Fed. R. Civ. P. 23, committee comment ("The new rule requires approval only if the claims, issues, or defenses of a certified class are resolved by a settlement, voluntary dismissal, or compromise."). In at least one case, a party contended that, although the 2003 amendments to the Federal Rules of Civil Procedure clarified that Rule 23 applied only to certified classes, putative class actions that fell under Class Action Fairness Act (CAFA) still required court approval, and prevented a plaintiff from voluntarily dismissing a case under Rule 41, and subsequently refiling in a more favorable state forum. *See* Adams v. U.S.A.A. Casualty Ins. Co., No. 16-3228, slip op. at 19–22 (8th Cir. July 25, 2017). The Eighth Circuit disagreed, holding that Congress rejected a version of CAFA that prevented the practice of refiling in state court. *Id.* at 21–22.

7. Lewis v. Vision Value, LLC, No. 1:11-cv-01055-LJO-BAM, 2012 WL 2930867, at *3 (E.D. Cal. July 18, 2012) (internal citations omitted); *see also* Eastham v. Chesapeake Appalachia, LLC, No. 2:12-cv-615, 2013 WL 3818549, at *2 (S.D. Ohio 2013).

8. *Lewis,* 2012 WL, at *3 (citing Diaz v. Trust Territory of Pac. Islands, 876 F.2d 1401, 1407 n.3 (9th Cir. 1989).

some states still use pre-2003 language in their version of Rule 23.[9] Finally, it is possible (but unlikely) that a court might also apply scrutiny to instances when a party attempts to amend a complaint under Rule 15 to remove the class action allegations, or where the plaintiff files a motion to dismiss a party under Rule 21.[10]

For the defendant, it may be important to ensure that the action will be dismissed rather than simply having a new class representative substituted. There is also the danger of an absent class member (sometimes represented by counsel) moving to intervene and taking over the class action. Tolling is also important to consider when settling individually. The Supreme Court has held that the filing of a class action tolls the statute of limitations for putative class members, at least until the action is dismissed or class certification is denied.[11] The Supreme Court recently confirmed that *American Pipe* tolling applies only to successive individual actions, and does not allow subsequent and untimely "piggyback" class actions.[12] Nonetheless, several issues still remain unanswered regarding *American Pipe* tolling, such as, whether it applies cross-jurisdictionally.

Court Review of Class Settlements

Rule 23(e) provides that a district court may approve a class action settlement on a finding that it is "fair, reasonable, and adequate." For many years, courts seemed to quickly review and enthusiastically approve most class action settlements. Recently, though, courts have subjected class settlements to a higher level of scrutiny and there has been an increase in the number of class action settlements that are not approved. The larger number of class actions that have been filed certainly drives some of this scrutiny as does the increased public attention to the large amount of money involved—both the amount of damages and attorney fees. The increased activity of professional objectors who raise issues about settlements has also contributed to a more critical review of class settlements.

---

9. *See, e.g.,* ALA. R. CIV. P. 23; O.C.G.A. 9-11-23; 231 PA. CODE Rule 1714.
10. *See, e.g., In re* Cardizem CD Antitrust Litig., No. 99-MD-1278, 2000 WL 33180833, at *5 (E.D. Mich. Mar. 7, 2000); Richards v. Lesaffre Yeast Corp., 2008 WL 131203, at *1.
11. American Pipe & Construction Co. v. Utah, 414 U.S. 538, 554 (1974).
12. China Agritech, Inc. v. Resh, 138 S. Ct. 1800 (2018), 2018 WL 2767565 (June 11, 2018).

Courts' heightened scrutiny of class action settlements and their willingness to overturn a class settlement is illustrated by several recent appellate decisions. *In re Subway Footlong Sandwich Mktg. & Sales Practices Litig.*[13] began with a teenager posting on his Facebook page that his Subway "footlong" sandwich didn't measure up.[14] Asserting that Subway had been passing off 11-inch sandwiches as footlongs to all of its customers, lawyers across the country filed numerous class actions. They soon discovered, however, that all of Subway's unbaked rolls weigh the exact same amount and that most bake to the full 12 inches. Due to "natural—and unpreventable—vagaries in the baking process," some may not grow to their advertised length, but they nonetheless contain the exact same amount of bread.[15] What's more, no customer, "regardless of bread length, was cheated on the amount of ham or turkey, provolone or pepper jack," because those items are standardized.[16] The plaintiffs' lawyers abandoned their damages class, but reached an injunction class settlement under which Subway agreed to take certain measures to ensure that footlongs were just that, but also acknowledged that "because of the inherent variability in food production and the bread baking process," there could be no guarantees.[17] The district court approved that settlement, including $520,000 in attorney fees and $500 to each named plaintiff. The Seventh Circuit reversed, observing that both before and after the settlement, Subway customers were subject to the same small chance that the bread may not be as long as advertised. Because the injunctive relief was "utterly worthless," the court rejected the settlement and stated that "a class action that seeks only worthless benefits for the class and yields only fees for class counsel is no better than a racket and should be dismissed out of hand."[18]

Another noted example is *In re Hyundai and Kia Fuel Economy Litigation.*[19] There, the Ninth Circuit rejected a nationwide class settlement regarding allegedly misleading representations of fuel economy because the district court failed to analyze whether the variation among state laws that applied to class members caused Rule 23 predominance prong to fail. The Ninth Circuit also held that the district court failed to

---

13. 869 F.3d 551 (7th Cir.) (hereinafter *Subway*).
14. *Subway*, 869 F.3d at 553.
15. *Id.* at 554.
16. *Id.*
17. *Id.*
18. *Id.* at 556.
19. 881 F.3d 679 (9th Cir. 2018).

consider whether used car purchasers should have been included in the class without determining whether they were exposed to the misleading communications. Both the plaintiffs and defendants have petitioned the Ninth Circuit for rehearing en banc.

Similarly, in *In re Target Corporation Data Security Breach Litigation*, the Eighth Circuit Court of Appeals held that the district court failed to engage in the requisite "rigorous analysis" after an objector asserted that the settlement class included both individuals who had suffered concrete injury, and those who had not and, therefore, could not claim monetary compensation.[20] According to the objector, the proposed settlement was inadequate because individuals without concrete injury would be required to release the defendant without compensation. The court ultimately reversed the lower court's approval on the grounds that the district court did not sufficiently explain the adequacy of the settlement for individuals who might suffer from future injuries.

These cases exemplify the increased scrutiny of class action settlements at both the trial court and appellate court stages. Indeed, these cases indicate that class counsel, during the negotiation stage, should take care not to negotiate terms that result in different segments of a single class being treated differently. Moreover, when a single class has multiple subgroups with potentially differing interests, a better practice is to break up the class into subclasses with separate representation. Indeed, in *Target*, that simple procedural solution probably would have satisfied the court, and saved the settlement.

Trap for the Unwary

Rule 23 states that court approval and notice are only required for certified classes. Therefore, under the Federal Rules, putative classes can be settled or voluntarily dismissed under Rule 41.

However, many state rules of civil procedure do not indicate whether settlement or voluntary dismissal of a putative class action requires notice, court approval, or other procedural safeguards. Thus, practitioners should familiarize themselves with the relevant state statutes, rules, and case law regarding the dismissal or settlement of putative class actions.

---

20. *In re* Target Corporation Data Security Breach Litig., 847 F.3d 608, 613–15 (8th Cir. Feb. 1, 2017).

PROTECTING THE SETTLEMENT: NEGOTIATING KEY TERMS

Although every negotiation over the settlement of a class action is different, the success or failure of any class settlement typically hinges on the negotiation of certain key terms. Moreover, unlike in non-class action litigation, the *way* that the parties go about negotiating the settlement may be almost as important as the substance of the settlement itself.

The Order of Negotiations

The propriety of a settlement often depends on how it was negotiated. The settling parties must establish that the negotiation was conducted at arms' length and was not the product of collusion.[21] Indeed, "[a] court determines a settlement's fairness by looking at both the settlement's terms and the negotiating process leading to settlement."[22] And when evaluating the negotiation process itself, courts examine a number of factors bearing on the fairness, reasonableness, and adequacy of the proposed settlement.

One factor is the phase of the litigation at which the negotiations take place. Courts have looked skeptically at settlements reached early in the litigation process—before class certification, sufficient discovery, or litigation that tests the strength of the claims or defenses.[23] On the other hand, "[i]f all discovery has been completed and the case is ready to go to trial, the court obviously has sufficient evidence to determine the adequacy of the settlement."[24] Settlement at a later stage ordinarily means that the parties have engaged in some discovery. Courts will infer that the plaintiffs' counsel has a solid understanding of the facts underlying the class claims and, therefore, will have an informed estimate of the value of the case.

The sequence of settlement negotiations is also important. Specifically, one red flag that can undermine proposed settlements is the order

---

21. *See, e.g.,* Moulton v. U.S. Steel Corp., 581 F.3d 344, 351 (8th Cir. 2009); Wal-Mart Stores, Inc. v. Visa U.S.A., Inc., 396 F.3d 96, 116 (2d Cir. 2005).

22. *Visa U.S.A., Inc.,* 396 F.3d at 116 (citing D'Amato v. Deutsche Bank, 236 F.3d 78, 85 (2d Cir. 2001)).

23. *See, e.g.,* Bickel v. Sheriff of Whitley City, No. 1:08-CV-102-TLS, 2015 WL 1402018 (N.D. Ind. Mar. 26, 2015).

24. 4 W. RUBENSTEIN, NEWBERG ON CLASS ACTIONS § 11:45, at 129 (2002). *See also* Visa U.S.A., Inc., 396 F.3d at 118.

in which negotiations take place. It is a best practice to conduct settlement negotiations in two stages. First, the parties should reach agreement on a settlement in principle on class relief and, only then, address attorney fees. Courts have consistently considered attorney fee negotiations that occur early in the negotiation process to be a red flag.[25] Early attorney fee negotiations could suggest that class counsel prioritizes the recovery of their own fees over the interest of absent class members. On the other hand, delaying the question of attorney fees too long carries a risk of blowing up an otherwise good settlement if the amount sought is not what the defense anticipated.

Some parties hold a separate mediation over attorney fees to avoid any inference of impropriety. Parties can also agree to forgo negotiations regarding attorney fees, electing instead to present a figure to the reviewing court, and litigate the issue. Of course, this method introduces a risk to plaintiffs' counsel that the court will approve a lower amount than counsel would like, and a risk to the defendant that the court will approve a higher amount.

When there are multiple class actions pending in different jurisdictions, it may also matter which case is the vehicle for seeking approval of a class settlement. Courts may see a red flag if the settlement appears to be a so-called reverse auction. This occurs when the defendant negotiates a global settlement in the weakest case, with plaintiffs' counsel lacking leverage, expertise, or ethics, and which seeks to bind class members from other cases with stronger counsel.[26]

Perhaps the most effective way to protect a proposed settlement is to mediate the case and to require, as part of the parties' agreement with the mediator, that she testify regarding the adversarial nature of the mediation. Mediation introduces a neutral third party who can inform the court, under oath, that the parties negotiated the settlement at arm's length. Although the imprimatur of a mediator will not guarantee that the settlement will gain court approval, it can go a long way toward proving to the court, over the protest of objectors, that the settlement process itself was conducted fairly.

---

25. *See* Manual for Complex Litigation, Fourth, § 21.7 ("[T]he simultaneous negotiation of class relief and attorney fees creates a potential conflict. Separate negotiation of the class settlement before an agreement on fees is generally preferable.").

26. *See* RUBENSTEIN, *supra* note 24, § 13.57.

Settlement Term Sheet

The final product of the negotiation can be extremely complex, and must address several intertwining issues. Thus, it is a best practice for each party to begin the negotiations with a proposed term sheet. This term sheet will frame the structure of the ultimate agreement and serves as an efficient way to guide negotiations going forward. The term sheet itself will address each material term of the final class settlement including the definition of the settlement class (if a class has not already been certified), whether the settlement will be paid from a common fund, or will be a claims-made settlement, the disposition of unclaimed proceeds, proposed payment dates, and the form and manner of notice to absent class members. The final settlement will sometimes include appendices, including an exemplar notice form, a motion to the court for approval of the settlement, and a proposed order approving the settlement.

Typical Contents of Settlement Term Sheet

- A proposed class definition for the settlement class
- The type of proposed class (e.g., Rule 23(b)(2) or (b)(3) class)
- A time period for the class
- A time period within which claims must be made on the settlement fund
- An agreement regarding who will pay for notice
- Some details about the method and content of the notice
- An agreement regarding who will administer the settlement
- The amount of the class fund
- Agreement about the settlement funding (claims made vs. common fund vs. coupons/discounts)
- The formula used to determine individual claim amounts
- An agreement regarding the distribution of unclaimed funds.
- The identification of cy pres recipients (if any)
- Proposed incentive awards to class representatives
- A description of any prospective or injunctive relief and the mechanism for monitoring compliance
- An agreement regarding the scope of the release
- An agreement that operates to terminate the settlement should the court not approve the settlement.
- An agreement that either party may terminate the settlement if a certain number of class members opt out ("blow up" provision)

Settlement Classes and Certification

As part of settlement approval, the court must certify a settlement class (unless an identical class has already been certified). Often, class actions are litigated as uncertified putative class actions, and certification of the settlement class occurs concurrently with final approval.[27] Thus, during the negotiation process, the parties will often negotiate the specific class definition or definitions (if there are multiple settlement classes). That definition dictates who will receive notice and (possibly) compensation, and which future claims will be released. The class definition also determines the preclusive effect of the settlement. Thus, reviewing courts pay special attention to the putative settlement classes during final approval of the settlement.

Although at the final approval stage, the parties to an uncertified class action lawsuit will jointly request[28] that the class be certified for settlement purposes, the court is not relieved of its duty to rigorously analyze the Rule 23 factors. These factors are evaluated in the same way as in a litigated certification motion except for the "manageability" factor because "the proposal is that there be no trial."[29] Thus, there is nothing for the court to "manage." Class certification for settlement purposes "demand[s] undiluted, even heightened[] attention" to Rule 23, "to protect absentees by blocking unwarranted or overbroad class definitions."[30] For instance, often courts analyze the Rule 23 adequacy prong more vigorously for purposes of settlement class certification due to a potential heightened risk of collusion. Indeed, the Supreme Court in *Amchem Products* has noted that a single class representative would not suffice when two subclasses had competing interests.[31]

> "When a court is asked to certify a class and approve its settlement in one proceeding, the Rule 23(a) requirements designed to protect absent class members 'demand undiluted, even heightened, attention.'"
>
> *In re.* Literary Works in Electronic Databases Copyright Litig., 654 F.3d 242, 249 (2d Cir. 2011) (quoting Amchem Prods., Inc. v. Windsor, 521 U.S. 591, 620 (1997)).

An important case illustrating the trend toward a heightened level of scrutiny in the area of settlement approvals, and the certification of

---

27. *See, e.g.*, RUBENSTEIN, *supra* note 24, § 13:51.

28. Out of an abundance of caution, some defense counsel prefer the plaintiff to make the motion for certification and approval. Defense counsel will then join the motion but make clear that they dispute the merits and are joining the motion for purposes of settlement alone.

29. Amchem Products, Inc. v. Windsor, 521 U.S. 591, 620 (1997).

30. *Id.*

31. *Id.* at 627.

a settlement class, was issued by the Second Circuit Court of Appeals in mid-2016.[32] In *MasterCard*, a case involving credit card interchange fees, and the means by which Visa and MasterCard process those fees, the parties agreed to a settlement after ten years of litigation that would result in $7.25 billion for an opt-out class, and injunctive relief for an injunction class. However, objectors asserted that the class representation was inadequate, resulting in a settlement that failed to protect the interests of absent class members. Noting that, when a settlement approval occurs at the same time as class certification, a determination of adequacy requires heightened attention, the court recognized that the opt-out class and the injunction class had adverse interests: "[t]he former would want to maximize cash compensation for past harm, and the latter would want to maximize restraints on network rules to prevent harm in the future."[33] While, in most instances, the use of a mediator cures issues of collusion between the plaintiffs' and defense counsel, the *MasterCard* court held that "even an intense, protected, adversarial mediation, involving multiple parties, including highly respected and capable mediators and associational plaintiffs, does not compensate for the absence of independent representation."[34] Thus, because "[u]nitary representation of separate classes that claim distinct, competing, and conflicting relief create[s] unacceptable incentives for counsel to trade benefits to one class for benefits to the other in order somehow to reach a settlement," the court reversed the trial court's judgment approving the settlement.[35]

Common Fund versus Claims Made Monetary Settlements

The most common ways to structure monetary settlements are:

1. Non-reversionary common fund, with automatic distribution;
2. Non-reversionary, claims made, common fund;
3. Reversionary claims made common fund; and
4. As-made (i.e., no fund but defendant pays claims made).

---

32. *In re* Payment Card Interchange Fee and Merchant Discount Antitrust Litig., 827 F.3d 223 (2d Cir. June 30, 2016), *appeal docketed*, No. 16-710 (U.S. Nov. 29, 2016) (hereinafter *MasterCard*).

33. *MasterCard*, 827 F.3d at 233.

34. *Id.* at 235 (internal quotation marks omitted).

35. *Id.* at 234, 240.

When the parties agree to a monetary settlement fund, the defendant agrees to deposit the settlement funds into an account. From there, a claims administrator will either pay all class members automatically or pay claims based on an agreed-upon formula that allocates the distribution of the money from the settlement account to individual claimants. Attorney fees for class counsel are typically paid out of the common fund account, subject to court approval.

There will inevitably be some unpaid funds in a class settlement. Thus, counsel must address the question of what do with unclaimed funds. As discussed in more detail later in the chapter, there are several solutions to this question.

Some settlements, commonly known as "claims as-made" settlements, do not involve a common fund and do not have a specific amount that is distributed into a settlement account. Rather, the parties will agree to a claims formula and instruct the claims administrator to distribute the funds on a claim-by-claim basis, sometimes up to a maximum amount. Rather than depositing the funds into an account, the defendant directly pays the claims or funds them in tranches. Because the defendant will retain the difference between the claimed amount and the agreed maximum amount, there is no need to negotiate a provision that deals with unclaimed funds. Moreover, attorney fees are often paid separately from the maximum available amount for claimants. This leaves more money available for recovery by class members.

Claims as-made settlements can be beneficial to certain individual claimants in some circumstances. Defendants that compensate claimants through a claims as-made settlement might agree to a more generous claims process and provide larger claims amounts per claimant because the defendant expects to receive far fewer claims with a claims as made process. A defendant may not want to attract unneeded attention or collateral litigation by challenging claims pay-outs, or enacting procedural hurdles.

Some will argue that a claims as-made settlement can more accurately approximate the overall value of the case to the class because the defendant only pays class members who assert that they have truly been injured. On the other hand, this assertion is only true if injured class members have adequate notice of the claims process and are not forced to jump through unnecessary hoops or produce copious documentation in order to make a claim.

For instance, recently, several class action lawsuits have been filed asserting deceptive food labeling practices. However, it's arguable that these lawsuits have been filed on behalf of a class of persons who never bothered to read the labels at all and, therefore, have no cognizable injury. A claims as-made settlement process in this type of litigation accounts for the problem of plaintiffs who do not feel as though they have been injured because, theoretically, they will not take the time to file a claim on the settlement.

Claims Processing

Courts have criticized and refused to approve class settlements that include a claims process that makes it difficult to make a claim or receive payments from the settlement. Courts suspect that a burdensome and complicated process is a red flag of collusion between class counsel and the defendant who may be trying to minimize the net settlement payout. This is particularly troublesome if the settlement is a claims as-made settlement or a monetary fund settlement with a reverter provision. In both of those situations, the defendant has an incentive to reduce the number and amount of claims that are made and paid.

In *Eubank v. Pella Corp.* the Seventh Circuit reversed the approval of a settlement for, among other reasons, the obstacles placed on a member of the class to receive any settlement payment.[36] The court noted that the claim form for class members was twelve pages long for a maximum payout of $750 and a thirteen-page claim form and a required arbitration process was required for the $6,000 claim form. The settlement did not provide for the shifting of legal fees in a successful arbitration, so it was unlikely claimants would have the assistance of counsel.[37] The court was not surprised that only 1,276 claims were filed in response to 225,000 notice that had been sent to class members.[38] The court rejected as erroneous the district court's finding that the expected settlement fund would be $90 million, when actual claims filed as of the date of the trial court's opinion totaled a little more than $1 million.[39]

---

36. 735 F.3d 718, 725 (7th Cir. 2014).

37. *Id.* at 726.

38. *Id.*

39. *Id. See also* Manual for Complex Litigation, Fourth, § 21.61 cautioning courts to look at settlements that "impos[e] such strict eligibility conditions or cumbersome claims procedures that many members will be unlikely to claim benefits, particularly if the settlement provides that the unclaimed portions of the fund will revert to the defendants."

Because of concerns like this, counsel should avoid constructing settlements that contain unnecessary claims redemptions processes.[40] But, a claims process is necessary when (1) class members cannot be identified and are unknown; or, (2) when class members must provide information to establish eligibility for an award or to establish the extent of damages because neither the defendant nor a third party has that information.

A class action defendant will be keenly interested in a typical claims rate in a class action settlement because most "as made" settlements have no cap on the number of claims, creating the potential of large exposure to the defendant. Plaintiffs will want to ensure that the claims rates are as high as possible. In 2012, pursuant to the Dodd-Frank Act, the Consumer Financial Protection Bureau (CFPB) conducted a study to analyze the effect of mandatory arbitration clauses in consumer financial contracts for products such as banking and credit card accounts.[41] In doing so, the CFPB examined 419 consumer class actions settlements between 2008 and 2012, and determined that the average claims rate was 21 percent, with a median of 8 percent. Although a 21 percent claims rate in a consumer class action would not be unexpected, the number could vary based on multiple factors, and the CFPB study only examined a limited cross section of class action settlements: consumer class actions within a five-year period. Claims rates could be much higher in a commercial class action, or in a class action that involves a sophisticated, or insular group of class members. Indeed, with the advent of social media, with its potential for the viral spread of information, there is a possibility that a class consisting of a group with strong social ties and a social media presence could result in higher claims rates. A relatively new development is the advent of claim-filing companies or aggregators that will sometimes seek out claimants and assist them in making their filings (this is especially true for classes of commercial entities but can exist in other classes). Additionally, the potential for a higher recovery will likely result in a higher claims rate. Another factor that will affect the claims rate is the actual form of the notice to the class. Of course, the longer the claim period, typically the higher the

---

40. RUBENSTEIN, *supra* note 24, § 12:17 ("[B]ecause distribution of class proceeds is difficult to accomplish if claiming is required, the best practice in most cases is to create a system for distributing the class's funds without the necessity of any claiming process, much less a cumbersome one.").

41. Alison Frankel, *CFPB Arbitration Study a Powerful Vindication of Consumer Class Actions*, 18 No. 19 CONSUMER FIN. SERVICES L. REP. at 3 (2015).

Claims Rate Factors

Factors that tend to drive up claims rates:

- Commercial class actions
- Higher recovery amounts per class member
- Small class
- Geographically concentrated class (such as workers in a single factory)
- Strongly cohesive class
- Third-party involvement (such as claim filers or labor unions)

Factors that tend to drive down claims rates:

- Consumer class actions
- Low recovery amounts
- Larger classes

ultimate claims rate (although a period that is too long can result in claimants forgetting and not filing). Typically claim filing is highest earlier in the claims period and at the very end of the claims period.

Scope of the Release

A critical term in any settlement is the scope of the claims released. But in class action settlements, a very broad release can be a red flag that catches the attention of the court. This can arise in two contexts—an overly broad class definition or an overly expansive release from liability for conduct outside of the claims asserted in the complaint. In negotiations, the defendant will want to expand the scope of the release both in terms of the number of individuals who release claims, the number of claims released, and the time frame with which claims are released. Courts tend to scrutinize the scope of the release with great care.

Typically, settling parties will specify that class members agree to release all claims pled in the complaint. Courts will sometimes allow the parties to agree that the settlement covers transactions, conduct, and occurrences broader than those alleged in the actual lawsuit.[42] However, to the extent that the release covers legal theories that were not raised in the complaint, defendants will seek to include a catchall clause that releases any and all claims arising out of the conduct, transaction, or occurrence underlying the lawsuit to the broadest extent allowable under the law.[43]

One particular risk to defendants of settling a class action is the possibility that a significant number of class members will opt out of an approved settlement. A disproportionate number of opt-outs reduces the preclusive value of the settlement to the defendant. Thus, defendants

---

42. *See In re* Initial Pub. Offering Sec. Litig., 226 F.R.D. 186, 190 (S.D.N.Y. 2005).
43. *See, e.g., In re* Celera Corp. Shareholder Litig., 59 A.3d 418, 432 (Del. 2012).

should consider negotiating a provision that allows the parties to terminate the agreement if a certain number (for instance, 5 percent of the potential settlement class members) of potential class members opt out of the class, known as a "blow up" provision. For plaintiffs, these provisions are fairly low risk unless there is reason to believe that opt-outs may be solicited by another set of counsel. Additionally, the parties can agree to a provision that neither side will encourage potential class members to opt out. Finally, counsel will need to consider whether the specific triggering numbers of the "blow up" provision should be included in the settlement agreement that will become a public document. It is a legitimate concern that if the trigger numbers are public, it will encourage other attorneys to organize an opt-out effort. To address this concern, the settlement agreement can contain the "blow up" provision, but the triggering numbers are included in a confidential side letter that is not part of the public filings.[44]

Unclaimed Funds

In every monetary class settlement, there will be some leftover or residual funds. This is because some class members cannot be located or they do not cash their checks. In other cases, interest will have accrued during the claims process or the administrative costs turn out to be lower than predicted. When the residual funds are large enough, the preferred approach is to make a second distribution pro rata to those class members who can be found. Before doing so, however, the parties or claims administrator will want to ensure that the second round of payments will be large enough so that the administrative costs are justified and the checks are sufficiently large that they are likely to be cashed. In other words, it may be unwise to spend $2 per class member to generate and mail a check for less than $1, which is unlikely to be cashed and will fail to fully diminish or even reduce the residual funds.

The amount of residual funds in most class actions (i.e., employment discrimination, wage and hour, securities, antitrust, ERISA) is generally quite low. The amount of unclaimed funds is sometimes significant in

---

44. *See, In re* Warfarin Sodium Antitrust Litig., 212 F.R.D. 231, 253, 2002–02 Trade Cas. (CCH) ¶ 73791 (D. Del. 2002), *aff'd*, 391 F.3d 516, 2004–02 Trade Cas. (CCH) ¶ 74632 (3d Cir. 2004) ("The notice did not need to include details such as . . . the confidential 'opt-out' threshold beyond which defendant reserved the right to withdraw from the settlement (irrelevant to members' opt-out decision)"), *aff'd*, 391 F.3d 516 (3d Cir. 2004).

consumer cases, however, where claims rates vary and may stay below 20 percent, leaving a large amount of the fund to be disposed of.

Reverter Clauses

When the settlement proceeds are paid into a fund, one way to address residual funds is to include a reverter clause in the settlement agreement, allowing the unclaimed money to return to the defendant. However, courts often see reverter clauses as red flags, and some federal courts will not approve a reversion of settlement fund proceeds to a defendant.[45] This is, in part, because it may create an incentive for the defendant to negotiate an unnecessarily complicated claims filing process or otherwise deter class members from filing claims (a particularly sensitive issue in employment class actions). Some argue that a reverter clause may also undermine the deterrent nature of the class action device.[46] Moreover, even if the lawsuit was filed in a jurisdiction that does not prohibit reverter clauses outright, the defendant may spend time and money effectuating the return of unclaimed class money following the expiration of the claims period.

A similar provision that deals with funds set aside for an attorney fee is a "kicker provision," which requires that unapproved attorney fee funds will return to the defendant. Like reverter clauses, courts are skeptical about these types of clauses because the result of a court disapproving some of the proposed attorney fee is a reduction in the amount of the common fund available for payment to the class. For instance, in two Seventh Circuit cases, the court overturned an approved class settlement, in part, because of settlement provisions that returned any unapproved attorney fees to the defendant rather than to the class.[47] This reasoning, however, should not apply to settlements in which the defendant pays the attorney fee separately from the payments to the class; for instance, a claims made settlement or a settlement in which the payment of attorney fees is on top of the common fund.

---

45. One appellate judge has opined that a reverter clause is the preferred method of dealing with residual funds. *See* Klier v. Elf Atochem North America, Inc., 658 F.3d 468, 481–82 (5th Cir. 2011) (Jones, J. Concurring).

46. For an excellent discussion of the pros and cons of reverter clauses, see RUBENSTEIN, *supra* note 24, § 12.29.

47. Eubank v. Pella Corp., 753 F.3d 718 (7th Cir. 2014); Pearson v. NBTY, Inc., No. 12-1245, 2014 WL 6466128 (7th Cir. Nov. 19, 2014).

Cy Pres

In a class action, cy pres refers to the distribution of settlement funds to a charitable organization rather than member of the class. The concept derives from trust law where the goal is to provide funds to an alternative recipient as close as possible to the original, intended recipient. Until recently, the use of cy pres relief was routinely approved by many courts, as a simple, efficient way to distribute settlement funds when it is impossible or very costly to identify or locate class members or when there are residual funds after one or more distributions. However, recent concerns about cy pres awards have caused them to become a red flag, attracting close judicial scrutiny. Courts look to see whether the class really cannot be directly compensated and examine whether the recipient of the award, (the mission of the charitable organization) is aligned with the interests of the class and the underlying purpose of the class action.

There are two circumstances in which settling parties typically use cy pres. The most common use of cy pres is when residual funds remain after one or more rounds of class member distribution have reduced the fund to the point where further distribution is unwarranted. In these situations, courts will approve cy pres when the charitable institutions closely match the underlying purpose of the litigation and have the same geographic reach as the class.

The second and more controversial use of cy pres occurs when the class members cannot be identified or the amount of their losses is too small to economically justify distribution. This type of cy pres is the subject of close scrutiny because the class members will receive no direct compensation but the class attorneys and the charitable organizations do, and the defendant receives a complete release of claims. It can be particularly questionable if the judge, counsel, or the parties are connected to or have control over the charitable organization. Yet there are circumstances when either the actual damages are infinitesimally small per class member, or the cost per-person of distributing checks is greater than the actual amount of money that the individual class member will receive. In these circumstances it is not economically viable to distribute money to the class, and cy pres may be a better way to deliver a benefit to class members, though only indirectly. While class members do not directly recover, the defendant will still be forced to disgorge some measure of the gains from the allegedly illegal conduct, which can be seen by some as consistent with the deterrent and punitive aspects of the class action device.

A good starting point is the American Law Institute's factors for utilizing cy pres, included in its Principles of Aggregate Litigation.[48]

Parties who wish to include a cy pres element to their settlement agreement should consider whether their settlement is appropriate for cy pres relief under the ALI factors. The ALI's *Principles*, released in 2010, primarily recommend that courts distribute settlement funds to class members through a pro rata distribution if at all possible. However, recognizing that often times this is not possible, the ALI recognizes three specific circumstances where cy pres is proper:

1) Where individual class members cannot be identified
2) Where individual distributions are so small that they are not economically feasible, and
3) Pro rata distributions of settlement funds would be so small so as to be economically infeasible

If cy pres is necessary, then the parties should "identify a recipient whose interests reasonably approximate those being pursued by the class."

PRINCIPLES OF AGGREGATE LITIGATION § 3:07 (2010)

This emphasis on aligning the recipient to the interests of the class is paramount: parties cannot agree to simply give residual funds to any random charity and expect the reviewing court to approve the settlement. Rather, there must be a nexus between the interests of the class and the recipient organization. First, and perhaps most obviously, the recipient of a cy pres distribution should be involved in work related to the underlying allegations in the lawsuit. For instance, in *Koby v. ARS National Services, Inc.*, a case involving debt collection phone calls, the Ninth Circuit reversed a magistrate's approval of a class action settlement, in part, because the cy pres provision authorized a $35,000 payment to a veterans' organization located in San Diego, California.[49] The court held that there was no indication that the class was made up of a large number of veterans, or that the charity worked to protect individuals from unfair debt collection practices. Likewise, in a 2011 case involving breach of electronic communications privacy against AOL, the parties agreed to make cy pres distributions to the Legal Aid Foundation of Los Angeles, the Boys and Girls Clubs of Santa Monica and

---

48. PRINCIPLES OF AGGREGATE LITIGATION § 3:07 (2010).
49. Koby v. ARS National Servs., Inc., 846 F.3d 1071, 1080 (9th Cir. Jan. 25, 2017).

Los Angeles, and the Federal Judicial Center Foundation.[50] The court rejected the cy pres provision, in part, because the charities had nothing to do with the underlying claims of Internet fraud. On the other hand, in *In re Google Referrer Header Privacy Litigation*, a case involving purported Internet privacy violations, the district court approved a cy pres distribution to six nonprofit organizations that had "a record of promoting privacy protection on the internet, reach and target interests of all demographics across the country . . . and [were] capable of using the funds to educate the class about online privacy risks."[51]

Similarly, because the ultimate goal of cy pres recovery should be to provide an indirect benefit to class members, it follows that the work of the recipient organization should have the same geographic reach as the class members. For instance, in both the *AOL* and *Koby* class action lawsuits just discussed, the court rejected the cy pres distributions because, although the classes were national in scope, the charity recipients were limited to the Los Angeles and San Diego areas, respectively.[52]

Thus, typically, when the parties include a cy pres provision in a settlement agreement, they should be prepared to demonstrate to the court:

1. That it is not feasible to distribute settlement funds directly to class members (the difficulty of identifying class members, high cost of distribution).
2. The rationale why the proposed distribution aligns with the interests of the class. This includes both aligning the geographic scope of the class and the cy pres recipient and the underlying objectives of the claims that were made in the case.

Notably, the Class Action Fairness Act (CAFA) expressly recognizes the possibility of cy pres. It allows the court, in its discretion, to approve the distribution of the value-equivalent of unclaimed coupons "to 1 or more charitable or governmental organizations, as agreed by the parties."[53] However, under CAFA, the final attorney fee cannot be based on the value of those unclaimed coupons, even if that value was converted to money and donated to a charity or government organization.

---

50. Nachshin v. AOL, LLC, 663 F.3d 1034, 1040 (9th Cir. 2011).
51. *In re* Google Referrer Header Privacy Litigation, 87 F. Supp. 3d 1122, 1132 (N.D. Ca. 2015), *aff'd*, 869 F.3d 737 (9th Cir. 2017).
52. *Koby*, 846 F.3d at 1080; *Nachshin*, 663 F.3d at 1040.
53. 28 U.S.C. § 1712(e).

Escheat

Some settlements provide that unclaimed money will escheat to the state. While this may be appropriate in some types of cases, it does not benefit class members and is effectively a windfall to the government. Practitioners should also be specific in all settlement documents to avoid the potential of a state later claiming that undistributed funds should escheat to the state even without a court order. Practitioners should research state unclaimed property laws that may be applicable to class settlement residuals in their case.

Incentive Awards for Named Plaintiffs

Most consumer class actions, and a significant number of commercial and other non-consumer class actions, are filed on behalf of class members whose claims are worth less than the cost of litigation. Indeed, one purpose of the class action device is the vindication of small value claims. Therefore, because the named plaintiffs must have claims that are typical of other claimants, the claim of the named plaintiffs will likely also be small and the named plaintiffs should be entitled to no more damages than any other class plaintiff. However, it has become typical in many class settlements to provide for the payment of "incentive awards" to the named plaintiffs. Incentive awards can be red flags of a problematic settlement when there is a large disparity between what is received by the named plaintiff and what other members of the class receive.[54]

Named plaintiffs act as fiduciaries for the class and are expected to make certain sacrifices in order to vindicate the rights of their fellow class members. Named plaintiffs are the only class members who will be required to place their name prominently in the public record. Named plaintiffs in employment litigation risk retaliation, including job loss and future bad references. Moreover, named plaintiffs will often be required to provide answers to discovery, produce documents, submit

---

54. In Ratcliffe v. Experian Info. Solutions, Inc., 715 F.3d 1157, 1164 (9th Cir. 2013) the named plaintiffs would receive "conditional incentive awards" worth $5,000 (compared to between $26 and $750 for class members), but only if they explicitly supported the settlement. The court noted "[i]nstead of being solely concerned about the adequacy of the settlement for the absent class members, the class representatives now had a $5,000 incentive to support the settlement regardless of its fairness and a promise of no reward if they opposed the settlement. The conditional incentive awards removed a critical check on the fairness of the class-action settlement, which rests on the unbiased judgment of class representatives similarly situated to absent class members." Id.

to depositions, and attend court hearings. Thus, serving as a named plaintiff can result in significant risks, and expenditure of time and effort, and it is appropriate to compensate them for that effort when the effort has contributed to a recovery for the class.

Typical class action recoveries are not a sufficient incentive for most individuals to serve as a named plaintiff. Consequently, class action settlements often include an enhanced award for named plaintiffs, which must be independently approved by the court.[55] Incentive awards can range between $1,000 and $20,000 per named plaintiff, but also can be significantly higher.[56] Good practice will include contemporaneously documenting and then demonstrating in the record, that the named plaintiffs expended a considerable amount of time participating in the litigation.

Addressing incentive awards at the *proper time* is extremely important, and can go a long way toward avoiding the appearance of impropriety, and the efficacy of later objections. Specifically, the safest and best course of action is to put off any discussion of incentive awards until after the class relief has been negotiated.[57]

> Class representatives should not agree to a proposed incentive when they initially hire class counsel, and absolutely should avoid a contractual term whereby they condition their support for a settlement agreement upon a specific incentive award.

Notice

Settlement notice is fundamental to informing class members of the settlement terms and their options: participating, objecting or opting out. A proposed notice program that is inadequate is a red flag that attracts extra scrutiny to the settlement. Objectors often target settlement notice, in large part, because purported notice deficiencies have been fertile ground for courts to reject proposed settlements. Further, aggrieved parties can collaterally attack a settlement, even after the settlement has been approved, and proceeds have been paid out.[58] Obviously, the idea

---

55. *See, e.g.,* Espenscheid v. DirectSat USA, LLC, 688 F.3d 872, 875 (7th Cir. 2012).
56. *See* 2 McLAUGHLIN ON CLASS ACTIONS § 6:28 (13th ed. 2016) ("there is near-universal recognition that it is appropriate for the court to approve an incentive award payable from the class recovery").
57. *See* Berry v. Schulman, 807 F.3d 600, 614 (4th Cir. 2015).
58. *See, e.g.,* Juris v. Inamed Corp., 685 F.3d 1294, 1312–13 (11th Cir. 2012).

that a good class action settlement can be challenged and overturned after approval is nightmarish for the parties, unnamed class members, and counsel. Consequently, parties to class action litigation must take extreme care to make sure that notice is adequate.

> Notice is often the first and central part of any attack by objectors.

Rule 23(e) requires that the parties send notice "in a reasonable manner to all class members who would be bound by the proposal."[59] This notice provision has several purposes.

> The principal purpose of this provision is "to ensure that absentee class members, for whom settlement will have a preclusive effect, have an opportunity to review the materials relevant to the proposed settlement and to be heard or otherwise take steps to protect their rights before the court approves or rejects the settlement."[60]

In the event that a litigation class has already been certified, the notice might be sent in order to allow individuals who had previously opted out to rejoin the class for settlement purposes.

Best Practice

Often, members of the putative class will be difficult to locate, and there may be no good class list with names and addresses. While this complicates the notice process, there are ways to ensure that the notice plan passes constitutional muster. First, practitioners should consider supplementing mailed forms with other types of notice, such as publication in a magazine or newspaper. Practitioners may also consider purchasing internet advertisements. Second, at the settlement approval phase, parties should consider offering an expert (usually someone associated with the settlement administrator) to testify regarding the efficacy of the supplemental notice.

Although there are no "rigid rules to determine whether a settlement notice to the class satisfies constitutional or Rule 23(e) requirements, the settlement notice must 'fairly apprise the prospective members of the class of the proposed settlement and of the options that are open to them in connection with the proceedings.'"[61] The Manual for Complex

---

59. FED. R. CIV. P. 23(e)(1).
60. *In re* Nat'l Football League Players Concussion Injury Litig., 775 F.3d 570, 583 (3d Cir. 2014) (citing 2 MCLAUGHLIN ON CLASS ACTIONS § 6:17 (10th ed. 2013)).
61. Wal-Mart Stores, Inc. v. Visa U.S.A., Inc., 396 F.3d 96, 114 (2d Cir. 2005) (quoting Weinberger v. Kendrick, 698 F.2d 61, 70 (2d Cir. 1982)).

Litigation provides a more fulsome list of what the notice should accomplish:

- define the class and any subclasses;
- describe clearly the options open to the class members and the deadlines for taking action;
- describe the essential terms of the proposed settlement;
- disclose any special benefits provided to the class representatives;
- provide information regarding attorney fees;
- indicate the time and place of the hearing to consider approval of the settlement;
- describe the method for objecting to (or opting out of) the settlement;
- explain the procedures for allocating and distributing the settlement funds, and, if the settlement provides different kinds of relief for different categories of class members, clearly set forth those variations;
- explain the basis for valuation of nonmonetary benefits if the settlement includes them;
- provide information that will enable class members to calculate or at least estimate their individual recoveries, including the size of the class or any subclasses; and
- prominently display the address and phone number of class counsel and how to make inquiries.[62]

In addition to the preceding list, the Federal Judicial Center has released exemplar notices that cover some types of cases.[63] Like all Rule 23 notices, the settlement notice should be written in "plain, easily understood language."[64] Some litigants find these exemplar notices to be longer, and more complicated than necessary to provide sufficient notice. Thus, some parties elect to draft their own Rule 23 notice forms.

Generally, notice need not disclose every detail of the pending litigation, but should inform class members of the "big picture," describe the terms of the settlement, direct them to court filings for more detailed

---

62. *Manual for Complex Litigation*, § 21.312, (4th ed.) (some parentheticals omitted).
63. Federal Judicial Center, The Federal Judicial Center's "Illustrative" Forms of Class Action Notices, www.fjc.gov (follow "Class Action Notices Page" hyperlink).
64. Fed. R. Civ. P. 23(c)(2)(B).

Trap for the Unwary

When mailing notice forms, practitioners must be mindful of class members' privacy concerns. For instance, there has been recent litigation regarding class action notice mailed to HIV patients. *See* Alison Frankel, *KCC sues Aetna, blames Gibson Dunn in HIV settlement notice fiasco*, Reuters (Feb. 7, 2018), https://www.reuters.com/article/legal-us-otc-aetna/kcc-sues-aetna-blames-gibson-dunn-in-hiv-settlement-notice-fiasco-idUSKBN1FR2WB. Specifically, the notice forms "included transparent windows displaying not just the names, addresses and claim numbers" of class members, "but also the first sentence of the settlement notice, which included the words, 'when filling prescriptions for HIV medications.'" *Id.* This illustrates the fact that any time practitioners are handling class action litigation involving health care or other sensitive topics, great care should be taken to avoid revealing sensitive information.

---

information, and invite class members to attend the fairness hearing.[65] Moreover, at least one court has found that due process does not require that an opt-out form be included in the notice, so long as the notice describes simple steps for opting out.[66] Additionally, if the settlement requires class members to make a claim, then the notice should either include a claim form, or provide easy access to a claim form—such as through a website. More importantly, the notice should recite that the class member's failure to return the proof of claim form will not only result in a waiver of their right to the class proceeds, but will also bind them to the settlement.

Best Practice

The parties may use a firm that specializes in developing notice plans in class action litigation, particularly where addresses are not readily available. These firms have developed an expertise in ensuring that the notice reaches the highest number of class members, and therefore, conforms with the requirements of Rule 23. Typically, these firms handle all aspects of the notice process, including:

- Assisting in the development of a notice plan that comports with legal notice requirements
- Providing detailed analytics and data regarding response rates
- Assisting in the design of notice forms so that they are easy for class members to understand

---

65. *See* 2 McGLAUGHLIN ON CLASS ACTIONS § 6:17 (13th ed. 2016).

66. *See, e.g.*, Patrowicz v. Transamerica HomeFirst, Inc., 359 F. Supp. 2d 140, 152 (D. Conn. 2005).

- Assisting in the design of opt-out and opt-in forms
- Assisting in the design of claims forms
- Providing affidavits describing the effectiveness of the notice plan
- Assisting in the design and implementing websites (which typically include notice and claim forms)
- Publishing notice in newspapers and other publications
- Locating class members for the purpose of mailing notice
- Mailing relevant notice forms, processing undelivered notices and remailing as appropriate

Perhaps the most efficient, inexpensive, and effective way to protect a proposed settlement from objection over notice issues is to set up a publicly accessible website that contains all of the relevant information regarding the litigation. Indeed, some judges consider this form of notice to be mandatory. The parties can provide a link to this website through either an e-mail to the class, physically mailed notice, or both. The key is to be overly inclusive so as to avoid any implication that the parties' attorneys are trying to hide any piece of information.

A settlement website is one of the best methods for ensuring that notice is adequate. The parties should be *overly inclusive* about what information is accessible. At the very least, the following documents should be included:

- The long form notice
- The short form notice
- Key filings in the underlying litigation
- An explanation about the scope of the release
- The notice plan
- Any expert testimony
- Opt-out forms, if any
- Claims forms, if any
- An explanation, in simple, accessible language, of the proposed settlement
- Contact information for class counsel
- A Frequently Asked Questions page explaining the settlement, and the process for recovery, in layman's terms.

Scheduled for likely approval in late 2018, a proposed amendment to Rule 23 will explicitly allow notice through e-mail.[67] Specifically, the

---

67. *See* COMMITTEE ON RULES OF PRACTICE AND PROCEDURE OF THE JUDICIAL CONFERENCE OF THE UNITED STATES: PROPOSED AMENDMENTS TO THE FEDERAL RULES OF APPELLATE, BANKRUPTCY, CIVIL, AND CRIMINAL PROCEDURE, at 211–12 (2016).

proposed rule states that notice can be sent "by United States mail, electronic means, or other appropriate means."[68] The Committee on Civil Rules of Practice and Procedure recognized that notice should be analyzed for each case, considering the demographics of each class and the expense. Electronic notice (properly done) can in many instances be far more effective than traditional mail. Some consumers simply throw their notice forms away with other junk mail. Moreover, e-mail notification is also highly beneficial to classes where the aggregate recovery by the class is small and can be repeated with virtually no additional costs. The cost of a traditional mailed notice is extremely high, and can constitute a large percentage of the overall fund in smaller value class actions. E-mail notification can exponentially increase the monetary recovery by individual class members.

Of course, this proposed rule does not require e-mail notice, and the committee comments recognize that some classes will have limited or no access to the Internet.[69] Thus, as with any other kind of notice, the parties should consider the demographics of the putative class, and determine whether they have good, working e-mail addresses for class members. For instance, e-mail notification is less likely to be effective for a class consisting of elderly class members, indigent persons, or other individuals who might have limited access to the Internet.

Determining Attorney Fees

The plaintiffs' attorney fees are a major red flag for courts reviewing the fairness of a class action settlement. Rule 23(h) regulates the procedure for approval of attorney fees in the class action context,[70] and requires that the requesting party file a motion under Rule 54(d)(2). Class counsel must provide "notice to class members in a reasonable manner."[71] When fees will be awarded as part of a settlement, many circuits require that the motion for attorney fees be filed before the deadline for objections, and have held that filing the motion after the deadline for objections is a violation of Rule 23(h).[72] However, even

---

68. *Id.*

69. *Id.* at 219.

70. The rule applies to both class actions and putative settlement classes. Fed. R. Civ. P. 23(h) advisory comm. n.

71. Fed. R. Civ. P. 23(h)(1).

72. *See, e.g., In re* Nat'l Football League Players Concussion Injury Litig., 821 F.3d 410, 446 (3d Cir. 2016); *In re* Mercury Interactive Corp. Securities Litig., 618 F.3d 988, 993 (9th Cir. 2010).

when this practice is not required, plaintiffs may opt to file a motion for attorney fees prior to the deadline for objections to avoid the risk of an objector raising this issue on appeal. Although the rule does not require formal hearings, the court is obligated to make findings of law and fact regarding attorney fees under Rule 52(a).[73]

It is useful to imagine the negotiation of class action attorney fees as a mini-version of the larger settlement negotiation because, just like with the class action settlement, counsel must take care that both the substance of any attorney fee agreement, and the process by which the parties might agree to an attorney fee, reflect an arm's length negotiation. Indeed, courts have an "independent obligation to ensure that the award, like the settlement itself, is reasonable, even if the parties have already agreed to an amount."[74] This is because, as claimants to a settlement fund, class counsel can find itself "adverse to the interest of the class in obtaining recovery."[75] Rule 23 requires courts to make a reasonableness determination regardless of whether or not the fees are taken from a settlement fund.[76] At the point in which attorney fees are being determined, "there is often no one to argue for the interests of the class . . . ."[77] Adding to this thicket of potential issues is the possibility of negative media attention garnered by purportedly high attorney fees in class action settlements.

There are multiple proven ways for counsel to craft a settlement agreement that is protected against a challenge on the grounds of improper attorney fees. In terms of process, the parties should avoid discussing the settlement of attorney fees at the outset of negotiations. Courts often view with suspicion proposed attorney fees that were reached early in the process.

In terms of *substance*, there are two common ways to calculate attorney fees: the lodestar method and the percentage of the fund method.

The Lodestar Method

One approach to determining a reasonable fee is the lodestar method, in which the fee is determined by multiplying a reasonable hourly rate for similar attorneys in the relevant geographical area by the number of

---

73. Fed. R. Civ. P. 23(h)(3).

74. *In re* Bluetooth Headset Products Liab. Litig., 654 F.3d 935, 941 (9th Cir. 2011).

75. Rawlings v. Prudential-Bache Properties, Inc., 9 F.3d 513, 516 (6th Cir. 1993).

76. *See, e.g.,* Gascho v. Global Fitness Holdings, LLC, No 2:11-cv-436, 2014 WL 1350509, at *32–33 (S.D. Ohio 2014).

77. *Id.*

hours reasonably expended by class counsel.[78] This method "produces an award that roughly approximates the fee that a prevailing attorney would have received if he or she had been representing a paying client who was billed by the hour in a comparable case."[79] Once the court determines this "lodestar" amount, it can then adjust the figure applying a multiplier that represents factors such as the ultimate benefit to the class, the risk assumed by class counsel in taking the case, and the performance of the attorneys.[80] However, counsel must provide adequate substantiation for a multiplier request.[81]

There is some authority that the lodestar method of computing attorney fees is inappropriate for common fund cases, and should only be used for class actions when fee shifting is authorized by statute, such as civil rights claims brought under 42 U.S.C. § 1983.[82] However, most circuits give federal district courts "flexibility to choose between the percentage and lodestar methods in common fund cases . . . ."[83]

The parties must decide during attorney fees negotiations whether the fees will be paid out of the class settlement fund, or whether the defendant will pay the fees *in addition* to the settlement fund. An attorney fee payment that does not deplete the settlement fund carries with it less risk that the court will disapprove the fee award. However, a defendant must weigh this benefit against the risk of greater exposure, especially in a claims as-made settlement, where a high claim rate could result in higher than predicted exposure.

---

78. *See* Lindy Bros. Builders, Inc. of Philadelphia v. American Radiator & Standard Sanitary Co., 487 F.2d 161, 167–68 (3d Cir. 1973); *see also* SUFI Network Servs. v. U.S., 785 F.3d 585 (Fed. Cir. 2015); Couser v. Comenity Bank, 125 F. Supp. 3d 1034 (S.C. Cal. 2015); Hernandez v. Immortal Rise, Inc., 306 F.R.D. 91 (E.D.N.Y.2015); Dikeman v. Progressive Exp. Ins. Co., 312 Fed. App'x 168 (11th Cir. 2008).

79. Perdue v. Kenny A. *ex rel.* Winn, 559 U.S. 542, 551 (2010).

80. *See, e.g., In re* Sterling Foster & Co., Inc. Securities Litig., 238 F. Supp. 2d 480, 487 (E.D.N.Y. 2002).

81. *See, e.g.,* Dungee v. Davison Design & Dev., No. 16-1486, 2017 WL 65549 (3d Cir. Jan. 6, 2017) (vacating a class action attorneys fee of $1.1 million because counsel failed to justify the application of a 4.35 multiplier enhancing the lodestar calculation).

82. *See, e.g.,* Blum v. Stetson, 465 U.S. 886, 900 n.16 (1984) ("Unlike the calculation of attorney's fees under the 'common fund doctrine,' where a reasonable fee is based on a percentage of the fund bestowed on the class, a reasonable fee under § 1988 reflects the amount of attorney time reasonably expended on the litigation."); Staton v. Boeing Co., 327 F.3d 938, 965 (9th Cir. 2003); Williams v. Rohm and Haas Pension Plan, No. 4:04-CV-0078-SEB-WGH, 2010 WL 1644571, at *1 (S.D. Ind. 2010).

83. Union Asset Management Holding A.G. v. Dell, Inc., 669 F.3d 632, 644 (5th Cir. 2012).

The Percentage of the Fund Method

"[U]nder the percentage of the fund method, the court simply determines a percentage of the settlement to award the class counsel."[84] Similar to the lodestar method, the parties can determine whether the attorney fee amount will come out of the common fund itself, or whether it will be paid on top of the common fund. In determining a proper percentage, courts analyze a multiplicity of factors including

- the time and labor expended by counsel,
- the quality of representation,
- the risk of the litigation,
- the complexity of the litigation,
- the size of the litigation,
- the relationship of the requested fee to the settlement,
- the amount of attorney fees in similar litigation,
- the market rate for legal fees, and
- public policy concerns.[85]

Although the most important factor weighed by the courts is the benefit of the settlement to the class,[86] courts are mindful of the potential of a windfall for counsel who manage to negotiate a particularly large settlement amount for their class. Thus, courts have recognized that larger settlements often necessitate a smaller percentage attorney fee recovery.[87]

In many jurisdictions, courts considering a percentage of the fund award will cross-check the final award against the lodestar.[88] Courts engage in a cross-check analysis in order to "avoid windfall fees, i.e. to 'ensure that the percentage approach does not lead to a fee that

---

84. Lonardo v. Travelers Indem. Co., 706 F. Supp. 2d 766, 789 (N.D. Ohio) (citing *In re* Sulzer Hip Prosthesis and Knee Prosthesis Liab. Litig., 268 F. Supp. 2d 907, 922 (N.D. Ohio 2003)).

85. *See* Wal-Mart Stores, Inc. v. Visa, USA, Inc., 396 F.3d 96, 121 (2d Cir. 2005); *In re* Synthroid Marketing Litig., 264 F.3d 712, 718 (7th Cir. 2001); Gunter v. Ridgewood Energy Corp., 223 F.3d 190, 195 (3d Cir. 2000); *In re* Union Carbide Corp. Consumer Products Business Securities Litig., 724 F. Supp. 160, 163 (S.D.N.Y. 1989).

86. *See, e.g.*, Redman v. RadioShak Corp., 768 F.3d 622, 633 (7th Cir. 2014).

87. *See, e.g.*, Goldberger v. Integrated Resources, Inc., 209 F.3d 43, 52 (2d Cir. 2000); *In re* Synthroid Marketing Litig., 110 F. Supp. 2d 676, 684–85, (N.D. Ill. 2000); Erie County Retirees Ass'n v. Cnty. of Erie, Pennsylvania, 192 F. Supp. 2d 369, 381 (W.D. Pa. 2002).

88. RUBENSTEIN, *supra* note 24, § 15:89.

represents an extraordinary lodestar multiple.'"[89] Thus, even if plain-tiffs' counsel is expecting to obtain an award from the fund, it is criti-cal that they carefully track their time over the course of the litigation. Additionally, prior to the fairness hearing, the parties should perform their own lodestar cross-check and submit it to the court, rather than having the court perform the analysis on its own.

One potential issue regarding the calculation of attorney fees involves how courts measure the overall benefit to the class for pur-pose of determining a percentage of the common fund. In *Redman v. RadioShak Corp.*, the Seventh Circuit questioned the overall value to the class of a class action settlement, and severely reduced the attorney fee award.[90] Following the fairness hearing, the reviewing district court valued the *RadioShak* settlement at $4.1 million, consisting of $830,000 for class member claims, $1 million in attorney fees, and $2.2 million in costs. Thus, under the district court's math, the attorney fees consisted of about 24 percent of the common fund, which is within the normal 25 percent range of class action attorney fees.

Judge Richard Posner, however, fundamentally disagreed with this calculation. Rather, Judge Posner posited that the amount of money that courts should evaluate in calculating an attorney fee ratio is the amount that directly goes to the benefit of class members, and admin-istrative costs, including the enormous cost of notice, should not be included in this amount. Thus, the court held that the *actual* ratio of attorney fees to overall benefit was approximately 55 percent, since the value of the claims was only $830,000. Moreover, Judge Posner held that the $830,000 number was itself suspect because the benefit to the class came in the form of $10 coupons. The court, therefore, reversed the trial court's settlement approval, with a suggestion that the parties reduce "the relative shares of the settlement received by class counsel" without increasing the overall value of the settlement.[91]

Judge Posner further admonished the parties, insisting that "the reasonableness of a fee cannot be assessed in isolation from what it buys . . . [n]o one would think a $1 million attorney fee appropriate compensation for obtaining $10,000 for the clients . . . ." Put differently, under Judge Posner's formulation, class counsel is compensated solely

89. *In re* Enron Corp. Securities, Derivative & ERISA Litig., 586 F. Supp. 2d 732, 751–52 (S.D. Tex. 2008) (quoting *In re* Cendant Corp. Litig., 264 F.3d 201, 285 (3d Cir. 2001)).

90. *Redman*, 768 F.3d at 622.

91. *Id.* at 632.

for its role in obtaining a direct, monetary benefit to class members, and not at all for their role in discouraging future misconduct by both the defendant, and other entities tempted to act similarly.

Very few courts outside of the Seventh Circuit have followed Judge Posner's logic, and the vast majority of courts who use a percentage of the fund method to determine attorney fees continue to use the entire amount of the settlement.[92] For instance, in a recent case out of the Eighth Circuit, the court approved a $2.8 million attorney fee award that was based on a "percentage of the benefit" method of calculation.[93] The court calculated the "benefit," in part, by including $750,000 in fund administration costs. In doing so, the court recognized that the Seventh Circuit, in *RadioShak*, cast doubt on the practice of characterizing fund administration, and similar costs, as "benefits to the class."[94] However, the court also noted that the Ninth Circuit takes a different approach, allowing the district court to include the cost of administration where those costs are justifiable.[95] Ultimately, the Eighth Circuit sided with the approach taken by the Ninth Circuit, holding that it was "in keeping with the deference our court affords district courts in awarding attorney fees."[96]

The 25 Percent Benchmark

Regardless of the method used by the court to determine the reasonableness of attorney fees, by far the most important benchmark evidencing reasonableness is whether the amount and/or percentage of the proposed attorney fee is consistent with other cases in the relevant jurisdiction. Although the numbers will vary on a case by case basis, many courts will consider a benchmark amount of around 25 percent of the common fund, or benefit to the class, to be reasonable.[97] However,

---

92. *See, e.g.,* McDonough v. Toys R. Us., Inc., 80 F. Supp. 3d 626, 654 n.27 (E.D. Pa. 2015); Lee v. Enterprise Leasing Co.-West, No. 3:10-CV-00326, 2015 WL 2345540, at *10 (D. Nev. May 15, 2015).

93. *In re* Lifetime Fitness Inc. Telephone Consumer Protection Act (TCPA) Litig., 847 F.3d 619 (8th Cir. Feb. 2, 2017).

94. *Id.* at 623.

95. *Id.* (citing Staton v. Boeing Co., 327 F.3d 938, 975 (9th Cir. 2003)).

96. *Id.*

97. *See, e.g., In re* Black Farmers Discrimination Litig., 953 F. Supp. 2d 82, 98 (D.D.C. 2013) ("[A]s a general matter, a majority of common fund class action fee awards fall between twenty and thirty percent.") (internal quotation marks omitted); Camden I Condominium Ass'n, Inc. v. Dunkle, 946 F.2d 786, 744 (11th Cir. 1991) ("[t]he majority of common fund fee awards fall between 20% and 30% of the fund."); *see also* Russ M. Herman, Stephen J. Herman, *Percentage-of-Benefit Fee Awards in Common Fund Cases*, 74 TUL. L. REV. 2033, 2044–45 (2000).

when a proposed attorney fee award exceeds the 20 to 30 percent benchmarks, some circuits require trial courts to engage in an even more enacting level of scrutiny. For instance, in the Eleventh Circuit, fee award requests exceeding 25 percent of the common fund must be analyzed under an 11-factor test.[98]

> **Best Practice**
>
> Typically, the plaintiff's counsel should aim for their attorney's fee request to be around 25 percent of the common fund, or the benefit to the class. Any more can invite additional judicial scrutiny, and can pose a risk to the settlement.

On the other hand, as noted earlier, cases that result in an especially large recovery, a "mega-fund" case, often result in an attorney fee representing a percentage of the common fund lower than 25 percent. Indeed, one study found that in cases awarding classes $500 million to $1 billion between 2006 and 2007, "the mean and median awards were both 12.9% of the fund."[99] The lower percentage avoids a windfall for class counsel, and reflects that a large settlement may be the result of factors not attributable to class counsel's work.

Clear Sailing Provisions

A clear sailing provision is a settlement clause in which the defendant agrees not to contest a proposed attorney fee up to a certain amount. Because attorney fees are ultimately subject to a determination by the court, they carry some risk for both parties. From the defendant's perspective, this type of provision can be a valuable settlement tool acting as an implicit ceiling on the amount of attorney fees that can be awarded. And for the plaintiffs' counsel, clear sailing provision means that their litigation adversary is not going to be fighting about this issue. However, some courts see clear sailing provisions as a red flag of collusion because they deprive the court of the adversary process on this

---

98. *See* Faught v. American Home Shield Corp., 668 F.3d 1233, 1243 (11th Cir. 2011) (applying the "*Johnson* factors test," which requires courts to examine (1) the time and labor required; (2) the difficulty of the issues; (3) the skill required; (4) the preclusion of other employment by the attorney because he accepted the case; (5) the customary fee in the community; (6) whether the fee is fixed or contingent; (7) time limitations imposed by the client or circumstances; (8) the amount involved and the results obtained; (9) the experience, reputation, and ability of the attorneys; (10) the undesirability of the case; (11) the nature and length of the professional relationship with the client; and (12) awards in similar cases).

99. Brian T. Fitzpatrick, *An Empirical Study of Class Action Settlements and their Fee Awards*, 7 J. EMPIRICAL LEGAL STUD. 811, 839 (2010).

issue. [100] Nonetheless, clear sailing provisions are important tools to get some settlements done. And courts are willing to approve settlements with this feature when the agreement was reached at arms-length, does not reduce the common fund,[101] and counsel can factually support the reasonableness of the proposed fee.

Injunctive Relief, Monitoring, and Compliance

Some class actions are brought, in whole or in part, to challenge an allegedly illegal corporate or governmental policy or practice and seek prospective injunctive relief to stop its continued use. Far more than a monetary judgment, the prospect of a court order regulating company operations can seem particularly intrusive and disruptive. A negotiated settlement may offer a defendant the opportunity to modify its practice in a manner, and on a timetable, that better accommodates its ongoing business. At the same time, plaintiffs' counsel may decide that the defendant will be more likely to comply with the policy changes if the terms are negotiated rather than imposed by a court. Non-monetary settlement relief may take many forms depending on the type of case, for example, corrective public statements in a false advertising case, goals and timetables in a hiring discrimination case, management training and improved recordkeeping in an off-the-clock wage and hour dispute, or structural corporate reforms or additional disclosures in corporate litigation. However, a settlement involving largely injunctive relief can also be a red flag indicating a problematic class settlement when it involves the class giving the defendant a release in exchange for meaningless changes in the defendant's conduct, that cost it very little, and does little for the class.[102] Accordingly, when seeking judicial

---

100. *See, e.g.*, Eubank v. Pella Corp., 753 F.3d 718 (7th Cir. 2014).

101. *See* Blessing v. Sirius XM Radio, Inc., 507 Fed App'x 1, 6 (2d Cir. 2012) (presence of a clear sailing provision was not grounds to vacate a fee award because the "fee was negotiated only after settlement terms had been decided and did not . . . reduce what the class ultimately received."); *see also In re* Bluetooth Headset Products Liability Litig., 654 F.3d 935, 947 (9th Cir. 2011); Waters v. Intern. Precious Metals Corp., 190 F.3d 1291, 1293 n.4 (11th Cir. 1999).

102. *See In re* Subway Footlong Sandwich Mktg. and Sales Practices Litig., 869 F.3d 551 (7th Cir. 2017) (A settlement that results only in a benefit for class counsel and no meaningful relief for the class "is no better than a racket." *Id.* at 556. The court found that it was cynical to suggest the injunction, "a set of procedures designed to achieve better bread length uniformity," provided value. *Id.* at 556-57.); Pearson v. NBTY, 772 F.3d 778, 787 (7th Cir. 2014) ("A larger objection to the injunction is that it's superfluous—or even adverse to consumers. Given the emphasis that class counsel place on the

approval of a settlement that involves injunctive relief, counsel should be prepared to demonstrate the real value of that relief to the members of the class. This is particularly important if plaintiffs' counsel is going to seek an award of attorney fees based on the claimed value of the injunctive relief that the litigation produced.[103] When an injunction is part of the settlement relief, class counsel may need some means of ensuring that, once the settlement is approved, the defendant fulfills its obligations as agreed. One method can be periodic reports prepared by the defendant and filed with counsel and/or the court. In other cases, a third-party monitor is appointed to inspect, review data, or evaluate complaints. The settlement will need to address the selection, duties, and compensation of the monitor.

A key term for negotiation is how the parties address a dispute that arises concerning compliance. Plaintiffs do not want to have to file a new lawsuit for breach of the settlement. The agreement can authorize the plaintiffs to file a motion for contempt with the court or a special master, just as would occur in a litigated proceeding, or proscribe other alternative dispute resolution mechanisms. If the court will be the final arbiter of compliance, then the court must agree to retain jurisdiction for that limited purpose and the judgment must so state. The agreement should also address whether attorney fees are available for the compliance motion and on what basis (e.g., lodestar with cap, flat fee, prevailing party).

THE SETTLEMENT APPROVAL PROCESS

The most distinctive aspect of class action settlements is the role of the court, which, unlike in non-class action litigation, takes an active role

---

fraudulent character of [defendant's] claims, [defendant] might have an incentive without an injunction to change them. The injunction actually gives it protection by allowing it, with judicial imprimatur (because it's part of a settlement approved by the district court), to preserve the substance of the claims by making—as were about to see—purely cosmetic changes in wording which [defendant] in effect is seeking judicial approval of. For the injunction seems substantively empty.").

103. Merger and acquisition litigation in Delaware often concluded with settlements in which the corporation agreed to supplemental disclosures that were not material or helpful to shareholders in exchange for a release of claims and the payment of attorney fees. The Delaware Chancery Court brought this litigation to an end by rejecting disclosure only settlements because they do not provide the plaintiff shareholders any meaningful consideration to warrant a release of claims. *In re* Trulia, Inc, Stockholder Litig., 129 A.3d 884, 887 (Del. Ch. 2016).

as a fiduciary for the class. The role of the court as a fiduciary is necessitated by the peculiar procedural posture of the parties during class action settlement: both class counsel and defense counsel are working hand-in-hand to highlight the benefits of the settlement while downplaying the agreement's weaknesses.[104] Accordingly, Rule 23(e) requires the court to make a substantive determination that the proposed settlement will adequately compensate absent class members.

Procedurally, courts will examine the merits of a proposed settlement in two phases: preliminary approval and final approval.

Preliminary Approval—New Attention

The first step toward final settlement of a class action is a motion for preliminary approval, which has become a critical phase of a putative settlement. For litigants, preliminary approval by the court signals that the proposed settlement falls within the range of acceptability, and gives the parties permission to send the requisite notice to class members regarding the settlement. Although the purpose of preliminary approval is for the court to determine whether notice should be sent to class members regarding the settlement, courts tend to take this step very seriously, and will not normally "rubber stamp" a proposed settlement. This is a significant change from past practice, and is different from the approach of many state courts. Rather, courts are increasingly using preliminary approval to ensure that the settlement itself is substantively acceptable. This is because the preliminary approval stage is likely the only opportunity that a reviewing court will have to efficiently provide input into the substance of the settlement. During this process, the reviewing court does not have the power to rewrite settlement terms itself but it can suggest changes, condition preliminary approval upon the inclusion of some clause or modification of the settlement, signal to the parties that final approval will be more likely if certain items are included, or deny preliminary approval without prejudice. Such suggestions or signals typically cause the parties to make changes to the proposed settlement and refile for preliminary approval. It is more difficult for a court to affect the terms of a settlement in this way once it has given the settlement preliminary approval, because the parties will have provided notice to the class of the settlement terms and perhaps initiated a claims process, often at significant expense. So

---

104. *See* MANUAL FOR COMPLEX LITIGATION § 21.61, at 309.

the preliminary approval stage is the best chance for the court to play a role in crafting the settlement.[105]

> Many courts see preliminary approval as one, if not the only, opportunity for the judge to effectively modify the proposed settlement, since it is extremely difficult to make any alterations or changes after preliminary approval.

At the preliminary approval phase, the parties must establish to the court that the proposed settlement meets a baseline of fairness, reasonableness, and adequacy such that the parties can begin the process of notifying class members of the proposed settlement itself, their opportunity to opt out, object, and attend the final fairness hearing. The court will also review the settlement, as well as the parties' conduct in negotiating the settlement, to ensure that the negotiations were conducted at arm's length, and were not collusive. Put differently, the court will typically issue a preliminary approval of a proposed class settlement

> if the preliminary evaluation of the proposed settlement does not disclose grounds to doubt its fairness or other obvious deficiencies, such as unduly preferential treatment of class representatives or of segments of the class, or excessive compensation for attorneys, and appears to fall within the range of possible approval . . . .[106]

At this preliminary stage, the court will not need the volume of information needed at final approval, however, the court will need *some* information about the class, and courts will typically not preliminarily approve a class settlement based on the ipse dixit of counsel.[107] Therefore, practitioners should, at the very least, consider including the following information and documents in their motion for preliminary approval of the settlement:

- the settlement agreement;
- the proposed notice forms;
- information about the proposed administration of claims;
- an affidavit or declaration by counsel describing the process of settlement negotiations;

---

105. As discussed later, under CAFA, when the putative settlement is submitted to the court for preliminary approval, this filing triggers a duty to report information about the proposed settlement to appropriate state and federal authorities within ten days.

106. *In re* Vitamins Antitrust Litig., Nos. MISC. 99-197(TFH), MDL 1285, 2001 WL 856292, at *5 (D.D.C. July 25, 2001).

107. *See, e.g.*, Martin v. Cargill, Inc., 295 F.R.D. 380, 386 (D. Minn. 2013).

- an affidavit or declaration by a mediator describing the mediation process and attesting that the negotiations were conducted at arm's length;
- the brief in support of the motion for preliminary approval;
- information about the anticipated petition for attorney fees;
- a draft proposed final judgment order;
- a proposed schedule for opt-outs, objections, and the final fairness hearing.

As part of the notice provisions, the parties should propose a date for the final settlement hearing. Although courts have held that a fairness hearing can be held as early as 30 days after notice is mailed to class members, as will be discussed later, CAFA mandates that the fairness hearing must be held no earlier than 90 days after the parties send notice to certain state and federal officials. Thus, because CAFA requires the parties to send notice to certain state and federal officials no later than ten days after the proposed approval is filed with the court, the fairness hearing will generally take place at least 100 days after the motion for preliminary approval is filed.

If the class has not been certified, the parties will usually file a joint motion for conditional certification of the class for settlement purposes in addition to the motion for preliminary approval. Prior to 2003, Rule 23 provided for conditional certification of a class for settlement purposes. However, the 2003 amendments removed the conditional certification provision. This omission, however, has not stopped courts from effectively granting "conditional" class certification for settlement purposes.[108] Moreover, the Manual for Complex Litigation continues to instruct judges to "make a preliminary determination that the proposed class satisfies the criteria set out in Rule 23(a) and at least one of the subsections of Rule 23(b)."[109]

> Because it is not guaranteed that the court will approve the settlement, the defendant, by stipulating or agreeing to class certification, risks waiving the right to oppose class certification at a later date. Defense counsel should include language in the settlement agreement reserving the defendant's right to object to class certification should the court decline to grant final approval.

108. *See, e.g.,* Nelson v. Mead Johnson & Johnson Co., 484 Fed. App'x 429, 432 (11th Cir. 2012).
109. MANUAL FOR COMPLEX LITIGATION, Fourth, § 21.632.

One important effect of conditional approval involves competing cases in other jurisdictions that arose out of the same facts as the conditionally approved lawsuit. Once a court conditionally certifies a class, it is indicating that it has jurisdiction over absent class members, including those who have filed competing cases in other jurisdictions. In the event that counsel attempts to move forward with the competing case, a party to the conditionally certified class action may elect to ask the judge in the competing case to enjoin the parties from proceeding.[110] As noted earlier, the court will also be alert to the presence of a "reverse auction," where the defendant has negotiated a favorable settlement in the weakest case that binds class members in stronger cases.

To be sure, during preliminary approval, some courts choose to engage in the rigorous Rule 23 analysis that is traditionally reserved for final approval,[111] and some courts even make the decision regarding whether or not to certify the class itself at the preliminary approval stage.[112]

The Federal Rules Advisory Committee has proposed amendments to Rule 23 that will likely be effective on December 1, 2018. The amendments aim to front load the approval process, requiring courts to conduct a rigorous review of the settlement before ordering notice to the class. Under amended Rule 23(e)(3), notice should be ordered only if "giving notice is justified by the parties' showing that the court will likely be able to: (i) approve the proposal under Rule 23(e)(2); and (ii) certify the class for purposes of judgment on the proposal." This language will likely slow down the approval time line and, depending upon the complexity of the case and the discretion of the court, could lead to multiple hearings, multiple rounds of briefing, or even proposed changes to the settlement from the court (since changes are likely easier to obtain in the settlement structure before a preliminary approval order). If there are non-parties watching the docket (or the legal press) or if there are regulators who are interested, it could lead to battles at this preliminary approval stage that previously only occurred at the final approval stage.

The comments to the proposed changes emphasize the importance of the preliminary approval and encourage the submission of documents in support of the settlement at the preliminary approval stage,

---

110. Antisuit injunctions raise complex legal issues of which practitioners should be aware. RUBENSTEIN, *supra* note 24, § 13.19.

111. *See* Smith v. Professional Billing Management Servs., Inc., No. 06-4453(JEI), 2007 WL 4191749, at *2 (D.N.J. Nov. 21, 2007).

112. *See* Orvis v. Spokane City, 281 F.R.D. 469 (E.D. Wa. 2012).

including information on the attorney fees arrangement. Because the scope of the comment is so broad, it is useful to quote the key portions:

> The decision to give notice of a proposed settlement to the class is an important event. It should be based upon a solid record supporting the conclusion that the proposed settlement will likely earn final approval after notice and an opportunity to object. The parties must provide the court with information sufficient to determine whether notice should be sent . . . should ordinarily provide to the court all available materials they intend to submit to support approval under Rule 23(e)(2) and that they intend to make available to class members . . . if a class has not been [previously] certified, the parties must ensure that the court has a basis for concluding that it likely will be able, after the final hearing, to certify the class . . . the court cannot make the decision regarding the prospects for certification without a suitable basis in the record . . . . A basis focus is the extent and type of benefits that the settlement will confer . . . that showing may include details of the contemplated claims process and the anticipated rate of claims . . . the settlement agreement ordinarily should address the distribution of those funds . . . . The parties should also supply the court with information about the likely range of litigated outcomes, and about the risks. . . . Information about the extent of discovery completed in the litigation or in parallel actions . . . provide information about the existence of other pending or anticipated litigation . . . . The proposed handling of an award of attorney's fees under Rule 23(h) ordinarily should be addressed in the parties' submission to the court. In some cases, it will be important to relate the amount of an award of attorney's fees to the expected benefits to the class. One way to address this issue it to defer some or all of the award of attorney's fees until the court is advised of the actual claims rate and results. . . . The court may direct the parties to supply further information . . . . The court should not direct notice to the class until the parties' submissions show it is likely that the court will be able to approve [the settlement].[113]

Fairness Hearing and Final Approval

Once the reviewing court grants preliminary approval, the parties will arrange to send notice to the class informing individuals of their right to opt out, or file a written objection to the settlement, or do nothing and be bound by the settlement. The notice will also give class members

---

113. Comm. on Federal Rules of Civil Procedure, *Preliminary Draft of Proposed Amendments to the Federal Rules of Civil Procedure* 221, *available at* http://www.uscourts .gov/sites/default/files/2016-08-preliminary_draft_of_rules_forms_published_for_public _comment_0.pdf.

the date of the judicial fairness hearing, and inform them of their right to attend and to object in person. Prior to the fairness hearing, typically, on an agreed upon date, the parties will submit a motion for final approval of the proposed settlement and, if necessary, a motion to certify the class. The court must rigorously analyze the proposed settlement, thus, the parties will submit a large volume of material to the court, generally consisting of:

- the motion for final approval of the settlement;
- Brief in support of the motion for final approval that, if necessary, refutes any arguments raised by objectors;
- declarations of the attorneys laying out, in detail, the course of negotiations and assuring the court that the negotiations were held at arm's length;
- declarations of a mediator attesting that the negotiations were held at arm's length;
- reports or declarations by experts attesting to the value of non-monetary benefits to the class;
- declarations from the attorneys or the firm coordinating notice (such as a claims administrator) describing the notice process, and attesting that the parties complied with CAFA's notice provisions;
- statement from the claims administrator describing the claims administration process;
- a summary of discovery exchanged to establish that the parties were sufficiently informed of the underlying facts of the lawsuit prior to entering, or during settlement negotiations;
- if necessary, a motion for class certification and accompanying evidence establishing that the class satisfies the Rule 23 prerequisites;
- a petition to the court by class counsel requesting attorney fees;
- a proposed final judgment order approving the settlement and, if necessary, certifying the class and/or retaining jurisdiction for future compliance.

Once the court has reviewed this information and considered any objections, the court will make the final decision regarding whether or not to approve the settlement and, if necessary, certify a settlement class. As far as approval of the settlement is concerned, the court's benchmark for determining whether or not approval is merited is whether the settlement is fair, reasonable, and adequate.[114]

> The use of expert testimony during the final approval process is a common practice. Expert testimony can help a reviewing court understand how the proposed settlement is objectively fair, reasonable, and adequate, and how the processes underlying the settlement were appropriate. For instance, parties should consider using experts to
>
> - Help the court understand the value of non-pecuniary relief to the class as a whole;
> - Help the court understand the issues underlying a complex or technical case;
> - Explain to the court, in statistical terms, the risk to the class of proceeding with the litigation rather than settling;
> - Calculate total damages to the class, and explain how the proposed settlement fairly compensates the class;
> - Explain the process of providing notice to absent class members, and how that process was calculated to inform as many class members as possible about the proposed settlement.

Several specific "tests" have developed within the different circuits that help to guide district courts when making fairness determinations. For instance, courts within the Fifth Circuit evaluate settlements based on the so-called *Reed* factors, which are

> (1) the existence of fraud or collusion behind the settlement; (2) the complexity, expense, and likely duration of the litigation; (3) the stage of the proceedings and the amount of discovery completed; (4) the probability of plaintiffs' success on the merits; (5) the range of possible recovery; and (6) the opinions of the class counsel, class representatives, and absent class members.[115]

The Sixth Circuit utilizes a similar test, which adds a seventh factor: whether the settlement is in the "public interest."[116] Other circuits evaluate additional disparate factors such as "the reaction of the class to the settlement,"[117] "the amount offered in settlement[,]" "the presence of a

---

114. FED. R. CIV. P. 23(e)(2).
115. Reed v. Gen Motors Corp., 703 F.2d 170, 172 (5th Cir. 1983); *see also* Union Asset Management Holding A.G. v. Dell, Inc., 669 F.3d 632, 639 n.11 (5th Cir. 2012).
116. *See, e.g.,* UAW v. Gen. Motors Corp., 497 F.3d 615, 631 (6th Cir. 2007).
117. *See* McReynolds v. Richards-Cantave, 588 F.3d 790, 804 (2d Cir. 2009).

governmental participant[,]"[118] "the ability of the defendants to withstand a greater judgment,"[119] and "the risks of maintaining a class action
through trial."[120] It is essential that counsel understand the test that is used
in the relevant jurisdiction, and the case authority that has developed
around those tests, prior to submitting their settlement for final approval.

The proposed Rule 23 amendments include their own set of factors
to consider for approval of a class settlement. The comments explain
that the new list of factors are not intended "to displace any factor"
but instead to "focus the court and the lawyers on the core concerns
of procedure and substance that should guide the decision whether
to approve the proposal." First, the court must consider whether "the
class representatives and class counsel have adequately represented
the class" and whether "the proposal was negotiated at arm's length."
The rule comments note that the court may consider whether a mediator was involved and suggest that the court pay "[p]articular attention"
to the treatment of attorney fees "with respect to both the manner of
negotiating the fee award and its terms."[121]

Next, the court must consider whether "the relief provided for the
class is adequate" taking into account "(i) the costs, risks, and delay of
trial and appeal; (ii) the effectiveness of any proposed method of distributing relief to the class, including the method of processing class-member
claims; (iii) the terms of any proposed award of attorney's fees, including timing of payment; and (iv) any agreement required to be identified
under Rule 23(e)(3)." Further, the court must determine whether the
"proposal treats class members equitably relative to each other."[122]

These factors, and the comments, could have a substantial impact on
court involvement in the settlement process, and the length of time and
costs of any approval. For instance, in the comments to the proposed
rule, the committee notes that measuring the proposed relief "may
require evaluation of any proposed claims process; directing that the
parties report back to the court about actual claims experience may be

---

118. *In re* Bluetooth Headset Products Liab. Litig., 654 F.3d 935, 946 (9th Cir. 2011).

119. *In re* Prudential Ins. Co. America Sales Practice Litig. Agent Actions, 148 F.3d
283, 317 (3d Cir. 1998).

120. *See, e.g.,* Pichler v. UNITE, 775 F. Supp. 2d 754, 758 n.5 (E.D. Pa. 2011).

121. Fed. R. Civ. P., *Preliminary Draft of Proposed Amendments to the Federal Rules of
Civil Procedure*, at 224–25, *available at* http://www.uscourts.gov/sites/default/files/2016
-08-preliminary_draft_of_rules_forms_published_for_public_comment_0.pdf.

122. Federal Rules of Civil Procedure, *Preliminary Draft of Proposed Amendments to the
Federal Rules of Civil Procedure* 214, *available at* http://www.uscourts.gov/sites/default
/files/2016-08-preliminary_draft_of_rules_forms_published_for_public_comment_0.pdf.

important." Further "the relief actually delivered to the class can be a substantial factor in determining the appropriate fee award" suggesting that some settlement structures may delay the award of attorney fees (much less their payment). Moreover, the comments suggest that the court should examine the details of the claims process: "often, it will be important for the court to scrutinize the method of claims processing to ensure that it facilitates filing legitimate claims."[123]

Objectors

In December 2016, a class of aggrieved plaintiffs filed a class action in the Northern District of Illinois against several law firms and lawyers, claiming, among other things, that their practice of "professionally objecting" to amicable class action settlements amounted to a violation of the Racketeer Influenced and Corrupt Organizations Act.[124] Although this case has since been dismissed,[125] it is indicative of the acrimony that exists between lawyers who, in many instances, spend years crafting a class action settlement, and "professional objectors"—lawyers who have made a career out of obtaining a side agreement to drop an objection made on behalf of a "client."

The ability of a class member to object to a proposed settlement is fundamental to the class action device.[126] Unnamed class members do not have any real effect on the progression of the litigation. And, when the settlement is being negotiated, they do not have any input in determining the value that they will receive in exchange for a full release of their claims. The Federal Rules, therefore, provide class members with an opportunity to object to the settlement as the mechanism by which they can have some input to comport with due process principles.

Specifically, after the court has preliminarily approved the settlement, counsel must send notice to absent class members informing them of their right to object to the settlement or opt out of the settlement entirely. Notice and a right to opt out are required for money

---

123. COMMITTEE ON RULES OF PRACTICE AND PROCEDURE OF THE JUDICIAL CONFERENCE OF THE UNITED STATES: PROPOSED AMENDMENTS TO THE FEDERAL RULES OF APPELLATE, BANKRUPTCY, CIVIL, AND CRIMINAL PROCEDURE, at 213–14, 224–25 (2016).

124. Edelson PC v. The Bandas Law Firm PC, et al., No. 1:16-cv-11057 (Dec. 5, 2016)

125. *Id.* (objections for personal gain are "vexing" and "distasteful[,]" and "[g]aming the rules of the legal system solely for personal self-enrichment wastes the time and money of courts and attorneys, wrests funds away from deserving litigants and tarnishes the public's view of the legal process").

126. FED. R. CIV. P. 23(e)(5).

damages classes under Rule 23(b)(3). However, notice is also permissible in mandatory classes under Rule 23(b)(1) or (b)(2). Rule 23(e)(1) requires notice of settlement "in a reasonable manner to all class members who would be bound by the proposal" without distinguishing among the types of class actions. Typically, the preliminary approval order will provide a method for class members to object, including a deadline for objections and a deadline for providing notice of an intent to appear personally at the final fairness hearing, as well as a deadline to opt out of the settlement (assuming such an option is available).

> Under proposed amendments to Rule 23, class members must state, with additional specificity, the grounds for their objections. This provision attempts to combat the problem of boilerplate objections ("objection must state whether it applies only to the objector, to a specific subset of the class, or to the entire class, and also state with specificity the grounds for the objection"). Additionally, the amendments require a hearing and court approval for any payment for withdrawing an objection, or "forgoing, dismissing, or abandoning an appeal from a judgment approving the proposal."

If a class member chooses to opt out of a class or a settlement, he or she no longer has a protectable interest in the settlement and, therefore, cannot object.

> Even if the parties have negotiated at arm's length, avoided collusive activities, and followed all of the best practices in negotiating and presenting the settlement, objectors have the ability to hold up the agreement through an appeals process that could take years to resolve. This will significantly delay relief to class members, who will become more difficult to locate with the passage of time. Similarly, class counsel will be unable to recoup any of their costs, or obtain attorney fees for a significant period of time. Defendants also do not have the benefit of the settlement release and its res judicata effect on other similar litigation.

Generally, objections fall into four broad categories: (1) public interest organizations or state regulators making substantive points intended to improve the settlement (for instance, the relief provided, the notice, the scope of the release, or the scope of injunctive relief);[127] (2) lawyers

---

127. For example, Theodore Frank is the director of litigation and the director of the Center for Class Action Fairness at the Competitive Enterprise Institute and has been characterized as a "professional objector to hollow class-action settlements." *In re* Subway Footlong Sandwich Marketing and Sales Practices Litigation, 869 F.3d 551, 553 (7th Cir. 2017).

involved in competing actions seeking to call the court's attention to the other cases or in some cases to derail a "reverse auction" (such objections are sometimes substantive and sometimes merely self-interested); (3) individuals (who sometimes do not fully grasp the settlement terms but who sometimes raise valid substantive issues); and (4) professional, serial objectors (generally seeking to exploit the leverage of delaying the settlement to extract a payoff). When an objector raises a valid objection that ultimately confers a material benefit on the class, a court may award attorney fees, but such awards are rare.[128] Courts are reluctant to award attorney fees to objectors when they suspect that their motive is entirely economic and self-serving.[129]

Proposed Rule 23 amendments may help deter frivolous objectors. These proposed changes will increase the amount of effort required, and thus the transaction costs, to object to a settlement and later appealing the approval of that settlement. It remains to be seen how effective these changes will be since it is the threat of increased court involvement that gives objectors leverage in the first place.

Under the proposed amendments, class members must state, with additional specificity, the grounds for their objections. This provision attempts to combat the problem of boilerplate objections ("objection must state whether it applies only to the objector, to a specific subset of the class, or to the entire class, and also state with specificity the grounds for the objection"). Additionally, the amendments require a hearing and court approval for any payment or "consideration" for withdrawing an objection, or "forgoing, dismissing, or abandoning an appeal from a judgment approving the proposal." The comments emphasize that the term "consideration" should be "broadly interpreted, particularly when the withdrawal includes some arrangements beneficial to the objector counsel."[130]

One method to diminish the leverage held by prospective objectors is to incorporate a quick-pay provision in the settlement agreement. A quick-pay clause provides that class counsel will receive attorney fees and expense reimbursement payments promptly upon court approval,

128. *See, e.g.,* Rodriguez v. Disner, 688 F.3d 645 (9th Cir. 2012).
129. *See, e.g.,* Lonardo v. Travelers Indem. Co., 706 F. Supp. 2d 766, 804 (N.D. Ohio 2010).
130. Comm. on Federal Rules of Civil Procedure, *Preliminary Draft of Proposed Amendments to the Federal Rules of Civil Procedure* 230, *available at* http://www.uscourts.gov/sites/default/files/2016-08-preliminary_draft_of_rules_forms_published_for_public_comment_0.pdf

and will refund these payments in the event that the settlement is set aside or the award is reduced on appeal. With class counsel receiving immediate payment, an objector cannot leverage potentially years of delay in counsel's reimbursement simply by filing an appeal, thereby discouraging bad faith appeals. A study of 2006 federal court class action settlement found that some 35 percent contained a quick-pay provision, as compared with some 37 percent that explicitly withheld payment of class counsel fees until all appeals were exhausted.[131]

However, at least to the extent that class counsel is not known to be well capitalized, some defendants may find the risk of nonpayment to be unacceptable, at least without adequate assurances or guarantees of repayment. Quick-pay is also more common in certain areas of the law (for instance, securities litigation).

A better solution may be to place the transaction cost of objecting onto the objector himself or herself. Courts have, in some circumstances, required objectors to pay an appeal bond as a condition for appealing a judgment approving a settlement.[132] However, courts are split regarding whether such a bond may be imposed at all and what the amount of the appeal bond should be—with some courts assessing a bond amount as high as $9 million, and others assessing a bond as low as $800.[133] Because of the high variability of potential appeal bonds, and the likely effectiveness of requiring a substantial bond on deterring frivolous appeals and, therefore, frivolous objections, some commentators have proposed rules that would tie the amount of an appeals bond to the full cost of the appeal on both the class and the defendant, and making the bond a requirement for an appeal.

Counsel should consider asking the district court to approve objection requirements tailored to flagging the professional objector—such as a requirement that the objector list each case in which he, she, or their counsel have filed class action settlement objections or a requirement that the objector disclose the financial arrangement between the

131. Brian Fitzpatrick, *The End of Objector Blackmail?*, 62 VAND. L. REV. 1623, 1642–43 (2009), http://vanderbiltlawreview.org/articles/2009/11/Fitzpatrick-The-End-of-Objector-Blackmail-62-Vand.-L.-Rev.-1623-2009.pdf). Anecdotally, the use of quick-pay provisions appears to have increased over the past decade, and to be more readily agreed to by sophisticated defense counsel who understand its value in deterring professional objectors.

132. *See* John E. Lopatka & D. Brooks Smith, *Class Action Professional Objectors: What to Do About Them*, 39 FLA. ST. U. L. REV. 865, 908–18 (2012).

133. RUBENSTEIN, *supra* note 24, § 14:16 (listing exemplar cases).

objector and his or her counsel. Some parties seek inclusion of a provision in the preliminary approval order permitting counsel to seek leave of court to depose an objector before the final fairness hearing in appropriate circumstances.

In all events, however, the parties should take care to avoid imposing unreasonable roadblocks that unduly burden class members' right to object. Similar to a burdensome claims process, obstacles to class members who wish to object to the settlement can be a red flag for heightened judicial scrutiny of the settlement. Settlements should be designed so that objecting class members have a reasonable means to express concerns about the proposed settlement. Those means should not be exorbitantly time consuming, costly, or unreasonable in light of the value of the settlement.

The objection protocol should provide that objectors must file any notice of objections and supporting materials by a deadline sufficiently in advance of the final fairness hearing to permit the parties to file written responses before the hearing.

CAFA COMPLIANCE AND COUPONS

In addition to Rule 23(e), practitioners must be aware of the provisions of CAFA that govern class action settlements. This section provides a general overview of CAFA compliance regarding notice and coupons in the settlement context. However, a more detailed discussion of the subject can be found in the ABA CAFA strategy guide.[134]

CAFA has wide-ranging breadth, and regulates certain forms of notice, and the creation of coupon settlements. On their own, CAFA's notice and coupon settlement provisions significantly affect the way in which the parties typically negotiate settlement terms. In addition, CAFA also proscribes geographical discrimination and losses by class members. These provisions, however, are rarely relevant in the settlement context. Thus, this section will address CAFA's regulation of coupon settlements, and the CAFA-specific notice provisions, both of which shape the contours of settlement negotiations.

---

134. THE CLASS ACTION FAIRNESS ACT, LAW AND STRATEGY 295–322 (Gregory C. Cook, ed. 2013).

Coupon Settlements

Congress, in enacting CAFA, was concerned with the use of coupons to settle class actions.[135] In such settlements, class members receive a coupon or voucher that allows them to purchase a good or service from the defendant, which raises several concerns, including that class counsel, rather than the class, is obtaining the primary benefit of the settlement and the settlement is just a thinly veiled marketing scheme for the defendant's products. In addition, as one court noted, coupon settlements "often do not provide meaningful compensation to class members; they often fail to disgorge ill-gotten gains from the defendant; and they often require class members to do future business with the defendant in order to obtain compensation."[136]

However, CAFA does not actually prohibit coupon settlements. Rather, it sets particular requirements on their use. Indeed, despite Congress's criticism of coupon settlements, they remain a useful tool for practitioners, and can often help lead to a beneficial class settlement. For instance, some settled class action lawsuits are the result of underlying claims of questionable legal merit. Defendants will often settle the case because, despite the likelihood of success on the merits, the costs of defending the case outweighs the cost of settlement. In these instances, the availability of coupon settlements allows for a measurable benefit to the class, because the alternative would likely be no class benefit whatsoever. Similarly, there are instances in which the defendant is in poor financial condition and a large monetary settlement is simply beyond its means. It does class members no good to bankrupt the class action defendant. Thus, the best option could be to provide coupons, even though those coupons may provide a marginal benefit to both the class members and the defendant.

Definition of "Coupon Settlement"

Congress did not define the term "coupon settlement." Congress did, however, offer some examples of problematic settlements that led to the passage of CAFA that include (1) a settlement whereby cruise ship patrons received a $30 to $40 discount for a future cruise while class counsel received almost $900,000 in fees, costs, and expenses; (2) a settlement where a Chicago restaurant gave class members $1 off coupons

---

135. S. Rep. No. 109-14, at 5–6.
136. Figuerosa v. Sharper Image Corp., 517 F. Supp. 2d 1292, 1302 (S.D. Fla. 2007).

while class counsel received cash compensation; (3) a settlement involving unsafe cribs where class members received either a crib repair kit or a $55 coupon towards the purchase of another product from the company; and (4) a settlement involving an airline where class members received vouchers for $25 to $75 off the price of future travel while the lawyers were paid approximately $25 million in fees.[137]

These examples certainly provide a decent guideline for Congress's intent when it comes to the meaning of "coupons," but in practice, the multiplicity of different forms of non-pecuniary relief can complicate the determination of what is and isn't a "coupon." Courts generally define the term as a settlement "that provides benefits to class members in the form of a discount towards the future purchase of a product or service offered by the defendant."[138] This definition seems straightforward enough, and settlements that provide a "coupon" to class members that gives them a discount on a good or service are clearly "coupon settlements" for purposes of CAFA. However, some settlements have features that operate effectively as "coupons," but aren't obviously "coupon settlements." Moreover, in most cases, parties cannot avoid the CAFA rules on coupons by using alternative labeling—that is, by calling the "coupon" a "voucher," or something similar. For instance, courts have described pre-paid shipping envelopes,[139] airline vouchers for free drinks,[140] gift cards,[141] and a limited-time free pass to a health club[142] as "coupons" for purposes of CAFA. On the other hand, some courts *have* found that "vouchers" for free merchandise (as opposed to a "coupon" for a discount) did not count as "coupons" for purposes of CAFA,[143] and some cases have held that settlements that give class members an option of either taking cash or another form of non-pecuniary relief is not a "coupon settlement."[144]

---

137. S. Rep. No. 109-14, at 1518.
138. Radosti v. Envision, EMI LLC, 717 F. Supp. 2d 37. 35 n.16 (D.D.C. 2010).
139. Synfuel Technologies, Inc. v. DHL Express (USA), Inc., 463 F.3d 646 (7th Cir. 2006).
140. *In re* Southwest Airlines Voucher Litig., No. 11 C 8176, 2013 WL 5497275 (N.D. Ill. June 20, 2014).
141. Reibstein v. Rite Aid Corp., 761 F. Supp. 2d 241, 255 (E.D. Pa. 2011).
142. Silver v. LA Fitness Intern. LLC, No. 10-2326, 2013 WL 5429293 (E.D. Pa. Sept. 27, 2013).
143. *See, e.g.,* Foos v. Ann, Inc., No. 11cv2794 L(MDD), 2013 WL 5352969 (S.D. Cal. Sept. 24, 2013).
144. *See, e.g.,* O'Brien v. Brain Research Labs, LLC, No. 12-204, 2012 WL 3242365 (D.N.J. Aug. 9, 2012).

Although there is no consensus regarding the precise meaning of "coupon," the most important factor in determining whether an agreement is a "coupon settlement" is whether the settlement requires class members to spend more money in order to obtain a benefit. Courts also consider whether the settlement requires class members to continue to do business with the defendant in order to obtain the benefit, whether the settlement will actually result in a significant pecuniary loss to the defendant, whether the settlement will actually render a benefit to the defendant, and whether the coupon is transferable.

Approval of Coupon Settlements

Coupon settlements are not per se improper. However, counsel should consider the following steps to improve the chances that such a settlement will pass judicial muster:

- The coupons are freely transferrable.
- They have no "use-by" date.
- The coupons are stackable (i.e., multiple coupons can be used for a single transaction).
- The coupons are not limited to a certain good, or category of goods.
- The coupons contain as few restrictions as is practicable.
- The coupons are easily redeemed.

Heightened Scrutiny

CAFA mandates a hearing, and written court findings regarding whether a coupon settlement is "fair, reasonable, and adequate for class members."[145] Of course, other than the requirement that the fairness finding be "written," this mandate is entirely duplicative of Rule 23's requirement that the court hold a fairness hearing regarding the entire settlement. Nevertheless, courts have held that this duplication signals that courts should apply heightened scrutiny to coupon settlements.[146] Courts examine several factors to determine whether a coupon settlement is appropriate, including whether the coupons are transferable, can be converted to cash on a secondary market, compare favorably with deals available to the general public, and are likely to be

---

145. 28 U.S.C. § 1712(e).
146. *See, e.g.*, Reed v. Continental Guest Servs. Corp., No. 10 Civ. 5642(DLC), 2011 WL 1311886 (S.D.N.Y. Apr. 4, 2011).

redeemed.[147] As a result of this increased scrutiny, courts are much less inclined to treat the face value of the coupons as a basis for the overall value of the settlement.

Practitioners can take several steps to improve the chances that a coupon settlement will overcome judicial scrutiny. The key to a successful coupon settlement is to be generous regarding the redemption process, and the limitations placed on the coupons. It should be as easy as possible for class members to obtain and redeem the coupons. Likewise, the coupons should generally be freely transferrable, stackable, and not limited to a certain category of goods and services, and they certainly should not be limited to the purchase of the product that purportedly malfunctioned in a products liability class action. Finally, the parties should not place severely restrictive time limitations on the use of the coupons—it is a best practice for coupons to be redeemable for a year or longer.

Attorney Fee Considerations

One of Congress's chief concerns in passing CAFA was the prevalence of high attorney fees in coupon settlements. It is undeniable that the optics of this are bad—the lawyers get a healthy monetary reward while class members receive coupons or vouchers for a modest discount on the purported offender's goods or services. However, despite the questionable optics, often, class counsel expend considerable time and effort ensuring that class members get *some* benefit—especially in instances in which the plaintiffs have a weak case. Thus, CAFA still allows for an attorney fee in instances where the parties agree to coupon relief, however, it severely curtails the potential fee recovery.

Under CAFA, when a coupon settlement provides for an attorney fee that is a percentage of the recovery, that percentage must be based on the value to class members of the coupons that are *actually* redeemed by class members rather than the number of coupons that were issued.[148] Because actual redemption rates are typically low, CAFA has resulted in lower attorney fees in coupon settlements. Of course, this feature of CAFA also provides a strong incentive for class counsel to ensure that coupons are easy for class members to redeem.

---

147. NEWBERG ON CLASS ACTIONS § 12:13 (5th ed.) (citing BARBARA ROTHSTEIN AND THOMAS E. WILLGING, FEDERAL JUDICIAL CENTER: MANAGING CLASS ACTION LITIGATION: A POCKET GUIDE FOR JUDGES 18 (3d ed. 2010)).

148. 28 U.S.C. § 1712.

Because attorney fees in coupon settlements must be determined based on the amount actually redeemed, it is typically impossible for a court to finalize an attorney fee until the coupons' redemption period has expired. This can be highly problematic for class counsel, who may have to wait an additional year or more before they are compensated for their work. This also creates tension between the interest of the class in a long coupon redemption period, the corresponding best practice of creating a long redemption period, and class counsel's interest in receiving compensation for their work in a reasonable period of time.

This conflict and the increase of judicial scrutiny has operated to reduce the number of coupon settlements. However, there are at least two options that parties can use to ensure a faster payment of attorney fees while providing for a longer redemption period. First, the parties can ask the court to authorize periodic payments that are based on the value of coupons redeemed during the period. Second, CAFA authorizes the use of experts to create a projection of the value of potentially redeemed coupons.[149] Thus, the parties could request that the court authorize a contingent attorney fee based on a projection of the potential value of coupons.

Another, perhaps more appealing option for avoiding the problems associated with percentage of the fund attorney fees in coupon settlements is to avoid the percentage of the fund method altogether. Under CAFA, coupon settlements that do not provide that attorney fees will be determined as a percentage of the fund require that the court base the fee upon the time counsel reasonably expended, and the court can use a lodestar with multipliers.[150] CAFA reiterates the preexisting requirement that the court approve coupon settlement attorney fees based on the lodestar method, however, there is no indication that courts will more heavily scrutinize lodestar based attorney fee requests under 28 U.S.C. § 1212(b). That being said, the issue of large attorney fees in coupon settlements doesn't disappear when the attorney fee is calculated based on the lodestar method, and courts will sometimes look to the benefit conferred on the class when calculating the attorney fee. As a result, courts will typically consider the ultimate value to the class, leading to attorney fee awards that roughly match an award determined by the value of redeemed coupons.

---

149. *Id.* § 1712(d).
150. *Id.* § 1212(b).

CAFA Notice

CAFA requires that the parties provide notice of proposed class action settlements to appropriate federal and state officials. Specifically, each defendant participating in a proposed settlement must serve notice of the settlement on "the appropriate State official of each State in which a class member resides and the appropriate Federal official."[151] This notice must be served "not later than 10 days after a proposed settlement of a class action is filed in court."[152] This is an extraordinarily fast turnaround requirement—practitioners have only ten days after filing a motion for preliminary approval to send notice to any relevant state or federal officials. Thus, practitioners should have their notice mailings largely prepared prior to the filing of the proposed settlement with the court.

Failure to send the notice could result in class members not being bound "by a settlement agreement or consent decree in a class action if the class member demonstrates that the notice required under subsection (b) has not been provided."[153] Additionally, CAFA's notice requirement effectively lengthens the process of settlement approval by mandating that an "order giving final approval of a proposed settlement may not be issued earlier than 90 days after" the service of notice on state and federal officials.[154] Thus, taken together, CAFA's notice rules require parties to quickly send notice to "appropriate . . . official[s]" only to wait for the court to issue a final order approving the settlement.

The notice requirement also potentially changes the strategic calculus regarding the defense of class action litigation and potential settlement. Under CAFA, in order to settle a case, the parties have to inform multiple regulatory agencies about potential wrongdoing by the defendant. In many cases, this provision introduces considerable additional risk. While CAFA does not give these regulatory agencies standing to

---

151. *Id.* § 1715(b).

152. *Id.*

153. *Id.* § 1715(e). Failure to send notice to "appropriate officials," however, is not necessarily fatal to a proposed settlement. Rather, the typical result of failure to strictly comply with CAFA's notice requirements is additional delay in final approval. Parties who make a good faith effort to comply will likely not be punished by the court. For instance, parties may simply request a stay of final approval of the settlement to allow for the parties to serve proper notice. *See generally* THE CLASS ACTION FAIRNESS ACT, *supra* note 127, at 305–07 (2013).

154. 28 U.S.C. § 1715(d).

intervene in the lawsuit, many regulators might be tempted to take additional regulatory, or even criminal action against defendants based on the underlying allegations in the class action lawsuit. Thus, it might make a defendant unwilling to remove a class action to federal court and/or to settle a class action due to the potential for state and federal regulatory interference. Accordingly, defense counsel must inform their clients that the settlement of class action either filed in or removed to federal court could result in regulatory disclosure.

Identifying Appropriate Officials

Although CAFA requires that notice be served on "appropriate" state and federal officials, CAFA does not specify which officials are "appropriate." For federal officials, notice should be served on the Attorney General of the United States.[155] Where the defendant is a bank, either foreign or domestic, the appropriate official is "the person who has the primary Federal regulatory or supervisory responsibility with respect to the defendant, if some or all of the matters alleged in the class action are subject to regulation or supervision by that person."[156] For state officials, the defendant must inform "the person in the State who has the primary regulatory or supervisory responsibility with respect to the defendant, or who licenses or otherwise authorizes the defendant to conduct business in the State, if some or all of the matters alleged in the class action are subject to regulation by that person." If there is no regulator that matches this description, then the defendant must notice the state attorney general.[157]

Frequently, class action defendants are regulated by several overlapping administrative entities. CAFA creates a "safe harbor," allowing defendants to provide notice to "the appropriate Federal official and to either the State attorney general or the person that has primary regulatory, supervisory, or licensing authority over the defendant."[158] However, it is generally a best practice for practitioners to over-notify, even if it is unclear whether the specific regulator has jurisdiction over the particular entity.

---

155. Generally during CAFA's duration, DOJ has not taken any action on settlements. This has recently changed and the Department has announced it will be more active in the future.

156. 28 U.S.C. § 1715(a)(1)(A)–(B).

157. Id. § 1715(a)(2).

158. Id.

Contents of the Notice

CAFA delineates the items to be provided to state and federal regulators. There is no statute or regulation requiring that these materials must be provided in hard copy form, therefore, it is much more cost effective to provide electronic copies to state and federal regulators. The list of materials to be provided is relatively straightforward:

- The complaint, any amended complaints, and any materials filed with the complaint(s);
- Notice of any scheduled hearings;
- Proposed or final notification to class members of their right to request exclusion, or a statement that no such right exists, and the proposed settlement of the class action;
- Any proposed or final class action settlement;
- Any contemporaneous side agreements between class counsel and counsel for defendants;
- Any final judgment or notice of dismissal;
- If feasible, the names of class members who reside in each state and the estimated proportionate share of the claims of such members to the entire settlement; or, if not feasible, a reasonable estimate;
- Any written judicial opinion pertaining to the class settlement, or dismissal of the case.[159]

CONCLUSION

Settling a class action is not simple. Any class settlement requires careful attention to detail from the beginning through the end and for each of the many required documents. Practitioners should be especially alert to potential conflicts of interest within the class and especially careful when negotiating attorney fees. With all of this said, the vast majority of class settlements are still approved and there are many available resources to assist practitioners in this process.

---

159. *Id.* § 1715(b).

10

Trial Plans

Andrew J. McGuinness and James M. Finberg

T o trial plan or not to trial plan? That is the question. Of course, every class action practitioner (plaintiff and defense) should plan for trial, but should one (or both) parties submit to the court a document called a "trial plan," usually in connection with a motion for class certification?

Before we get to that question, let's start with the basics. What is a trial plan? While that question is explored in depth in this chapter, a trial plan—in simplest terms—is a roadmap that tells the judge which issues will be tried, in which order, and based on what evidence.

So, is a trial plan required? Some judges insist upon them, as is their prerogative. Writing in 2004, the authors of the Federal Judicial Center's Manual for Complex Litigation (Fourth) took a somewhat agnostic approach:

> The judge must decide whether the proposed Rule 23(b)(3) class will be manageable. For the most part, courts determine manageability by reviewing affidavits, declarations, trial plans, and choice-of-law analyses that counsel present[1]

---

1. In a separate section, § 22.318 at 362, the MANUAL touches on trial plans in the mass tort context—a matter beyond the scope of this book. However, some courts (especially in the Fifth Circuit) have cited case law regarding trial plans applied in that context to

The Advisory Committee's note to the 2003 amendment to Rule 23 was more supportive of trial plans:

> A critical need is to determine how the case will be tried. An increasing number of courts require a party requesting class certification to present a "trial plan" that describes the issues likely to be presented at trial and tests whether they are susceptible of class-wide proof.[2]

The Eleventh Circuit Court of Appeals, in dicta, has gone even further:

> We do not mean to say that submission of a trial plan by the plaintiff is necessarily a prerequisite, as a matter of law, for a finding of superiority in every case. Nonetheless, a plaintiff seeking class certification bears the burden of establishing each element of Rule 23, which includes superiority in Rule 23(b)(3) cases, and courts must consider how a case will be tried as part of the superiority assessment. Accordingly, the proposal of a workable trial plan will often go a long way toward demonstrating that manageability concerns do not excessively undermine the superiority of the class action vehicle. Moreover, there is a direct correlation between the importance of a realistic, clear, detailed, and specific trial plan and the magnitude of the manageability problems a putative class action presents. We therefore recommend that district courts make it a usual practice to direct plaintiffs to present feasible trial plans, which should include proposed jury instructions, as early as practicable when seeking class certification.[3]

Given this "recommendation," it might be that class counsel practicing in the Eleventh Circuit who do *not* give strong consideration to the submission of a trial plan with the certification motion will be questioned on adequacy grounds.[4] In fact, this may be wise advice to a plaintiff counsel in any court, thus taking away such an argument from defense counsel. Further, defense counsel is likely to characterize

---

consumer and commercial class actions. This chapter focuses on Rule 23(b)(3) damages class actions, where a showing of superiority (and therefore manageability) is required. *Id.*, § 21.142 at 236.

2. A portion of this passage from the Advisory Committee's 2003 Note was quoted by the panel in what many consider an important class action decision, *In re. Hydrogen Peroxide*, as part of an argument outlining the possible need to resolve certain merits issues essential to certification prior to the certification decision. *In re* Hydrogen Peroxide Antitrust Litig., 552 F.3d 305, 312 (3d Cir. 2008). The court articulated no explicit mandate for trial plans in *In re* Hydrogen Peroxide, however.

3. *Vega v. T-Mobile USA, Inc.,* 564 F.3d 1256, 1279 n.20 (11th Cir. 2009) (citations omitted).

4. An example of a district court in the Eleventh Circuit citing to plaintiffs' trial plan in granting class certification is *In re* Checking Account Overdraft Litig., 307 F.R.D. 656 (S.D. Fla. 2015).

the trial as an unmanageable series of individualized, person by person, determinations that will consume months of trial time. A trial plan directly responds to this type of argument. Still, trial plans are optional absent an express order of the court, as indicated by the sources cited earlier and as expressly held in at least one published appellate decision.[5] Some state courts also encourage trial courts to review trial plans when making class certification determinations.[6]

In sum, trial plans are a *tool*, born out of Rule 23(b)(3)(D)'s express "manageability" factor for assessing superiority, in recognition that it is plaintiff's burden to establish that the requirements for class certification are met under the well-established "rigorous analysis" requirement discussed in Chapter 7, Class Certification Strategy. Given the critical importance of class certification, the encouragement of courts and commentators for the submission of a trial plan, and plaintiffs' burden, plaintiffs should carefully weigh the benefits of submitting a trial plan against any perceived disadvantage.

COMPETING STRATEGIC CONSIDERATIONS
Plaintiff's Perspective

Class counsel should begin developing a trial plan from the outset. Attention to how the case will be tried will inform important pre-trial milestones, including designation of named plaintiffs, articulation of the type and scope of claims, case budget, selection of experts, discovery, and class certification strategy.

From the outset—as early as the Rule 26(f) case planning meeting and report—class counsel must be attentive to answering the court's questions about how the case will be tried. A number of considerations will likely factor into class counsel's approach as to when and how to demonstrate the manageability of a trial:

- Scope of the claims/damages;
- Sophistication of opposing counsel;

---

5. See Feder v. Elec. Data Sys. Corp., 429 F.3d 125, 139–40 (5th Cir. 2005). Additionally, a prominent complex litigation practitioner, William Isaacson of Boies Schiller Flexner LLP, who has tried a number of high-profile class actions in recent years representing both plaintiffs and defendants, reports that he does not routinely submit trial plans, but does provide estimates of how long the trial will be, witness lists, etc., and prepares internal trial plans on how the case will be presented.

6. *See, e.g.,* Duran v. U.S. Bank, 51 Cal. 4th 1, 29 (2014).

- Proclivities of the trial court;
- Circuit law;
- Breadth of discovery record; and
- Relative strength or weakness of plaintiffs' proposed certification.

It is possible that some combination of these or other case-specific factors may push counsel to eschew a separate, formal trial plan (unless requested or required by the court). For instance, for a modest claim of a type that is frequently certified, where the trial court, opposing counsel, and circuit law are not likely to criticize absence of a formal trial plan, class counsel might legitimately prefer to avoid giving her opponent a tangible target to shoot at in the opposition brief. Why fight about jury instructions when a jury trial might be over a year away? Also, if discovery is nascent and the evidence (and even the theory of the case) are still under development, a premature attempt to outline witnesses and proofs may do more harm than good.

But in most cases class counsel should view the crafting of a tangible trial plan as an opportunity, not a burden. Thinking through the trial plan early on in the case forces class counsel to determine what evidence she will present on each element of the case. It will ensure development of a plan to obtain that evidence in discovery and investigation. A thorough trial plan shows the court that plaintiffs have thought through how they will present their case at trial, in a manageable fashion, so that the judge will understand the feasibility of the trial being proposed. If plaintiffs can do so, it will substantially advance their goal of class certification. If, on the other hand, defendants can persuade the court that the trial would face insurmountable manageability problems, they will have gone a long way toward defeating certification.

Defense Perspective

Because plaintiffs bear the burden of proof of establishing manageability, it is unlikely that the defense would propose a trial plan—at least in the first instance. Instead, the defense is more likely to (1) criticize the plaintiffs' failure to submit a trial plan (if they do not do so); or (2) attack plaintiffs' plan as either incomplete, unrealistic, unmanageable, or violative of defendant's right to defend the claims of all class members.[7]

---

7. *But see* Chapter 7, Class Action Strategy, at note 19, discussing Mullins v. Direct Digital, LLC, 795 F.3d 654, 664 (7th Cir. 2015) (district courts should deny certification based on manageability concerns only as a "last resort," and then only late in the case).

Defendant may want to push for submission of a trial plan at the certification phase in a situation where the complexity of the case, dissimilarities in necessary proofs, uniqueness of potential defenses among putative class members, and other intractable complexities exist. Doing so will give the defense a more tangible proposal to attack in opposition. Defendants' interest in encouraging a trial plan submission at the class certification phase has been summarized as follows:

> For a defendant, [a trial plan] can be a useful tool in bringing to light practical manageability problems in adjudicating the claims on a classwide basis. [I]n jurisdictions in which there is no express rule or precedent [requiring a trial plan], it may be difficult to educate a judge about what a trial plan is or why it may be useful in ensuring that the case is manageable as a class action for trial. Therefore, a defendant has two hurdles to overcome in getting the judge to order a trial plan; 1) explain what a trial plan is, why it is different than a scheduling or trial management order, and why it might be useful; and 2) then convincing the judge to exercise his or her discretion to order one.[8]

CONTEXT: THE TRIAL OF CLASS AND COLLECTIVE ACTIONS

Because of the large number of witnesses, documents, and issues involved, trials of class action cases can present challenges not presented by trial of an individual's claims. Before certifying a class under Federal Rule of Civil Procedure 23(b)(3), a trial court must consider the "difficulties in managing a class action," including whether trial of the case is practicable. In considering whether trial of a class action is practicable, trial courts often consider procedural devices, such as bifurcation of trial issues under Rule 42, or certification of specific issues under Rule 23(c)(4). If a court bifurcates issues for trial, it must ensure that the trial plan does not violate the Seventh Amendment's Re-examination Clause.[9] Although it is fairly well established that differences in

---

For an example of a request for a trial plan demonstrating the infeasibility of a class trial, *see* Espenscheid v. DirectSat USA, LLC, 705 F.3d 770, 775–76 (7th Cir. 2013) (Posner, J.)

8. Deborah R. Hensler, Nicholas M. Pace, Bonita Dombey-Moore, Beth Giddens, Jennifer Gross, & Erik K. Moller, *Class Action Dilemmas: Pursuing Public Goals for Private Gain*, RAND Corporation (2000), http://www.jstor.org/stable/10.7249/mr969icj.

9. *See* Gasoline Products v. Champlin Ref. Co., 283 U.S. 494, 500 (1931). This issue— and the historical precedents for bifurcation, use of statistical sampling, and other common class trial plan innovations—are helpfully explored in L. Walker, *A Model Plan to*

individual class members' damages do not preclude class certification,[10] and that bifurcation of liability and damages issues does not run afoul of the Seventh Amendment since those sets of issues are usually distinct and separable,[11] the trial court must be careful to ensure that a defendant has an opportunity to present individual defenses.[12]

The contours of the Seventh Amendment bifurcation issue is summarized as follows. Unless waived, the district court must preserve a litigant's right to jury resolution of claims at law, even if they are joined with equitable claims as permitted by Federal Rule of Civil Procedure 18. This is so even where the legal claim may be characterized as "incidental" to the relief sought.[13] However, a single jury does not have to determine both liability and damages where these issues are separable and distinct,[14] which may not be the case in negligence-based state law actions. In such cases, issues such as contributory negligence and proximate cause may impact both liability and damages determinations.[15] Similarly, a jury verdict that establishes liability for breach of contract but not the dates of formation and breach, or whether claimant fulfilled a duty to minimize damages, is not separable from damages.[16] These principles suggest careful attention be paid to the structure of jury verdict forms for class trial plans that propose bifurcation of liability and damages to be tried by separate juries.

Resolve Federal Class Action Cases by Jury Trial, 88 Va L. Rev. 2, 405–45 (Apr. 2002), http://www.jstor.org/stable/1074002.

10. *See, e.g.*, Tyson Foods, Inc. v. Bouaphakeo,136 S. Ct. 1036 (2016); Blackie v. Barrack, 524 F.2d 891, 905 (9th Cir. 1975); *In re* Whirlpool Corp. Front Loading Washer Prod. Liab. Litig., 722 F.3d 838 (6th Cir. 2013); Butler v. Sears, 727 F.3d 796 (7th Cir. 2013).

11. *See, e.g.*, Robinson v. Metro-North Commuter R.R. Co., 267 F.3d 147, 169 (2d Cir. 2001); *Butler*, 727 F.3d at 811.

12. *See, e.g.*, Wal-Mart v. Dukes, 564 U.S. 338, 366 (2011) (defendant entitled to individualized hearings to determine employees' eligibility for backpay under Title VII); Duran v. U.S. Bank, 59 Cal. 4th 1, 25 (2014) ("[A] class action trial management plan must permit the litigation of relevant affirmative defenses, even when these defenses turn on individual questions.") (wage and hour class action).

13. *See* Dairy Queen, Inc. v. Wood, 369 U.S. 469 (1962).

14. Gasoline Prods. Co. v. Champlin Ref. Co., 283 U.S. 494 (1931).

15. *See In re* Rhone-Poulenc Rorer Inc., 51 F.3d 1293 (7th Cir. 1995) (reversing trial court's certification of an issue class to determine special verdict of negligence in an "extraordinary" mass tort case involving HIV infection of the blood supply).

16. *Gasoline Products*, 283 U.S. at 499.

The trial of a class action will often involve the presentation of statistical proof.[17] Frequently, it will also involve anecdotal evidence[18] or representative testimony.[19] Trial of liability issues will often include testimony from defendant company witnesses and documents.[20] Class trials frequently involve competing expert testimony.

How the trial is structured will depend upon the subject matter of the claims and the specific factual issues in dispute, and the evidence regarding those issues. In general, if common evidence is relevant to prove common issues, then it is sensible and practicable to try those issue in a single phase of the trial.

POSSIBLE ELEMENTS OF A TRIAL PLAN

The standard trial practice advice, "Keep the presentation as simple as possible—but no simpler," applies to trial plans.

Standard Trial Plan Elements

Trial plans often contain some or all of the following:

- Identification of the common issues to be determined. Examples:
  - "Did defendants form an agreement in restraint of trade with respect to the sale of aluminum pipe in the United States between January 2015 and March 2016?"
  - "Did defendant cause a probability of confusion in marketing its water bottles as BPA-free?"
- If discovery has sufficiently progressed, identification of possible witnesses (by name or category) that plaintiffs plan to call, including experts
- Other common proof (e.g., documents) that plaintiffs plan to present in their case in chief to establish defendants' liability
- A description of any representative evidence to be offered on common issues

---

17. *See, e.g.*, Teamsters v. United States, 431 U.S. 324 (1977); Bell v. Farmers Ins. Ex., 87 Cal. App. 4th 805 (2001); *see also* Kaye v. Freedman, Reference Guide on Statistics in Reference Manual on Scientific Evidence (3d ed., 2011); Nagareda, *Class Certification in the Age of Aggregate Proof*, 84 N.Y.U. L. Rev. 97, 117, 151 (2009).

18. *See, e.g., Teamsters* at 338.

19. *See, e.g., Bouaphakeo*, 136 S. Ct. at 1043–44, 1046–47; Morgan v. Family Dollar, 554 F.3d 1233 (11th Cir. 2008); Anderson v. Mt. Clemens Pottery, 328 U.S. 680 (1946).

20. Morgan v. Family Dollar, 551 F.3d 1233, 1247–58 (11th Cir. 2008).

- If there are subclasses, Rule 23(c)(5), identification of same and of the witnesses, and proof directed to the claims of the subclass
- If plaintiffs seek certification of an issue class, Rule 23(c)(4), then identification of the witnesses and categories of proof directed to that issue, and an identification of the issues that are not resolved by class adjudication and a proposal of how they will be resolved
- If the plaintiffs propose bifurcation of liability and damages (or other issues), then a description of the proposed phases of issues to be tried
- Preliminary proposed verdict forms covering each common issue, each subclass, each issue class, and/or each phase determination (e.g., liability, damages)
- A discussion of whether plaintiffs propose to determine damages on an aggregate or individualized basis. If the former, a description of the plan of distribution or for the determination of a plan of distribution.[21] If the latter, a description of the proposed procedure (i.e., individualized hearings; submissions of proofs, etc.) for individualized damages determinations
- If defendant is entitled to individualized determinations of liability (e.g., for back-pay eligibility in a disparate impact Title VII case[22]), a proposed mechanism of administering such hearings
- If appropriate, proposed key jury instructions

With a reminder that trial plans are necessarily case-specific, a gathering of sample trial plans, opinions discussing them, and related materials can be found in the online Appendix at www.ambar.org /class-action-survey.

Because of the growing significance of considerations of bifurcation (effectively an issue class as to liability), and use of representative evidence, to trial plans, a more detailed discussion of these topics follows.

---

21. *Bouaphakeo* suggests that a plan of distribution need not be approved until after trial. 136 S. Ct. at 1049–50 (rejecting defendant's argument that an acceptable plan must be developed "prior to judgment" where jury awarded aggregate damages prior to the court's approval of a plan of distribution).

22. In Title VII class actions, disparate treatment claims and disparate impact claims are often tried together, but treatment claims are jury claims, and impact claims (and back pay) are tried to the judge. One needs to handle this carefully in order to avoid Seventh Amendment problems.

Bifurcation

Bifurcation is a tool frequently used to manage class action trials. Rule 42 provides that "[f]or convenience, to avoid prejudice, or to expedite and economize, the court may order a separate trial of one or more separate issues, claims, cross claims, counter claims, or third-party claims." The tests for determining whether bifurcation is appropriate balance economy and possible prejudice.[23]

District courts have broad discretion in determining whether or not to bifurcate.[24] One constraint on that discretion is that the bifurcation plan must not run afoul of the Seventh Amendment's prohibition on a second jury re-examining issues decided by a first jury.[25]

The most common form of trial bifurcation in class actions is the separation of liability issues and damages issues, with liability issues resolved first.[26] The first phase of trial addresses the defendant's liability to the class using collective evidence. The specifics will vary by the type of case. Securities fraud, antitrust, product defect, employment discrimination, and wage/hour cases have all been bifurcated into liability and damages phases.[27] In *Tyson Foods v. Bouaphakeo*,[28] the U.S. Supreme Court suggested that bifurcation of liability and damages issues might be appropriate in some class action cases.

If the class representatives fail in establishing liability, there is no need for a damages phase. If they succeed, the parties might settle. If they do not settle, the trial court will have to decide the most

---

23. *See* 9A WRIGHT & MILLER, FEDERAL PRACTICE AND PROCEDURE, Civil 3d, § 2388 (2008).

24. *See* 4 *Newberg on Class Actions* (5th ed. 2014) § 11:5, at 18, n.10 and cases cited therein.

25. Compare Robinson v. Metro-North Commuter R.R. Co., 267 F.3d 147, 170 (2d Cir. 2001) (finding no Seventh Amendment violation with bifurcation of employment discrimination class action into liability and remedy phases), *with In re* Rhone-Poulenc Rorer 51 F.3d 1293, 1303 (7th Cir. 1995) (finding that trial plan under which one jury would first determine the common issues of negligence and subsequent juries would determine comparative negligence and proximate cause violated the Seventh Amendment's Reexamination clause).

26. *Newberg on Class Actions, supra* note 25, § 11:8 at 27; *id.* § 11:6.

27. *See, e.g., In re* Farmers Ins. Ex. Claims Representations Overtime Litigation, 336 F. Supp. 2d 1077 (D. Or. 2004), *rev'd on other grounds*, 481 F. 3d 1119 (9th Cir. 2006) (wage/hour); Butler v. Sears 727 F.3d 796 (7th Cir. 2013) (product defect); *In re* New Motor Vehicles Canadian Export Antitrust Litigation, 522 F.3d 6, 28 (1st Cir. 2008) (antitrust); Eisenberg v. Gagnon, 766 F.2d 770 (3d Cir. 1985) (securities fraud); Stender v. Lucky Stores, 803 F. Supp. 259, (N.D. Cal 1992) (gender discrimination).

28. 136 S. Ct. 1036, 1050 (Mar. 22, 2016).

appropriate way of resolving damages issues. Resolution of damages issues can be either through an aggregate approach or an individualized approach.[29]

In cases where damages flow from a liability determination, bifurcation of trial might not be necessary or appropriate. For example, in a securities fraud case involving a stock traded on an efficient market, the efficient market presumption, recognized in *Basic v. Levinson*,[30] typically permits a single trial of both liability and damages. Many class trials are not bifurcated.[31]

Plaintiff's Perspective on Bifurcation

As a strategic matter, counsel for plaintiffs might not want to bifurcate liability and damages. Doing so will not be necessary if damages can be proven through company records or expert testimony. Bifurcation of liability and damages only makes sense when one needs testimony from individual class members regarding damages, such as in a wage and hour case, testimony about the amount of time spent working off the clock where representative evidence is not available to establish defendant's aggregate liability.

Defendant's Perspective on Bifurcation

Defendants may wish to resist bifurcation where (1) the challenged conduct is seen as equivocal or otherwise non-egregious, and (2) damages are dubious or marginal. In this situation defense counsel might anticipate that a single jury will more likely find in defendant's favor or award only minimum damages in consideration of what counsel perceives as a weakness in at least half of plaintiffs' case.

However, where the conduct alleged is egregious (even if damages are dubious or marginal), a defendant might benefit from bifurcation—since the second jury will not be exposed to all the evidence of alleged wrongdoing. This could lead to a smaller damages award than in a

---

29. *Compare* Bell v. Farmers Ins. Ex., 87 Cal. App. 4th 805 (2001) (aggregate approach), *with In re* Farmers Ins. Ex. Claims Representations Overtime Litigation, 336 F. Supp. 2d 1077, (D. Or. 2004) (individual approach), *rev'd on other grounds*, 481 F. 3d 1119 (9th Cir. 2006).

30. Basic v. Levinson, 485 U.S. 224 (1988).

31. § 21.24, MANUAL FOR COMPLEX LITIGATION, Fourth (Federal Judicial Center 2004) ("Selectively used, this provision [Rule 23(c)(4)—discussed later] may enable a court to achieve the economies of class action treatment for a portion of a case, the rest of which may either not qualify under Rule 23(a) or may be unmanageable as a class action.").

single, non-bifurcated trial. Likewise, in a case perceived to have weak liability but heavy damages, a defendant might benefit from bifurcation so as to minimize the risk that a sympathetic jury will "stretch" to find liability and compensate the alleged victims.

Issue Certification under Rule 23(c)(4)

Rule 23(c)(4) of the Federal Rules of Civil Procedure "recognizes that an action may be maintained as a class action as to particular issues only." It has been used in a variety of types of cases, including employment cases, and "fraud or similar case[s] [where] the action may retain its 'class' character only through the adjudication of liability to the class; the members of the class may thereafter be required to come in individually and prove the amounts of their respective claims."[32] Rule 23(c)(4) may be appropriately used to decide class-wide issues before resolving individual issues.[33] However, there might be a circuit split as to the appropriate standard to apply for certification of an issues class, with an early Fifth Circuit decision[34] holding that the entire action must satisfy predominance rather than just the issues class; several of the other circuits have disagreed[35] and several have not reached this legal issue yet or have tried to chart a middle ground, while a more recent Fifth Circuit decision raises questions about the standard in that circuit.[36]

---

32. FED. R. CIV. P. 23 Advisory Committee Notes (1966); *see also* Simon v. Philip Morris Inc., 200 F.R.D. 21, 29–30 (E.D.N.Y. 2001) ("The framers of Rule 23(c)(4)(A) considered class actions brought under Rule 23(b)(3)—characteristically disputes that involve numerous individual proofs of causation and injury—particularly well suited for certification of fewer than all issues. Their conclusion follows from the fact that Rule 23(c)(4)(A) assists in satisfying Rule 23(b)(3)'s additional class certification requirements of predominance and superiority.").

33. *See* Chiang v. Veneman, 385 F.3d 256, 267 (3d Cir. 2004) ("[C]ourts commonly use Rule 23(c)(4) to certify some elements of liability for class determination, while leaving other elements to individual adjudication—or, perhaps more realistically, settlement.").

34. *See* Castano v. Am. Tobacco Co., 84 F.3d 734, 745 n.21 (5th Cir. 1996) (reversing certification of "what may be the largest class action ever attempted in federal court," comprised of "all nicotine-dependent persons in the United States" who bought cigarettes from defendants; issue classes could not be used to "manufacture" preponderance in (b)(3) class).

35. *In re* Nassau County Strip Search Cases, 461 F.3d 219 (2d Cir. 2006); Valentino v. Carter-Wallace, Inc., 97 F.3d 1227, 1234 (9th Cir. 1996).

36. The vitality of the *Castano* holding has been eroded by that court's more recent holding that the predominance requirement can be met if proceedings are structured to establish "liability on a class-wide basis, with separate hearings to determine—if liability is established—the damages of individual class members." *In re* Deepwater Horizon, 739 F.3d at 817. *See also id.* at 805 n.66 (favorably citing Butler v. Sears, Roebuck & Co., 727

In recent years, "issue classes" certified under Rule 23(c)(4) have gained prominence as a way to resolve common issues using common evidence in a single proceeding before turning to the thornier issues of relief.[37] Courts recognize the utility of 23(c)(4) for trying class-wide liability issues even where questions of damages require individual proceedings. In his oft-cited[38] opinion in *McReynolds v. Merrill Lynch, Pierce, Fenner & Smith, Inc.*,[39] Judge Posner noted that while "hundreds of separate trials may be necessary to determine which class members were actually adversely affected by . . . the [allegedly discriminatory] practices and if so what loss each class member sustained," Rule 23(c)(4) provided a means of determining, on a class-wide basis, "whether the challenged practices were unlawful."[40] The Seventh Circuit further observed that if the litigation were to proceed as separate, individual suits, the suits would be "more complex if . . . the question whether [the defendant] ha[d] violated the antidiscrimination statutes must be determined anew in each case."[41] Because "[t]he practices challenged in [*McReynolds*] present[ed] a pair of issues that c[ould] most efficiently be determined on a class-wide basis,"[42] the court of appeals reversed the lower court's denial of class certification "under Rules 23(b)(2) and (c)(4)."[43]

The Second Circuit has similarly encouraged courts to "take full advantage of [Rule 23(c)(4)] to certify separate issues in order to reduce the range of disputed issues in complex litigation and achieve judicial

---

F.3d 796, 799 (7th Cir. 2013)). *See also* Jenkins v. Raymark Indus., 782 F.2d 468, 471 n.4 & 473 (5th Cir. 1986) (affirming certification of asbestos personal injury claimant class to resolve common "state of the art" defense, leaving determinations of exposure, causation and damages to separate trials) (factually distinguished, but not overruled, by *Castano*). *In re Deepwater Horizon, Castano* and *Jenkins* each continue to be cited as good law by courts in the Fifth Circuit.

37. *See, e.g.,* Elizabeth Chamblee Burch, *Constructing Issue Classes*, 101 VA. L. REV. 1855 (2015), http://digitalcommons.law.uga.edu/fac_artchop/1049; Rebecca S. Bjork, *Recent Developments in Issue Certification Under Rule 23(c)(4) Require Courts to Focus on Manageability of Complex Class Actions*, BLOOMBERG BNA (2013); Patricia Bronte, George Robot, & Darin M. Williams, *"Carving at the Joint": The Precise Function of Rule 23(C)(4)*, 62 DEPAUL L. REV. 745 (2013).

38. *See, e.g.,* Bjork, *supra* note 38, at text accompanying notes 20–25 (discussing *McReynolds*); Bronte et al., *supra* note 38, at 754–57 (same); Michael C. Harper, *Class Based Adjudication of Title VII Class in the Age of the Roberts Court*, 95 B.U.L. Rev. 1099 (2015).

39. 672 F.3d 482 (2012).

40. *See id.* at 491.

41. *See id.* at 492.

42. *See id.* at 491.

43. *See id.* at 492.

efficiencies."[44] Specifically, in *Robinson* the court held that the district court abused its discretion in declining to certify the liability stage of a Title VII pattern-or-practice disparate treatment case:

> [L]itigating the pattern-or-practice liability phase for the class as a whole would both reduce the range of issues in dispute and promote judicial economy. For example, if the class should succeed and, even assuming that the remedial stage is ultimately resolved on a non-class basis, the issues and evidence relevant to these individual adjudications would be substantially narrowed. . . . If, on the other hand, Metro-North succeeds at the liability stage, the question of whether it engaged in a pattern or practice of intentional discrimination that injured its African-American employees would be completely and finally determined, thereby eliminating entirely the need for a remedial stage inquiry on behalf of each class member.[45]

More recently, the court in *Houser v. Pritzker* reached the same conclusion and certified a liability and injunctive relief class under Rule 23(c)(4) in a Title VII disparate impact case.[46] The plaintiffs in *Houser* brought a case against the U.S. Census on behalf of over 250,000 minority applicants, alleging that the census's applicant screening process is racially discriminatory. Plaintiffs sought both injunctive relief and monetary damages. The trial court found that the requirements for injunctive

---

44. Robinson v. Metro–North Commuter R.R. Co., 267 F.3d 147, 167 (2d Cir. 2001) (internal alterations and citation omitted). *See, e.g.*, Robert H. Klonoff, *The Decline of Class Actions*, 90 WASH. U. L. REV. 729, 809 (2013) (noting Second Circuit's historical support of issue certification).

45. *Robinson*, 267 F.3d at 168. Post Wal-Mart v. Dukes, 564 U.S. 338 (2011), several courts within the Second Circuit have recognized the continuing vitality of this holding of *Robinson*, and have held that *Robinson* applies with equal force to disparate impact cases as well. *See, e.g.*, Easterling v. State of Connecticut Dep't of Correction, 278 F.R.D. 41, 46 (D. Conn. 2011); The Vulcan Society, Inc. v. City of New York, 276 F.R.D. 22, 34 (E.D.N.Y. 2011); Jacob v. Duane Reade, Inc, 2015 WL 525697, at *3 (affirming, in a wage-and-hour case, Rule 23(b)(3) predominance was satisfied with respect to issue of liability alone); Fort Worth Employees' Ret. Fund v. J.P. Morgan Chase & Co., 301 F.R.D. 116, 136 & 142 (S.D.N.Y. 2014) (ordering issue certification where liability could be determined with common proof, but there was no method to calculate class-wide damages). Scholarly authority supports issue certification, as well. *See, e.g.*, American Law Institute, *Principles of the Law of Aggregate Litigation* § 2.02(a)(1) (2010) (advocating issue certification where it would "materially advance the resolution of multiple civil claims by addressing the core of the dispute in a manner superior to other realistic procedural alternatives"); Manual for Complex Litigation (4th) § 21.24 (2010) ("issues-class approach contemplates a bifurcated trial where the common issues are tried first, followed by individual trials on questions such as proximate causation and damages"). *But see* Hines, *Codifying the Issue Class Action*, 16 NEV. L.J. 625, 635–38 (2016).

46. Houser v. Pritzker, 2014 U.S. Dist. LEXIS 91451 (S.D.N.Y. 2014).

relief under Rule 23(b)(2) were met and certified a liability and injunctive relief class pursuant to Rule 23(c)(4), which would "materially advance the litigation and make the proceedings more manageable."[47] After resolution of the liability issues, the court can determine the best way to handle relief issues:

> If and when the litigation reaches that stage, the Court will have a number of management tools at its disposal to help resolve these issues. For example, the Court could appoint a special master to preside over individual damages proceedings, or could decertify the class after the liability phase and provide notice to plaintiffs as to how to proceed to prove damages. There is no need to decide at this time which avenue to pursue. What is important is that the Court has the tools to handle any management difficulties that may arise at the remedial phase of this litigation.[48]

Outside the employment context, appellate courts have applied the same reasoning in awarding or upholding Rule 23(c)(4) certification.[49]

In sum, the practice point is this: consider the possible advantages and disadvantages of bifurcation of liability and damages, or other possible issue class(es), in light of the governing standards in your jurisdiction.

The Teamsters Model

The Supreme Court sanctioned an important trial plan model for the phasing of a pattern-or-practice employment discrimination suit in *International Brotherhood of Teamsters v. United States.*[50] This model may be helpful in devising trial plans in other substantive areas as well. As is typical in Title VII pattern-or-practice suits, the question of individ-

---

47. *Id.* at 85.

48. *Id.* at *85–86 (citation omitted).

49. *See In re* Deepwater Horizon, 739 F.3d 790, 816 (5th Cir. 2014) (certification can be "accomplished by means of multi-phase trials under Rule 23(c)(4), which permits district courts to limit class treatment to 'particular issues' and reserve other issues for individual determination"); Butler v. Sears, Roebuck & Co., 727 F.3d 796, 800 (7th Cir. 2013) ("[A] class action limited to determining liability on a class-wide basis, with separate hearings to determine-if liability is established-the damages of individual class members, or homogenous groups of class members, is permitted by Rule 23(c)(4) and will often be the sensible way to proceed."); *In re* Whirlpool Corp. Front-Loading Washer Prods. Liab. Litig., 722 F.3d 838, 860 (6th Cir. 2013) ("Where determinations on liability and damages have been bifurcated, *see* FED. R. CIV. P. 23(c)(4), the decision in *Comcast*—to reject certification of a liability and damages class because plaintiffs failed to establish that damages could be measured on a classwide basis—has limited application.").

50. 431 U.S. 324, 360–62 (1977).

ual relief does not arise until the plaintiffs first demonstrate class-wide liability, that is, that the employer has followed an employment policy of unlawful discrimination[51]—which is essentially the same sort of bifurcation that occurs under Rule 23(c)(4).[52]

Courts have commonly bifurcated *Teamsters* pattern-or-practice cases under Rule 42(b).[53] At least one court, however, has tied the *Teamsters* bifurcation procedure to Rule 23(c)(4).[54] In *Robinson v. Metro-N. Commuter R.R. Co.*, the Second Circuit held that the lower court erred in failing to bifurcate the pattern-or-practice claim and to certify the liability stage of the claim under Rule 23(b)(2).[55] In so doing, the court relied upon Rule 23(c)(4)(A),[56] noting that "[d]istrict courts should take full advantage of th[is] provision to certify separate issues in order . . . to reduce the range of disputed issues in complex litigation and achieve judicial efficiencies."[57] Whether applied in conjunction with Rule 42(b) or Rule 23(c)(4), *Teamsters* provides an accepted process for bifurcation in pattern-or-practice cases. In *Wal-Mart*, the Supreme Court expressly reaffirmed continuing validity of the *Teamsters* procedure.[58]

Under the *Teamsters'* procedure, if the plaintiffs succeed in the liability phase in establishing that discrimination was the company's standard operating procedure, then there is rebuttable presumption that all class members were victims of the discriminatory policy and practice. The defendant has the opportunity in the relief stage to rebut that inference and establish that a particular individual was treated as he or she was for legitimate, nondiscriminatory reasons.[59] In *Teamsters*, the government used statistical evidence to establish a pattern and practice of discrimination.[60] The defendant had an opportunity to rebut the government's statistics. The government also bolstered its statistical evidence

---

51. *See id.* at 361.
52. *See, e.g.*, United States v. City of New York, 07-2067, 2013 U.S. Dist. LEXIS 166616, *7–8 (E.D.N.Y. Oct. 28, 2013) (describing procedure for special masters to determine class members' eligibility for damages).
53. *See, e.g.*, Eastland v. Tennessee Valley Auth., 704 F.2d 613, 616 (11th Cir. 1983).
54. Robinson v. Metro-N Commuter R.R. Co., 267 F.3d 147 (2d Cir. 2001), *abrogated on other grounds* by Wal-Mart Stores, Inc. v. Dukes, 131 S. Ct. 2541 (2011).
55. *See Robinson*, 267 F.3d at 167.
56. In 2007, Rule 23 was amended to make "stylistic" changes, and what had been 23(c)(4)(A) and (B) were respectively changed to 23(c)(4), addressing issue classes, and 23(c)(5), addressing subclasses. *See* Committee Notes to Fed. R. Civ. P. 23 (2007).
57. *Id.* (internal quotation marks omitted).
58. *Wal-Mart*, 131 S. Ct. at 2552, 2555.
59. *Teamsters* at 361.
60. 431 U.S. at 337–40.

with the testimony of over 40 specific instances of discrimination that "brought the cold numbers convincingly to life."[61]

While *Teamsters* concerns discrimination claims, Title VII case law can serve as persuasive precedent for analogous approaches in other types of cases. For instance, in *Bouaphakeo*, the U.S. Supreme Court re-affirmed that statistical evidence (statistical analysis based on time studies pertaining to a subset of the class) and representative testimony can be used to establish both aggregate liability and damages in class and collective actions. The Court noted that the specific use of statistical evidence and representative testimony will depend on the evidence being introduced and the issue for which it is being introduced: "Whether and when statistical evidence can be used to establish class wide liability will depend on the purpose for which the evidence is being introduced and on the 'elements of the underlying cause of action.'"[62]

Representative Testimony

A central component of any class trial is the evidence offered by individual named and absent class members. Each side must evaluate how to maximize the effectiveness (or mitigate the impact) of such testimony.

In *Anderson v. Mt. Clemens Pottery Co.*,[63] the U.S. Supreme Court recognized the appropriateness of representative testimony from a few collective action members in the trial of a collective action. In *Morgan v. Family Dollar*, the Eleventh Circuit re-affirmed the continuing validity of that holding, emphasizing the "general rule" that "not all employees have to testify to prove overtime violations."[64] In *Morgan*, seven of the 1,424 collective action members testified. In addition to representative testimony, plaintiffs presented testimony from company managers and evidence from company documents, including payroll records.[65] Similar to the anecdotal testimony in *Teamsters*, the representative testimony in *Morgan v. Family Dollar* was only a portion of the evidence plaintiffs used to prove liability and entitlement to damages.

---

61. *Id.* at 330.
62. Tyson Foods, Inc. v. Bouaphakeo, 136 S. Ct. 1036, 1040 (2016).
63. 328 U.S. 680, 687–88 (1946).
64. *Family Dollar*, 551 F.3d at 1279.
65. *Id.* at 1247–58.

Plaintiffs' Perspective on Representative Testimony

How many class members the plaintiffs call as witnesses in a class action trial is subject to a number of strategic considerations. If the class member testimony is simply anecdotal, and meant to bring other evidence to life, then there is no set number that needs to be called. The witnesses who are called should be articulate and sympathetic. The jury should identify with them and believe that they suffered a real harm.[66]

Whether unnamed class members who testify at trial are deposed before they testify is an issue that should be clarified at a pre-trial conference. If trial witness lists are exchanged after the close of discovery, it might be that the defendant does not get to depose the absent class member trial witness. In some class action trials, class counsel called unnamed class member witnesses at trial whom defendants had not deposed.[67] Some judges, however, might insist on the exchange of preliminary witness lists before the close of discovery, or might allow depositions of trial witnesses disclosed after the close of discovery.

Beyond absent class member testimony, plaintiffs must carefully consider additional evidence concerning absent class members. Experts, for example, frequently provide testimony regarding the class as a whole, to determine liability or damages. In planning this testimony, class counsel should consider whether, and to what extent, it may "open the door" to defense introduction of absent class member testimony that may be exculpatory.

Defendant's Perspective on Representative Testimony

The experiences of absent class members might be used strategically by defendants as well. In a representative action, such as a class action, the claims of the named plaintiffs are supposed to be tried to "stand in" for absent class members.[68] Rule 23 is

> designed to ensure that "the common bond between the class representatives' claims and those of the class is strong enough so that it is fair for the

---

66. Because an expert witness will need to testify to a valid scientific basis for any evidence based on a statistical sample, in most class action cases the testimony of class members will only be anecdotal, and not part of a precise statistical sample.

67. *See, e.g., In re* Farmers Ins. Ex. Claims Representations Overtime Litigation, 336 F. Supp. 2d 1077 (D. Or. 2004); Pryor v. KBR, JAMS Ref. No. 1100052926, (N.D. Cal. JAMS Nov. 2013); and Keller v. CSU, CGC 490977 (S.F. Sup. Ct. Apr. 2015).

68. *In re* Pharm. Indus. Average Wholesale Price Litig., 582 F.3d 156, 195 (1st Cir. 2009) ("class-action litigation often *requires* the district court to extrapolate from the class representatives to the entire class") (emphasis in original).

fortunes of the class members to rise or fall with the fortunes of the class representatives."[69]

It is for this reason that the trial court is to "rigorously" analyze the requirements of commonality, typicality, and adequacy before certifying the case for class treatment.

Nevertheless, some trial courts have permitted defendants to present testimony regarding absent class members' experiences with the product, service, or conduct at issue. Defendants may argue to the trial judge that class counsel has "cherry picked" named plaintiffs to present a distorted view of class liability, and that defendant should be permitted to depose and call some number of absent class members to present a more balanced record.

The experiences of absent class members may be a focus of defense argument or testimony even if absent class members are not called. A prominent example is the bellwether trial on behalf of a class of Ohio residents in the front-loading washing machine case, *Glazer v. Whirlpool*. Defendant obtained a ruling shortly before trial that plaintiffs were required to prove that each of 21 models of defendant's washing machines were defective—including models not purchased by the named plaintiffs. This permitted defense counsel during trial—in opening, cross examination of plaintiffs' experts, and closing—to argue that plaintiffs had failed to sustain their burden as to models purchased by absent class members (and that this failure doomed the plaintiffs' entire claim).[70]

Each case is unique, but for trial plan purposes it is important to recognize that the issue of testimony, other proof, and argument concerning absent class member at trial is one that raises a number of issues that can significantly impact either plaintiffs or defendants. It is a topic with which most trial judges are not likely to be intimately familiar. Class and defense counsel would do well, therefore, to look for opportunities to advocate and to set the permissible boundaries well in advance of trial.

---

69. Cooper v. Southern Co., 390 F.3d 695, 713 (11th Cir. 2004) (citation omitted), *overruled in part on other grounds*, Ash v. Tyson Foods, Inc., 546 U.S. 454 (2006). *See also* Hansberry v. Lee, 311 U.S. 32, 42–43 (1940) ("It is familiar doctrine of the federal courts that members of a class not present as parties to the litigation may be bound by the judgment where they are in fact adequately represented by parties who are present . . . .").

70. Plaintiffs filed a post-trial appeal claiming error in part on this basis. Glazer v. Whirlpool, Inc., Case No. 14-4184 (6th Cir. Dec. 3, 2014). The case settled on appeal.

CONCLUSION

Like most civil cases, class action cases most often settle before trial. But there have been enough class action trials, in cases involving a sufficient variety of claims, to know that trials of class actions are manageable in many cases.[71]

To assist the trial court in understanding whether and how a class trial would work, a trial plan submitted with the motion to certify is a useful tool. Of course, the trial plan will also provide the defendant a concrete opportunity to persuade the court how and why the plan submitted by the plaintiff falls short—by presenting manageability issues or violating the defendant's right to defend particularized issues not subject to common proofs. From both the plaintiff and defense perspective, the sooner a trial plan is proposed, the sooner the parties can focus their legal theories, discovery, expert witness development, and case strategy to further their respective clients' interests.

---

71. See "Roundup of Recent Class Action Trials, 2016 to 2018," E. Cabraser and F. Vincent (Feb. 28, 2018), ABA Litigation Section, Class Actions & Derivative Suits committee Winter 2018 newsletter, *available at* https://www.americanbar.org/groups/litigation/commit tees/class-actions/articles/2018/winter2018-roundup-recent-class-actions-trials-2016-2018. html (membership required). *See also, e.g.*, Krakauer v. Dish Network L.L.C., No.1:14-CV-333, 2017 WL 2455095 (M.D.N.C. June 6, 2017) ($20 million TCPA verdict); *In re* Apple Ipod Itunes Antitrust Litigation, Case No. C 05-00037 (N.D. Cal. 2014) (defense verdict); Gutierrez v. Wells Fargo Bank, 704 F.3d 712 (9th Cir. 2012) (affirming in part and reversing in part finding of liability based on state law consumer protection statute after two-week bench trial); Velez v. Novartis Pharm. Corp., Case No. 04-9194 (S.D.N.Y. 2010) ($253 million employment discrimination verdict); *In re* Scrap Metal Antitrust Litig., 527 F.3d 517 (6th Cir. 2008) (affirming verdict and $20 million damages award); *In re* Farmers Ins. Ex. Claims Representations Overtime Litigation, 336 F. Supp. 2d 1077 (D. Or. 2004), *rev'd on other grounds*, 481 F.3d 1119 (9th Cir. 2006) (vacating $52.5 million FLSA bench trial verdict); *In re* High Pressure Laminates Antitrust Litig., No. 00 MDL 1368 (CLB), 2006 U.S. Dist. LEXIS 29431 (S.D.N.Y. May 15, 2006) (denying motion Rule 50 motion after plaintiffs' proofs in antitrust case, prior to defense verdict); Cnty. St. Clair v. Ford Motor Co., Illinois 20th Circuit Court (2004) (trial court case no. unknown); on appeal, 355 Ill. App. 3d 1209, 319 Ill. Dec. 318, 885 N.E.2d 589 (2005) (defense verdict in Ford Motor Company Police Interceptor products liability class action brought on behalf of Illinois police); Stender v. Lucky Stores, 803 F. Supp. 259 (N.D. Cal. 1992) (bench trial of Title VII race and gender discrimination claims); *In re* TFT-LCD (Flat Panel) Antitrust Litigation, MDL No. 1827 (N.D. Cal 2012) (antitrust); in *In re* FPI/Agretech Securities Litigation, MDL No 763 (D. HI 1990) (jury verdict of $25 million in favor of class against accounting firm in securities fraud action).

11

How to Properly Use and Attack Experts in Class Actions

Fred B. Burnside and Rebecca J. Francis

"Expert evidence can be both powerful and quite misleading because of the difficulty in evaluating it. Because of this risk, the judge . . . exercises more control over experts than over lay witnesses."[1] These principles hold equally true in the class action context, where expert testimony is often critical at multiple stages of the litigation: at class certification, to show whether the proposed class can satisfy commonality and, in a class action seeking damages, the predominance of common questions; at the merits stage, to assist in determining whether the class has shown class-wide liability (such as causation or the fact of injury); and at trial, to evaluate whether the class can establish damages on a class-wide basis, without violating the defendant's due process rights. Because class certification often occurs before discovery has closed, class action litigants face the challenge of identifying, at an early stage of the litigation, what type of expert testimony "will help the trier of fact to understand the evidence or to determine a fact in issue," and what type of

---

1. Daubert v. Merrell Dow Pharms., Inc., 509 U.S. 579, 595 (1993).

expert will be effective in communicating or debunking the information at issue in a helpful way.[2]

In this chapter, we provide an overview of some of the ways in which plaintiffs and defense counsel may choose to use experts in class actions, the types of experts that are often used, application of *Daubert* at the class certification stage, and issues surrounding the use of experts at trial. In doing so, we have focused on federal law, because of the abundance of cases, the guidance from the U.S. Supreme Court, and the fact that many states find federal class action cases and rules persuasive. Plaintiffs and defense counsel, however, should always consult the applicable local and state law and rules in deciding whether, when, and how to use expert testimony in class action litigation.

> Experts are often critical at multiple stages of litigation: at class certification, to show whether the proposed class can satisfy commonality and, in a class action seeking damages, the predominance of common questions; at the merits stage, to assist in determining whether the class has shown class-wide liability (such as causation or the fact of injury); and at trial, to evaluate whether the class can establish damages on a class-wide basis, without violating the defendant's due process rights.

DETERMINING THE NEED FOR AND TYPE OF EXPERT

The first question both plaintiffs and defense counsel face is whether an expert is needed and, if so, what type of expert. In evaluating these issues, counsel should analyze their litigation strategy and budget, the potential exposure, the client's goals, the type of expert appropriate for the stage of litigation, and the substantive areas of expertise that could be relevant. In particular, because experts can be expensive, defense counsel should consider whether a corporate representative (fact witness) could effectively address some or all of the topics that would otherwise be covered by an expert—without appearing unduly biased—potentially obviating the need for a costly expert witness.

---

2. FED. R. EVID. 702(a).

Consulting/Non-Testifying Experts versus Testifying Experts

Generally speaking, there are two types of experts: consulting/non-testifying experts, and testifying experts. The difference between these two is material. A consulting/non-testifying expert will not appear in the proceedings but may advise counsel, interpret evidence, or assist in developing litigation strategy. Under Federal Rule of Civil Procedure 26(b)(4)(D), the opposing party cannot take discovery of a consulting/non-testifying expert's opinions or knowledge, except on a showing of "exceptional circumstances." As a result, counsel's communications with a consulting/non-testifying expert should remain work-product protected and not subject to disclosure.

In contrast, Federal Rule of Civil Procedure 26(a)(2) requires parties to identify testifying experts who will submit testimony into the court record, including by providing signed written reports that describe the bases for the opinions stated in the reports, the data considered, professional qualifications, and compensation (among other things), and live testimony. Opposing counsel may depose a testifying expert.[3] In addition, while a testifying expert's draft reports are work-product protected under federal law (but not necessarily state law), not all communications between counsel and a testifying expert receive such protection.[4] Counsel should always consult the applicable rules to understand the scope of potential discovery into the communications and information exchanged with consulting/non-testifying and testifying experts, and into a testifying expert's prior drafts.

Counsel should ensure compliance with any court order or rule establishing deadlines for disclosing testifying experts. Similarly, defense counsel in particular should be mindful of the risks of not disclosing rebuttal experts until a rebuttal deadline. A judge could exclude such an expert, or strictly limit their testimony to purely rebuttal testimony, even if the defendant does not bear the burden of proof on the issues on which the expert intends to opine.

When to Use Expert Testimony

Once counsel understands whether the case requires a consulting or testifying expert (or both), plaintiffs and defense counsel must each consider the stage of the proceeding at which to use expert testimony.

---

3. FED. R. CIV. P. 26(b)(4)(A).
4. FED. R. CIV. P. 26(b)(4)(B)-(C).

At class certification, the focus is on whether the proposed class satisfies the standards for certification in Rule 23. As one commentator has emphasized, "[E]xpert testimony and analyses often are an important part of the class certification submission of both the proponent and opponent of class certification."[5] This is particularly true in proposed damages class actions under Rule 23(b)(3), as well as in class actions in many substantive areas of law, such as antitrust, securities, environmental, and employment/labor class actions.

While the Rule 23 analysis will often overlap with certain merits considerations, both plaintiffs and defense counsel should analyze whether additional or different expert testimony will be required to prove or defend the merits post-certification, whether at summary judgment or at trial. Parties may decide they need additional or different expert testimony for a variety of reasons: class certification and merits analyses generally raise different questions; class certification often occurs before merits discovery has completed; or the court may have certified a narrower or differently defined class than that which plaintiffs originally proposed, among other possible scenarios. In these circumstances, both plaintiffs and defense counsel must remain particularly mindful of the deadlines in the case schedule or under the rules for disclosing testifying experts.

Areas of Expertise, Qualifications, and Scope

In addition to evaluating the need for a consulting versus testifying expert, and for assessing the stage of the proceedings at which the expert opinions will be needed, counsel must determine the area of substantive expertise required. Common areas of substantive expertise for class actions include statisticians, economists, securities and commodities experts, engineers, medical and epidemiology experts, environmental experts, survey experts, and social scientists. Expert testimony is not appropriate or admissible on legal conclusions, however, such as whether the proposed class satisfies the certification requirements in Rule 23, or what the legal standards or requirements are for the class to prevail on the merits of the claims.

Once counsel has decided on the area of expertise needed, counsel must evaluate the expert's qualifications, scope of testimony, and

---

5. 1 Joseph M. McLaughlin, McLaughlin on Class Actions § 3:14, at 469 (13th ed. 2016).

credibility, to prepare for defeating a challenge under *Daubert v. Merrell Dow Pharmaceuticals, Inc.*, and ultimately, for persuading the fact finder. Under Federal Rule of Evidence 702, an expert must be qualified "by knowledge, skill, experience, training, or education," must use "reliable principles and methods," and must "reliably appl[y] the principles and methods to the facts of the case." Counsel should thoroughly research a potential expert's experience providing expert testimony, as well as the expert's qualifications and substantive expertise. An expert who has been excluded from providing similar testimony, or who is a serial expert, may be particularly vulnerable to a *Daubert* challenge, or may lack the credibility needed to be effective.

USES FOR EXPERTS IN CLASS ACTIONS

Once counsel determines a need for an expert witness and the type of expert witness needed, counsel must decide how to use the expert, and how to prepare for challenges to the admissibility of expert testimony. We address these subjects in more depth in this section.

Use of Consulting Experts in Pre-filing Investigation or Early Case Evaluation and Discovery Planning

Plaintiffs' counsel may need to retain a consulting expert to assist with pre-filing investigation, and both plaintiffs and defense counsel may decide an expert's assistance with early case evaluation and discovery planning outweighs the financial cost of retaining a consulting expert. For instance, a consulting expert could assist plaintiffs' counsel in pleading plausible allegations of commonality and predominance, including in beginning to set the stage for how the class might attempt to prove liability and, if relevant, damages, on a class-wide basis. In turn, a consulting expert could assist defense counsel in identifying, early on, strengths and weaknesses in plaintiffs' proposed class definition and in plaintiffs' liability or damages theories, advise on public perception or public relations concerns, and assist in evaluating potential exposure, the last of which can often be critical in determining defense strategy.

Examples of ways in which the right consulting expert might assist counsel in the pre-filing and early case assessment stages include:

- Researching publicly available materials and information, such as publicly available data about health care reimbursement rates, consumer complaints/reports in product liability/consumer class actions, false advertising complaints with the Better Business Bureau in false advertising class actions, publicly disclosed securities/commodities/trading information;

- Reviewing manuals and technical service bulletins, employer policies, insurance plans, or medical records;
- Reviewing materials obtained through FOIA or public records act requests; and/or
- Conducting surveys or tests.

An expert who assists in such pre-filing investigation efforts may also be well equipped to help counsel identify categories of information to seek from opposing and third parties in discovery. This, in turn, would assist counsel in preparing for early conferences with the court, or with opposing counsel, on how discovery should proceed, including whether discovery should be phased, the extent to which third-party discovery will be needed, and the nature and scope of information to be requested from and exchanged between the parties. From a defense perspective, early insight into the type of discovery that might be needed could help the defendant in obtaining a more offensive position on discovery, rather than the reactionary, defensive position that too often occurs.

In addition, depending on the scope of information available to the expert and the extent to which the expert can reach opinions pre-filing, plaintiffs' counsel may want to consider whether to include the expert's opinions or findings in the class action complaint. Doing so could help insulate the class action complaint from challenges under Rule 12(b)(6) to the sufficiency of the allegations, or to early motions to strike class allegations, but could also expose the expert to broader discovery than would otherwise be allowed for purely consulting experts. On the flip side, in certain technical or complex cases, a defendant intending to respond to a complaint with an answer might also consider attaching an expert report rebutting allegations in the complaint. Again, doing so could expose the expert to discovery, but that risk may be outweighed by the potential benefit of developing a counter narrative early in the case.

As mentioned earlier, consulting experts whom counsel do not intend to designate as testifying experts are generally subject to heightened work-product protections and need not be disclosed in the manner required for testifying experts. This gives counsel and the expert additional flexibility in determining the ultimate role in the case for the expert, without inhibiting their ability to work together to identify areas of investigation and theories to pursue. However, if counsel decides to use the consulting expert as a testifying expert, counsel must comply with the applicable disclosure and discovery rules and deadlines. Further, if counsel supplies a declaration or affidavit from the consulting expert in support of a motion filed with the court, the consulting expert's opinions and the facts known to him/her may become discoverable.[6] And, at least some federal courts have held that when the testifying expert relies on the consulting expert's expertise to form the report, the consulting expert's facts and opinions prepared in anticipation for of litigation or trial may become discoverable.[7] Counsel should always review and understand the law of the relevant jurisdiction to ensure attorney-client privileged and work-product protected information remains protected.

Role for Experts at Class Certification

In many class actions, expert testimony will play a central role at class certification, as plaintiffs attempt to demonstrate they can prove complex claims and theories, such as antitrust price-fixing, unpaid wages, product liability, or securities fraud claims, through common proof. Meanwhile, defendants mainly face the task of attempting to debunk the methodologies and principles on which plaintiffs' expert relies to show neither establishes a means of proving absent class members' claims through common, generalized proof. Courts, then, are often placed in the position of having to assess expert submissions even before merits discovery has completed. This section addresses plaintiffs' strategy, defendants' strategy, disclosure of experts, and the application of *Daubert* at the class certification stage.

Plaintiffs' Strategy for Using Experts at Class Certification

In a series of class action decisions since 2011, the U.S. Supreme Court has made clear that courts should not grant class certification where the plaintiff:

---

6. *See, e.g.*, Positive Techs., Inc. v. Sony Elecs., Inc., 2013 WL 1402337, at *2–3 (N.D. Cal. Apr. 5, 2013) (discussing cases).

7. *See, e.g.*, Uncommon, LLC v. Spigen, Inc., __ F. Supp. 3d __ , 2018 WL 1469049, at *10 (N.D. Ill. Mar. 26, 2018) (collecting cases); Dura Auto. Sys. of Ind., Inc. v. CTS Corp., 285 F.3d 609, 614 (7th Cir. 2002).

(a) attempts to use statistical, survey, or anecdotal evidence and a "trial by formula" theory to circumvent the lack of a common policy or other common questions; or

(b) fails to identify, in proposed Rule 23(b)(3) classes, a methodology for proving class-wide damages on the claims to be certified; or

(c) proposes, in a Rule 23(b)(3) class only, a methodology for proving class damages that could not be relied on in individual litigation.[8]

The Court has repeatedly emphasized that Rule 23

"does not set forth a mere pleading standard." Rather, a party must not only "be prepared to prove that there are *in fact* sufficiently numerous parties, common questions of law or fact," typicality of claims or defenses, and adequacy of representation, as required by Rule 23(a).[9]

These decisions have arguably heightened the bar for class certification. It is now clear that plaintiffs "'must affirmatively demonstrate . . . compliance' with Rule 23" with evidence.[10] Similarly, the Court has clarified that to engage in the "rigorous analysis" required under Rule 23, courts may well need to "probe behind the pleadings" to the underlying merits.[11] Although this does not mean plaintiffs must prove at class certification that they will or are likely to win on the merits, it does mean courts must consider the merits when necessary to rigorously analyze the Rule 23 certification factors.[12] The Court's recent class certification decisions may well have caused expert testimony to assume an increasingly important role for plaintiffs at the class certification stage.

Plaintiffs' counsel should therefore carefully analyze the class action factors for which expert testimony may be needed, and the substantive area of expertise that will provide the best fit for the liability and damages theories plaintiffs intend to present. A closer examination of the successes and pitfalls of plaintiffs in the *Dukes*, *Comcast*, and *Tyson Foods* cases illustrates well the strategy considerations plaintiffs must make

8. *See* Wal-Mart Stores, Inc. v. Dukes, 564 U.S. 338, 355–56, 367 (2011) (lack of a common policy); Comcast Corp. v. Behrend, 569 U.S. 27, 34 (2013) (failure to identify methodology for proving class-wide damages for liability theory); Tyson Foods, Inc. v. Bouaphakeo, 136 S. Ct. 1036, 1046–47 (2016).

9. *Comcast*, 133 S. Ct. at 1432 (quoting *Dukes*, 564 U.S. at 350).

10. *Id.* (quoting *Dukes*, 564 U.S. at 350).

11. *Id.* (quoting *Dukes*, 564 U.S. at 350).

12. *See Tyson Foods*, 136 S. Ct. at 1049 (recognizing merits determinations remain for the jury); Kleen Prods. LLC v. Int'l Paper Co., 831 F.3d 919, 931 (7th Cir. 2016) ("the fact that class certification decisions must be supported by evidence does not mean that certification is possible only for a party who can demonstrate that it will win on the merits").

in developing expert testimony on class certification, and the ways in which plaintiffs may seek to use expert testimony to satisfy Rule 23's requirements. We discuss each of these cases and the lessons to be learned from them.

Dukes: Trial by Formula—Part 1 In *Dukes*, the Court reversed certification under Rule 23(b)(2) of a nationwide class of employees alleging discrimination under Title VII because the class had failed to prove commonality under Rule 23(a)(2). There, plaintiffs alleged Wal-Mart discriminated against female employees, but Wal-Mart had no such common policy. Rather, it gave local supervisors discretion over employment matters.[13] To prove common questions of law or fact under Rule 23(a)(2) despite the lack of a common policy, plaintiffs presented (a) anecdotal reports of discrimination, as well as (b) statistical evidence of pay and promotion disparities at the regional and national levels, offered through a statistician and labor economist, and (c) the expert testimony of a sociologist, who had conducted a "social framework analysis" of Wal-Mart's "culture" and "personnel practices."[14] The Ninth Circuit envisioned a scenario where a "sample set of class members would be selected, as to whom liability for sex discrimination and the backpay owing as a result would be determined in depositions supervised by a master."[15]

> The percentage of claims determined to be valid would then be applied to the entire remaining class, and the number of (presumptively) valid claims thus derived would be multiplied by the average backpay award in the sample set to arrive at the entire class recovery—without further individualized proceedings.[16]

The Court found the anecdotal evidence insufficiently representative, rejected the statistical evidence as failing to "raise the inference" of a company-wide policy of discrimination "at the store and district level," and viewed the sociologist's proposed methodology to be an improper "Trial by Formula."[17] In particular, the Court criticized the "Trial by Formula" approach because it would allow class members to use statistical evidence to gloss over variations in employment policies,

---

13. *Dukes*, 564 U.S. at 355.
14. *Id.* at 346.
15. *Id.* at 367.
16. *Id.*
17. *Id.* at 357–58, 367.

practices, experiences, and injuries, thereby enlarging class members' substantive rights (i.e., allowing them to obtain relief in a class that they could not obtain in an individual suit), in violation of the Rules Enabling Act, 28 U.S.C. § 2072(b).[18] In addition, the "Trial by Formula" approach improperly deprived the defendant of its right to "litigate its statutory defenses to individual claims."[19]

Tyson Foods: Trial by Formula—Part 2 When the Court accepted certiorari in *Tyson Foods*, the defense bar hoped the Court would categorically ban the trial by formula approach to proving aggregate damages. It did not. In *Tyson Foods*, workers at a pork processing plant brought a putative class action seeking compensation under Iowa's wage statute, and a collective action under the Fair Labor Standards Act (FLSA), for time spent donning and doffing protective gear. To recover on their claims, plaintiffs had to prove that (1) their time spent working—inclusive of donning and doffing—exceeded 40 hours per week; and (2) Tyson did not compensate them fully for that time.

At the class certification stage, Tyson argued that because the donning and doffing time varied among employees, some class members would not meet the 40-hour threshold necessary to sustain a claim, barring certification. Plaintiffs, however, presented an expert providing statistical evidence about the time it took employees to don and doff. Although the study showed some variation in donning and doffing times, including significant variation between two departments, the expert opined on the average donning and doffing times for employees in each of the departments. The district court certified two classes, finding "there were common questions susceptible to classwide resolution, such as 'whether the donning and doffing of [protective gear] is considered work under the FLSA," and whether such work is compensable and not de minimis.[20]

At trial, plaintiffs' industrial relations expert presented representative evidence of the average time it took employees to don and doff protective gear in certain departments, which he based on employee testimony, video recordings, and a study he conducted of 744 videotaped observations.[21] A second expert used this average to opine on the

---

18. *Id.* at 367.
19. *Id.*
20. *Tyson Foods*, 136 S. Ct. at 1043.
21. *Id.*

estimated amount of uncompensated time each employee worked, and to identify some 212 employees who did not meet the 40-hour threshold.[22] Plaintiffs argued their expert testimony supported an aggregate damages award of $6.7 million.[23] The jury returned a special verdict form, cutting the damages award by more than half, awarding around $2.9 million to the class, and Tyson appealed.[24]

The key issue before the Supreme Court was whether plaintiffs could use statistical evidence to prove that, inclusive of donning and doffing time, the workers were working over 40 hours per week without overtime pay. Tyson argued the time spent donning and doffing varied significantly among the individual plaintiffs, even within departments, making it impossible to prove liability class wide (even before reaching the issue of allocating damages) without representative sampling, which Tyson argued was not permitted. The Supreme Court disagreed, declining to adopt a categorical ban on such representative evidence. It reasoned that its long-standing precedent in FLSA actions, starting with *Anderson v. Mt. Clemens Pottery Co.*,[25] creates a presumption in favor of employees when an employer fails to keep the records necessary to resolve a labor dispute. Under *Mt. Clemens*, in these circumstances an FLSA plaintiff will be deemed to have

> carried out his burden if he proves that he has in fact performed work for which he was improperly compensated and if he produces sufficient evidence to show the amount and extent of that work as a matter of just and reasonable inference.[26]

In other words, in the context of an FLSA case where the employer admitted it failed to keep records sufficient to allow computation of donning and doffing times, the Court has sanctioned the use of statistical analysis "to fill an evidentiary gap."[27]

But the Court clarified that even then, plaintiffs may not rely on representative evidence to prove class claims unless each class member could have relied on that same sample to establish liability in an individual action.[28] And it reached the rather unremarkable conclusion

---

22. *Id.* at 1043–44.
23. *Id.* at 1044.
24. *Id.*
25. 328 U.S. 680 (1946).
26. *Id.* at 1047 (quoting *Mt. Clemens*, 328 U.S. at 687).
27. *Id.*
28. *Id.* at 1046–47.

that "[w]hether a representative sample may be used to establish class-wide liability will depend on the purpose for which the sample is being introduced and on the underlying cause of action."[29] So, while *Tyson Foods* suggests representative evidence may be appropriate in some FLSA actions, "[t]he fairness and utility of statistical methods in context other than those presented [in *Tyson Foods*] will depend on facts and circumstances particular to those cases."[30]

Comcast: *Damages Model Must Derive from Liability Theory—Part 3*

Despite the open-endedness of *Tyson Foods*, plaintiffs' counsel should be careful to avoid reading *Tyson Foods* so broadly as to run afoul of *Comcast*, which requires plaintiffs to show that their model for proving and calculating damages on a class-wide basis flows from the liability theory on which they base their claims. In *Comcast*, a class of over two million current and former Comcast subscribers alleged Comcast committed various antitrust violations and "proposed four theories of antitrust impact," three of which the district court rejected.[31] At class certification, plaintiffs relied on the testimony of an expert who had "designed a regression model comparing actual cable prices in" the particular market with hypothetical prices to prove predominance.[32] The expert did not, however, "isolate damages resulting from any one theory of antitrust impact"—that is, the expert did not devise a methodology that calculated aggregate damages flowing from the only antitrust impact theory remaining in the case.[33] As a result, the Court held the expert's "model [fell] far short of establishing that damages are capable of measurement on a classwide basis."[34] In the Court's words: "[A]t the class-certification stage (as at trial), any model supporting a plaintiff's damages case must be consistent with its liability case, particularly with respect to the alleged anticompetitive effect of the violation."[35]

---

29. *Id.* at 1049.
30. *Id.*
31. 133 S. Ct. 1426, 1430–31 (2013).
32. *Id.* at 1431.
33. *Id.*
34. *Id.* at 1433.
35. *Id.* (quoting ABA Section of Antitrust Law, *Proving Antitrust Damages: Legal & Economic Issues* 57, 62 (2d ed. 2010)).

Post-Dukes, Tyson Foods, and Comcast—Part 4 *Dukes, Tyson Foods,* and *Comcast* provide some general guideposts for plaintiffs seeking to use expert testimony to establish the Rule 23 elements at class certification:

- Plaintiffs may not use representative or statistical evidence to demonstrate the ability to prove liability or damages on a class-wide basis where doing so would simply circumvent necessary individualized issues, and/or prevent the defendant from exercising its right to assert individual statutory defenses;[36]

- Plaintiffs cannot rely on representative or statistical evidence where they could not do so to prove liability and damages in an individual suit (note, this may also require showing that plaintiffs would also have to rely on representative or statistical evidence even in an individual suit, because the defendant failed to keep records as statutorily required or otherwise failed to keep the individual records necessary for plaintiffs to prove their claims without resort to representative evidence);[37]

- Plaintiffs seeking to rely on representative evidence outside the FLSA context must show that their duties and/or experiences were so similar that, as in an FLSA matter, reasonable inferences could fairly be drawn based on the representative evidence;[38]

- Plaintiffs' proposed damages model must be connected to the injury/liability theory (e.g., in a case alleging consumers paid inflated prices because of misrepresentations, plaintiffs should make sure their experts consider both the supply and demand

---

36. *See, e.g.,* Campbell v. Nat'l R.R. Passenger Corp., __ F. Supp. 3d __ , 2018 WL 1997254, at *31 (D.D.C. Apr. 26, 2018); Senne v. Kansas City Royals Baseball Corp., 315 F.R.D. 523 (N.D. Cal. 2016), *reconsidered in part* 2017 WL 897338 (N.D. Cal. Mar. 7, 2017), *appeal pending* No. 17-16276 (9th Cir.).

37. *See, e.g., In re* Celexa & Lexapro Mktg. & Sales Prac. Litig., 315 F.R.D. 116, 118 (D. Mass. 2016), *appeal denied* No. 16-8024 (1st Cir. Dec. 7, 2016); *In re* Myford Touch Consumer Litig., 2016 WL 7734558, at *18 (N.D. Cal. Sept. 14, 2016), *reconsidered in part* 2016 WL 6873453 (N.D. Cal. Nov. 22, 2016).

38. *See, e.g., In re* Myford Touch Consumer Litig., 2016 WL 7734558, at *18 (N.D. Cal. Sept. 14, 2016), *reconsidered in part* 2016 WL 6873453 (N.D. Cal. Nov. 22, 2016) (allowing for representative evidence in warranty, product liability, and state consumer protection act claims where differences in how much each class member paid for the product were "unlikely to be material").

sides of the transaction), and must show that damages could be calculated on a class-wide basis;[39]

- In addition, while *Dukes* and *Tyson Foods* refused to categorically ban the use of representative evidence to demonstrate commonality and predominance, plaintiffs' counsel should be mindful whether a potential expert's methodology can adequately account for variations among absent class members.[40]

Defendants' Strategy for Using Experts at Class Certification

At the class certification stage, defense counsel must decide whether the best strategy will be to solely bring a *Daubert* challenge to plaintiffs' expert and otherwise poke holes in the expert's methodologies, or whether to also present defendant's own expert testimony. In some cases, expert testimony (whether limited to rebuttal testimony or not) can help the defendant show that plaintiffs have not satisfied the elements for certification under Rule 23, such as by helping the defendant demonstrate individualized issues concerning causation and injury, or lack of manageability. However, because, as discussed more fully later, courts are increasingly willing to engage in a more robust *Daubert* analysis at the class certification, defense counsel may find simply attacking plaintiffs' expert testimony a more cost-effective strategy.

> Expert testimony (whether limited to rebuttal testimony or not) can help the defendant show that plaintiffs have not satisfied the elements for certification under Rule 23, such as by helping the defendant demonstrate individualized issues concerning causation and injury, or lack of manageability.

First, however, and regardless whether the defendant offers its own expert testimony, defense counsel should analyze whether the plaintiffs' expert

(a) proposes a methodology that would allow the plaintiffs to circumvent fatal variations among class members, as in *Dukes*;

---

39. *See, e.g., In re* NJOY Consumer Class Action Litig., 120 F. Supp. 3d 1050, 1074–75 (C.D. Cal., Aug. 14, 2015); Victorino v. FCA US LLC, __ F.3d __, 2018 WL 2967062, at *16 (S.D. Cal. June 13, 2018).

40. *See, e.g.,* Angeles v. U.S. Airways, Inc., 2017 WL 587658 (N.D. Cal. Feb. 13, 2017) (decertifying because post-certification evidence showed individualized issues during donning/doffing periods).

(b) seeks to use representative or statistical evidence on which plaintiffs could not rely in individual suits;

(c) does not tie damages to the plaintiffs' liability theory; or

(d) relies on representative or statistical evidence that does not tie to the class as defined.

In addition, defense counsel should carefully evaluate plaintiffs' showing under all the class certification elements in Rule 23, and avoid any inclination to succumb to plaintiffs' framing of the questions and issues.

Second, defense counsel should cross-examine the plaintiffs' expert and should carefully evaluate the pros and cons of filing a *Daubert* motion—indeed, after *Tyson Foods*, the defense bar may be inclined to file *Daubert* motions whenever a plaintiff submits expert testimony in support of class certification. This is because in *Tyson Foods* the defendant neither filed a *Daubert* motion nor submitted rebuttal expert testimony, but rather simply argued "that the varying amounts of time it took employees to don and doff different protective equipment made the lawsuit too speculative for classwide recovery," and that the plaintiffs' expert's "study overstated the average donning and doffing time."[41] In affirming class certification, the Supreme Court emphasized:

> Representative evidence that is statistically inadequate or based on implausible assumptions could not lead to a fair or accurate estimate of the uncompensated hours an employee has worked. Petitioner, however, did not raise a challenge to [plaintiffs'] experts' methodology under *Daubert*; and as a result, there is no basis in the record to conclude it was legal error to admit that evidence.[42]

Put simply, defense counsel's failure to launch a *Daubert* challenge at class certification may well have been a near-fatal decision.[43]

Third, regardless whether defense counsel decides to challenge plaintiffs' experts under *Daubert* or to submit rebuttal expert testimony,

---

41. *Tyson Foods*, 136 S. Ct. at 1044.

42. *Id.* at 1048–49.

43. *See also* Kleen Prods. LLC v. Int'l Paper Co., 831 F.3d 919, 931 (7th Cir. 2016) (affirming class certification and writing, "Defendants did not challenge [plaintiffs'] experts under *Daubert* and Federal Rule of Evidence 702, and so we accept their reports for what they are worth at this stage."); Mednick v. Precor, Inc., No. 14 C 3624, 2017 WL 2619139, at *9 (N.D. Ill. June 16, 2017) (denying motion to reconsider order granting class certification and writing, "Precor did not raise a *Daubert* challenge to Plaintiffs' expert testimony in this case, and the Court declines to subject the testimony to that review *sua sponte*.").

counsel should analyze other ways in which to distinguish *Tyson Foods*. For instance, although some courts have applied *Tyson Foods* outside the FLSA context,[44] the Court in *Tyson Foods* relied heavily on FLSA case law in affirming the use of representative evidence, and that case law explicitly allows for inferences to be drawn against the employer where, as in *Tyson Foods*, the employer failed to keep statutorily required records. And as discussed earlier, defendants should look for ways to show that the evidentiary gap between class members is too wide and the variations too large to justify using representative evidence to establish the elements of Rule 23.

Timing of Disclosing Class Certification Experts

Rule 26 does not provide a separate deadline for disclosure of experts whom parties intend to use on class certification. Because class certification generally occurs before merits discovery has concluded, the rules do not require the parties to disclose their class certification experts before filing their class certification briefs and, therefore, the parties will not have had an opportunity to depose and cross-examine those experts until then. Both plaintiffs and defense counsel should therefore evaluate the best strategy for dealing with the timing of expert disclosures and discovery. For instance, if the parties and court agree to phasing discovery between class and merits, counsel should consider requesting that the court include separate deadlines for disclosure of class certification experts and merits experts. Alternatively, counsel might prefer to build in extra time in the class certification briefing schedule to allow for depositions of any experts relied upon in class certification briefing.

Failing to plan ahead for the timing of disclosure and discovery on class certification experts risks costly and time-consuming rounds of motions in limine, at best, and exclusion of critical expert testimony, at worst. Further, courts expect the parties to cooperate, as much as reasonably possible, on discovery matters, and to approach issues such as expert disclosures and timing with transparency. As a result, even if a court denies a motion to exclude expert testimony disclosed for the first time in a class certification brief, the party filing that brief may lose

---

44. *See, e.g.,* Vaquero v. Ashley Furniture Indus., Inc., 824 F.3d 1150, 1155–56 (9th Cir. 2016) (applying *Tyson Foods* to case involving claims under California's minimum wage and hour laws); *In re* Myford Touch Consumer Litig., 2016 WL 7734558, at *17–18 (N.D. Cal. Sept. 14, 2016) (applying *Tyson Foods* to case involving breach of warranty, product liability, and state consumer protection act claims), *reconsidered in part* 2016 WL 6873453 (N.D. Cal. Nov. 22, 2016).

credibility with the court if the timing of the disclosure suggests a lack of cooperation or transparency.

Applicability of Daubert

Federal courts have "evolved toward near-universal acceptance that the requirements of *Daubert* and Rule 702 apply with full force at the class certification stage."[45] This evolution stems in no small part from the Supreme Court's decisions in *Dukes* and *Comcast*, in which the Court emphasized the need for rigorous analysis of the Rule 23 criteria, especially for (b)(3) classes. In addition, in *Dukes,* the Court cast "doubt" on the notion that *Daubert* does not apply at the class certification stage.[46]

A court may admit expert testimony if:

(a) the witness is "qualified as an expert by knowledge, skill, experience, training, or education";

(b) the expert's testimony is relevant, that is, "will help the trier of fact to understand the evidence or to determine a fact in issue"; and

(c) the testimony and its methodology are reliable and "reliably applied" to the facts in the case.[47]

Under *Daubert,* courts play a gatekeeping function, and may consider various factors in determining whether the proposed expert satisfies Rule 702. These factors include whether the expert's theory or technique is generally accepted in the relevant expert community, whether the theory has undergone peer review or publication, whether it can or has been tested, any known potential error rate, and the existence of standards or controls.[48]

As the Court indicated in *Tyson Foods,* "[r]epresentative evidence that is statistically inadequate or based on implausible assumptions" is not admissible under *Daubert.*[49] On the other hand, once a court finds

---

45. McLaughlin on Class Actions § 3.14 at 472 (citing *In re* Blood Reagents Antitrust Litig., 783 F.3d 182, 187–88 (3d Cir. 2015); Messner v. Northshore Univ. HealthSystem, 669 F.3d 802, 812 (7th Cir. 2012); Ellis v. Costco Wholesale Corp., 657 F.3d 970, 982 (9th Cir. 2011); Blades v. Monsanto Co., 400 F.3d 562, 575 (8th Cir. 2005); *In re* Initial Public Offerings Securities Litig., 471 F.3d 24 (2d Cir. 2006); Sher v. Raytheon Co., 419 Fed. Appx. 887 (11th Cir. 2011)).

46. 564 U.S. at 354.

47. Fed. R. Evid. 702; *see also* Daubert v. Merrell Dow Pharmaceuticals, Inc., 509 U.S. 579, 590–91 (1993).

48. *Daubert,* 509 U.S. at 593–95.

49. *Tyson Foods,* 136 S. Ct. at 1048–49.

expert testimony admissible under *Daubert*, the weight it should receive and the persuasiveness of it are "the near-exclusive province of the jury."[50] So, the questions before a court on a *Daubert* motion at the class certification stage may include, depending on the nature of the challenge, whether the expert is sufficiently qualified, whether the proposed testimony is relevant to the Rule 23 factors and class certification analysis, and whether the proposed methodology is reliable.

> So, the questions before a court on a *Daubert* motion at the class certification stage may include, depending on the nature of the challenge, whether the expert is sufficiently qualified, whether the proposed testimony is relevant to the Rule 23 factors and class certification analysis, and whether the proposed methodology is reliable.

Some commentators have suggested that the federal circuits apply varying levels of *Daubert* analysis at the class certification stage.[51] Because, however, the federal courts appear to have accepted that *Daubert* applies at the class certification stage, plaintiffs and defense counsel litigating in federal courts may be better served by focusing on whether the subjects of proposed expert testimony are relevant to the Rule 23 factors, and whether the methodology is reliable and reliably applied to those factors, rather than on the subtleties in the degree of analysis applied across the circuits. As always, counsel litigating in state courts should research the applicable jurisdiction's treatment of *Daubert* challenges at the class certification stage, discussing federal case law by way of analogy.

In any event, plaintiffs' counsel should be careful not to fall into the trap of relying too heavily on experts, for "[i]t is reversible error to certify a class simply on the basis that proffered expert analysis is admissible."[52] Plaintiffs and defense counsel alike should focus on an expert's methodologies, including the construction of the sample, the reliability of the

---

50. *Id.* at 1049. *See also* Monroe v. FTS USA, LLC, 860 F.3d 389, 401 (6th Cir. 2017) (under *Daubert*, the issue is "the admissibility of representative evidence," not the "sufficiency" of it; approving use of representative evidence in FLSA case where, among other things, defendant did).

51. *See, e.g.,* Newberg on Class Actions § 7:24 (5th ed., Dec. 2016 update) (describing First, Third, Fifth, and Eighth Circuits as applying a "limited *Daubert*" analysis, and the Second, Fourth, Seventh, Ninth, and Eleventh Circuits as applying a "full" or "serious" analysis).

52. McLAUGHLIN, *supra* § 3:14 at 478 (citing Am. Honda Motor Co. v. Allen, 600 F.3d 813, 818–19 (7th Cir. 2010); *In re* Hydrogen Peroxide Antitrust Litig., 552 F.3d 305, 323 (3d Cir. 2006)).

method (such as whether, in the instance of sampling, recall, self-interest, or non-response biases may have affected reliability), the reliability of the application to the facts, and the presence of individualized issues and/ or variations among policies. In addition, since *Comcast*, courts applying *Daubert* at the class certification stage will scrutinize whether the proposed expert testimony is consistent with plaintiffs' damages theory and measures damages attributable to that theory only.[53]

Finally, given merits discovery often has not closed by the time the parties litigate class certification, plaintiffs and defense counsel alike should remain mindful of the fact that a *Daubert* hearing on the admissibility of expert testimony on the Rule 23 factors may not preclude a later *Daubert* challenge to the same expert's proposed testimony at trial. By the same token, if the court admits expert testimony on class certification and certifies a class, and if the expert intends to present additional testimony on the merits, plaintiffs must be sure to timely supplement the expert's report, triggering potential supplementation by the defendant.

Role of Experts at Trial

Experts play as significant a role, if not more so, at trial as at class certification. At trial, a certified class will often rely on expert testimony to prove class-wide liability and in Rule 23(b)(3) classes, aggregate damages. Whether or not the defendant offered expert testimony at class certification, the defendant will likely need an expert to be available to help debunk the class's expert's testimony or, possibly, to propose an alternative damages model and calculation. The parties may use the same expert opinions at class certification and at trial, but often they will not, requiring a second round of expert disclosures, reports, and discovery.

Daubert *Challenges*

Class and defense counsel will therefore need to prepare for *Daubert* challenges at trial, which will require working with their respective experts to improve the chances of defeating or prevailing on such challenges. As mentioned, counsel should not shy away from launching a second *Daubert* challenge to an expert that the opposing party offered at class certification, when the expert intends to offer additional or different expert testimony at trial.

---

53. *See, e.g.*, Goldemberg v. Johnson & Johnson Consumer Cos., 317 F.R.D. 374, 394 (S.D.N.Y. 2016).

At trial, the court will apply the same factors under Federal Rule of Evidence 702 and *Daubert* to the admissibility of the proposed expert's testimony, but may engage in a more robust analysis than at class certification, depending on the jurisdiction. In addition, the court will be focusing on the relevance of the proposed testimony to the merits and damages, and the reliability of the methodology and its application on those subjects—as distinguished from the focus on the Rule 23 criteria at class certification. This may mean that counsel for both parties need to prepare their experts for *Daubert* challenges somewhat differently than at the class certification stage.

Defense counsel should therefore be prepared to attack proposed expert testimony and methodologies that would:

(a) gloss over individualized experiences and/or the lack of a uniform policy;

(b) attempt to bridge evidentiary gaps too wide to allow for just or reasonable inferences;

(c) allow class members to prove liability and/or damages using proof on which they could not otherwise rely if suing individually;

(d) rely on composite examples, rather than actual plaintiffs or class members;

(e) result in mini test trials; or

(f) propose a damages methodology that does not derive from the liability theory on trial.

Likewise, class counsel should be prepared to attack proposed expert testimony and methodologies that would attempt to reargue any of the class certification factors, challenge the class's theory of liability, or minimize damages.

Bifurcation

Sometimes, parties or the court will suggest bifurcation or phasing of a trial. The typical bifurcation is between liability and damages, although Rule 23(c)(4) might allow a trial phase for an issue alone. Counsel for both parties should consider the impact of bifurcation on the extent and scope of expert testimony. *Tyson Foods* exposed the risks and benefits of bifurcating the liability and damages phases in Rule 23(b)(3) classes. On the one hand, doing so may make it easier for plaintiffs to obtain class certification, because liability questions can often be framed as common questions, and courts often conflate the fact of damages (i.e., injury), which should preclude certification when individualized, with the amount of damages, which should not preclude certification, even when individualized. On the other hand, a defendant who does not insist on or agree to bifurcating the proceedings may end up facing a much higher damages award than otherwise. Expert testimony may also need to be more precise if proceedings are bifurcated and if bifurcation could expose problems in the expert's opinion to the court and perhaps to the jury.

Damages

In damages class actions under Rule 23(b)(3), counsel for both parties should evaluate whether to provide expert testimony that proposes an alternative damages model or calculation. Defense counsel should weigh alternative models against the option of relying solely on a rebuttal expert, whose testimony debunks the plaintiffs' expert's damages methodology and calculations. Juries often want to "split the baby," and an alternative damages model and calculation could make it easier for the jury to award something less than the greatest possible damages amount. If damages can be calculated on a class-wide basis without individualized assessments (such as in cases involving automatic damages set by statute, or a common refund of the same amount across the class), forcing the jury to make an "all or nothing" decision could increase the defendant's odds of obtaining a complete victory—depending on the strengths and weaknesses of the underlying claims—because an "all or nothing" approach would, in an un-bifurcated case, force the jury to decide whether the class has proven liability in the first instance. Proposing alternative damages models and calculations poses both risks and benefits, and the appropriate scope of expert testimony should be carefully considered.

CONCLUSION

Today, experts are part of virtually every class certification. Both plaintiffs and defendants should spend considerable attention in selecting and working with their experts, and with understanding and attacking the other side's experts. Often experts are the deciding factor for the court in determining if predominance can be satisfied or whether the matter is manageable.

Table of Cases

E

F

G

K

Meaunrit v. The Pinnacle Foods Grp., LLC, No. C 09-04555 CW, 2010 WL 1838715 (N.D. Cal. May 5, 2010), 128–129 n.123

Mednick v. Precor, Inc., No. 14 C 3624, 2017 WL 2619139 (N.D. Ill. June 16, 2017), 381 n.43

Menowitz v. Brown, 991 F.2d 36 (2d Cir. 1993), 115 n.72

In re Mercury Interactive Corp. Securities Litig., 618 F.3d 988 (9th Cir. 2010), 316 n.72

Merrill Lynch, Pierce, Fenner & Smith, Inc. v. Haydu, 675 F.2d 1169 (11th Cir. 1982), 79 n.137

Mervyn v. Atlas Van Lines, Inc., No. 13 C 3587, 2015 WL 12826474 (N.D. Ill. Oct. 23, 2015), 172 n.74

Messner v. Northshore Univ. Health Sys., 669 F.3d 802 (7th Cir. 2012), 244 n.75, 254 n.108, 383 n.45

Meyers v. Nicolet Rest. of De Pere, LLC, 843 F.3d 724 (7th Cir. 2016), 67 n.92, 125 n.107

In re Midwest Milk Monopolization Litig., 386 F. Supp. 1401 (J.P.M.L. 1975), 282 n.65

Miller v. Ghirardelli Chocolate Co., 912 F. Supp. 2d 861 (N.D. Cal. 2012), 132 n.138

Mills v. Foremost Ins. Co., 511 F.3d 1300 (11th Cir. 2008), 225 n.14

Minkler v. Kramer Labs., Inc., No. CV 12-9421-JFW FFMX, 2013 WL 3185552 (C.D. Cal. Mar. 1, 2013), 100 n.10

Mocek v. Allsaints USA Ltd., 220 F. Supp. 3d 910 (N.D. Ill. 2016), 125, 126

Mollicone v. Universal Handicraft, Inc., No. 216CV07322CASMRWX, 2017 WL 440257 (C.D. Cal. Jan. 30, 2017), 136 n.160

Monroe v. FTS USA, LLC, 860 F.3d 389 (6th Cir. 2017), 384 n.50

Moore-Dennis v. Franklin, 201 So. 3d 1131 (Ala. 2016), 50 n.32

Moore v. Wyeth-Ayerst Labs., 236 F. Supp. 2d 509 (D. Md. 2002), 260 n.8

Mora v. Harley-Davidson Credit Corp., No. 1:08-CV-01453-AWI, 2012 WL 1189769 (E.D. Cal. Apr. 9, 2012), 61–62 n.69

Moreno v. Autozone, Inc., No. C-05-4432 MJJ EMC, 2007 WL 2288165 (N.D. Cal. Aug. 3, 2007), 176 n.90

Morgan v. AT & T Wireless Servs., Inc., 177 Cal. App. 4th 1235, 99 Cal. Rptr. 3d 768 (2009), 66 n.88, 109 n.42

Morgan v. Family Dollar, 551 F.3d 1233 (11th Cir. 2008), 353 n.19, 353 n.20, 362, 363

Moser v. Holland, No. 2:14-CV-02188, 2016 WL 426670 (E.D. Cal. Feb. 4, 2016), 188

Moses H. Cone Mem'l Hosp. v. Mercury Constr. Corp., 460 U.S. 1 (1983), 40 n.1, 84, 85 n.167

Moulton v. U.S. Steel Corp., 581 F.3d 344 (8th Cir. 2009), 296 n.21

In re MTBE Products Liability Litig., 241 F.R.D. 185 (S.D.N.Y. 2007), 262 n.13

Mullins v. Direct Digital LLC, 795 F.3d 654 (7th Cir. 2015), 33, 137 n.164, 228 n.19, 246, 350 n.7

Munning v. Gap, 2017 WL 733104 (N.D. Cal. Feb. 24, 2017), 130 n.131

Muzquiz v. W.A. Foote Mem'l Hosp., 70 F.3d 422 (6th Cir. 1995), 151 n.4

Index

417